DATE DUE

DE , 79			

DEMCO 38-296

MODERN KOREAN LITERATURE

KOREAN CULTURE SERIES

General Editor: Chung Chong-wha,
Professor of English and Director,
Anglo-American Studies Institute, Korea University, Seoul

KOREAN CLASSICAL LITERATURE
Edited by Chung Chong-wha

LOVE IN MID-WINTER NIGHT: KOREAN SIJO POETRY
Edited by Chung Chong-wha

MEMOIRS OF A KOREAN QUEEN: Lady Hong
Edited, introduced and translated by Choe-Wall Yang-hi

THE SHAMAN SORCERESS: Kim Dong-ni
Translated by Shin Hyun-song and Eugene Chung

THE WAVES: Kang Shin-jae
Translated by Tina L. Sallee

MODERN KOREAN LITERATURE
Edited by Chung Chong-wha

MODERN KOREAN LITERATURE

An Anthology 1908–65

Edited by

CHUNG CHONG-WHA

KEGAN PAUL INTERNATIONAL
London and New York

W, England
USA: 562 West 113th Street, New York, NY 10025, USA

Distributed by
John Wiley & Sons Limited
Southern Cross Trading Estate
1 Oldlands Way, Bognor Regis
West Sussex, PO22 9SA, England

Columbia University Press
562 West 113th Street
New York, NY 10025, USA

© Kegan Paul International 1995

Set in 10/12pt Times by Intype, London
Printed in Great Britain by TJ Press, Padstow, Cornwall

ISBN 0 7103 0490 0

British Library Cataloguing in Publication Data

Modern Korean Literature: Anthology,
1908–65. – (Korean Culture Series)
I. Chung, Chong-wha. II. Series
895.708004

ISBN 0–7103–0490–0

US Library of Congress Cataloging in Publication Data
Modern Korean literature: an anthology, 1908–1965 / edited by Chung
Chong-wha.
468 pp. 22cm. — (Korean culture series)
ISBN 0–7103–0490–0
1. Korean literature—20th century—Translations into English.
I. Chung, Chong-wha. II. Series: Korean culture series (London,
England)
PL972.6.M63   1994   94–9433
895.7'08004—dc20   CIP

CONTENTS

Preface   ix
Notes on the Authors   xv
Notes on the Editor and the Translators   xxiii

Introduction: Modern Korean Literature 1908–65   xxv
Chung Chong-wha

Part 1: 'Meetings and Farewells' and other stories   1

The Camellias   3
    Kim Yujong (translated by Chung Chong-wha)
Shower   9
    Hwang Sun-won (translated by Chang Wang-rok)
The Marsh   20
    Kim Dong-ni (translated by Chung Chong-wha)
The Flood   29
    Han Mal-suk (translated by Kim Dong-sung)
The Young Zelkova Tree   38
    Kang Shin-jae (translated by Shin Hyun-song)
The Rock   60
    Han Mu-suk (translated by Chung Chong-wha)
Meetings and Farewells   76
    Yi Sang (translated by Chung Chong-wha)

Picture of a Shaman Sorceress 82
  Kim Dong-ni (translated by Chung Chong-wha)
The Wings 104
  Yi Sang (translated by Moon Hi-kyung)
The Night Outing 124
  Kim Sung-ok (translated by Eugene Chung)

Part 2 'The Crag' and other stories 139

The Red Hills: A Doctor's Diary 141
  Kim Dong-in (translated by W. E. Skillend)
Snow 147
  Hwang Sun-won (translated by W. E. Skillend)
Dogs in the Village beyond Hills 150
  Hwang Sun-won (translated by Bob Donaldson)
Spring, Spring 171
  Kim Yujong (translated by W. E. Skillend)
The Buckwheat Season 185
  Yi Hyo-suk (translated by Shin Hyun-song)
The Fire 197
  Hyun Chin-kon (translated by Katherine Kisray)
A Lucky Day 204
  Hyun Chin-kon (translated by Chung Chong-wha)
The Crag 215
  Kim Dong-ni (translated by Chung Chong-wha)
The Afternoon of Mellow Persimmons 223
  Sohn So-hi (translated by Angela Chung)
The Tale of Kim Takbo 233
  Yi Mun-gu (translated by Shin Hyun-song)

Part 3 'Winter, 1964, Seoul' and other stories 261

Echoes 263
  O Yong-su (translated by W. E. Skillend)
A Betrayal 298
  Oh Sang-won (translated by Kim Chong-wun)
Two Reservists 314
  Kim Dong-ni (translated by Chung Chong-wha)
Retreat 322
  Hwang Sun-won (translated by Chung Chong-wha)
Winter, 1964, Seoul 331
  Kim Sung-ok (translated by Chung Chong-wha)

Contents

A Journey to Mujin 348
Kim Sung-ok (translated by Moon Hi-kyung)
The Heir 373
Suk Ki-won (translated by Kathryn Kisray)
Laughter 389
Choi In-hun (translated by Lee Sang-ok)
The Revelation 403
Sunwu Hwi (translated by Chung Chong-wha)
Obscurity 427
Yi Kwang-su (translated by Lyndal Weiler)

PREFACE

CHUNG CHONG-WHA

In compiling this anthology I have based the criteria for selection on historical as well as literary merits. In the ninety-odd years of modern Korean history since the opening of the old Korea to western influences at the turn of the century, the country has produced many talented writers. As soon as a new kind of literature was launched in 1908 an amazing number of the then young writers started writing under the strong influence of western literature, producing stories and poems of remarkable quality. Within a couple of decades of the start of the new literature, there emerged writers in their late teens and early twenties, who had managed to absorb the new concepts of literature from the west through Japanese translations and then grafted the newly acquired conventions and tools upon their traditional sensibility.

These writers are represented in this anthology by Yi Kwangsu, Kim Dong-in, Hyun Chin-kon and Kim Yu-jong. Yi Kwang-su's 'Obscurity', Kim Dong-in's 'The Red Hills', Hyun Chin-kon's 'The Fire' and 'A Lucky Day', and Kim Yu-jong's 'The Camellias' and 'Spring, Spring' all mark important historical moments in the development of modern Korean literature. Their achievement shines out more remarkably in the light of the historical fact that they bravely discarded the Chines literary conventions that had had formed the basis of the cultural heritage of the country for some three to four thousand years, and also of the fact that these young writers produced, within less than two decades of the absorption of foreign literary conventions, works which are not mere imitations but powerfully original products of the imagination.

Among the group Yi Kwang-su is the first pioneer of the new literature; he is followed in the line of seniority by Kim Dong-in, Hyun Chin-kon, and Kim Yujong. It is no coincidence that the literary achievement of these writers became more refined and more original as the upstart tradition of modern Korean literature moved on. If Kim Dong-in's 'The Red Hills' and Hyun Chin-kon's 'The Fire' and 'A Lucky Day' are more important in a historical sense, Kim Yu-jong's 'The Camellias' and 'Spring, Spring' are certainly more significant in terms of literary value. If there is a cliché'd pattern of human movements in 'The Fire' and 'The Red Hills', one sees human psychology at work in depth in 'The Camellias' and 'Spring, Spring'.

Along with Kim Yu-jong, many truly talented writers emerged in the 1930s. They include Yi Hyo-suk, Yi Sang, and Kim Dong-ni. By the time the generation of Yi Hyo-suk, Yi Sang and Kim Dong-ni began writing, the new literature of Korea had reached such a level of sophistication and maturity, that one can safely regard the 1930s as the period when the two decades of investment in an entirely different tradition flowered. If Yi Kwang-su, Kim Dong-in, and Hyun Chin-kon were the pioneers of the budding age of the new tradition, Kim Yu-jong, Yi Hyo-suk, Yi Sang, and Kim Dong-ni are the real founders of modern Korean fiction. One sees the echoes of Yi Hyo-suk's 'The Buckwheat Season' in Hwang Sun-won's 'Snow', 'The Shower', 'Dogs in the Village beyond Hills', and more strongly and more recently in O Yong-su's 'Echoes'.

Yi Sang's 'The Wings' is one of the first Korean stories to explore the intricate patterns of life. The story is the very first psychological fiction of the modernist movement, which opened up a new direction in the writers' concern with the depths of human heart. Already by the 1930s, slightly more than twenty years after the first initiation of the new tradition of literature, the story-telling conventions of the Korean novel had gained a great diversity in the structuring of human relationships, while the linear structure of plot took an inward movement into the dark cave of the human heart.

What Yi Sang initiated was further developed by the other writers who came after him, among whom Choi In-hun and Kim Sung-ok stand out. In 'Laughter', 'The Night Outing', 'A Journey to Mujin', and 'Winter, 1964, Seoul', the authors went into the dark recesses of the human heart and analysed the deeper meanings of life that they found in the cave of symbolic language and allegoric metaphors, which was highlighted in Kim Sung-ok's Kafkaesque world of Seoul in the bleak cold winter of 1964. In 'Winter, 1964, Seoul' Kim Sung-ok created a highly symbolic world of human behaviours which are hidden under the surface of verbal cognition, producing a truly wonderful work of art in allegorical language.

Another great writer who emerged in the wake of Yi Sang was Kim Dong-ni, whose 'Picture of a Shaman Sorceress' echoes Greek tragedy. There is in the story a strong suggestion of incestuous relations between mother and son, and between half brother and half sister, two of whom perish under the working of fate manifested in the clash of foreign imported Christianity and indigenous Buddhism-Shamanism, represented by the son and the mother. Kim Dong-ni employs the same theme in 'The Crag', in which the powerful working of fate against fragile human beings is symbolically intimated in the death of a leper woman on a crag.

Kim Dong-ni's theme represents a typical Korean view of life and the universe in which the individual in his confrontation with a powerful adversary, be it Nature or the social system, is always crushed and frustrated. This is what Sohn So-hi and Han Mu-suk portray in 'The Afternoon of Mellow Persimmons' and 'The Rock'. In both stories the theme of renunciation is powerfully dominant, as is typical of most Korean stories where the hero's challenges to and triumphs over mighty opponents are markedly missing. 'The Afternoon of Mellow Persimmons' and 'The Rock' both end with the protagonists in a state of sad frustration and unfulfilled regret. The echo of sad tunes in most Korean stories is largely due to the absence of the hero's challenges and his triumphs in the final defeat.

Sunwu Hwi's 'The Revelation' is another case where this

theme of frustration and renunciation is powerfully presented. The central character in the story gives in to the tyranny of political reality without challenge when the occasion arises, leaving a scar of deep regret in his heart. The author in a sense seems to present an aesthetic of sadness on the themes of frustration, renunciation and regret.

However, there are exceptions. Yi Hyo-suk, Kang Shin-jae and Han Mal-suk are examples of such writers. 'The Buckwheat Season' rejects a sad ending; it ends on a strong hint of happy reunion, refusing to accept the work of fate. In 'The Young Zelkova Tree' the hero and heroine defy their adversary presented in the form of social conventions, and the story ends on a happy note. So does 'The Flood', where the young married couple are united by the force of passion in a kind of challenge against the forces of Nature. Yi, Kang and Han disclose another kind of tradition in modern Korean literature in the midst of the main stream of regret and resignation.

I have here selected thirty stories on the basis of their historical interest and literary worth, each representing a monumental moment in the history of modern Korean literature. I have grouped them into three parts; the ten stories in the first part are put together on the basis of their common theme. This section offers historical and social view of the Korean experience of man confronting woman. The innocence and purity in the man-woman relationship presented in 'The Camellias', 'Shower, 'The Marsh', and 'The Flood' take different forms in the other stories; the relationship becomes more sophisticated and complex in 'The Rock', 'Meetings and Farewells', 'Picture of a Shaman Sorceress', and 'The Night Outing'. For this reason I have not grouped the stories in the chronological order of their publications.

The ten stories in the second part are classified together on the basis of common subject matter; they all deal with old Korea or the old Korean way of life. If one is looking for the old Korea of bygone days, one may look at the patterns of life in 'Snow', 'Dogs in the Village beyond Hills', 'Spring, Spring', 'The Buckwheat Season', or 'The Fire'. 'The Tale of Kim Takbo' reveals a glimpse of the traditional forms of life in the country, which is gradually disappearing in the face of industrialization and internationalization.

The third group of stories reveals modern Korea in the process of change. Seven stories in the group are about the time of the Korean War and soon after. 'Two Reservists' and 'Retreat' describe the direct war experience, while 'Echoes' recounts the building of life from the ashes of war, faintly echoing Patrick White's *The Tree of Man*. 'Winter, 1964, Seoul', 'A Journey to Mujin', 'The Ballad of Mong-gum-po', and 'Laughter' narrate the trauma that hit the people directly and indirectly in the wake of war. 'A Betrayal' relates the political chaos at the time of the liberation of the country from the Japanese Occupation and the victimization of the individual by political intrigues during the period. 'Obscurity' portrays symbolically the diverse faces of Korean people in the prison cell of Japanese Occupation.

All the thirty stories may serve as social documents. Indeed, from the time of ideological chaos following the independence of Korea in 1945 up to the fall of the USSR in the 1980s, modern Korean literature has been powerfully swayed by Marxist ideology one way or another. The social function of literature was emphasized by the neo-Marxists who began to speak out in a strong voice after the Korean War, and markedly more so in the 1970s and 80s when the country experienced endless fights against military dictatorships under the banner of student demonstrations.

Literature certainly has an important role to play in its portrayal of the relations between society and individual people, and it has a particularly vital social function in developing or underdeveloped countries. Korea, from 1908 when the new modern literary tradition began until 1965 when Kim Sung-ok wrote 'Winter, 1964, Seoul', was an underdeveloped country desperately struggling to develop. Modern Korean literature has played a very significant role in enlightening, enhancing, enriching and enfranchizing people's view of life.

However, the stories I have selected in this anthology are not just historical documents. They represent the peak of literary achievements by great and gifted writers in the first half of this century. It is indeed amazing to find so many talented writers producing so many powerful works of art in a short span of just over fifty years between 1908 and 1965. This anthology of thirty stories is an invitation to readers to grasp

how much Korea has attained in the process of its modernization and internationalization.

Finally a word about the translation of Korean stories into
English. There can be many different levels of translations
into a foreign language. At the lowest level there is the strict
literal translation of matching word for word. Then there is
the method of faithful restatement, the translator producing
the original in readable language of his own. And finally there
is the transposition of the original into the freest idioms of the
target language, one good example of which is Pound's *Cathay
Poems*. In this anthology I have adopted the second method,
attempting to provide faithful reproduction of the original in
readable English, but there are several stories in which the
translators have employed a much freer approach to the orig-
inals to make them more easily understood by the readers;
they have edited certain parts of the text and modified some
of them to make the stories more presentable, but this was
done with full consultation with the authors. 'The Rock', 'The
Afternoon of Mellow Persimmons', 'Two Reservists' and
'Retreat' are stories in this category. In many ways translation
is the transplantation of a delicate flower into another soil.
Sometimes the flower needs careful nurturing when it is
removed from one place to another.

NOTES ON THE AUTHORS
BY ORDER OF THEIR BIRTH

Yi Kwang-su was born in 1892 in Chongju, North Pyongan Province. Orphaned at the age of 10 he went to Japan to study when he was 13. He graduated from Waseda University with a bachelor's degree in philosophy and art. On his return home he began to work as a journalist and in 1917 wrote 'Indifference', the first western-style novel in the country, which became an immediate great success. On the publication of this novel all the young writers followed Yi's suit, thus opening a new literary era and making him the founding father of modern Korean literature in the field of the novel. Before he was kidnapped to North Korea at the outbreak of the Korean War he was a pioneer and the most popular patron of modern literature, and he remained as the most influential writer of his era until the untimely termination of his career. His brilliant record was marred by his collaboration towards the end of the Japanese Occupation, which is partly exposed in Sunwu Hwi's 'The Revelation'. Over 34 years Yi wrote about 60 novels, poems, stories, personal and critical essays, but his main contribution to modern Korean literature is his achievement as a novelist and story-writer. Among his best-known works are *The Pioneer, The Leader, Resurrection, Prince Ma-ui, The Sad Life of King Dan-jon, The Soil, Affection, Admiral Yi Sun-shin, Life of a Woman, Death of Reverend Yi Cha-don, Love* and *Won-hyo, The Great Priest*.

Kim Dong-in was born in 1900 in Pyongyang, North Korea. With money from his rich father he was sent to Japan to study fine arts when he was in his teens. He returned to Seoul from Tokyo without finishing his studies to become involved in literary activities. In 1918 he became a founding member of the first literary magazine in the country, symbolically called *Creation*, where he published his first story, 'Sadness of the Weak'. As a contemporary of Yi Kwang-su, he was very much Yi's rival. While Yi was deeply committed to enlightening his readers, Kim engaged himself in aesthetic writing, although he wrote in the naturalistic conventions, to which most of his stories belong, such as 'His Toes Resemble Yours' and 'Potatoes'. Among his well-known novels are *Spring in Wunhyon Palace* and *Those Young People, Suyang the Great*. Kim died in 1951.

Hyun Chin-kon was born in 1900 in Taegu, North Kyungsang Province. He studied German in Tokyo, but came back to Korea to become a journalist and started writing stories. In 1920 he made his literary debut with a story called 'The Victim', which he published in *Gaebyuk*, another pioneering magazine published in the wake of the opening of the country to the west, *Gaebyuk* meaning the creation of the earth. Along with Yum Sang-sup he was a champion of realism, and wrote most of his stories on the subject of the sufferings of the poor and the underprivileged, as shown in 'The Fire' and 'A Lucky Day'. His most renowned stories are 'An Impoverished Wife', 'Wine Offering Society', 'The Corrupt', 'Death of Grandmother' and 'Love Letters and Matron B'. He also wrote novels, among which the best-known is *The Tower of the Shadowless*.

Yi Hyo-suk was born in the county of Chinbu, Kangwon Province, in 1907. He studied English literature at the Japanese Imperial University in Seoul. He began writing stories in Korean and Japanese while he was a student at the Imperial University. His first Korean story was 'The City and the Ghost', published in 1928, which was followed by 'Personal Letters from the North Pole' (1931) and 'The Sea near the Russian Territory' (1931). At the beginning of his writing career, he wrote stories on the theme of social commitment, but with the publication of 'The Pig' in 1933 he began writing stories with a more lyrical colour, drawing his subject matter from the countryside, an example of which is 'The Buckwheat Season' (1936). In the third and last phase of his career he explored the world of sensual experiences, showing his indebtedness to D. H. Lawrence, exemplified in 'Bun-nyo' (1936) and *The Flower Pot* (1937). Among his well-known stories, apart from 'The Buckwheat Season', are 'The Emperor' (1939), 'Bun-nyo' (1936), 'The Roses are Sick' (1938), 'Autumn and the Wild Goat' (1938), and 'The Sacred Picture' (1937). He died of meningitis in Pyongyang in 1942 where he was professor of English at Sungshil College.

Kim Yu-jong was born in 1908 in Kangwon Province. After a brief spell at a college of arts in Seoul and a wasteful attempt at gold-mining, he began his creative life by publishing 'The Shower' (1933), 'No Touch' (1935) and 'Spring, Spring' (1935). His literary career ended two years later when he died in 1937. He left one unfinished novel and twenty-five short stories, among which 'The Camellias' (1936), 'A Traveller in the Countryside' (1936), 'Chastity' (1936), 'A Sad Story' (1936) and 'A Spring Night' (1936) are widely known. In Kim Yu-jong's stories one is constantly confronted with a strong nihilistic view of life, due to his unhappy personal life (his mother died when he was six, and his father when he was eight, and since then he had an unsettled life), yet he tries to present a sense of humour as the most powerful feature of his art.

Yi Sang, one of the most gifted writers of the 1930s, was born in Seoul in 1910. His real name was Kim Hae-kyong. He was trained as an architect and worked in his professional field briefly. He adopted the name of Yi Sang, according to one of the numerous popular legends that surrounded him, during this period when a worker at a construction site called him by mistake 'Mr Lee', which in Japanese is pronounced as 'Yi Sang'. But when ill-health put an end to his work in the Architectural Department of the Japanese Colonial Government, he started writing poems and stories. When in 1934 he published 'The Bird's Eye View' series, one of the most obscure and difficult poems of modern Korean literature, he was both abused and praised. He wrote what may be termed 'confessional' poems and stories revealing his indebtedness to Dadaism, Symbolism, and Surrealism. 'Meetings and Farewells' (1936) and 'The Wings' (1936) are examples of this confessional trend. He was also a gifted painter. He died of tuberculosis in Tokyo in 1937 when he was only twenty-seven.

Kim Dong-ni was born in Kyungju in North Kyungsang Province in 1913. He is one of the most influential writers in modern Korean literature in that he has written so many powerful stories on the theme of man's relationship with his indigenous soil, Nature, the universe and Fate, which makes his work mystical and philosophic, as is well portrayed in 'Picture of a Shaman Sorceress' (1936) and 'The Crag' (1936). He is an autodidactic writer having had little formal education, but he has enjoyed a position as one of the respected senior writers of South Korea since 1945. It was Kim Dong-ni who, through his critical essays, defended literature from the Marxist theories of the political role of art at the time of the political and ideological chaos of the post war period of 1945–49. He persistently stressed that literature could not be mobilized for political propaganda, firmly basing his notion of literature on what he himself terms humanism. He made his debut in 1935 with 'Hwarang's Descendants' and in 1936 'The Mountain Fire'. Among his well-known stories are 'The Story of the Yellow Earth' (1938), 'The Moon' (1947), 'The Evil Spirit of Post Horse' (1947), 'Two Reservists' (1950), 'The Retreat from Hungnam' (1956), 'A Life-Size Buddha' (1959), 'The Marsh' (1964), and 'The Cries of Magpies'. Among his best-known novels are *Saphan's Cross* (1957), *History of Freedom* (1959), and *The Sea Wind* (1962). He has also published books of poems and critical essays. He has served as the president of the Korean Academy of Arts and Letters, and of the Korean Novelists Association.

O Yong-su was born in South Kyungsan Province in 1914 and studied in Japan. He taught at high schools for a long while before he began his career as a professional writer. When he published 'The Wild Berries' (1949) his portrayal of country life was enthusiastically welcomed. He more or less remained as a writer of local colour to the end of his life. He died in 1980. Among his well-known stories are 'A Seaside Village' (1953), 'Light and Dark' (1958) and 'Echoes' (1959)

Hwang Sun-won, another senior writer of the South Korean literary world, was born in Daedong County in South Pyungan Province in 1915. He studied English literature at Waseda University in Japan. He published poems before he turned to writing stories. With the publication of 'The Stars' in 1941 he began his literary career as a highly acclaimed writer of local colour portraying the simple life of farming people in the remote countryside and using the strong local dialect of Pyongan Province, features of which are well seen in 'Snow' (1944), 'Dogs in the Village beyond Hills' (1948) and 'Shower' (1953). During and after the Korean War he began reflecting the trauma of war in stories like in 'Retreat'. In his later works he has become more urbane in his subject-matter and shown interest in the immediate realities of social life in big cities. This concern has become markedly prominent in novels like *Cain's Descendants* (1959) and *Trees Stand on Cliff* (1960).

Sohn So-hi was born in 1917 in Kyong-sung, North Hamkyung Province. She made her debut when she published 'Goodbye to Tapir' and 'The Day Before' in 1946, but her literary reputation was established with the publication of a book of stories called *The Story of Rira*. Her concerns in her writing were diverse, but from the beginning of her career she was dedicated to exploring the delicate inner world of her female characters and to expounding the fate of women in traditional society, a good example of which is 'The Afternoon of Mellow Persimmons'. She was a prolific writer and published 7 books of stories and 8 novels, among which the novels *The Valley of the Sun* and *The South Wind* and the collections of stories *The Season of Iris* and *That Sound of Jackdaws* are widely known. She died in 1987.

Hahn Mu-suk was born in Seoul in 1918. In 1942 her first novel, *The Woman Who Raises the Lamp*, was chosen at a competition organized by the magazine, *The New World*, as the best novel by a hitherto unknown writer; but her reputation as a promising writer was widely recognized in 1948, when he novel, *History Flows On*, was published, as a prize-winning story at a competition organized by the *Kukje Daily*. She went on to publish many books of stories and several novels, among which *The Moon Halo, A Place for Festivity and Fate, Everything Among Us, In the Depths of Emotion* and *Meeting* are representative. In most of her works she sensitively endeavours to catch the subtle waves of emotion in the hearts of her characters. She died in 1992.

Sunwu Hwi was born in 1922 in North Pyongan Province. He was trained as a school teacher like the narrator in 'The

Revelation', which was largely based on real characters. After a brief spell as a journalist and teacher, he joined the army in 1949 and in 1958 he was discharged, upon which he returned to the newspaper world. His first story published in the *New World* in 1955 was 'A Ghost', but he was unanimously recognized as one of the most promising writers of the time when in 1957 his story, 'The Flame' was awarded the Literature and Arts prize. He won one of the prestigious Dong-in Literary Prizes in the same year. He wrote many stories about the man of action, reflecting his belief in nationalism and patriotism, which is well seen in the titles of such stories and novels like 'Terrorists' (1956), 'Geese and Insignia' (1958), and *The Standard Bearer Without a Banner* (1959). He died in 1986.

Kang Shin-jae was born in Seoul in 1924. She studied at Ewha Woman's University. She made her debut in 1949 when 'The Face' was published in the influential literary magazine *Munye* (Literature and Arts). She won the Korean Women Writers Association Prize in 1967 and the Grand Prize of the Chung-ang Culture in 1984. She was President of the Korean Women Writers Association and is a member of the Korean Academy of Arts and Letters. Among the collections of her stories *The Comic Picture, The Mood of Journey, The Young Zelkova Tree* and *Fairy Tale for a Bleak Day* are widely known, and among her novels, *The Dandelions of the Imjin River, The Waves, This Splendid Sadness, Today and Tomorrow* and *Princess Sado* are her major works.

Oh Sang-won was born in 1930 in North Pyongan Province. He studied French Literature at Seoul National University. In 1953 his play, *Rusty Splinters* won the best prize at a competition. In 1955 with 'Respite' he won a major literary prize. He was heavily influenced by André Malraux and Sartre: their traces are manifest in his works, 'A Betrayal' being a good example. He published one novel, *A Record on the White Sheet* (1957), but his reputation largely depends on his short stories, among which 'The Witness' (1957) and 'A Medal' disclose his interest in people trying to overcome the wounds of the Korean War. He died in 1985.

Suh Ki-won was born in Seoul in 1930. He studied business management at Seoul National University, but he did not finish the course. He served in the air force, and on discharge he worked as a journalist at various newspapers and news agencies. In 1956 he published his first story, 'A Blank Map', with which he discussed his obsession with the trauma of the Korean War and its effect on people. Like Oh Sang-won and Choi In-hun he belonged to the war generation, and his subject matter was largely drawn from what he personally experienced during the 1950–3 War in Korea. Among his best known stories are 'The Dollar Story' (1957), 'The Plotting Family' (1958), 'The Moonlight and Famine' (1959), 'Today and Tomorrow' (1960), 'The Four Limb Exercise' (1960), 'Embrace in Such a Mature Night' (1961), 'The Heir' (1963), and 'The Love Song' (1963). Suh later served in the government as an information officer, and became president of the mighty government-owned Korean Broadcasting System and *Seoul Daily*. In his later works his concerns became wider, dealing with various social issues. He wrote several historical novels.

Han Mal-suk was born in 1931 in Seoul and studied linguistics at Seoul National University. Her first story, 'Cliff of Myth', was published in 1957. She was awarded the 1964 Modern Literature Prize for her story 'Traces' and the first Korean Creative Writing Prize for her story 'Promise With God'. She has published five book of stories, *Cliff of Myth* (1960), *Under This Sky* (1964), *Promise With God* (1968), *Melancholy of Journey* (1978), and three novels, *The White Journey* (1964), *Beautiful Soul Music* (1983), and *Time of Groping* (1986).

Choi In-hun was born in 1936 in North Hamkyong Province. At the outbreak of the Korean War he moved down south and began to study at the Law School of Seoul National University, but did not finish. In 1959 he published 'The Rise and Fall of the Grey Club' and 'The Story of Roul'. With the publication of *The Plaza* his literary reputation was firmly launched. 'The Nine Cloud Dream', a novella (1962), 'Christmas Carol' (1963), *The Grey Man*, a novel (1963), 'Laughter' (1966), 'The Voice of the Governor-General' (1967), 'One Day in the Life of Mr Kubo, the Novelist' (1969) are some of his major works. He is a writer deeply preoccupied with the philosophic problems of life. He teaches creative writing at an arts college in Seoul.

Kim Sung-ok was born in Japan in 1941. He studied French literature at Seoul National University. In 1962 the publication of his prize-winning story 'A Life Exercise' marked the start of his professional writing career. He became one of the most promising writers since the Korean War when he published,

'A Journey to Mujin' and 'A Cup of Tea' in 1964, and in 1965 'Winter, 1964, Seoul', which won the prestigious Dong-in Literature Award. 'Zero Chapter, the Moonlight of Seoul' won the first Yi-sang Literature Award in 1977. He has shown interest in writing scripts for films. He wrote the script of Kim Dong-in's 'Potatoes' and directed it.

Yi Mun-ku was born in 1941 in South Chungchung Province and studied the creative writing at Sorabul College of Arts. Yi is a socially committed writer, concerning himself with the theme of social injustice, and therefore he draws his stories mainly from the life of the underprivileged in the setting of countryside farms or seaside fishing villages as is powerfully represented in 'The Tale of Kim Takbo' (1968). His social concerns sometimes bring him to the construction sites in cities where the miserable life of the underdogs calls for attention, of which 'The Ballad of Mong-gum-po' is an eloquent example.

NOTES ON THE EDITOR AND THE TRANSLATORS

Chung Chong-wha is a professor of English and Director of the Anglo-American Studies Institute, Korea University, Seoul. He studied at Seoul National University and the Universities of Bristol and Manchester. He is the editor (and co-translator) of *Modern Far Eastern Stories* and *Modern Korean Stories* published by Heinemann Educational Books and *Meetings and Farewells* published by Queensland University Press, Australia, and St Martin's Press, New York. Currently he is the general editor of Kegan Paul's Korean Culture series (in which his translation of Korean classical *sijo* poems was published under the title of *Love in Mid-Winter Night*, winning the 1986 grand literary prize of Korea. Chung's latest book are *Anthology of Modern Korean Poems* published by the East-West Publications, London, and *Anthology of Korean Classical Literature* published by Kegan Paul International, London.

Chang Wang-rok is a professor of English at Hallim University, Chunchon, Korea. He has translated many stories by Hwang Sun-son.

Angela Chung is a professor of English at Hankuk University of Foreign Studies, Seoul.

Eugene Chung, a graduate of Cambridge University, works for a Swiss bank.

Bob Donaldson studied Korean language at Brigham Young University.

Kim Chong-wun was formerly a professor of English at Seoul National University, and is currently the president of the University.

Kim Dong-sung was formerly a professor of English at Seoul National University and later became a Minister for Information.

Kathryn Kisray lives in Cambridge.

Lee Sang-ok is a professor of English at Seoul National University.

Moon Hi-kyung is a professor of English at Korea University, Seoul.

Shin Hyun-song is a professor of Economics at the University of Southampton and was formerly a fellow at University College, Oxford.

W. E. Skillend was a professor of Korean Studies at London University. He is the author of *Korean Classical Novel*.

Lyndal Weiler is a graduate of Griffith University, Australia, specializing in Korean language.

INTRODUCTION: MODERN KOREAN LITERATURE 1908–65

CHUNG CHONG-WHA

A definite demarcation line for the start or end of a literary movement or period is not usually easy to draw. Who today dares put forward the year 1900 as the obvious commencement of twentieth-century English or French literature, or as the very last year of the nineteenth-century literature? Henry James, for instance, died in 1916 and wrote most of his major works before 1899 except his last three great novels (*The Wings of a Dove* in 1902, *The Ambassadors* in 1903 and *The Golden Bowl* in 1904). Though *Portrait of a Lady* was published in 1881 and *The American* in 1877, who would classify him without qualm as a nineteenth-century writer or an 'eminent Victorian'? A cultural phenomenon, an artistic tendency or a literary epoch is never artificially created, nor factitiously terminated.

However, modern Korean literature offers an exception to this rule. In November 1908 suddenly a completely new literature was born. Choi Nam-sun, one of the pioneers in the westernization of the country, published a new kind of work in the first literary magazine in the history of Korea. Choi Nam-sun's 'From the Sea to the Boys' was published in Choi's magazine, *The Boys*; it was the very first western-style poem written in free verse, and it marked the end of traditional poetry and the beginning of modern literature.

Traditionally Korean literature had been nurtured and

developed under a strong influence from Chinese literature. Although the indigenous *sijo* tradition had long kept a fine heritage, the main stream of poetry had been practised in the strict Chinese notion of the genre. The forms, conventions, images and even themes were largely drawn from the Chinese, and the poems had to be written in Chinese characters. This was the inevitable cultural consequence of a socio-political climate where the medium of learning was the study of Chinese classical texts and all civil servants and the educated class had to memorize Chinese classical poetry.

With his first western-style poem Choi bade farewell to this classical tradition of Korean literature and his attempt received a nation-wide response immediately. All the young writers of the time followed Choi's suit. They avidly read western literature and wrote their works in a western style, imitating one movement after another. They had completely discarded the long-established Chinese tradition, which can be traced back to at least 17 BC when the first recorded poem in Chinese, 'The Song of the Yellow Birds', was written. Amazingly the Korean reception of the west was uncritical, almost to the degree of fanaticism.

What they tried to do in their acts of imitation was of a revolutionary nature. By denouncing the traditional practice of writing, styles and forms, by renouncing references and phrases drawn from classical Chinese, and by departing from the Chinese heritage altogether, the westernization movement took on a radical character. When Yi Kwang-su, another leading light of the period, introduced the western mode of writing in the field of the novel and short stories as his fellow poet, Choi Nam-Sun, had done in poetry, he was referred to as a 'brave Don Quixote' by another fellow writer, Kim Dong-in, in his 'Essay on the Modern Novel':

> Yi Kwang-su's first literary work was a declaration of revolt against his society. He was a brave Don Quixote. He proclaimed war on Confucianism, on aged parents, and on the traditional idea of marriage. In fact, this brave Don Quixote rebelled against the ideas of morality, against all the social systems and principles as well as codes of behaviour – anything which had been regarded as right in the past.

Yi Kwang-su's monumental achievement culminated in his writing of *Indifference* in 1917, in which he not only practised the new form of the novel but preached the reformation of the existing political structure and social values. It was to this novel that Kim Dong-in was referring when he described him as a 'brave Don Quixote'. But he was a more organized idealist and with the book he became the most popular writer of his time.

However, what Choi Nam-sun and Yi Kwang-su accomplished in literature was not an isolated cultural phenomenon. It has to be seen as part of a series of political and social ventures with organized planning, among which the most noted was the short-lived *Kabo Reformation* (declared in 1894) with its manifestoes declaring the abolition of rigid class differences, the abandonment of serfdom, the legalization of the remarriage of widows, the modernization of government organizations, the training of students abroad, and the independence of the nation from China.

Korea on her path towards modernization needed a complete break from China, politically, socially and culturally, and the only solution for this was to get closer to the west directly or through Japan. Choi Nam-sun and Yi Kwang-su were students in Japan, learning the advanced ideas of the west through Japaneses translations, and their notion of modernizing the county was embodied in their search for a new literary tradition based on western concepts of literature.

For Korean writers the western literatures were a treasure trove. Their search for great wealth led on from the discovery of one literary movement to another, one master to another, and one school to another. It was an age of revelations and discoveries, perhaps comparable to the Age of Discovery – geographical – in the 1660s. They discovered the English romantic poets, Zola and Flaubert, Tolstoy and Dostoevsky, Shakespeare, Goethe, Baudelaire and Verlaine, Yeats and Eliot . . . all the literary giants of the west the Japanese translations made accessible at last. And almost concurrently the waves of naturalism, realism, romanticism, symbolism, decadence, and many other movements swept the nation. Writers and poets eagerly declared their allegiance to one movement after another. Choi Nam-sun wrote his first free verse in imitation of Byron's *Childe Harold's Pilgrimage*, Yi Kwang-su became a champion of Tolstoy's moral humanism, Hyun Chin-kun and Kim Dong-in adopted realism as their literary principle, and Yi Sang wrote his poems and stories under the mixed influence of symbolism, romanticism, decadence, and Dadaism. Even the tune of the first national anthem was an adaptation from the Scottish song *'Auld Lang Syne'*. What is unique about the Korean westernization process was that there was not a single voice of criticism raised. In a sense the cultural climate of the country was so totally anti-traditional that a kind of vacuum was created in the negation of the past, and the vacuum syphoned into itself any small particle of enlightenment from western literature.

Among western literatures Britain and France attracted Korean writers and poets most powerfully. Byron was translated often in Choi Nam-sun's magazine and even his biography was serialized. Chaucer, Milton, Swift, Shelley, Tennyson, Carlyle, Oscar Wilde, Yeats, Hardy, Kipling, Eliot and Lawrence were also introduced or translated in *The Boys* and other literary magazines that followed. To this list American poets like Poe, Longfellow and Whitman should be added. Tagore's English poems also gained popularity.

A true appreciation of Shakespeare was a relatively later phenomenon, but the impact of English literature and culture was felt as early as 1886. When Emperor Kojong had his birthday on 25 July of that year the congregation of Sae-moonan Church composed 'The Emperor's Birthday Song' using the melody of 'God Save the King'; even the words of the birthday song were written so as to fit the tune. Behind the composers were the American missionaries who found the British national anthem – also the American anthem 'My Country 'tis of Thee' – expedient for the Korean occasion and made use of it for their missionary ends.

Missionaries hoped to use church hymns and Anglo-American songs to attract more people to the church. The popularity of some hymns and songs soon exceeded the aims of the plan and spread widely outside the church; hymns were adapted among the people for songs that incited the spirit of independence and enlightenment, songs that satirized social corruption, or songs that warned the nation of the dangers of Japanese colonialism. The songs themselves opened a new genre in the literary field by adopting a similar Japanese form and paved the way for the coming of the new poetic tradition. 'From the Sea to the Boys' is in this sense a stage beyond the songs. The two forms were clearly different; the songs were quatrains with the strict arrangement of seven and four syllables in each line, whereas the new poetry was in the form of free verse. These forms were alien to the indigenous notions of poetry, but the widely popular church hymns and songs prepared the Korean audience to accept another foreign tradition.

The mood of the time was to welcome anything new and foreign, which was well reflected in Choi Nam-sun's 'A World Tour' written in the form of a song published in 1914. The poet sends a character called Choi Kun-il on a tour of the world. He visits European cities and subsequently goes to America, where he is overwhelmed by the scenic beauty and rich cultural history:

> Climbing across the Pyrenees
> I now got to Bordeaux,
> Surrounded by the fragrance of roses and olives,
> The port, world famous for exporting grapes.
>
> I set a boat on the Bay of Biscay
> And visit Nantes famous for shipbuilding
> And then travel along the Loire
> Calling upon various Saracen ruins.
>
> Joyfully I arrive at Orleans Castle
> Where Jeanne d'Arc's miracles took place.
> A few hours further north
> Lies the Capital City that I long to see.
>
> Dear Paris, though this is the first time I see you,
> I've heard of you so much
> I know you are the centre of the world civilization
> And a paradise on earth.

Although this song sounds alike a guidebook to world history and geography, it was the articulation of a young poet's mental journey to the roots of western civilization and literature; Choi

Nam-sun's homage to the birthplaces of his new literary tradition.

Choi Nam-sun's magazines, first *The Boys* and later, when Choi was in his youthful twenties, *The Youth*, carried a great number of English and French poets in translation. The major literary magazines that appeared and disappeared during this first period of modern Korean literature allowed a generous space to Anglo-American and French poets. *The Beginning, The Creation, The Ruins, The Rose Village, The White Tides, The Venus,* among sixty-odd others, published Tennyson, Yeats, Arthur Symons, Eliot, Baudelaire, Valéry and Verlaine. When *Dance of Agony,* the first book of western poetry in Korean translation, was published in 1921, its effect was powerfully felt among Korean poets. The book carried 21 poems by Verlaine, 10 by Gourmont, 6 by Baudelaire, and 6 by Yeats. Yi Kwang-su commented on the book and said that 'the mode of young poets became a dance of agony not only in their expressive method but their thought and spirit'. Yi Kwang-su thought that the 'achievement of Kim Uk', the author of the book and a poet himself, 'in the building of new Korean poetry will be remembered forever with this single book.' Yi Kwang-su's assessment was correct; Kim Uk's main contribution to modern Korean poetry by this book was to teach the coming generation what a good poem should be like.

The process of westernization from Choi Nam-sun onward began to blossom soon after Kim Uk's *Dance of Agony.* Within the first decade of Choi's initiation many good poets emerged under heavy influences of Anglo-American and French poets. Park Jong-hwa, Hong Sa-yong, Byun Yung-no, Yi Jang-hi, Yi Sang-wha, No Ja-young, Yang Ju-dong, Hwang Sukwu and others wrote romantic poems, expressing their feelings exuberantly and indulging in the sentiments of solitude, despair, death and tears.

Critics of Korean literature tend to see every decade as a new era. There is some truth in this with regard to this eventful period. The first decade up to 1920 saw the rise of a new literature under the leadership of Choi Nam-sun and Yi Kwang-su. It was the cradle period of the new tradition, preceeding the second decade of the 1920s. Choi Nam-sun and Yi Kwang-su were in their late teens and twenties. The names of their magazines, *The Boys* and *Youth*, testify to this. The other magazines like *The Beginning, The Creation* or *The Ruins* also reflect the germinating age of the modern literature or the death of the old one.

The second decade is the period of growth with poets of the post-*Dance of Agony* period and prose writers like Hyun Chin-kun, Kin Dong-in, Yum Sang-sup, Chu Yohan, Park Jonghwa and Na Dohyang. This decade happened to be a time when the Japanese colonial policy adopted a more relaxed political course as the result of the nationwide anti-Japanese upheaval of 1 March 1919. The Japanese colonial government in Korea changed its policy from military to cultural rule, and as a result there were more lively literary activities. It was in this period that various literary groups published their own journals and magazines. It was also the time when the second wave of Korean writers and poets returned from Japan with much deeper contacts with western literature.

It is remarkable that it took very little time – only about two decades – to create a solid new literary tradition. When modern Korean literature entered its third decade, it produced a good many great writers and poets. Yi Sang published *Meetings and Farewells* in 1936 and his sensational poem 'A Bird's Eye View' in 1932, Yi Hyo-suk wrote *The Buckwheat Season* and Kim Yu-jung *The Camellias* in 1936. The same year saw the publication of Kim Dong-ni's *Picture of a Sorceress*. In fact, the year marked a vintage year of modern Korean litera-ture. Kim Hwan-tae, a critic, has called that year the beginning of another epoch in Korean literature, though the next decade until the end of the Japanese occupation of the country in 1945 was a dark age for Korean writers, whose activities were extremely limited under the coercive measures of the Japanese colonial policy. It could be referred to as the withering period, an unfortunate disaster for the rapid growth and development of the new literature, when the Japanese colonial government tried to suppress not only the nationalistic sentiment but Korean literature and language themselves. Writers were forced to show loyalty to the Japanese war cause and even had to promote Japanese imperialism through their writing, or else they had to stop writing. Young writers were subject to draft and mobilization and many died in Japanese prisons for their acts of defiance.

The end of the war in 1945 brought about a breakthrough. With direct contacts with American literature, and through it, European literatures, Korea went through a period of rehabilitation and reawakening when Korean writers were swept by a second wave of western influence. Through the 1960s and 1970s, Korean literature developed along with the new literary fashions, movements and experiments of the west. No European or American vogue went without leaving some substantial traces in Korea; Eliot came and left loud echoes, new criticism dominated the Korean literary scene for some tiem. Sartre made extentialism felt in Korean sentiment, and even Lukács gathered force. Now in the 1980s and 1990s Structuralism, Deconstruction and Post-Structuralist theories and other current literary phenomena are all palpably reflected in the sensitive minds of Korean writers.

Except during the war years of 1950–3 and the lean years of economic rehabilitation until the late 1960s when Korean literature kept pace with political and economic hardships, modern Korean literature has been greatly enriched and developed by contact with western sources. New ideas and experiments in the west have made enormous contributions to make Korean literature diverse and maturer. New criticism helped Korean critics and scholars look at literature in a rigorous fashion, and Lukâcs and neo-Marxism made a group of Korean writers approach their source material in a wider historical and social context.

However, in spite of the big role the west has played in shaping and developing a new literature, the powerful western influences have not affected the deeper reality of the Korean mentality. What Choi Nam-sun and Yi Kwang-su did in the initiation of a new tradition and what their followers did in expanding it denied the past and traditional values. But their negation remained only on the surface. What they wanted to destroy was the external political structure and the social system; some of this was well reflected in the manifestoes of the *Kabo Reformations*. What ran deeply in the heart of the people and what formed the backbone of the indigenous culture could not be completely abandoned, though part of it wanted improvement and renovation. Hence, although the first two decades were a period of anxious imitation and uncritical reception of western prototypes, writers and poets gradually came to see what to accept and what to reject. They slowly became critical of their blind absorption of western literatures and chose what they thought good for their own local climate and specific requirements. As early as 1924 Kim Uk himself, the author of *Dance of Agony* with its influential translations of French and British peotry, raised a voice of criticism against 'the cursory borrowing or western and Japanese poems.' In his review of the state of poetry in 1924 he wrote:

> The recent trend of poetry in the country makes me wonder if it is dressed in Korean costume without the Korean soul, which should be properly worded in the indigenous language. Korean poetry today looks very much like a figure in Western costume with the Korean top-hat or in Korean costume but in Japanese wooden clogs. No wonder Korean poetry had become a laughing stock in the eyes of the world. We must first of all retrieve the Korean soul that has been lost, without which poetry is nothing but a toy.

Kim Uk's suggestion was that the poet should write 'what is congenial to the nature of Korean language and the thoughts and feelings of Korean people' and insinuated that lyric forms should be adopted for this. He thought 'a short lyric poem was the most beautiful one', the best example of which he found in folk ballads and the *sijo*.

As a poet Kim Uk largely wrote short lyric poems with heavy emphasis on rhythmic effect, which was very much reminiscent of the folksy mood of the traditional *sijo*. Kim Uk's appeal to the traditional rhythms gathered forces from many leading poets and made a strong impact on the young emerging poets like Kim So-wol, who later became one of the best lyric poets of the country and opened up the lyric tradition on modern poetry.

It is interesting to speculate why Kim Uk changed his prowestern attitude and became a nationalistic poet. (It was only three years after the publication of *Dance of Agony* that he became critical of the following of western literatures). Critics vary on this, but my personal assessment is that his ability to translate more French and English poetry was limited (his linguistic ability being rather doubtful), his personal preference for short lyrical forms found the western tradition of epic poetry not to his taste (he made clear his displeasure with 'dramatic and historic epics'), and tiring of his previous stance he became more sympathetic to the nationalistic movement that had been spreading fast since the failure of the 1 March 1919 upheaval against the Japanese colonial rule.

The political climate of the time was certainly all for the awakening of a national spirit. The Society for the Study of Korean Language was established in 1921 and there was a movement for the creation of a national university in opposition to the establishment of a Japanese Imperial university. Some writers and poets began exploring the traditional culture and rediscovering its literary treasures. Yi Kwang-su tried his hand at the *sijo* using some legends of old Korea, and Hong Sa-yong published some folk songs which he collected from the southern provinces.

Amongst this, Kim Dong-hwan became the most successful folk poet when he published 'Night at the Northern Border' in 1925. Kim Dong-hwan subsequently wrote about the life and customs in the northern towns, with which he succeeded in invoking homesickness for the snow-covered North and stirring nationalistic feeling for the motherland. His shorter, earlier poem, 'Pointing at the Red Star' (1924), is a good example of Kim's evocation of the atmosphere of a small town in the far north (where he came from) and his masterful presentation of old Korea and the hard life of the common people:

> In the north country it snows day and night.
> Whenever snow pours down from the grey sky
> I see the North buried in snow.

> . . . . .

> The north country is cold. In this cold night
> Smuggler's horse cart is heard passing by the river
> Submerging the sounds of bells
> In the ice-grinding sounds.

> Oh, snow is falling again, white snow is

Falling silently on
The removal cart bound for the cold north

Winter here is perhaps symbolic of the difficult time under
the Japanese occupation. The whole mood of the poem is bleak
and cold in its outlook, in contrast to other nationalistic peoms;
for example, Yi Sang-hwa, a poet from the south, tried to
portray the state of the nation in a spring scene in his famous
'Does Spring Return to the Plundered Field? (1926), the first
line of which starts: 'Now it is somebody else's land, does
spring return to the plundered field?' The revealing title and
the first line imply everything the poet wishes to say. Unlike
Kim Dong-hwan, Yi Sang-hwa was much more positive in his
regard to this homeland, and insinuates the cultivation of the
land, ending the poem thus:

Get me a hoe
I'd like to tread and sweat
On this soft soil rich as buxom breast.

Like a child by the river
My imprudent soul, why do you run endlessly?
What are you looking for? Where are you going? Tell me
why.

Soaked in green smells
Amidst green laughter and green sorrow
I walk on whole day, limping. Perhaps I'm struck with
spring spirit.

But now . . . the field is plundered and even spring may get
stolen.

In the last line the poet imparts his determination to keep
spring for himself (and his subjugated fellow countrymen).
What makes the poem successful is that the lively and hopeful
mood of the last stanza (in which the poet seems to say,
'though my land is taken away, I shall not let them steal my
spring'.) agrees with the general tone of the poem, which is
wonderfully rich and youthful in its mood. The whole poetic
design comes alive in the green imagery ('Soaked in green

smell/Amidst green laughter and green sorrow') and with the
sensual tone (I'd like to tread and sweat/On soft soil as rich
as a buxom breast').

Yi Sang-hwa's green phase is representative of this period.
Korean literature had just come out of the first decade of its
cradle period, during which Choi Nam-sun, Yi Kwang-su, Kim
Uk, Chu Yo-han and other poets and writers put the literary
tradition on a sound footing. In this second decade Korean
literature began to show signs of lively growth, by becoming
more conscious of the artistic refinement of form, by gaining
diversity in its poetic approaches, and by becoming more critical of the indiscriminate reception of outside influences. By
the time Yi Sang-hwa, Kim Dong-hwan, Kim So-wol, Kim
Dong-in, Park Jong-hwa came alone and shaped modern
Korean literature into a more aesthetic structure, the new
tradition had reached another phase of growth and development. However, for maturity it had to wait for the next generation of poets and writers like Yi Sang, Chung Ji-yong, Suh
Jung-ju, Kim Dong-ni, and Yi Hyo-suk.

Maturity came in the third decade which saw the flowering
of the twenty-odd years of experiments. While absorbing vigorously rudimentary techniques and other devices from the west
and Japan, the writers of the first and second decades tested
the craft on their native subjects for the best course of the
future of Korean literature and paved the road for the coming
of the third generation. And indeed the 1930s (possibly from
the latter part of the 1920s with the appearance of Han Yong-
woon and Kim So-wol) produced many talented poets and
writers who knew how to handle confidently the tools of their
craft.

But they were not just highly skilled technicians. They had
an advanced sense of art and possessed a mature view of life.
The weaning from foreign influences and the awareness of
their national inheritance coincided with their becoming more
competent and mature artists. When Han Yong-woon wrote
'Artist' in 1924 and called himself 'an unskilled painter' and
'an incompetent singer' (though the object of his artistic
creation should be taken at a symbolic level), the statements
were in a sense indicative of the first stage of a new literature
trying to develop from an immature state. By the early 1930s,

however, with the appearance of Yi Sang, Chung Ji-yong, Kim Ki-rim, Kim Dong-ni and Yi Hyo-suk, the new tradition began to show signs of entering adulthood. The sentiments of solitude, despair, love and death were dispensed with, and the 'green phase' of youthfulness changed into a thoughtful and critical outlook on life. Poets started searching for the meaning of life. The general trend of poetic concern was an analytical examination of selfhood.

Many poets showed an interest in the subject, and Yoon Dong-ju, Yi Sang and Suh Jung-ju all wrote poems called 'A Self Portrait'. While Yoon's picture was nacissistic, the analysis of selfhood in Yi and Suh was more objective and unflattering. They saw a ridiculous and pitiful figure of the self, which could perhaps represent the true portrait of Koreans during the hardship period of the Japanese occupation. When Yi Sang saw the reflection of himself in a mirror, he came to realize the impossible reality of not being able to penetrate into the true identity of his real being; he only had a replica or an opposite of himself and hence he thought it regretful that he could not examine the depths of his inner self:

There is no sound in the mirror.
There is no world more quiet.

I have ears even in the mirror,
Two ears which regretfully cannot hear me.

I am a left-hander in the mirror
Who cannot shake hands with me.

Though because of the mirror I cannot touch me in the
     mirror.
If it were not for it, how would I have met me in the
     mirror?

I do not have a mirror now, but in it there is always me.
Though I cannot be sure, he will be absorbed in his solitary
     affairs.

The me in the mirror is so tryly me opposite
And yet so totally my replica.

It is regretful that I cannot worry about and examine me in
the mirror.

What makes this poem a monumental piece is the poet's cool
ability to detach himself and scrutinize his being in a clinical
way. The fact that Yi Sang realizes limits in the attempt is
itself an achievement of a sort. Yi Sang's 'Self-portrait' in this
sense makes a good contrast to Yoon Dong-ju's mild and self-
indulgent megalomaniac 'Self-portrait':

Turning the hill along the paddy field
I go to the lone well, alone, and look quietly in.

In it the moon shines, the clouds float, and the sky
Spreads, the blue wind blows and autumn is there.

And also there is a man.
Somehow hating him, I turn away.

Having turned away I become sorry for him
And I go back and find him still there as before.

Again I go away, hating the man
Whom I begin to miss having turned away.

In the well the moon shines, the clouds float, the sky
Spreads, the blue wind blows, autumn is there.

And there is a man like a memory.

The dominant mood of the poem is an adolescent love and
hatred of the self. The poet is not in the least interested in
self-analysis, and perhaps incapable of it. The well, in which
'the moon shines, the clouds float, the sky/Spreads, the wind
blows, autumn is there', only serves as a means of indulging
in an adolescent fantasy for something far beyond. Yet he sees
his reflection in the water, but the encounter does not lead
him to glimpse the deeper reality of the self; the image in the
water only incites a nostalgic memory, thus reducing the poetry
to a juvenile daydream and narcissistic self-love. The young

poet has not matured enough to face himself and find out the truth of his real identity.

Suh Jung-ju, on the other hand, in his 'Self-Portrait', disclosed a mature posture; there is no symptom of juvenile narcissism. In his self-examination Suh penetrates into the truth of the self deeper than the two poets above:

> Father was a serf, who did not come home far into the night.
> There were only Granny, old as a leek root, and a jujube tree.
> Mother with another child was dying for an apricot – protected by the dirty walls.
> Under a kerosene lamp I was a mother's boy with dirty finger nails.
> And rich hair and big eyes, taking after Mother's Father,
> Who had not come back from the sea since the year of the horse.
>
> For twenty three years the better part of what raised me was the wind.
> I am more ashamed of myself the longer I live.
> Some read a criminal in my eyes,
> Some detected an idiot in my mouth,
> Yet I will regret nothing.
>
> Even in a glorious bright morning,
> A few drops of blood are mixed
> In the sweat of poetry on my forehead.
> I have come along panting like a sick dog
> With the tongue drivelling in the sun and the shade.

Suh's courage in facing an ugly picture of himself, tracing his links to serfdom, exposing his childhood background of dire poverty, and expressing a dull and uninspiring form of existence reveals very much an adult's outlook on life. Whether the poet's ancestors were slaves or not, whether there are elements of the criminal or idiot in him, is not important here. (One detects a trace of Baudelairian influence, which the poet himself has acknowledged.) What matters here is the poet's realistic stance to his art and the mature and bold view of reality, with which Suh Jung-ju emerged as one of the most important poets in modern Korean literature. He marked a peak in the three decades of adopting a new tradition and nurturing and developing modern literature in Korea. From Suh Jung-ju onward Korean poetry entered a new stage of maturity and enrichment.

The quest for the real identity of the self still goes on in present-day Korean literature. It is the continuation of what Suh and his generation tried to do. The image of the serf, when reflected in the distorted mirror of the withering age of Japanese occupation, looked extremely ingnominious and pitiful, and yet the servile figure of a subjugated Korean dominated the concern of the writers and poets of this miserable period. It was perhaps a deliberate act of self-analysis and self-criticism. Instead of dreaming of something other than himself, instead of drawing a romantic and narcissistic figure of the self, writers turned towards self-deprecation, portraying themselves as weak, sad and oppressed characters, often in despair. Naturally the literature of this period was characterized by sadness, anxiety and misery.

This mood of sadness persisted in the works of the next decade following the end of World War II when Japan surrendered and withdrew from Korea. It was a time of rehabilitation, but instead of rejuvenation and cheerfulness at having recovered the country from their oppressors, the writers were not liberated from the mood of resignation and melancholy which continued on into the next decade with the Korean War and its aftermath. The country became culturally lively from its contact with the United States and Europe. It was a period of cultural reawakening, but the shock of the war deepened the prevailing mood of resignation and sadness. The war ravaged the country and paralysed the people, and the writers and poets suffered from its devastation. The war at the same time offered abundant source material for great tragedies, but most writers wrote stories about its victims. What they depicted in their works was not a brave challenge to their adverse circumstances, nor a bloody fight to overcome them. They almost seemed to indulge in sadness and suffering.

This love of sad stories is a major feature of much Korean literature. From classical literature onward sentiments of sadness and melancholy have predominated. In classical poetry birds in spring did not chirp but cried. Throughout the long course of Korean history there had been plenty of tragic stories, but when they were transformed into works of art they always fell short of tragedy in the true sense of the term and remained as melodramas. This non-tragic approach to tragic source material expresses a typical eastern mode of thought that does not allow people to make war with the greater opposing forces. Eastern philosophy – mainly Taoism and Buddhism – advocate the renunciation of the world and a return to nature. Therefore, there was a reconciliation before war, peace before a tragic end. The heroes and heroines in various tragic situations resigned themselves to frustration. This is why one seems to hear the sad tune of '*Auld Lang Syne*' at the end of every sad story.

This is also why the picture of the protagonist is always weak and gloomy. As time went on, however, the quest for the self became the search for 'what I was' rather than 'who I was' and the exploration was conducted in a more penetrating manner and broader context. The obsession of the 1970s and 1980s with social evils and political wrongdoings is in fact part of this exploration of the self in a larger framework. In doing this, writers seem to be trying to define the protean identity of the true Korean.

The quest for the self and the real Korean identity goes on. Modern Korean literature has only a short history of 70-odd years since the creation of the new literature in the 1910s by Choi Nam-sun and Yi Kwang-su. It is still a young literature which needs to learn much from the west; modern prose literature, for example, still follows the classical romance tradition. This leaves it short of reaching the logical coherence of realism. The developing tradition has not yet produced a Tolstoy, a Proust, a Joyce or a Lawrence, but it has given birth to many talented writers and poets and many major writers seem to be on the way, who will eventually succeed in presenting a great picture of a true Korean.

Part 1

'MEETINGS AND FAREWELLS' AND OTHER STORIES

THE CAMELLIAS

KIM YUJONG

Translated by Chung Chong-wha

Once again our rooster was being mauled. It was after lunch
when I was about to go out to gather wood that I heard the
violent fluttering sound of roosters from behind the house.
Startled, I went round to the foot of the hill and found the
two roosters, as I feared, in a bloody fight again. Jomsun's
rooster, as sturdy as a badger with a big strong head, was
pecking at our small rooster; the big one jumped into the air,
bit the head of our little one mercilessly, moved back a little bit
and then rapped its neck, fluttering its wing as if it were aware
of the elegance of its fighting style. The little one, whenever it
was attacked, put its beak onto the ground and shrieked wildly.
There were streams of blood running from old wounds that
had been cut open again. Watching this, I felt the blood rush
to my head. I wanted to run over and hit the big rooster with
my stick, but I changed my mind; instead I thrashed the air
with the stick.

Jomsun must have done it to get at me. I couldn't understand
why the girl wanted to bully me so badly. I had done nothing
wrong in refusing the potatoes she offered me four days ago.
Why the hell did the girl interfere with my fence-building
instead of going to pick her greens? She came tiptoeing up to
me from behind and said, 'Hello! Are you alone?' Until the
day before we had not been on speaking terms, pretending to

3

ignore each other. Why this sudden change of heart? Anyway, how dare she talk to a man while he was at work? We were not small children; she was as big as a pony herself.

'Of course I'm alone. I don't work in groups,' I answered curtly.

'Do you enjoy your work?' she asked. 'Why not make the fence when the summer starts?' She giggled, trying to hide it with both her hands. I didn't see anything funny there. I wondered if the warm weather was beginning to addle her brains. As if to confirm my suspicion she fished her hand from beneath her apron, keeping an eye on the house, and opened her palm right under my nose. There were three potatoes, still warm.

'You don't have these at home, do you?' As if she was doing me a great favour, she told me to gobble them right there, saying if someone saw us she would be in trouble. 'Potatoes are really nice in spring, you know,' she said.

'I don't eat potatoes. You can have them,' I said, not even turning to look at her, and reached over my shoulder to push the potatoes away. She didn't move. I heard a panting sound from behind me and then turned my head. I had never seen her darkish face go so red in my three years in the same village. There was anger in her eyes and then tears, while she stared at me. She picked up her basket, her mouth tightly shut, and ran off towards the bank of a paddy field.

Village elders used to tease her, saying, 'They should marry you off?' And she would retort without a tinge of embarrassment, 'Don't you worry, sir. When the time comes I will marry someone.' She never seemed to be bashful in situations which might have made someone her age feel timid. She was the last person to show tears because she felt frustrated or angry. It would have been more her style to hit me across the back with her basket.

Since that incident she had used all her wits to torment me. Granted, I was not polite refusing her potatoes – but what right did she have to say, 'You don't have these at home, do you?' Why couldn't she give me them nicely? Because her father was the bailiff and we were only tenant farmers under his supervision, we always had to be humbly polite and attentive to him and his family. When we first came to the village and we had no house, it was due to her father's favour that we got a bit of land and built our present house on it. When we were short of rice or barley, my parents went to Jomsun's for help. Father and Mother would praise her parents for their kindness; and yet Mother would warn me not to get involved with Jomsun, saying that if a boy and girl of sixteen were seen together by a villager 'it wouldn't be nice'. She had a point there; if I really did get involved with Jomsun, her parents wouldn't like it, and we'd end up with no land to farm and no house to live in. So why the hell did this girl try to bully me to death?

The evening of the day she had run off in tears, I was coming home after gathering wood when I heard the shrieking sound of a hen. At first I thought that somebody was killing a chicken for the pot, so I paid no attention and carried on past Jomsun's house. I looked over the fence and was shocked to see Jomsun, sitting on the earthen floor of the inner quarters, holding our hen tightly in her apron and hitting it as hard as she could, yelling, 'Bloody animal, drop dead! Drop dead!' She wasn't just hitting it on the head, but punching it in the guts as if she wanted to damage the ovaries. I shook with rage. I looked round to make sure that there was no one in the house, then hit the fence with my stick as hard as I could and shouted, 'What the hell are you doing, trying to make our hen stop laying?'

But she didn't look surprised at getting caught. She just kept on beating the hen and yelling, 'Drop dead! Drop dead!' As she wasn't scared, I could tell that she had waited for my return from the hill before she began to beat up our hen. I realized that I was in a bad spot; I couldn't go into the house and fight a girl. All I could do was to whack her fence each time she hit our hen, as I knew that the more I beat the fence the shakier it would become. And yet I knew I couldn't win.

'You bitch! Do you really want to kill our hen?' Staring at her as viciously as I could, I shouted at the top of my voice. Only then she came towards the fence and threw the hen at my head. 'Filthy! Filthy!' she spat out. To show her I was really disgusted and angry I strode off along the fence. But the fluttering hen landed on me, dropping some muck on my forehead; and I could tell immediately that not only were the ovaries damaged, but all its insides were out of order. I heard the girl curse at my back, 'You fool! You idiot!' That was quite enough, but she went further: 'Your father's a eunuch, isn't he?'

'What? My father's a eunuch?' I was going to shout at her, but when I turned round I couldn't see Jomsun's head over the fence. As soon as I turned back again, I heard her swear at me. I was so angry I didn't even feel the pain in my toe when I stubbed it on a stone and it began to bleed. In the end tears shot up in my eyes.

But Jomsun's bullying didn't end there. When there was no one around she would bring her cock to our house and start a cock-fight. She knew that their big, aggressive cock would win the fight. Our little one's head would get badly pecked, with blood running around both eyes. When our cock wouldn't come out to fight, she would use bird seed to coax it out.

I just couldn't let things go on like this. I had to think of a way to retaliate. One day I took our cock to the pot where chilli paste was preserved. I was told once that when you give chilli paste to a cock, it works as wonderfully as feeding an adder to a sick bull. I scooped out a dishful of chilli paste and pushed it to the cock. It seemed to like the paste and gobbled up nearly half the dish. As I thought it would take a while for the chilli to work on the cock, I left it in the coop.

During a short break after I had carried two piles of manure to the field, I took the cock out of the coop. Everybody seemed to be in the fields except Jomsun, who was crouching down doing something – either sorting rags or rearranging old cotton wool. I went to the field where Jomsun's cock was roaming about, and I let our cock loose, waiting for what would happen. The two cocks lost no time getting into a fight. The big cock managed first to pounce on our little one, which fluttered its wings and jumped into the air, rising and falling a few times. But finally our cock made a big soaring jump, and while it was coming down it scratched its opponent's eyes with its claws and pecked at its head. The big one seemed surprised and retreated a few steps. Our cock didn't miss the opportunity; it swiftly charged at the cringing enemy and pecked again at the head. Blood started running from the wounds.

What a thought! All you needed for a cock fight was a chilli paste! I became quite elated. I saw Jomsun watching, with a frowning face, from the other side of the fence. I began to slap my backside with both my hands, feeling great, and shouting, 'Well done! Bravo!'

But soon the situation was reversed and I became disconcerted. The big cock suddenly rebounded as if it wanted to even the score, and struck back, pecking violently. This time Jomsun was triumphant and began to laugh as loud as she could. I couldn't stomach it any longer. I picked up our cock and returned home. I regretted not having fed it more chilli. I went to the chilli pot and gave more paste to our defeated champion Perhaps due to excitement the cock refused to take any more of the stuff. I had no choice but to force it to lie back while I pushed a cigarette holder into its beak. I mixed the paste with water and then poured the hot liquid through the holder. The cock seemed to find it too hot and began to sneeze, but I decided that was better than having its old wounds re-opened.

However, after two dishfuls of the chilli water, the sprightly cock became still and dropped its head on the ground. This was awful. I was afraid of my father catching me at this. I took the fowl back to the coop and left it there until this morning.

And the cock was taken to a fight yet again. That girl Jomsun must have sneaked into our house while there was no one about and taken the ailing cock out. I was worried about the effects of the chilli water, and yet I couldn't afford to skip the wood gathering. While I was cutting dead pine branches, I kept wanting to choke Jomsun to death. I decided I'd hit her on the back with my stick as hard as I could, and hurried down to the village.

While I was nearing our house I was surprised to hear the sound of a reed pipe, and stopped short. I saw yellow camellias on a rock at the foot of the hill, and Jomsun playing the reed pipe among the flowers. What was more surprising was the fluttering sound of the cocks coming from where she sat. The girl must have brought out the cocks to the path where I was bound to pass by, in the hope that she would catch my eye and get me going again.

There she was playing the reed pipe nonchalantly, as if nothing was happening. I was so infuriated that I felt tears gushing up in my eyes. I didn't have time to put down the wood I was carrying on my back; I just threw it down and dashed to the scene of the cock fight with my stick.

When I came nearer I saw, as I had half expected, our little cock almost bitten to death, while Jomsun was playing the pipe undisturbed. That really make me fly into a rage. At one time I had thought, like other people in the village, that Jomsun was a pretty girl who worked hard to help her mother round the house, but now looking at her I found she had the eye of a little fox.

Without hesitation I ran to the big cock and hit it hard with my stick. The thing dropped dead on the spot. By the time I realized what I'd done, Jomsun came at me with the nastiest eyes she could make and I fell over backwards.

'You bastard! What right do you have to kill someone else's cock?'

'So what?' I said, standing up.

'Do you realize whose fowl it is?' She gave me a shove and I fell over again. I felt ashamed of my rash behaviour and yet I was angry. But I was also afraid; the result of this incident would be losing our land and our house. I sat up weakly and burst into tears, hiding my eyes with my sleeve.

'You won't do it again, will you?' Jomsun came to me and whispered. It was like hearing the voice of a saviour.

'No, I won't do it again,' I readily answered, wiping away tears, though I didn't know what she meant by 'do it again'.

'If you do it again, I'll bully you to death.'

'No I won't do it again, I promise.'

'Don't worry about the cock, I won't tell my father.'

As if she was pushed by something from behind, she fell on me, and both of us tumbled into the camellias. I felt dizzy with the fragrant smell of the flowers.

'Be quiet!'

'Don't worry.'

A few minutes later I heard Jomsun's mother calling her, irritated, Jomsun! Jomsun! Where has that girl gone in the middle of her sewing?'

Scared, Jomsun stole out from the flowers and ran down towards the village, and I crawled along the rock towards the peak of the hill.

SHOWER

HWANG SUN-WON

Translated by Chang Wang-rok

The boy knew who the girl was when he saw her by the brook.
She was playing with the running water, dipping her hand into
and splashing it. She was a great-grandchild of the old scholar
Mr Yun of Sodang village. It seemed as if she had never seen
such a brook in the big city of Seoul where she had come
from.

She had played with the water there for some days on her
way home from school. Until the previous day she had always
squatted at the edge of the brook, but today she was squatting
on one of the stepping stones, near the edge, that crossed the
brook.

The boy sat on the bank waiting for her to step back to the
edge of the brook so that he could walk across the stones to
the other side. By chance a man approached, and when the
girl stepped back to make way for him the boy followed him
across.

The following day the boy showed up at the bank a little later
than usual. But again she was squatting on the stepping stone
in the middle of the brook. This time, though, she was not
playing with the water but was washing her face with it. She
had rolled up the sleeves of her pink sweater, exposing the

9

glistening whiteness of her forearms to match the nape of her neck.

After washing her face, she looked into the water for a long time, perhaps at her reflection. Suddenly she stopped at the water as if to capture a tiny fish that was passing. The boy had no way of knowing whether she had noticed him watching her from the bank. She kept on clutching at the water in front of her. More often than not she had missed what she wanted to catch, but, intrigued by her game, she did not give up. To all appearance she would not budge until someone came along, as on the previous day.

Then she picked up something from the bottom of the stream. It was a white pebble. She rose to her feet, pebble in hand, and hopped across the stones to the other side of the brook. She then turned toward the boy and threw the stone in his direction, shouting, 'You silly boy!'

Instinctively the boy stiffened. The girl fled, her short hair bouncing behind her. She followed a path into the clump of tall reeds along the bank and disappeared. The tips of the swaying reeds shone radiantly in the autumn sunlight.

For quite a long time, he waited anxiously for her to emerge from the other side of the reeds. He stood on tiptoe and kept watching, but she did not appear. Then he noticed at one spot a wisp of reed tops moving, and soon she was back in sight on the other side, holding an armful of the flower-like seed pods from the tops of the reeds. She was walking slowly ahead, and her load hid her head so that it looked as if a bundle of flowers was walking through the field in the clear bright sun.

The boy remained where he stood until the walking flowers disappeared from sight. He looked down at the pebble she had hurled at him. It had dried. He picked it up and put it into his pocket.

He came to the brook the next day a little later than usual and the girl was nowhere to be seen. He felt relieved. And so it was the following day. But when on succeeding days he did not meet the girl, he felt an emptiness in his heart. He had meanwhile fallen into the habit of fingering the pebble in his pocket.

One day he sat on the same stepstone the girl had used and dipped his hands into the water and washed his face as she had done. He looked into the water. It reflected his deeply tanned features which he decided he didn't like. He cupped his hands and tried to scoop the image up again and again until he felt someone approaching. He stood up, surprised. It was her, coming across the stream. She must have been hiding and watching. The boy started to run. One foot missed a stepping stone and fell into the water with a splash. He ran on.

He wished to hide himself, but there were no reeds or any other cover on this side. The buckwheat patches were too low. As he ran across them the aroma of the pinkish-white flowers struck his nostrils. For a second he felt faint, then a salty liquid reached his tongue from his upper lip. His nose was bleeding. He ran on, wiping the blood with his hand. He seemed to hear her shouting, 'You silly boy! You silly boy!'

It was Saturday. When the boy arrived at the brook, she was squatting there on the opposite edge of the stream, playing with the water. He had not seen her for some days. He started to walk across the stones, pretending not to notice her. He took care not to miss the stepping stones, as he had done before, and managed to cross the brook safely.

'Hey, you,' she called.

Pretending not to have heard, he walked up the bank.

'Say, what's the name of this shell?' she asked, catching up with him.

He turned around in spite of himself. His eyes met hers. They were clear and dark-brown. He quickly glanced at the thing in her palm.

'Silk clam.'

'What a pretty name!'

They were now at a fork in the path. She had to go down about one and a half kilometres one way and he nearly two kilometres in the other direction. The girl stopped.

'Ever been to the other side of that hill?' she asked, pointing ahead to the swell of land across the field.

'Oh, no.'

'Let's go there together, shall we? I've been bored to death since I came to the countryside from Seoul.'

'It's farther than you think it is.'

'It can't be too far,' she retorted. 'When I lived in Seoul, we

11

used to go on picnics pretty far away.' Her eyes wore a derisive expression.

The boy and the girl started along the narrow path between the rice paddies. Farmers were harvesting golden rice. In some of the paddies stood scarecrows with strings attached to them. The girl pulled the end of the one of these strings, which she found attached to the side of the path. The startled sparrows flew away. The boy suddenly remembered that he was supposed to have gone straight home to do his chore of chasing away sparrows in the rice paddies near there.

'What fun it is!' the girl exclaimed in delight. The birds flew away, dancing away from the scarecrows waving their arms operated by the string she pulled. He noticed a small dimple appearing on her left cheek.

The girl saw another scarecrow some distance away. She started running there to pull its string. The boy ran after her, forsaking his sense of obligation to help his father on such a fine day as this.

He caught up with her, ran beside her, and then ran ahead. His face stung a little every time a flying locust hit it. The clear blue sky seemed to whirl before his eyes. He felt dizzy. He gazed at the eagle circling over him and realized that that was why the sky was spinning and why he was getting dizzy.

He looked back. She was pulling the string of the second scarecrow he had run past. This one was a more animated dancer than the previous one.

There was a ditch at the end of the rice paddies they had run across. The girl, who had caught up with him, jumped over it before he did. From there started fields of various crops other than rice. Stacks of Indian millet stood sparsely in the field they were passing.

'What's over there?' the girl asked, pointing to a rugged thatched platform atop four tall poles, a ladder leading to it.

'It's a watchtower for the melon field.'

'How are the musk-melons here?' she asked. 'Are they very sweet?'

'Sure. And the watermelons are the best.'

'I wish I could eat one.'

The boy entered a radish patch nearby, pulled up two radishes, and brought them to her. They were still too young, but the boy pulled the leaves off of them and gave her one. As if

12

to show her how, he bit off the top of his radish and, digging his thumbnail into it, peeled off the white skin. Then he bit into it noisily.

The girl followed suit, chewed a few mouthfuls, then tossed the radish away. 'Oh, it's bitter!'

'You're right,' the boy agreed, and hurled his away.

They were much closer to the hill. The autumn maple leaves were dazzling. With a joyful shout, the girl ran toward the foot of the mountain. The boy stayed behind and picked flowers. Soon the girl joined him.

The boy gave her the bundle of flowers he had collected.

'Thank you,' she said. 'Tell me the names of these flowers, will you?'

'This is a daisy,' he started, 'and this one is a bush clover, and these are bellflowers.'

'I didn't know that bellflowers were so pretty,' the girl said admiringly. 'I like the purple ones better than the white ones. And what is the name of this yellow flower that looks like a tiny umbrella?'

'It's called *matari*,' the boy replied.

The girl repeated its name and held up the flower by its stem, in the manner of putting up an umbrella, and smiled with a blush. Slight dimples creased her reddened cheeks.

The boy left her and started collecting flowers again. When he returned, he sorted out only the fresh and wholesome ones before handing them to her.

'Don't throw any away,' she ordered as she gratefully received the second handful of flowers.

Soon they climbed up the maple-and-pine-covered hill. They uttered cries of joy when they reached the hilltop, from which they could view a rocky valley with a broad, winding brook and some farmhouses huddled in groups under poplars at the foot of the hills beyond. Otherwise the landscape looked pretty much the same as that on the side of the hill from which they had just come.

The boy and the girl turned around and, finding an oblong rock a few steps before them, went and sat there as if by tacit agreement.

A quiet descended all around. The hot autumn sun seemed to circulate the aroma of drying grass.

'Tell me the name of the flower over there,' she said, pointing to a little steep slope below which some pinkish-violet flowers peeped out from under clusters of pods on tangled vines.

'They are the flowers of arrowroots,' the boy explained.

'Oh, they're just like wistaria,' she said. 'There's a trelissed wistaria in my school in Seoul. Those flowers remind me of the girls I used to play with there.'

So saying, she rose to her feet and climbed down toward the base of the steep slope and pulled at one of the thick flower-vines. But it didn't yield to her efforts. She strained further and slipped, screaming. Her hand snatched a vine and held it.

The boy flew over and, seizing her outstretched hand, pulled her to safety. He regretted that he hadn't gone to fetch the flower for her.

He was shocked at the sight of blood oozing through a scratch on her right kneecap. He knelt down and, putting his lips to the spot, started sucking the blood. An idea occurred to him, and he excused himself and ran away to get something.

The boy came running back, out of breath. 'Let's put this on the wound. It will help,' he said, applying some pine resin to the scratch.

He then climbed down to the same spot where she had been, and, seizing the same vine with the clusters of flowers, bit it off. In the same way, he collected some more flower clusters. He handed them to the girl. 'How is your cut?' he asked.

'It's all right now,' she said. 'Thank you.'

'There's a calf down there in the clearing,' the boy reported. 'Let's go and look.'

It was a little brown calf, so young that it didn't have a nose-ring yet. He grabbed the reins close to its muzzle and scratched its back with his other hand to please it. Then he leaped up adroitly and landed astride the animal's back. The calf started trotting around the stake to which it was tethered. As it kept on circling, the white face of the girl, her pink sweater and dark blue skirt, the spray of wildflowers in her hands – all suddenly blurred into one whirling multi-coloured circle. He became dizzy, but he was so proud of his feat, which the girl from Seoul could not possibly imitate, that he forced himself to stay on.

'Boy, what are you doing here?' he heard a man shouting.

An old farmer with a long beard, evidently the owner of the calf, emerged from a clump of sword grass.

The boy slid off the back of the calf. He was sure that the farmer would scold him for riding the little calf whose back was still tender. But the old man merely studied the boy and said, 'Hurry back home, children, before a shower catches you.'

Indeed, a huge column of rain clouds appeared overhead. Things were astir. A gust of wind whistled through the bushes. Then the sky, the trees, the ground and everything around them turned dark violet.

While they were descending the hill the boy and the girl heard raindrops pattering on the broad oak leaves. The boy felt a big drop or two chill the nape of his neck. Then down came the rain in sheets, almost blocking the view before them.

When they finally reached the foot of the hill, they saw through the rain a watchtower looming ahead in the field. Soaking wet, they ran to the solitary shelter but found it in bad shape, its tattered straw-thatched roof leaking freely and its posts tilting. However, the boy found one dry spot in it and led the girl there. Her lips had turned purple and her shoulders were shaking. The boy took off his cotton jacket and put it around her. She looked at him gratefully, water dripping over her eyes, but did not say anything. She then began to sort out the crushed and broken flowers from the bundle she still held.

The roof began to leak even where the girl stood, so that the place no longer served as a shelter. The boy looked out, thinking. The next moment he dashed out to one of the stacks of tall sorghum stalks about twenty metres away and stuck his hand inside to see if it was dry. He then fetched some bundles of stalks from the nearest stacks for additional protection. Feeling secure, he beckoned to the girl.

Inside the conical stack there were no leaks, but it was dark and there was not enough room for both of them. Putting her inside, he stayed out in the rain. A mist of steam rose from his shoulders.

Almost in a whisper, the girl asked him to come inside. He said that he was all right. But she insisted, so he edged in backwards. His back crushed the flowers she was holding, but she didn't mind. The sudden smell of the boy's wet body surprised her, but she didn't turn her face away. Her trembling seemed to ease somewhat from the body heat of the boy.

All of a sudden the steady pattering of the shower on the sorghum stack stopped, and in no time it had grown light outside. They left the gloom of their temporary abode, and ahead of them sunlight was pouring down on the amber rice fields.

They walked up to a ditch, where there was a noisy flood of muddy water. The ditch was too wide to jump across, so the boy rolled up his trousers and turned his back toward the girl. Without a word she allowed him to carry her piggy-back. 'Omuh!' exclaimed the girl when she saw the water come halfway up his thighs, tightening her hold around his neck.

By the time they returned to the brookside where they had started, the sky was blue again and without a speck of cloud, as if it had had no knowledge of the shower that had just passed.

The boy did not see her for days after that. Every day when he reached the brook on his way home from school he looked around, but she was nowhere to be seen. He looked for her in the schoolyard and peeped into the fifth-grade girls' classroom, but neither brought him the sight that he desired so much.

Then one day, when he got to the brook, his fingers busy with the white pebble in his pocket, there she was, squatting on the edge of the far side of the brook. As he crossed the brook he felt his heart beating fast.

The girl rose. 'I've been ill,' she said. She did look ill – pale and thinner.

'Because of the shower we had the other day?' he asked, worried. She nodded. They were walking side by side.

'Are you all right now?'

She shook her head. 'Not quite yet.'

'Why, then, you should be in bed, shouldn't you?'

'But it's boring staying home so long. So I came out.... What fun it was that day, though.'

She looked down at her pink sweater and said, 'I don't know where I got this. This spot doesn't seem to want to come off.'

The boy saw a dim dark-brown smudge on the hem of her pink sweater. The girl looked up. The familiar dimples appeared on her flushed cheeks. 'What do you suppose made this spot?'

The boy kept staring at it, puzzled.

'Yes, I know now,' she said. 'You remember when you carried me on your back? It came from that.'

He blushed.

At the fork, she said. 'By the way, this morning they picked these at home.' She held out a handful of jujubes to him. 'They're going to use them for ancestral rites on the harvest moon day.'

He hesitated.

'Come on, have some,' she insisted. 'They're very sweet. They say my great-grandfather planted the tree.'

He held out his cupped hands and took them. 'Wow! They're really big.'

'Did you know we're moving out of our house after the harvest moon?'

The boy had heard villagers talking about how the Yun family's business had failed in Seoul and how the grandson had had to sell his house there and come back here to his father's house in the country. It now appeared that the family was hard-pressed financially and was obliged to sell this house as well.

'I don't know what it's all about, but I just hate moving,' she complained. 'It's what the grown-ups do and I can't help it.' A sad look appeared in her eyes, something he had not seen before.

They parted, and as he walked back home he mulled over the news of her moving away from the village. He could not describe how he felt, but somehow the jujubes she had given him did not taste as sweet as they should have.

That night the boy crept into the walnut grove of Old Man Toksoe and climbed a tree. During the day he had taken note of the branch that had the most walnuts, and now he beat the nuts off this branch with a pole. He was frightened by the loud sound of the falling nuts hitting the ground. He became desperate and struck the branch hard again and again, to get all the good nuts.

On the way back home he felt his way along carefully, staying in the shadows cast by the three-quarter moon. It was the first time he had ever felt thankful for the shadows.

The boy ran his hands over his bulging pockets. It didn't bother him at all that people say you can get a bad itch from shucking the burrs from walnuts with your bare hands. The walnuts from Old Man Toksoe's house were supposed to be the best ones in the area, and the boy's only thought was that he must get some to the girl right away for her to try.

But then, he suddenly remembered that he had forgotten to ask her to come again to the brook as soon as she got better before they moved away. What a silly fool he was. What a silly fool.

When he returned from school the next day he saw his father dressed up to go out, holding a chicken in his hands. The boy asked him where he was going, but his father, ignoring his question, said to his mother, 'I wonder if this hen is big enough.'

She handed him a straw-mesh beg. 'It's been cackling for days now looking for a place to lay its first egg,' she said. 'Not quite so big yet, but it's fat all right.'

The boy turned to his mother and this time asked her where his father was going.

'He's going over to the Yuns in Sodang Village to give them this chicken for an offering at their ancestral rites.'

'Why not the big speckled rooster, then?'

His father gave a jocular laugh and said, 'Son, this one has more substance.'

Embarrassed, the boy threw down his bundle of books, went out to the stable, and spanked the rump of the bull as if to kill a gadfly.

The water in the brook became clearer as the autumn deepened. One day the boy crossed the brook on his way back from school and stopped for a while at the fork where he had last parted with the girl. From the reed bush where he lingered the village looked much closer under the transparent blue sky.

The boy had heard the grown-ups say that her family was moving to Yangpyong tomorrow to run a small shop. The boy fingered the walnuts in his pocket with one hand, and impulsively tore off reed tops again and again with his other hand.

That night, lying awake alone, he was still thinking of her leaving him and the village. He tried to decide whether or not to go to the village to see them depart. If he did, would he be able to see her? . . .

He was about to doze off when he heard a voice saying, 'What a terrible thing to happen!'

His father had returned and was talking to his mother. 'The Yuns are really in a bad way,' he went on. 'They had to sell all the fields they owned, and then the house they've lived in for generations. To make matters worse, old Mr Yun's great grandchild died.'

'Oh, that's too bad,' the mother said, making a clicking sound with her tongue. 'That little girl from Seoul was their only grandchild, wasn't she?' She was sewing under a kerosene lamp.

'Right,' his father replied. 'They also had two boys, but both died a long time ago.'

'How unfortunate they are with their children!'

'That's what I was going to say.' The father was puffing on a small bamboo pipe. 'They say that the girl had been sick for quite a few days, but the family couldn't afford to give her the medical care she needed. Their family line is cut off now. But you know, she must've been an extraordinary girl – she said, just before she died, "When I die, please bury me in the clothes I'm wearing now." '

THE MARSH

KIM DONG-NI

Translated by Chung Chong-wha

Suk has come to the marsh again, his heart pounding rather heavily. Full of strange expectation and curiosity, he ran to the marsh through the barely field where barley plants stand taller than his height.

Would he cross the marsh today? No, he wouldn't; he wouldn't dare. He is still afraid of it. Then, from where does the strange expectation and curiosity stem? He can't tell. When he passes through the big barley field and comes to the top of a small hill where black coloured weeds grow thick and wild, he sees a wood, so far away that it seems to be in touch with the brim of the sky, and then suddenly his eyes sparkle and shine brightly. But only for a moment. The strange expectation and curiosity die out the moment the glitter in his eyes fades. His head drops, and his eyes stay on the sight of the bubbling bog and the surface of the marsh which is always covered with sea-lettuce. Dejected, sad, and motionless, he watches the bubbling bog and the marsh covered with sea-lettuce for a long time. The other end of the marsh is conjoined with another bubbling bog, and a heath stretches out at the end of it, reaching the foot of a steep hill. The wood is on the slope of this hill, the big and endless wood.

In the evenings the wood is canopied by beautifully coloured clouds. On a fine day the wood seems to constantly puff out patches of white, soft clouds. In the woods are numberless beautiful flowers and myriad birds sing. The grandfather lives there waiting for him with a basketful of sweet wild fruit.

'Take these, son. Help yourself, Suk.' The grandfather offers the fruit basket to Suk, who picks up one of the most red and ripe ones in his small hand, and then he runs towards the heart of the wood, following after a mysterious bird. Suddenly he stops, and picks up blue and yellow flowers, which he rubs on his face. How nice and lovely the fragrance of the flowers is!

But Suk lets the fruit and flowers fall on the ground, for he has heard something rise up through the green surface of the marsh. He doesn't know what it is. He hasn't seen it. The moment it soared up he was still in the wood, wandering, and the thing presently fell into water again.

What abides in the marsh? Occasionally, something arises from the surface of the marsh and then sinks in a second. Sometimes a big, white ring, a mercury-like, big white bubble appears on the green water, tearing sea-lettuce apart, and it instantly bursts out, making a small explosive sound. Perhaps it is the sound of an old and fearful sea-monster farting. Once he was told that the sea-lettuce is the best food for reptiles. Then in the marsh snakes and adders must be swarming. Once he saw an old toad, his lower jaw drooping and his eyes encircled by gold rings, slowly crawl out of the water to the earth of the bog, and wriggle for a while, spouting venom.

A leech in the marsh is as big as an earthworm. No sooner the leech of this kind touches one's skin than it gets to the innermost bones. Perhaps the marsh teems with more reptiles, insects, animals and monsters than Suk is aware of, more venomous, more horrible than he can imagine.

Suk once asked his father what dwells in the marsh, but the answer wasn't very informative. His father only said that, as others have commonly said, there are vipers and many other dreadful monsters and therefore no one dares to go near the swamp.

Indeed, there is no one around the marsh. Suk is always alone there. He very much wishes to ask someone how to get to the far-away wood across the marshy land, but no one is there to answer him. So he roams about the place alone and goes back home when it gets dark.

Suk does know where the marsh starts and where it ends.

There is a mountain to the north of it and a big river to the southeast of it. He just guesses that the marsh stretches in between the mountain and the river. Many times he tried to find a way to the wood in the direction of the steep mountain and the river. In his efforts to break through a thick wild bush where goose-fronds, wild-grapes and dayflowers are entangled and primitive-looking, he soon tired and became exhausted. In the midst of the wild plants, taller than he, he watched caterpillars, earthworms, frogs, crabs, and many others creep about here and there, uninterestedly.

Suk doesn't mind these insects much. Even lizards do not scare him. The only thing he is afraid of is the viper. If, by mistake and misfortune, he happens to tread on the tail of an adder, he will be bitten to death. Even if he is lucky enough to avoid vipers, there is no hope of his getting into the wood. At the end of the bush he will confront either the towering mountain or the wide river. Suk, nevertheless, exhausts himself in his efforts to pierce the bush, because he can not stay home.

Suk comes to the marsh, because he is restless and impatient. He is well aware that he can not cross the marsh. He is simply filled with strange expectations, curiosity for unidentified things.

The other day he heard Buni's mother talking to Buni in the kitchen.

'He's going to die like his mother.'

The mother and daughter didn't know that Suk was listening outside. Suk does not hold anything against Buni. He thinks it only natural for her to be cross with him since he bluntly refused her earnest entreaty not to go near the swamp. She might have told her mother of his visits to the forbidden place because she is really worried about him. She seems to believe that anyone who goes near the marshy land will be drowned. Suk, however, was puzzled by what Buni's mother said to her daughter; its meaning was beyond his comprehension. He simply interprets her remarks as nasty abuse directed against his own mother and himself.

Suk has been to the wood only once. It was with his mother when they went to see his grandfather, when he was two or three years old. Suk was carried on his mother's back, and they reached the wood, after they had climbed many hills and crossed the wide river by a small ferry-boat.

Still Suk can remember the occasion clearly: a deep and clear rivulet flowing by the inlet of the wood into the big wide river; age-old pines, furs, zelkova and oak-trees standing densely on the other side of the rivulet; a bare stump of a withered tree among these, reminding him of the carcass of a giant standing with his hands wide open.

Suk's mother crossed the bridge over the rivulet, carrying the child on her back, and went deep into the wood. Overhead the leaves of myriad trees covered the sky, and briars and nameless flowers were to be seen here and there. Suk got off from his mother's back and ran after the flowers. But his mother called after him.

'No, child. You might get lost in the wood.'

She held the child by the arm.

'Mummy, where is grandpa's house?'

'We ought to go further into the wood.'

Mother led him into the wood, cutting through wild flowers and trees.

'Mummy, do you really know where grandpa's house is?'

'Yes, I do. It is under the trees with big leaves.'

His mother seemed to have determined her path further and further into the wood according to the shapes of trees. But the trees with big leaves didn't seem to be near at hand, and to the boy the way seemed endless. The deeper they went in, the louder the birds sang, as if they were signalling to one another the trespassing of strangers. Suddenly the chirpings of birds made Suk afraid of the unknown wood. When he turned his head toward his mother, she immediately saw in his fear-sticken eyes that he was tired, and she said, 'Come, darling. Come to my back.'

Suk fell asleep on his mother's back, and when he opened his eyes he found he was inside his grandfather's hut. But the grandfather was not at home.

'Mummy, where is grandpa?'

'He went out to pick berries.'

'What berries?'

'You shall know when he comes back.'

'Where does he get them?'

'In the wood.'

'Are there many berries in the wood?'

'Yes, darling.'

His mother told him that she ate a lot of berries when she was a small child, as small as Suk himself.

'Did you live on berries in the wood?'

'No, child. Beside berries, there are potatoes, yams, corncobs, millets, and pumpkins.'

Suk's mother went into the kitchen and took out some potatoes from a wooden box, to wash them. When she came back from the well with cleaned potatoes, the grandfather had already come home, an old man, small in height, his eyes deeply hollowed and his face covered with a black beard. He offered Suk a basket filled with colourful plums, apricots and mulberries, with a smile on his purple lips amid the black beard. He said nothing, as if he were dumb.

'This is your grandfather,' said his mother to Suk, but the old man said nothing again; he only showed his purple coloured lips through the black beard. He took out well-ripened apricots and plums, and put them in Suk's hand. But when he turned to his mother, the old man opened his mouth and said, 'Yong-jin is dead.'

'Yong-jin?'

'It was last spring. Before he died, on his death-bed, he called your name once, so I am told.'

Suk's mother said nothing; she only stared into the old man's face, absent-mindedly, and in a minute tears welled out of her eyes and rolled down on her cheeks. Suk didn't understand why his mother shed tears on hearing the news of the death of a man called Yong-jin. He just turned his head away, spat out the seed of an apricot, and threw it over a zelkova tree.

The next day the grandfather disappeared into the wood as soon as he had finished breakfast, and in the evening he brought home the same berries but in greater quantity than before. Suk wanted to accompany his grandfather, but his mother wouldn't let him go to the deeper parts of the wood. Instead, he picked the flowers around the hut with his mother: the flowers, blue, white, red, or yellow, whose names were unknown even to his mother. The birds in the wood were different in colour from those in the village; and they were so free in their movements from branch to branch.

'Mummy, can you get me that bird over there, the bird with a long tail and red wings?'

'I can't fly like him.'

Suk spent the whole morning trying to catch the bird with red wings, but in vain. In the evening he told the old man of his abortive bird-catching adventure, and the old man, revealing his purple lips, said, 'You can live here with me in the wood, if you like.' And Suk thought that he wouldn't mind living with him if he could have the bird with red wings.

But Suk had to leave the wood and the old man two or three days later, to get back to his father, and again he was carried on his mother's back. The days he spent in the wood are now to him the happiest moments of his life, but they are also the source of grief and distress. No sooner had Suk returned home from the wood than his father welcomed his mother with cruel abuse. Suk didn't know why his father was so angry. He only vaguely guessed that his mother was not to go back to the wood, but why, he didn't know. Why his mother, so beautiful and gentle, should be treated like that by his father, was completely beyond the understanding of a boy of two or three years of age.

Today, by the marsh, Suk again thinks of the incident and still can't explain it to himself. Why did mother make father angry? Did she really deserve father's ill-treatment? Why didn't mother live with grandfather in the wood? Why did she marry father? How did father manage to find mother in such a remote place? Why did grandfather let mother leave him for father? Why has mother left home without a word? Why didn't she choose to fight back against father?

The night before she left home she had cried the whole night, holding Suk on her knees. (His father had refused to see her and hadn't stayed home then.) Around daybreak, Suk fell asleep, and his mother left home for good. The next day, a group of people went out to look for her, but no one told Suk the result of this search. However, Suk managed to hear that she had gone to a temple to become a nun, but people seemed to doubt the authenticity of this account.

To find out himself, he went to Paradise Temple, some two and half miles away, last spring, but no one there was able to tell him anything about his mother. After that Suk decided to disbelieve the rumour. He also decided, for fear of being flogged, not to let his father know about his visit to the temple. Whenever his mother is mentioned, his father becomes wild, and either beats him or shouts at him.

Last autumn Suk's father remarried after three years as a widower. His wife brought with her a girl, called Buni, of ten years of age, four years older than Suk. His father's new wife told Suk to call Buni 'Sister' but Suk has insisted on calling her by her first name, which makes his father's wife furious. She says, 'The brat is too damn stubborn.' Suk also has refused to call the woman 'Mother'. She is just 'Buni's mother', and this makes her hostile attitude to Suk worse. A kindly old woman in the neighbourhood tried to dissuade him from adopting an obstinate attitude, but Suk couldn't comply with her wishes. Suk thinks his father's new wife far too ugly.

But Buni is quite different from her mother. First of all she doesn't hate Suk. And she shares with Suk sweets which her mother has given her, edibles such as burnt rice, potatoes, and even wheat-gluten. Sometimes she gives the whole lot to him. She never tattles on him to her mother, even if he has done something wrong. Strangely, Suk's father does not like Buni which Suk finds difficult to understand. Suk's father causes Buni to become ill, and makes her do various rough tasks. On the other hand, Buni does not dislike her step-father, and always calls him 'Father' never 'Suk's Father' Suk sometimes feels that Buni is his real sister.

'Don't you hate your mother?' Suk often asks Buni.

'Why, she is my mother,' replies Buni. 'Why should I? Do you hate your real mother?'

Suk's eyes become wet whenever his mother is mentioned. His mother always stays in his heart, and many times he calls her in a whispering tone, and yet when someone refers to her and says 'Your mother' he finds it difficult to hold back tears. When Buni saw tear-drops in Suk's eyes, she said, giving him a small flute made of a barley plant, 'Now, please don't go near the marsh.' Her voice was soft and gentle, and there was a light of tenderness in her eyes. Suk felt that Buni could be his real sister after all.

'Promise me that you won't go near the marsh, please.' She sounded determined.

'Why, you scared of vipers?' Buni merely shook her head to convey a negative response.

'Are you afraid of the bog?'

She shook her again.

'Then, fearful insects?'

'No, I know all about these.'

'Then, what?'

'Perhaps your mother might...' She didn't finish, but she meant to say that, 'Perhaps your mother might have thrown herself into the marsh.'

However, Suk didn't understand why Buni had uttered an incomplete sentence. He more or less guessed that she meant to say that his mother had disappeared in tragic circumstances.

'Perhaps my mummy has gone to my grandpa. When you reach the marsh you can see the wood where he lives. They say that my mummy has become a nun, but it is a lie.'

Tearful, Buni looked into Suk's face, and said nothing.

Four days later, Suk ran again to the marsh, in spite of Buni's entreaties that he should not go there. Apprehensive that something might go wrong, she decided to follow him, and ran along the narrow winding path through the barely field. She caught sight of the lonely figure of Suk standing by the marsh. But she didn't dash to him straight away, fearing that he might take off into the wild shrubs. She hesitated for a while. An idea suddenly flashed in her mind. She cut a barley plant and made a small flute out of its stalk, and she began to play it, in the hope that the sounds of the flute would somehow make him come back to her. However, when he heard the flute, he just turned his head toward Buni and then moved his eyes away to the waters of the marsh, remaining where he was, motionless. Buni approached him, playing the flute the while, but Suk just sat there watching the far away wood, indifferent to the music of the flute. When she stood close to Suk, Buni said, offering the flute, 'Here, keep it.' Suk remained mute and deaf to her. Buni threw the barley-stalk flute into the marsh and held him by the arm gently. 'Let's go home,' she said.

As Buni tried hard to drag him homeward, Suk resisted her with all his strength, and at that very instant the edge of the bank collapsed and one of Suk's feet slipped into the bog. In a moment of panic she let him go, and the next moment the other foot slid into the bog as he exerted himself trying to get out. Overwhelmed with fear and confusion, Buni stretched her hand to Suk and tried to pull him out on to the crumbled edge of the bank. But the earth was too soft to withstand the weight of both of them. The harder she tried, the deeper they sank. When finally she slipped into the bog, Suk was already buried with only his head above the surface. While sinking deeper Buni grasped Suk's hand firm and hard. She held it as powerfully as she could, trying to pull him out.

THE FLOOD

HAN MAL-SUK

Translated by Kim Dong-sung

It continued to rain for four days, and the muddy water from the flooded river covered the rice paddies and the fields. Three more days of rain and Tashik's hut would be washed away.

Tashik stood on the porch and watched the whole village that stood upstream being swept away by the water. The straw roofing of huts floated by. Moth-eaten pillars were being carried off. Everything was rolling wildly down the river in the same direction: broken cabinets, torn-off doors, lids of pots ...

Tashik watched them silently.

His bride was sitting by the oven in the hut. She stared at her husband's back. She too was silent.

Several rats dashed out of the kitchen and onto the porch, climbed a beam there, came down again, and darted away. The bride could hear them squeaking underneath the porch. Rats are very sensitive to floods; their holes are the first to be destroyed by the water.

The bride continued to stare at her husband, too absorbed in him to worry about their hut.

They had been married the day before and had just spent their first night together. At breakfast she dared not look at his face. She was a bashful woman, and looked down while she ate. Perhaps he was shy also, for he too kept silent. However, he added two extra spoonfuls of cooked rice to her bowl.

29

There is a saying that two spoonfuls bring a man and his bride closer together, and she blushed as she thought of this.

She had only met him once before they were married, and all she had seen of him then was his feet. Nor could she see him last night in the dark. So she did not know what he looked like, even though they had already spent a night together. She knew that he was of medium height and that his body was strong. But she had not yet seen his eyes and nose and mouth, although once the matchmaker had said that there could hardly have been a more comely man.

She herself knew she was not very pretty. But she was dark-complexioned, and had heard it said in the village that the young men there maintained that her dark, dewy eyes made them feel numb and set their hearts pounding.

Their simple wedding took place ten days after they were engaged. Tashik had decided to marry her although he had never seen her before. He knew she was the eldest child in a large family. Her parents consented to the marriage. They were glad to reduce the number of mouths they had to feed, even by only one.

Because of the rain, nothing delicate was prepared for the wedding. There were only a plateful of rice cakes, two dishes of cooked rice, and two bowls of soup, all placed on the table in the hallway of the home of Mr Yi a landowner for whom Tashik worked. When the food was set before them, Tashik and the bride bowed to each other and became man and wife. There were no guests at the wedding, but Tashik was happy.

The bride had nothing to bring as a dowry, not even a piece of cloth. After the wedding ceremony, Tashik came across the hill to the hut with two spoons, two pairs of chopsticks, two bowls, a can of red-pepper mash, a can of soy sauce, and a cooking pot, which he carried on his back. The matchmaker and the bride followed him. On her head she carried two blankets and a pillow. This was their only bedding.

The rain let up for a moment, then it began falling harder and harder until it became a forceful downpour. The bride was startled as she suddenly became aware of the beating rain. She smiled to herself, glad that her husband did not notice her fear.

A small centipede fell to the floor and landed upside down, its white belly showing. It turned over. When it started to run away, moving its scores of legs, she crushed it with her foot. Another one fell. It landed on her shoulder. She brushed it off and stepped on it. The wet straw roof was infested with centipedes.

The hills nearby were so bare of trees that one could scarcely hear cicadas, even in midsummer. There had always been floods in the region, and no trees could grow. But at least there were no snakes. Floods are horrible, but snakes make them worse. Snakes as they are being washed away by the water cling to people. 'It is a good thing there are no snakes,' the bride said to herself.

More rats dashed out of the kitchen and darted under the porch.

The bride looked at her husband as he stood at the edge of the porch. His sturdy, well-tanned legs were greatly reassuring to her. She blushed as she thought of their first night together. And she could feel her heart pounding as she began to think of the evening ahead and what would take place again.

Tashik stood on the porch and continued to stare at the water. Since his childhood he had worked as a farmhand for Mr Yi. He was an honest man, and he worked hard; he knew Mr Yi was especially fond of him. A few days ago Mr Yi had come to the hut and found Tashik at work papering the walls with newspaper. Formerly the hut had been used by a forest guard. 'Well, well, you sure are in a hurry, aren't you?' Mr Yi said, laughing.

Tashik smiled as he remembered Mr Yi's good-natured remark.

More and more objects came floating by in the muddy, rapid water. A sauce jar drifted down and bobbed irregularly until it sank. Bundles of clothing, wet pillows, hooks and pans, an aluminium pot ... silently and swiftly they floated past and disappeared down the river.

Tashik only noticed the things he wanted most.

His eyes widened as he watched the debris float past. He would follow a floating object with his eyes until it was out of sight. Then he turned his head and looked upstream again, ready to follow another one.

Something white drifted by, and behind it came something bright and colourful. It was a blanket and a quilt! Perhaps

31

they had been bound together with straw ropes, for bits of straw cord floated in disarray alongside them.

'Bedding,' he mumbled to himself, 'bedding, bedding!' That was something he really needed. The blanket and quilt drifted closer to the hut. His eyes sparkled. Quickly he turned his head and looked back at his bride. Her dewy eyes met his. He wanted to speak but could say nothing. She covered her face with her hands, and he realized that this was the first time she had seen his face.

He turned and looked at the water again. 'Bedding,' he said again. The quilt and blanket were far out of reach by now. They floated away, now close together, now far apart. As soon as they were out of sight, Tashik looked upstream again.

'My husband, my darling . . .' he heard his wife saying softly.

But at that moment he cried out as if in battle, leaped from the porch to the ground, and dashed into the rain. Glancing quickly over his shoulder he noticed his bride jumping to her feet. But he kept running.

In no more than ten strides he reached the river and plunged in. 'Darling!' he heard his wife cry as he swam wildly towards midstream.

The rain began falling harder. It came in torrents.

Tashik swam directly into midstream and clutched at a large pigpen. He clung to it, and knew now that his wife would understand what he was doing. Surely she remembered what Mr Yi had said: 'I will give you a little pig soon. Let's see what you can do with it.'

The little pig will grow up. In six months it will be ready to bear young. Sometimes a pig has as many as five or six in a litter. They too grow up and bear. The males can be sold, the females kept. Sell the males and keep the females! One pig brings in ten or fifteen thousand *hwan*. And the droppings from the pigpen make the best manure. With pig manure the rice crop will be a better one.

He had not been able to get a pigsty. They are expensive, for they must be strong and well built. Otherwise the pigs break them and get away. Tashik wanted to be sure his pigs would not get away. What good are pigs if they escape, he thought as he grabbed one corner of the pigsty and tried to pull it ashore.

He pulled hard, but the pen was locked in the current. The swift water would not yield an inch.

The pigsty was made of logs about two feet long and several inches thick. They were fastened tightly together with wire. It was large enough for perhaps ten pigs. This would be perfect for us, Tashik thought.

'Come on, let's go!' he shouted, pulling at the sty. Water splashed all over his head. He wiped it from his face with one of his big, hardened hands.

The water was up to his waist. The river seemed to be boiling under the punishment of the pelting rain.

Somehow the waves pushed the pigsty up on the shore. 'Hurrah!' he cried, overjoyed. He scrambled up on the bank and pulled the pen towards him. But at the next moment another wave carried it back into the muddy water.

'Hey, wait a minute. Stop there!' he yelled, clinging to the pen. It rode on a surging wave and began to float wildly down the river. He could not let the pigsty go – if he did he might drown. Nor could he hold on to it either – how far would he be carried if he did? He was panicky.

He wanted to cry out for help, but that would be useless. There were no houses along the shore, and no one would be out in such a rain. Even his hut was out of sight now.

He looked for a raft. Often during the rainy season men ride along the swollen river on rafts, pulling things out of the water so they can sell them later. In a flood such as this one they make small fortunes.

The pigsty rolled and tumbled crazily in the flooded river. It would smack into a wave and Tashik would be splashed with a torrent of muddy water. He closed his eyes and mouth tightly to keep mud out of them. For a moment the water would be calm and the rain washed the mud off his face.

The low hills along the shore were utterly strange to him. He did not know where he was now. Only God knew how far downstream he had come.

He was too frightened now to worry about the pigsty. He could think only of getting back to shore somehow and going home.

A shiver shot through his whole body. Above anything else the cold was to be dreaded. He would not be able to swim if he became too cold. He was really afraid.

He looked around again and cried out for help. Suddenly he saw a raft not more than fifty yards away. There were two men on it. His eyes brightened.

He called out to them. But the men on the raft either did not hear him or pretended not to. They paid no attention at all. He remembered having heard someone say that the raftmen were heartless, and it angered him now. Money might be precious, but how can men ignore someone in danger?

'Hey there!' he yelled. 'Help! Help!' He let go of the pigpen and began swimming for the raft. But he had to swim against the current, which made the going twice as hard. The muddy water splashed mercilessly against his face, into his eyes and ears and nostrils. Tashik blew hard through his nose, lifted his head as high as he could, and kept on swimming.

After struggling against the current for some time, he looked up and found the raft floating farther and farther away. He was hot with anger. If he should ever reach the raft, he thought, he would throw those two bastards into the river!

But he kept swimming across the current towards the raft. He could scarcely control his direction. At last he was thrown onto a sandbar which was barely covered with water. He stood up, relieved to be out of the muddy water. He breathed deeply for a while, swinging his arms back and forth to get warm. He moved his arms rapidly, shook his head, and wiggled his whole body to loosen up his muscles. From where he was standing he could see that the swollen river had doubled its normal width.

It was not raining very hard now. He yelled at the raft once more.

'Help! You lousy devils, help!'

Neither man responded. One of them was pulling something out of the water with a hook.

'Help!' Tashik shouted.

Again there was no answer. He choked with anger.

It began to rain harder again. Suddenly the sandbar collapsed under his feet and he tumbled back into the water, startled. But the raft was much closer to him now, closer than either shore was. He swam feverishly and reached the raft. He grabbed for it and hung on until one of the men pulled him up.

Apparently they recognized him. 'Aren't you the newlywed

who works for Mr Yi?' one of them asked. 'What happened?
How do you come to be out here?'

Tashik did not try to answer. He was out of breath and
exhausted. He had even forgotten his determination to push
the raftmen into the water. He did not know them, but he
assumed they were villagers.

For a while he lay with his eyes closed, barely conscious. At
last he sat up and began to examine himself. Nothing was left
of his shirt except a little scrap of cloth which hung onto his
right shoulder. The rest of it must have been washed away.
The same thing had happened to his trousers. His leather belt
and a fragment of cloth which had clung to it were all that
remained around his waist. He was naked.

There were pots, pans, hoes, shovels, and all sorts of household utensils on the raft. But there was nothing to cover his
naked body.

'Where are we?' he asked at last.

'A little past Dang village,' one of the men answered.

So, he was not too far from his home after all. He looked
towards the shore and saw the hill which rose behind his hut.
He was just across the hill from his home; he had followed
the bend of the river which curves around that hill. He was
relieved.

It was getting dark. It must be well past the supper hour.
He had been in the water for nearly the whole afternoon.

'Say, young man,' one of the men on the raft asked him,
'you were married yesterday, isn't that right?'

'Yeah.'

'In this rain?'

'Yeah.'

The raft drew closer to shore. The men said they would let
Tashik off before they picked up anything else from the flood.

When the raft was almost at the shore, Tashik suddenly
spied the pigsty that he had been trying to salvage. It had been
washed up onto the bank. His face lit up and he jumped into
the muddy water.

'Thanks a lot,' he shouted to the astonished raft-men, dashing out of the water and across the river bank.

He pulled at the pigsty. But it was waterlogged and hard to
move. He realized he could never carry it home this way. He
looked for the place where the wire was knotted and loosened

the knot. The sty fell apart instantly. Then he tied the wood neatly together with the wire. And although the precious bundle of wood was very heavy, he dragged it behind him.

Naked, he headed home, pulling the wood all the way. He was shivering with cold. The rain was not chilly, but it stung him like pellets of ice after his long hours in the water. But it did wash the dirt off his body.

The bride burst into tears when he reached the hut. She must have cried a great deal, for he saw that her eyes were swollen. He looked at her and tried to smile, but he collapsed onto the floor.

She felt his body shiver violently. She put a blanket under him and covered him with the other one. But he kept shivering. There was nothing else to cover him with. She wanted to cry.

She tried to build a fire, but nothing would burn. She came back to him.

She watched the blanket shake as he shivered. Tashik was rocking with chills. He seemed to be out of his senses. The bride knew that her husband had to be warmed somehow. She tried to think of how she could give his body warmth.

She took his hands into hers. She felt herself blushing, but told herself that it was not a time to be shy. His hands were icy cold. Shocked and afraid, she frantically pressed her body against his and she massaged his hands. Her heart pounded. Then she thought she could warm his body with her own. But he shook more violently as she snuggled close to him.

Wildly she rubbed his body everywhere. Then she took off her blouse and pressed her breast against his. He kept shaking. In silent hysteria she tore off her skirt and underwear. She no longer felt bashful. All she could think of was how to make her husband warm. She pressed her naked body hard against the cold, naked body of her husband.

Gently now, she covered his whole body with hers. She tucked his shoulders under her armpits and covered his knees with her thighs.

She pressed her mouth upon his blue lips. His lips were ice-cold, his eyes tightly closed. He was completely unconscious.

With her own lips still upon his, she sensed his upper lip stiffen. They say the upper lip stiffens when one is about to die, she recalled. Her heart sank.

To prevent his upper lip from growing stiff, she began to

suck it and her husband's nose. With one hand she rubbed his body. She had no other way to warm him, no medicine, no fire. And there was no neighbour to help her.

Outside it was dark. The rain continued to fall.

'Don't die. Please, don't,' she repeated quietly, over and over again. She felt the tears flooding her eyes.

Her arms ached, and her lips ached too. But she kept on sucking.

Finally, his body began to get warm. But now it was becoming too warm. He became hot as a burning stove. He began to cry out incessantly, shouting unintelligible syllables. His mouth was burning, and now his lips became dry whenever she took her mouth away. She moistened his dry lips with her tongue.

All night it continued to rain.

As dawn came Tashik's fever began to subside. He awoke.

The bride made a bowl of gruel. Tashik sat up and washed his face. It seemed to have grown thinner during the night. Still, it was a full, strong face.

As she placed the gruel before him she looked up at him lovingly. He sat there and smiled timidly at her.

Outside the rain fell violently.

A centipede fell from the ceiling into the sauce jar on the table. Oh my goodness, she thought, even before he has touched the gruel. She was ready to cry.

But Tashik picked up the centipede with his thumb and forefinger and threw it out of the room. Then he poured the sauce in the gruel and swallowed the whole bowlful in one long gulp.

He pushed the table aside and seized her as she was about to rise to get him more. He held her tight.

Her dark, dewy eyes were inflamed. They were fastened against his eyes as her lips clung to his. She could scarcely breathe.

The rain kept falling, harder and with more force than ever.

THE YOUNG ZELKOVA TREE

KANG SHIN-JAE

Translated by Shin Hyun-song

He is always enveloped in a smell of soap. No, I'm wrong.
That isn't entirely true. I can't really say 'always'. It is when
he comes home from school, runs into the bathroom, and
comes out having battled and tussled with the water that he
gives off the smell of soap. Even as I sit motionless in front
of my desk with my back turned to him, I can feel him coming
towards me. I can anticipate beforehand what kind of a mood
he's in, and even tell what kind of an expression he's wearing
on his face.

Marching into my room in the T-shirt he's just changed into,
he would throw himself on the armchair, or else lean against
the window sill with his elbow, and turn to me and smile.

'What are you doing?' he asks.

It is on these occasions that he smells of soap, and it is
then that I realize that my saddest and most painful hour has
arrived.

As the sweet fragrant scent of soap starts to fill the air
around us, I feel a tingling sensation start to bubble up inside
and slowly diffuse through my whole body. Oh, I wanted to
tell him so . . .

'What are you doing?' As he throws that question in my
lap, he would open his eyes a little wider as a matter of course,
and gaze into my face. That gaze . . . I have often wondered

what it would be doing. Perhaps it's scanning my face, trying to read my countenance, or perhaps it's urging me to be just that little bit more jovial, or possibly, its purpose is no more than the mere expression of his uncontrollable mirth.

At these moments, something compels me to stare back into his eyes, despite the turmoil inside me as I focus all my available resources in an effort to stem the flood of grief and unmitigated agony.

I want to know ... I want to know what he sees when he looks at me. I throw myself yet again at the mercy of this question. Day and night, time after time, like timeless waves crashing into a timeless rock, this desire to know hurtles into me again and again. But each time I fail hopelessly in getting the answer. I cannot read the meaning in his eyes, and so yet again, I can feel my pain and sadness turn into something heavier and slowly sink to the bottom of my breast.

But the very next moment, I realize that I must bring myself down to that role where no embarrassment or awkwardness exist – that of his younger sister.

'Oh, are you back?'

I respond in as bright a tone as possible, sensing this is what he wants most. I also know that it would be cruel and ignoble of me, were I to act awkwardly here.

As if relieved with my reply, he gives himself a big stretch.

'Yeah, I'm tired out! You couldn't get me something to eat, could you?'

'Oh, you're impossible! I was just getting myself into the swing of this English composition homework.'

I stand up and walk away from the desk pretending to moan.

'Really? Let me have a look. I'll tell you if you could make it as a writer!'

'No, don't!'

I hide the notebook under a pile of other books and come downstairs. Opening the door of the refrigerator, I take out a frosted bottle of Coca Cola, together with some crackers and cheese.

As I arrange these on a plate, I am overwhelmed with a sense of joy – a 'secret' joy, hidden and unknowable. Why does he always come into *my* room to ask for something to eat, especially when he passes right by the refrigerator on his way? Even the laziest of dogs would have no trouble opening the fridge door, and if he really did want someone to fetch it for him, he would do better asking someone in the kitchen. Besides, anything would be better than asking me to do it. I mean, I always grumble, moan, and make him wait ages for his snack, and what's more, no one could be as clumsy as I am, spilling, and sometimes even tipping the whole thing over on the floor. Come to think of it, I really am very clumsy at doing things like that, no matter how much I try.

When I came back with the tray, he was looking out of the window at the runner rose, with the side of his face turned towards me. Sitting there deep in his reverie, I detected a calm and tranquil look in his eyes – a look that he doesn't show when he's near me. His face with its strong contours and darkish complexion is very appealing from this angle. And there is something about the way he looks when he is in private meditation that attracts me with its fascinating charm.

His well-sculptured head is as handsome as Apollo's must have been, and a few strands of his wavy hair lie intertwined over his forehead.

'I hear that curly haired people are violent by nature,' I told him once.

'No, that's not true. Really Suki, that's not right...' He protested in earnest when all I was doing was poking fun at him.

After having a rest in my room as usual, he picked himself up from his seat.

'Shall we play tennis?'

'Oh, okay.'

'Ah, I just remembered. I thought you were taking mid-term exams from tomorrow!'

'Oh, that, well ... it doesn't really matter.'

Frankly, I couldn't have cared less about them. I pulled out a drawer and took out a pair of white shorts and an orange-coloured shirt.

'You know, you'll fail with that kind of an attitude.'

Even as he said this he went out of the room to get the racquets.

The sun was shedding its fiery light, but a somewhat chilly wind could be felt from time to time blowing through the fresh greenness of the leaves.

We walked to the wall at the bottom of the hill and slipped into the yard opposite. I'd heard that this neighbouring estate used to be a part of the land held by the old royal family. The couple of old tile-roofed houses that sat in the estate were so far off that they were almost out of sight, leaving this side of the grounds, a big empty space.

Whatever motivated the people living in those houses, they certainly swept and polished at that piece of land.

'What a complete waste. It would make a first class tennis court. Yes! How about it?' I said one day sitting on the wall.

He wasn't very enthusiastic at first but later he walked over to the house and talked it over with the owners. The next day, we took some chalk, and a few days after that, we levelled the land and installed a net, making a complete tennis court out of the piece of land.

The owner, a grand old fellow, wasn't quite happy with how far we had gone, and protested as if anything could have been done about it. But he soon gave up. The next thing we knew, he would come out supported by his walking stick and watch us play.

I have always found it difficult to read the expression on an old face, but it was especially difficult with him. To spell it out, it was a face which seemed as if it was laughing one moment, and marvelling, another, at this curious game that unfolded in front of his eyes. And also at the same time, he looked as if he was a million miles away floating around in his own little world, somewhere beyond the sky.

Once or twice, at seeing my masterly skill at jumping over the wall, he opened his mouth as if to speak, but closed it again without saying anything. Possibly it was because I didn't look as if I'd pay attention to him... whatever he said. Anyhow, that place was an excellent place to while away our time.

A student of physics, he often seemed pressed with his work, but he wasn't a feeble-minded milk-sop who would shy away at the very mention of the word 'sport'.

I had been playing tennis before I came here, but the sudden improvement in my play is mainly due to him. One couldn't imagine my gratification when I realized just how much better he was than the coach I'd been learning from in the country.

I don't think I could really fall for anyone who is dull-headed, but at the same time, I'm not attracted by those that profess total separation from all physical activity. I think sport, in some of its aspects, shows without doubt, the very joy of living reflected in itself. The refreshing sweetness of the air as I run round the court in pursuit of the ball, is like nothing else.

But today, I really couldn't put racquet to ball. The only thing admirable on the court was his usual skill in pulling me along at my own pace, erratic as it was.

'Phew! I'm certainly not with it today, am I?'

'Oh, that's all right. I don't mind. I think it'd be a good idea to arrange a match with Jisu soon, don't you think so?'

As the sky turned a deep yellow, we picked the balls up and walked down to the mineral water spring. The icy water flowing out of a crack in the rock made our teeth numb with its coldness. It had a bitterish flavour.

We made dippers out of our hands and drank to our hearts' content, all the time holding our nostrils closed. A willow spread its graceful pea-green leaves over the rock, and an anonymous tree, covered in bright red flowers, was also spreading its branches over us.

We had always thought that it wasn't quite right for us to drink in such a rowdy manner in these surroundings, but still we continued.

'Drink up. They say it has medicinal qualities. Who knows, you might even benefit from some of its effects.'

'What for?'

'What for? Well, for a start, it might even make you a little better at tennis!'

At the spring we never failed to stir up some racket or other.

But today, we were surprised to find a gourd dipper placed on the edge of the rock. No doubt the old man had put it there.

'We'll have to be better behaved when we drink here from now on.'

'Yes, the guardian spirit of the mountain is watching over us.'

So we sat there and took a long break. We were never so

well behaved. He leaned forward and scooped up some water with the dipper and put it against my lips. He was wearing an unfamiliar face, deeply engrossed in some private thought, and it was carrying an expression so private, so personal... It was one of those he never shared with me.

I just took a sip and looked up at his face. He drank the rest slowly and deliberately. As he replaced the gourd dipper, I thought I saw for an instant fiery emotion shroud and blanket his face. He didn't answer my look. I was suddenly swept into utter confusion. But even in that state of amalgam and hodge-podge of feeling, I was aware of something strong and distinct. It was joy.

I threw my racquet over my shoulder and walked towards the wall.

Brother... He was my brother...

For me, this word is the very representation of absurdity and all things illogical. And I was the thing hopelessly entangled in its deadly web, hopelessly.

I jumped down from the wall which was taller than I was, and without casting back a glancc, I walked on through the garden. I was barefoot with my shoes in my hands. The bristly and yet soft texture of the grass was so exciting that I rarely wanted to lose it by wearing anything on my feet.

He likes to joke. If he were with me now, I bet he'd start teasing me. I remember once when we were walking side by side.

'Shall I fit a pair of soles on to your feet? Then you could go around everywhere without your shoes on!'

'You know, walking on grass barefoot always makes me feel as if I'm back home. No, rather, it makes me feel as if I've finally come back to my *self*.'

I would mumble a few words like this, but later that day, I would become all mixed up inside all of a sudden. So now-adays, I just keep my mouth closed like a stubborn old woman.

When I arrive at the terrace all sulky, seeing the purple rug laid across the wide room, the weighty pieces of furniture placed here and there, and the stillness floating around them, and when the fragrance of peonies in full bloom, the scent of lilac, and the smell of freshly mown grass combine to produce that intoxicating aroma, I feel the painful reality of my position slowly float up towards me in this purplish air. I cannot help but stand there flustered and frustrated as I open my eyes to the bitter irony of my situation. Were those fleeting moments of cheerfulness and joy in fact my grief and agony disguised?

Brother and sister . . .

Younger sister . . .

I hate these terms because they only invoke fear and aversion within me. The joy and happiness I have been feeling are definitely not permissible within these categorizations.

The irony that I experience in this purple-tinted air would be tinged with that little bit of sadness, and I would soon run out of courage to remain standing by his side. No doubt he would crack a few jokes blinking his ebony-coloured eyes and tell me in unspoken words to laugh and be merrier. Indeed, isn't this all he *can* do for me?

The strength of the elation that I'd felt earlier today had, I think, plunged me that much deeper into a sense of tragedy. I stood in front of the house daydreaming, and then slowly walked up on to the polished wooden floor of the house, puffing my cheeks out a little. The shiny wooden floor got marked by my footsteps, but funnily enough, I got a strange thrill seeing it being dirtied.

I had washed myself and was changing. I threw down a glance through the window. He was sitting on a bench underneath the wistaria vine, supporting his chin and looking into the bay tree forest. In the way he was directing his gaze, there was something which made him look awfully lonely.

Could it be that he was suffering from the same torment as I was? But then I was suddenly pushed by a streak of cruelty. Ha, but what use was there? What could be done?

I didn't turn on the light. I placed myself in a spot where I couldn't be seen from the outside, and watched him placidly.

It was only after darkness had blanketed the surroundings that he stood up from the bench. He looked up at my window and froze. He was there for some time before he finally disappeared out of sight.

I didn't turn on the light. Nor did I go downstairs for supper. Instead, I picked up the coffee cup that he'd sipped from and carefully, so carefully put it to my lips. Just as he had put the gourd dipper to his lips earlier.

What term would be the most appropriate referring to him? It is my fate to call him 'brother'.

It was late winter of the year before last, when ice and snow had sugared over the houses of Seoul, making them glitter like grated ice candy, that Monsieur Lee brought me (perhaps it would be better to say 'dragged' me) here.

Mother introduced 'him' like this.

'Suki, this is going to be your brother from now on. Say hello, he's called Hyon-kyu.'

I stood on the vivid purple carpet and inspected his face.

'Do you know, he's known as the genius of the College of Liberal Arts and Sciences at the University? Come to think of it, our Suki too, has quite a reputation back home of being a very accomplished young lady. Only, I think she's lost her feet a little coming to a place like Seoul. Try to get on well together, won't you?'

Mother's voice was soft and light, but her eyes appeared full of misgiving. I began to study the young man's eyes alertly.

He was wearing a brown V-neck pullover over a lighter coloured shirt. With those thick eyebrows of his and the look on his forehead, he gave the impression of being a little overbearing. But his eyes were cool and refreshing to observe, in that there was a sharpness and generosity. The sort of generosity that comes out of confidence.

The contours of his body seemed to show a neat propriety, but at the same time, seemed to expose a tough and stubborn character underneath. Only the lines around the chin and neck seemed sensitive and very delicate.

He looks normal enough, I thought. Height, shoulder breadth, and hmm, he does seem to have that certain quality suggestive of a genius . . .

All the time, I was giving him marks out of a hundred. But then, I wasn't so stupid as to judge the merits of someone on his outer appearance alone.

As I pierced his eyes with my look, the corner of his mouth twitched a little, like someone a little overcome by a flash of light in his eyes. He seemed a little embarrassed but at the same time, looked as if he was squeezing out a bitter smile against his will. Was it because he could look right through me? I suddenly feared that I was being probed under a detailed examination.

45

But at length, the tone in which he greeted me was simple to the extreme.

'Hello, I'm very glad that you could come. The house has been feeling a little empty recently...' and took me by the hand.

This only confirmed that he looked on me as a child, and probably, it was born out of his respect for my mother's feelings.

All so predictably, a great flood of relief and satisfaction could be seen surging over my mother's face, and I began to have some idea of the kind of connection that had been forged between this young man and my mother. It was an artificial mother and son relationship which obliged both parties to respect and venerate each other in all trivialities of everyday life.

Monsieur Lee seemed broad-minded enough, and appeared to take an easy-come-easy-go attitude in all aspects of his daily dealings, so that while all this was going on, he just stood there with a broad grin on his face, urging me to rest, saying how tired I must be.

Anyway, what is important is that from then 'he' has been able to call me by my first name without any inhibition. Sometimes, he would even call out, 'Hey, Suk!'

He has been very cordial and hospitable to me. Sometimes even too much so. When he was, it pained me a lot. Therefore, the fact that he had started to come to my room, be it to ask for something to eat, or ask me to put some medicine on his hands or somewhere, was a very significant change and a valuable one for me.

Be that as it may, I couldn't bring myself to call him 'brother', no matter how much I tried. At first it was because of the awkwardness arising from unfamiliarity, but later it was for another reason. This was many times harder than calling M. Lee 'father'. I'm not sure if I am a stubborn pig-headed ass, or worse still, someone who's lost control of reason for bashfulness. Which could I be, I wonder.

However, it appeared that Hyon-kyu and my mother recognized my peculiar predicament, and would phrase their questions in such a way that I would not have to struggle and twist trying to avoid that which I felt so abashed to say. In this

context, the only person who did put me into impossible posi-
tions from time to time was M. Lee himself.

I think in the little over a year that I've been here, I've
changed in many ways. I have learned to make the most of
my looks, and I've also grown a little taller and my skin seems
to have become a little whiter. Last year, I was voted 'Miss E
High School', and played Queen for a whole day. I had feared
that perhaps my bust would be too flat. So it was, that it was
I, more than anyone else, who was startled to find myself
winning, and by such a big margin as well. Mother was so
excited she didn't know what to do, and M. Lee bought me
an incredibly expensive watch. But 'he' didn't say much. Not
even a joke. All he did was utter one word of congratulation,
but even that, very shyly. Seeing him like this, I got a great
sense of satisfaction. I felt good.

I think my character has also undergone change. The girl
who used to have so many friends and who used to sing such
a lot has become, I think, a little more impetuous and a little
more aggressive since moving here. I think I can at last begin
to understand what is known so simply as the 'joy of life'.

The atmosphere in this house is very cosy and pleasant.
Also, because of the unusual circumstances which bind my
mother with M. Lee, there is that slight tinge of the romance
fused in it.

The district in which we live, is far from the hustle and
bustle of the city centre. And the way the creeping ivy, which
according to M. Lee was already thriving when he came, covers
the whole of this brick house, had a very comforting effect. I
could feel all these giving me a sort of solace that I had never
experienced before. What's more, he is always kind and polite
to mother, and M. Lee would express his greatest satisfaction
whenever I looked healthy and happy.

M. Lee was a tutor in economics at some university, and
was a plump and good-natured man. The reason I call him
'monsieur' even though he had no connections with France is
because he reminded me of a piteous father I once saw in a
French film. M. Lee is not pitiful. Indeed, he is very happy.
But it is exactly this perennial magnificence that seemed so
vulnerable. I fear that with just one slight mistake, he would
tumble down into utter misery and degradation.

In the tragedy of someone like Goethe's Werther, there is a

poignant beauty in the pain he suffers, but I have only fear as to what M. Lee's sadness would be like. I can only see a wretchedness. It was indeed fortunate that my mother was able to come and stand by his side.

Mother spent most of her time indoors, but she seemed happy enough. Her gentle tone of voice, so characteristic of her, had I think, grown even gentler. Only, it seemed she was suffering from guilt at the actual greatness of her bliss itself, and in consequence, would not go out very often and even strained herself not to laugh too loudly. But she was always in pleasant clothes and also indulged in a little bit of vanity with a little make-up on her face. This pleased me.

But however, I have an unanticipated anguish. My feelings towards Hyon-kyu are always weighing me down. Sometimes, when the distress becomes too strong to bear, I wish that I had never come here in the first place. But this wish doesn't last long. What if I die and never see him again in my life? I shudder at the thought. It didn't matter if nothing came to alter the situation. I was the happiest girl in the world by the mere fact that I had met him. And how could I ever exchange with anything else, the exhilaration that I feel, simply breathing next to him? But it is also true that I'm always under a shadow of anxiety and misery. To tell the truth, my sentiments change by the minute.

The fact that M. Lee is travelling abroad these days, seems to have lessened the weight of that burden on my shoulders a little. No longer am I obliged to feign happiness to please him every morning, or go downstairs to the dining room at the regular pre-arranged times.

'Please, Mum, just turn a blind eye to it until he returns, could you? You know how I hate being bound up in schedules. I'll eat when I want to, that's all right, isn't it?'

I negotiated as soon as M. Lee had left. But I knew only too well that the real reason behind this reluctance to go down to have regular meals was the fear that I'd soon be afraid to meet Hyon-kyu face to face. So it appeared that he was the only companion Mother had at supper table.

As the well-mannered young man accompanies Mother at the supper table, I gaze out blankly through the window at the falling sun. The little hamlets here and there composed of tiny dots that were once houses, the reflections on the lakes in the forest, and a winding river, all come rather blurred into my sight. Depending on the time of day and the weather, that river might show itself as clearly as a torch light would in the dark, or else, become milky and blurred beyond all recognition as if inside a thick opaque envelope of fog. At about the time the sky turns into a mellow grey from a purplish blue, the river merges itself with the warm grey clouds into one evanescent mass.

And here I was again, as usual, looking into the dark waters of the river and pressing myself that I had to find a way to free myself from this sticky web of entanglement. I wasn't in a position where I could leave myself at the mercy of those capricious propensities of my mind, and at the same time, I couldn't help holding contradictory inclinations as to the very nature of these propensities.

I don't feel guilty about being involved with Hyon-kyu, but taking into consideration the nature of the affinity between M. Lee and Mother, that sort of betrayal would almost certainly spell the utter destruction of all four of us. The harsh and dark sound of the word 'destruction' makes me shiver.

Before I had come here, I was staying at my grandparents', that is to say, my mother's parents', in the country. Even up until three or four years ago, Mother was able to stay with us as well, but when she went, it left just the three of us – my grandparents and me.

Of companionship, it is true that we had many hands working for us, and also guard dogs in the orchard, among them my favourite Bokdong, but I was always pursued and engulfed in emptiness. As a matter of fact, after Mother left us for Seoul, I had to endure great pain inside me. This was strange because all the time she was with us, I wasn't exactly overwhelmed with a feeling of security and contentment.

It had pained me every time I looked at her, still young and beautiful, just wasting her life away with us. On her lap was always a fine piece of cloth or some woollen thread, making something for me, and words of concern for my well-being never left her lips. But strangely, I found all this very irritating. I even felt hostility towards her sometimes. I wanted to tell her that she did not have to do all those things for me, but just live the life *she* wanted. To live for her own sake and not for mine. She should, I thought, get angry sometimes and scold me as the other mothers did. And it was the same with my grandparents. They also were too gentle with me.

I can't remember when this lifeless shadow-like existence of my mother had started. As far as I can reach back in time, to the time we had to come down to my grandparents' because of the War, that is, about ten years ago, and even before that when I was entering elementary school in Seoul, I was aware of something similar.

Concerning 'father', I know absolutely nothing. Someone once explained to me long ago that he'd died, but I remember I had the feeling this wasn't quite true. After the War, I was told again. This time, by my grandmother.

'Your father has passed away.'

There was something in the tone of voice that told me, this time it was for real. As I have figured it out, Mother and 'father' were probably separated when I was very young and somehow never got together again.

Anyway, all that I am sure about my father is that I have no knowledge *of* him, and hold no affections *for* him. This surname of mine, 'Yun', is the only thing I've inherited from him but even that, I can't help feeling, is just another surname, and a common one at that.

I don't know what happened to tie M. Lee to my mother, nor what drove him to visit her at the orchard.

That day I remember, I was straddling over the branch of an apple tree, munching an apple, when a slightly plump gentleman I'd never seen before was walking in our direction. He seemed to be hesitating a bit as he stopped outside the front gate, but then, seeming to muster up a little courage, took off his hat and walked in.

I dropped an apple seed when he was about to pass underneath the tree. He stopped and looked up. But as if in total confusion, I remember he didn't even smile. Later, as we were formally introduced to each other, it was plain that he had forgotten everything about that little informal welcome he had received earlier that day.

He went back without even spending the night, and it was

from then that I used to see Mother strolling about alone among the apple trees at night.

M. Lee came back once more, and not long after that, Mother left for Seoul.

One night, I was a little startled to hear Grandmother sobbing in the next room.

'If he'd only come and married her earlier... Then she wouldn't have had to go through all that suffering.'

'Now, what are you talking about? Then we wouldn't have Suki here with us.'

'Well, that's what's called fate. Oh, I don't know. I don't know whose fault it all is, but I don't think Kyung-ae was much to blame.'

It was a little funny to hear my grandparents refer to my mother by her first name instead of the usual 'the child's mother'. It made me smile as I ruminated over what her young days must have been like.

So, the grief at seeing my mother waste away was gone, and I even felt a certain contentment at seeing her become, what I thought, a little bit happier. But it was also true that I was desperately lonely without her.

Day and night, something drove me to sing. When I was coming home from school, when I was underneath the white blossoms of the apple tree, and also when I was in the yard, full of scarlet touch-me-nots, I had to sing.

'My dear child, people will laugh if you sing your head off like that, you know.' Grandmother would tell me sometimes, looking quite serious.

When Monsieur Lee came in late winter of the year before last and insisted on taking me with him, it was I who was startled, more than anyone. I could feel that my grandparents were somewhat hesitant, but they couldn't make any kind of a stand against the onslaught.

'The most important thing is that her mother wants it. She never says it outright, but I can always see it in her eyes.'

I was a bit tickled to see this all-too-sincere attitude of his. My grandparents appeared as if they had already been persuaded, and if he'd stopped talking for a minute, they would have given him their answer, but here he was, as though they would hold onto me with their lives...

As he threw a glance at me, I nodded a little, whence he stopped and put a broad grin on his face and took out his handkerchief and wiped the sweat off his brow. And this is how I came to be transferred to 'E High School for Girls'.

Monsieur Lee and Mother are husband and wife. The reason I find it difficult to call him my father is, I think, mostly because I have never got into the habit of uttering that word. But this is not to say that I dislike him. As a matter of fact, I feel a sense of security (and even a sense of fatherly watchfulness) in him – something that I had never been able to savour under Grandfather. But we are not related by blood.

It is the same with Hyon-kyu. In that respect, he and I are total strangers. The fact that he is a twenty-one-year-old young man and I am a seventeen-year-old girl is the simple truth, nothing more, nothing less. Why is it that I am not allowed to accept this so painfully obvious fact?

I don't want to give him away to anyone, never. Nor do I want to offer myself to anyone else. All I know is that the convention which ties us together shouldn't be.

Of course, I am hoping all the time that he's asking himself the same questions. Perhaps not the same 'pleasures', but at least the same 'sufferings'. So it is that anything, absolutely anything that has the slightest significance to this 'mutual suffering' of ours – the slightest memory, the most insignificant fleet of change in his countenance, the tiniest of observations, are all vividly recorded and stored for posterity. Ah ... Am I so destined never to savour the sweetness of happiness? Isn't happiness that thing whose sole reason for existence is for itself alone? Its *causa sui*?

The rich concentrated aroma of flowers comes floating in, wrapped in the opaque darkness of the early evening air. I fall face-down on the bed and drown myself in passionate tears.

'Suki, I happened to pick this up ...'

One Sunday morning, when I went downstairs, Mother was waiting for me with these words, holding up an envelope.

'What is it?'

I went a little closer. And although it was a little embarrassing, I stretched out my hand and tried to get it from her.

'Where did you manage to pick it up?'

'Not so fast. Could you seat yourself for a minute?'

Mother was pointing to the chair in front of me, trying to hide her obvious anxiety. I was hit by a wave of contempt, but I suppressed it and sat down as she ordered.

Jisu was minister K's son, and lived in that comic estate at the other side of the hill – that place with its walls like the Great Wall of China. He was a simple, rather bulky looking young man who was attending medical school somewhere, and played tennis with Hyon-kyu once in a while.

He used to cram his jeep with his younger brothers and sisters, from kindergarten upwards, and would drive them back and forth from school, himself.

I myself had received a couple of lifts in his jeep. Once I was with Hyon-kyu, so that I had no reason to refuse, and the other was when I was on my way home from town, and it would have been even more awkward had I refused the offer.

'I can't see the little ones today, where are they?'

'If they can fit themselves into my schedule, I cart them home, but otherwise, they have to make their way home by themselves. You know, it's just like a train with all its time-tables.'

It was not because this boy had written an unbecoming love letter that drew forth my cynicism. It was the slightly nonsensical attitude of Mother, puffing this thing up out of all proportion that caused it.

'That's funny, I wonder where it would have come from . . .'

'I found it under the bench in the vine.'

'Oh, now I remember, so I'd left it there!'

'What do you mean, "oh now I remember", you should be a little more prudent in your actions. Look for example at what you do after playing tennis. Your brother always seems to clear up after you.'

I only giggled in reply.

'Don't you at least think it is being discourteous to the person who sent it? Well, don't you think so?'

'Yes, you're right, Mum.' I took the envelope from her hand.

'Is it secret? Do you mind if I read it?'

'No, I don't mind. If it were anything I wanted to hide, do you think I would leave it lying around?'

I was becoming a little indignant.

'That's a relief. To tell you the truth, I'd already read it myself.'

'Oh, that's not very fair of you, Mum . . .'

'The only thing I want to tell you, Suki, is that anything, absolutely anything that bothers you in the least, don't just handle it by yourself but come and tell me at least the important parts and let's discuss it, okay? That's the way it's supposed to be, you know.'

As I stood listening, I became more and more depressed, and only wanted to leave that place as soon as possible.

'You know I'm always on your side, don't you, Suki?'

'Sure, Mum.'

I gave this automatic reply and slowly walked out of the house. I wondered how much she would be on my side if I went up to her and said, 'I am in love with your son!' How would she come to my aid then? This question was out of Mother's reach, and even that of Monsieur Lee.

I crumpled up the letter in my pocket and walked down the sloping meadow, getting myself quite wet up to the knees because of the dew. I walked in a direction from where I couldn't be seen. I passed the acacia grove, the barley field, and the shrubbery.

As I walked, I thought of Hyon-kyu and just how much our standing with each other had deteriorated recently into a gloomy, all time low. I was avoiding him like the plague because I couldn't endure the pain as I had to part joking, as if nothing existed between the two of us. So I would get angry with him for no reason, and this would stop him talking to me.

The birds were singing above, and the sky was a deep blue. It was as blue as the sea, and would reveal itself through the leaves in small patches. Summer was ripening.

The oak forest was concealing the direction where the swamp lay, so that I sat down on the grass, and fell into a deep reverie.

Shall I become a ballerina and sparkle like a gem on the stage? Although I had never heeded her, my instructor always reminded me that I should have ambition. If I did become a world famous dancer, when he comes with his plain-looking wife to watch me, he would be sorry, wouldn't he?

For a moment, this seemed a good idea, but it disappeared

as easily as it had come, as evanescent as a bubble on the surface of the water.

Then I'd think of becoming his servant and nothing more. Giving him everything and expecting nothing in return. But even before sadness had a chance to enter my heart, a tear drop had already rolled onto my foot.

I picked myself up to head back home. It was then that I heard leaves rustling behind my back, and a fine setter came out on a lead. At the other end of the lead was Jisu. The warm grey shirt seemed to go well with his robust body. Behind him came running a little boy and girl, both about ten, playing with some pebbles that they'd presumably picked up on the way.

Jisu seemed to panic a little when he saw me, but presently walked towards me revealing his white teeth.

'Good morning. Are you out for a walk?'

'Yes, I am. I was just on my way back.'

The children chattered and played between us. He gave the end of the lead to one of them and signalled them away.

We walked side by side for a long time without uttering a single word. But passing the acacia grove, he suddenly threw a question at me.

'Did you get my letter?' seeming a little embarrassed as he said this.

'Yes.'

'Aren't you giving me a reply?'

'Yes, well, I didn't really know quite how to write it out ...'

He nodded his head before the end of my reply out of embarrassment. I saw his ears get flushed with colour. He spoke again.

'But you know my feelings towards you?'

I told him that it was so. And I told him in the same breath that Hyon-kyu had wanted to play tennis with him, and he would come soon.

'Yes, I'll be there soon.'

He replied as if he had recovered a source of energy that he had lost. He began to whistle and whistled all the way up to the house.

'Thank you very much. It was wonderful this morning,' he

said, no sign at all of any awkwardness, and flicked off an insect that was crawling up my shoulder.

'Good bye, and don't forget to practise! We've improved a lot, you know . . .'

He nodded, biting his lips as if submerged in some thought.

I ran up the narrow steps and went straight to my room. I was whistling as Jisu had done. I felt that I mustn't lose my strength. My elbows and skirt were still giving off the fresh scent of the early morning dew and grass. I pushed open my half closed door and marched in.

There to my surprise, I found Hyon-kyu standing there staring at me. I wasn't startled only because of the fact that he did not normally come into my room without me there, but because he looked very angry.

I was stopped so suddenly in my path that I simply froze, not knowing what to do.

'Where have you been?' he asked, in a low, deliberate tone.

I remained silent.

'Did you leave that letter there on purpose so that I'd go and read it?'

He came a step closer. My face was nearly touching his chest.

'Where have you been, I said!'

I just closed my lips tighter. I felt contempt running through me. 'See if I ever tell you,' I thought.

He suddenly lifted his arm up and there was a sharp noise on my cheek. I felt something burst into flames, and instantly, pools sprang up in my eyes. But he went out without giving another look in my direction.

I turned my head towards the window and gazed out dumbfounded. I could see Jisu walking along the forest path. The spot where he had flicked the insect off me seemed so close, I could reach it.

A sudden awareness rushed through me like an electric current. I realized. I realized why Hyon-kyu had lost control of himself so completely. I felt as if my heart would burst open with the joy that was swelling up and expanding inside me. I threw myself on the bed and crouched up like a shrimp, legs on my chest. I didn't want any of this to escape. I wanted to keep every drop of this raging torrent of elation that I could hear rushing through me.

What am I to do?
We took a walk in the woods at night.
We held hands as we walked through the darkness.
And I let him embrace me.
What am I to do?
The answer to this question seemed harder to get as time went on. The only thing that could be said with any certainty was that I should stop seeing him at night.

Coming home from school, I was told that Mother was waiting for me in the main room. I suddenly felt faint. Did she know anything?

'Oh, are you back? But what's the matter with you, your face is almost blue! Are you ill?'

Mother put her hand on my forehead.

'You know, it's so hard to see you these days, what with your brother coming in so late and you so busy that I can only see you like this...'

Mother laughed a little as she spoke. But it was a smile of innocence. She hadn't found out.

'I got a letter today, and it looks as if I might have to go to America for some time. In fact for about a year. And if I do, I'll have to leave you by yourselves and... In fact I did send many replies refusing the offer, but...'

She turned away a little and continued.

'But what do you think? Your brother has already said yes,' she said, looking into my eyes again.

'It's fine by me as well,' I answered.

I was in a daze by this time with nothing but blackness in front of my eyes.

'Oh, thank you! We'll discuss the details tomorrow. But do you think I should ask the old woman from our uncle's to come and stay with you? Hmm, but even that seems a little useless.'

It was true. She would be of no use either here or there. Then what was going to happen between me and Hyon-kyu without Mother in the house? I felt the blood drain from my face at the thought. How was I to stop the might of my fate by merely refraining from seeing him at nights?

I couldn't get to sleep. I felt as if my whole nervous system was just one big wound: one that would bleed at the slightest touch.

The pain got worse as time went on, and it soon became unbearable. I left Seoul saying I was going to visit my grand-parents.

I told myself that I was never going to go back to school again. It seemed to me that my mind would only be allowed to rest if I put an end to all my hopes and make myself believe that my 'life', as such, was finished for good. It was painful, as painful as a knife carving flesh from my body. But what alterna-tive was there?

Every day, I climbed the hill at the back of the house. At about an hour's walk, there was a Buddhist nunnery. I wasn't very fond of temples. But walking a little farther, there was a slope where wild roses lay about in bushes and the refreshing greenness of the young trees would meet the wind face on.

I would sit there with the wind in my face. Between the young zelkovas, the mellow scent of wild roses was spreading, diluted by the wind.

I picked up a white flower petal and placed it on the hem of my turquoise dress, and many more on top of that, many more ... But they were soon bleached by the brilliance of the sky above and withered in the wind.

I lifted my head, and the next moment, I was up on my feet. It was Hyon-kyu. He was walking up the steep slope. His mouth was firmly closed and his expression was rather like that time when he once got angry with me. No, it was rather a sad face than an angry one.

He stopped a couple of yards in front of me. Suddenly, I felt as if I had been pushed into him. In fact, I was embracing the trunk of a young zelkova.

'That's right, Suki, don't let go of that tree. Just listen to me.'

He took a couple of steps back. There was something pathetic in his eyes.

'You must come back and go to school. Forget everything and continue school. I've told Mother to lease the house out. And I've found somewhere to go. You can stay at Mother's friends. Suki, though we'll have to live apart, there's still a way for us. Suki, can you understand?'

He planted his feet firmly into the ground. I was shivering a little holding the trunk in my arms.

'The things that happened between us, we know they're all true and we'll never be able to forget it or deny it. But we're parting so that we can be together again . . . Can you see? We still have a chance!'

I wiped my face with my fist.

'Can you see, Suki?'

I nodded to him. My eyes were welling over with tears. So my life wasn't over, after all! I could carry on loving him.

'Can you promise me that you'll come back? Tomorrow or the day after, as soon as possible.'

I nodded again.

'Thank you. Then I'd better be . . .'

He forced a pained smile on his face, and turning around, ran down the steep slope of the hill.

A gust of wind blew into my face. I was laughing with the young zelkova tree in my arms. Tears were rolling down my face, but I was laughing, laughter that was spreading and filling the blue void above. Ahh . . . I can still love him!

THE ROCK

HAN MU-SUK

Translated by Chung Chong-wha

There are too many 'I's. First, 'I' in my identification card;
Shin Sūng-kyun, age 34, address: Yonggang-dong, Map'o-ku,
Seoul. Second, 'I' on the conscription list. Third, 'I' in the
office; a certified architect, the chief of a section.

Besides these registered 'I's, there are other 'I's too. On the
wall of my room is hung a very cheap mirror. Whenever I
stand in front of it I find a different 'I'. I am not sure whether
it is due to the uneven surface of the mirror or due to the
uneven spread of mercury. However, all these different persons
are undoubtedly 'I'. Last Saturday I stood in front of the
mirror with no particular aim in mind, and to my great surprise
I found a horse's face in it. Instinctively I wanted to run away
from it, but the next moment I overcame my surprise and
remained there. This time I contracted my neck, and there
appeared a flat, widened face on the surface of the looking
glass. Then out of curiosity I stretched out my neck, and I saw
my nose longer than the length of a palm. When I turned my
face to the side I was really shocked, for I found my lips
twisted. I must have been laughing unconsciously. Now I deliberately tried to look angry, and there I found a calm and sad
face. It must have been getting dark. There was no sunshine
coming through the window. My eyes were expressionless and
sad, like those of an owl. My lips, which more often than not

60

are tightly closed, were half open. In short, I saw a very weak and lonely man with an utterly absent-minded face. I had never seen that face before, and yet strange as it was undoubtedly mine. Then I came to realize jokes I had made just for fun were beginning to bear some significance. But the angry and sad faces soon gave way to the twisted face which looked as if I were laughing at somebody. I tried to show an angry face again exactly as I had done before, but in the mirror I saw an entirely different face; the eyes under the broad forehead were gloomy and the lips, so sad and pathetic a few minutes ago, were tightly closed in a rather malicious expression. But all, everything was mine.

Were it not for my sister-in-law, who opened the door and called me to supper, I might have seen some more of my faces. As soon as she opened the paper-screened door, she shouted:

'Why, you are so concerned with your appearance! Dating with a lady?'

I couldn't hide the bitter smile on my lips. My sister-in-law is very sociable. She had quite a large number of friends with whom she runs a private financial club. I lost my wife and a son by an air raid and I now live under the same roof with my brother, and this is why I am quite well known among the group of ladies my sister-in-law sees. Whenever they gather they seem to talk about me:

'You see, my brother-in-law seems to have changed a lot since his serious illness. He now tries to look decent. He has never been like this before. The other day I saw him looking in the mirror, so absorbed. He must be very lonely, don't you think?'

In short, another different 'I' comes into existence every time they gather and talk about me. Hence all these different 'I's pile up, and, in the end, they have become a terrible burden to me and I can't cope with them all. Even I, myself, ask sometimes which is the real 'I' among so many.

I saw a rainbow over the river one day. It was very beautiful, and I felt ecstatic at its perfect beauty. It hung for only about five minutes, no longer. As soon as it vanished thin clouds appeared and floated like sands in the bare sky. Then I thought that life is as short as the rainbow and my existence is also destined to be brief and momentary. Until sometime ago I couldn't bear the thought that my life was utterly worthless and useless, the idea that there will be no vacant spot, after I perish, and there will be no change whatever on this earth; the sun will rise again and the sea will toss and leap as ever.

I had led a vacant and meaningless life for years and years, and I can't forgive myself for having to eat, to dress, to sleep, even after the sudden, tragic death of my wife and son. I have scolded myself for a long time that I took their death as a matter of course and that I got used to it.

My sister-in-law jokingly says that I am a loyal husband, but I am not, in fact, faithful to the deceased woman. Her idea that I do not want to marry again is utterly wrong and groundless. To tell the truth, I married my late wife just because my mother liked her, and naturally there was no love involved in the marriage. My married life was too short, and there wasn't time enough to love or hate each other. The child, too, died in infancy, just one hundred days old, and I didn't have time to be fond of him. To be honest, I sometimes even forget their faces.

There is one thing I cannot easily get rid of; it is the sound of their moaning on their death bed. My wife continued to cry out for about three days in spite of heavy haemorrhage. She was just twenty five years old. I could do nothing but watch them suffer and die in the terrible shower of cannon-balls. I myself had a bullet through my shoulder.

It was August 15th by the lunar calendar when my wife finally died. Wounded myself, I couldn't move: I only had to watch her stop breathing, with my son and nephew already dead in the next room. The clear moon shone through a hole made by an air-raid, and everything was quiet and still – it was a night of terrifying tranquillity and void where time didn't exist. And yet there was one sound; her moaning voice which came from the already unconscious body, and it sounded more like the suffering of a soul than a voice from a painful body. My heart was torn at the sight of a poor, helpless, weak mortal perishing in pain. I do not know if her voice continued to moan much longer for I soon lost consciousness. A few days later in hospital, I opened my eyes to find she had passed away. The first thing I heard on my waking was the heavy thumping of soldiers' feet and later I came to realize that it was a thousand pities that the whole tragic drama took place only three days before the retaking of Seoul by the UN forces.

Outside the heavy stamp of soldiers' marching and the rolling sound of tanks were met with the cheers of thousands and thousands of overjoyed citizens. My sister-in-law cried at the tragic fate of my family. But for my part I felt nothing. I just looked at her shabby and untidy figure, at the incessant undulating movement of her thin and bony shoulders. Gradually my eyes were filled with the moon beams that poured down through the hole of the ceiling of that empty night.

Ever since then this emptiness has become my reality. It seems that my heart was damaged by the bullet in my shoulder and had lost its proper function, for I now have no passion for despair, and only feel this great void.

Some years ago the wedding of my sister's daughter took place, but I didn't go. Naturally enough my sister was furious with me, because it was the biggest event in the life of her only daughter's, and my sister had lost her husband early in her marriage.

'How could you be so unkind and wicked?' I didn't go to the wedding, because I was not qualified as a human being, if a human being means a creature who sticks to happiness. Yet unqualified though I am, I am still alive, and days and months and years passed by. Perhaps we live before we think, or perhaps life possesses something which is beyond our comprehension even after we have undergone all its tragic elements.

Recently my sister-in-law has often said that I have changed a lot and that I have had an affair with a lady while I was at the Oksu Hermitage. I detest this sort of mean curiosity from a middle-aged woman. But in a way her teasing remarks are valid.

I left the Oksu Hermitage at nightfall and arrived in Seoul when it was quite dark. It was raining. As soon as I came home I threw myself on the bed without changing my clothes. Although I was dead tired I couldn't sleep. The rain in my heart fell more heavily than it did outside. The water of the rain formed a river in my heart and rippled.

Later my sister-in-law told me what had really happened on that night. She had thought it very unusual to see me come back as late as that, and so naturally opened the door of my room only to find tears in my closed eyes, and she had known that I was not asleep. Was I crying in bed? No, I wasn't. I just threw myself away into a river and above my head was a bare sky from which a rainbow had just vanished; I saw an indifferent sky and, suddenly, I came to accept the philosophy of indifference. I also came to realize that our salvation lies in this indifference to human desires and wishes, the indifference to the death of our dear ones. Perhaps I am changed as my sister-in-law points out. Certainly I am not what I was about a month and a half ago. I am no more than an empty human effigy. My vacant and hollow heart is filled up with love. I have experienced this valuable love, and the incomplete 'I' has become a complete one. I have become self-sufficient and I have become indifferent to the indifferent ways of this world.

However, I cannot help feeling uneasy from time to time before the various shapes of myself reflected in the uneven surface of the mirror. Whenever I feel uneasy I see an image of a rock appear in my eyesight, in relation with her. A rock stands between her and me.

The rock stands under an old zelkova tree on the lower ridge of a hill looking down at the Changja Lake. The path from this rock to the Oksu Hermitage on the higher ridge of Mount Chunma is rather flat and easy. So, as soon as one passes through, the wooded path of the hermitage one has to walk for some time towards the zelkova tree and the rock.

I used to take an early morning walk along the hillside path full of grass, wet with dew drops. Then early one morning I happened to notice a rock standing under the zelkova tree. From a distance the rock looked like some sort of symbol of fate and its contours in the setting sun seemed to tell the yearning and loneliness of a human being. But it wasn't until one late, windy autumn day that the rock occupied one corner of my heart. I was twenty four, young and strong, and I used to climb up the hill path – it took me only about half an hour to walk the three miles from the village to the hermitage. I climbed up that day with an excited feeling at the liberation of the country from under the Japanese yoke, but the excitement was mixed with the pain of torture and loneliness. Wind blew from all directions on to the hill, and, from time to time, a whirlwind formed. It wasn't quite dark yet, and I could see the Changja Lake in the twilight; the waves were high, and, to me, seemed alive. In the violent wind the zelkova tree by the lake appeared to be torn to pieces. With my back against the strong wind I proceeded towards the tree slowly. Whenever the branches of the tree swayed in the gale, the rock revealed its dark appearance. Suddenly an idea occurred to me that it was not the zelkova tree that was torn apart but the rock itself that was suffering in the wild weather.

Sometimes a mere gesture or a single, beautiful sound creates a myth. And the rock revealed its own myth at that moment. That the heartless rock possessed a myth is perhaps explained by the fact that someone had planted some vital force in it at some mysterious moment.

Long, long ago there lived a rich family at the place where now the lake lies. The master of the family was Pak Chang-ja, and the fact of his boundless money and power was put into a song and sung by the neighbourhood children. Yet the rich Pak was so stingy that he did not spare a single penny for the poor children.

One day a Buddhist monk came to the gate of the rich man and asked for alms. Pak Chang-ja called his servants and ordered them to beat him, instead of giving money. Chang-ja was not pleased the fact that a poor monk dared to come to his gate. When the monk got up after having been beaten mercilessly, a fair woman appeared and gave him something wrapped in cloth. She was the daughter-in-law of the family and what she had given was her share of cooked barley. The monk's face lit up, and he told the woman to flee from the house when a halo appeared around the sun at about midday three days later. He also warned the young woman not to turn back even if she heard some one calling her name. After that the monk disappeared. How the daughter-in-law spent her three days is not told in the legend. However, on the third day, she ran away from the house as soon as the halo started to loom up around the sun. When she finally reached the zelkova tree all by herself she suddenly heard terrible thunder behind her. She forgot all about the monk's advice and turned back to see, and she saw no house but a lake, reflecting the sun-halo. In a moment she herself was turned into a rock.

I cannot now remember who it was that told me the legend of the rock. When I told the story I felt as if I had told everything I wanted to tell. Feeling peaceful and happy I turned aside and saw Young-nan beside me. She did not say anything, she just cast her eyes down on the ground, which looked like leopard skin, due to the shadow made by the zelkova leaves. Without a word she touched the rock gently and cautiously, as a nurse feels a patient's pulse. I noticed her hand white and almost transparent.

It is ten years since the rock occupied a special place in my heart on that late, windy autumn day. Then the hill was covered with wild roses in full bloom and the rock bound by the vines of arrowroot. There was no chirping of wild birds. Everything was quiet. There was only the stir of the fresh May air, full of the odour of wild roses and grasses.

The May wind was fresh on my excited cheeks. I was indeed excited. I felt as if something hidden in my heart began to unveil itself, and it was a mixture of joy and surprise. No doubt some sort of season was on the verge of opening within me. If a miracle means an unexplainable phenomenon, it was certainly for me that I had met Young-nan at the Oksu Hermitage and she had rekindled the flame of life in me. Physically as well as spiritually I had not been well since the terrible war and since last spring I had been running a high temperature. By the time I got a bit better it was the beginning of summer. The temperature fell to normal but I still felt very weak and I stayed indoors. One day Sister Hejong paid an unexpected visit from the Osku Hermitage. She complained about her sciatica, which is rather common among Buddhist monks and nuns. Sister He-jong was a distant relation of my family; she was a sister-in-law of one of my sisters. She became quite friendly with my family when my late mother adopted Buddhism in her later days and she seemed to have heard something about me.

'You look pale and thin for a young man, *Namu kwanseum Posal.*' She rarely evoked the help of Buddhist Goddess, but she did that day. She stayed just one day and went back to her hermitage, leaving an invitation to me to visit and rest under her care. She promised to have a special room cleaned for me – in fact, a room in the arbour which she used to keep for specially favoured guests of hers. I appreciated her kind invitation, for I was feeling guilty over my sister-in-law who had been looking after me with the help of a little maid. My health didn't return and the so-called nervous breakdown developed, though it was not very serious or painful. So I made up my mind to go to the Oksu Hermitage. Sister He-jong was about forty when I first visited the hermitage with her nephew. She was then a woman with pure white skin, a lovely mouth and firm body. Besides Sister Hejong, there was one more cropped-haired nun in the hermitage who had lost her two children in a fire, and who had a burn on a temple. These two priestesses of almost the same age kept two helpers, one for gathering firewood and the other for cooking. My first impression of the hermitage was that of a mountain resort for unfortunate and beautiful women. The place made me forget that I was in a place of worship. The room she promised was a bit away from the main worship hall, and had once been occupied by a noble and well-known nun. It was by a crystal clear stream, from which the name of the hermitage came. It was not a big room and had a picture of Buddha on one side of the wall. I stayed in the room whenever I visited the hermitage. I like the room with a flower-bed of rhododendrons, chrysanthemums, lilies, and many other flowers, and a clear stream near by. On a wet day I could smell the rich fragrance of the various flowers. Whenever I came back to Seoul after a month or so at the hermitage I felt rather strange without hearing the rippling sound of the crystal clear stream.

However, when I actually went to the room this time, there was something strange in Sister Hejong's welcoming attitude. She took me to a room next to the main hall of worship and asked me to rest there. She was unusually talkative. I must have been tired, having walked along the hilly pine wood path. As soon as Sister Hejong left me alone. I fell asleep immediately.

I must have slept quite a while, for when I awoke I heard two people whispering in the next room. I couldn't catch what they had said but by the way they talked I could guess that they were hesitating to do something. I tired to listen to them more carefully, but to my disappointment the conversation stopped and the two went out of the room. Nuns are quiet. They are not even allowed to cough aloud. And naturally I became very curious to know what on earth they had been talking about. I sat up on the mattress for a moment. I felt dizzy. I had just lain down again when an old nun opened the door of the room. She was the one with a scar on her temple. She asked if I wanted the room lighted. Without answering I asked her if anything was wrong, and the old nun said no. But I insisted that things didn't seem all right and wanted to go back, requesting her explanation. The old nun hesitantly said:

'Your room is being taken by other people. They are also from Seoul. They came about three or four days ago . . .'

She didn't finish. As soon as Sister Hejong came back they had cleaned the room for me, and then these people had taken it. The old nun was really sorry for me. I asked her who they were.

'Well, they are Sister Hejong's niece and her husband. Look very rich.' She said sulkily, while she lighted the oil lamp. They were Young-nan and her husband. I wanted to leave the hermitage the very same night, but my temperature shot up that evening, perhaps due to the long walk on the hilly path. I had to be detained in the hermitage, but hoped I would leave the place as soon as I got better.

However, it was Young-nan's husband who left the place before me. One day a messenger came from Seoul and talked to the man. Two men left next day, leaving Young-nan behind. Young-nan moved to a room next to Sister Hejong's and I moved out to the guest room in the arbour where Young-nan and her husband had stayed.

Young-nan was a step-daughter of my elder sister, so I was her step-uncle. My sister was a kind person by nature, and she never discriminated between her step-daughter and her own children. Yet Young-nan's fragile appearance with fair skin, thin neck, and dark eyes made people think that they should be sorry for her Young-nan was rather quiet and gentle, and she loved her step-mother and half-brothers. As we grew older I felt awkward to be referred to as Young-nan's 'Uncle'. For my part I frequented my sister's house because it was also my closest friend's, Young-min. The last time I saw Young-nan, it was when her brother, Young-min, had gone to North Korea, so it must be seven or eight years ago.

Young-nan's father was stricken with a cerebral haemorrhage after his business had collapsed. I had gone to my sister's and I had found her on the floor, completely out of her mind. The children were in the garden, playing, and Young-nan was washing rice, looking thinner and leaner than before. She was rinsing the already clean rice again and again. I felt moved with pity to see my brother-in-law unconscious. But I felt more sorry to find Young-nan there, so fragile, and the image stayed in my heart for a very long time. Six months after my brother-in-law was stricken down with the cerebral hemorrhage, I was told that Young-nan had married an old, wealthy widower. I felt most miserable and sad at the news. They said that she sacrificed herself to save her sick father and two younger brothers. Soon after her marriage her father died and two years later one of her younger brothers died of diptheria. My sister fell into a helpless state and Young-nan extended assistance. But a series of disasters continued in the family. This time her elder son, her only remaining son, was taken by the North Korean Army and never came back, and my sister died of a broken heart in a refugee camp. Now Young-nan was left with no blood relations except Sister Hejong. Her noble act of sacrifice – throwing her young life away to marry a fat and rich man of her father's age, notorious for his cheating and prodigality – had turned out to be utterly meaningless.

However, I may be wrong to call her marriage a 'sacrifice', since a marriage sometimes consists merely of the combination of the two opposite sexes – male and female. I have had a very careful look at Young-nan's married life for years, and I have found out that she was very faithful and obedient to her old man. There has been no sign of complaint or regret, and I have felt betrayed and furious with her for no special reason. It was utterly beyond my understanding to find Young-nan so happy and content. Certainly there was no reason why she should be unhappy and sad either. Nevertheless, her self-satisfaction and seemingly settled life seemed bogus and fake. Young-nan seemed to care about her appearance very much. I can't tell whether it was due to the fact that she had enough money or because it was her nature to dress up in the best and the most expensive way, but this also made me mad. However, Young-nan has kept her fragile and girlish figure; she remained young. And yet whenever I see in her a mature woman of thirty years old I am endlessly tormented.

Sister Hejong told me that Young-nan had come to the hermitage to drink medicinal water for her poor health, but in fact she seldom drank at the well. Naturally I thought it odd that she didn't care for water until the cook – simple and honest – told me a different story about her coming to the hermitage. According to the cook, Young-nan's husband was notoriously lewd and promiscuous and had many mistresses. Recently he fell for a college girl of his granddaughter's age and had neglected Young-nan. Young-nan had got tired of it and escaped to the hermitage. To make a long story short her fidelity to her old husband was utterly meaningless. And it was indeed a terrible shock to me that Young-nan had not yet been registered as his legal wife after seven or eight years of marriage. I was also informed of the old man's flight to Japan to avoid a certain difficulty he had to face, leaving all the complications in Young-nan's hands. 'How dreadful!' the cook said and shook her head.

Yet Young-nan was as merry and happy as before when I saw her next morning at the well. Her face was so bright and fresh with a lovely smile that I couldn't believe she had been living in such a dreadful situation.

I decided to give up the resolution I had made that I would leave the hermitage as soon as I got better, and even after my temperature fell to normal I resolved to stay another month. Indeed my health had improved greatly during my stay in the temple. I felt endlessly refreshed at the sounds of *Sutra* being recited, the water running in the stream, and wild birds chirping. And yet I was lonely, the loneliness one comes to know when one falls on the street – the loneliness that I was thrown away into boundless space afflicted me and made me afraid of everything. And this loneliness drove me nearer to her, and when I saw her own affliction and despair, though just momentarily, I glimpsed another 'I' in her and eventually she became a part of me.

That evening we – Sister Hejong, Young-nan, and I – were in the main worship hall, mute and pensive, in the twilight. The lingering sunlight illuminated the five hundred Buddha's disciples and then moved over to the image of the Goddess just for a second, and I felt her rather than saw her. It was the image of a woman who suffered from all human afflictions rather than a goddess who poured out her mercy lavishly. Her half-opened eyes were full of sorrow, and her gilded body reminded me of an aged woman. The lotus flowers, on which her feet showing from the end of a garment of silk, were more like thorns. In short, I saw a woman in human affliction. I put my hands together in unconscious worship, in spite of myself, and I thought I was reciting the *Sutra* when I heard someone invoking the mercy of the Goddess. '*Namoo-kwanse-um-boh-sahl . . .*' It was almost like groaning sound full of sorrow and despair, the same moaning voice of my wife at her death-bed on the full moon night of August.

Twilight began to recede from the hall, and I saw the pale, beautiful eyes of Young-nan there, her eyes half shut, her face lifted up, and her mouth in the state of pronouncing the 'L' sound. It was Young-nan who had been reciting the *Sutra*. Her face was, like that of the Goddess, in affliction, and the next moment the Goddess and Young-nan became the same person. The one hundred and eight kinds of affliction taught by Buddha were momentarily revealed in the two women, one mortal and the other immortal.

To love is to have another 'I'; that is right. It was why I thought I was reciting the *Sutra* while in fact it was Young-nan who was calling the mercy of the Goddess and in the end I came to identify myself with her. It might have been a pure coincidence that a man who believed in the reality of emptiness had met a woman who had wasted her life in a meaningless sacrifice, in a small mountain temple. However, we came to realize that we loved each other, and when I was convinced of this fact I had to find Young-nan in the heart of my hearts where I myself had never been. For the first time in many, many years I felt a burning desire to live, to share my life with Young-nan.

It was a fine May morning. The bright sunshine dazzled the eyes, and the wind was gentle, passing over the grass and shaking the zelkova tree gently. The sky was blue without the one spot of cloud.

Young-nan didn't know the legend of Changja Lake. When she commented that the rippling movement of the surface of the water made her think that the lake was alive, I asked her if she knew the story of the family who had lived there, and of course her answer was negative. But she seemed not to listen to me carefully. absent-mindedly, she just felt with her hand the surface of the rock by the lake. When I finished the story she turned her head to the direction of the lake and asked, 'Do you think the legend has any message?'

'A message? Well, there might be one. Perhaps a kind of moral, I suppose.'

71

'Why then did God punish the kind daughter-in-law, too?'

'Well, that's a point, isn't it?'

'The centre of the legend is the rock, I suppose.' This time Young-nan turned her head to me and gazed into my eyes.

'Of course, yes. She is the only human being in the story.'

'And the only kind-hearted person, too.'

'Well, she is goodness itself.'

Young-nan did not say anything for a while. After a few minutes' silence, she said again, 'Then goodness is also punished as evil, I suppose.'

I was quite taken aback at the question. I eagerly searched her eyes, but she avoided mine. Looking at the rock, she asked again, 'Did you say that the daughter-in-law was the only human being in the family? Why?'

'Well, because she looked back.'

'Because she looked back?'

'By looking back she became a human being. But the subtlety of this legend is found in the fact that it is an incomplete moral story,' I said and put my hand on the rock. It was just a rough rock and nothing else. It didn't matter, in fact, whether it was rock or clay, or anything else. What mattered to me was Young-nan herself.

'Could she have been happy, if she didn't turn back?' Young-nan said in a low voice. She was asking herself rather than asking me.

'What is happiness? I don't know. But if she didn't turn back in the story there might have been something different.'

Young-nan remained in silence for sometime, and said slowly, putting stress on each word, 'She was so kind-hearted, and yet she was destined to become a rock.'

My eyes finally met hers, and I realized that she was looking into herself with her eyes. Without knowing I approached a step nearer to her and said, 'Why do you like to call such a thing destiny? Do you always call punishment destiny?'

Young-nan cast down her eyes and without a word rubbed her ribbon.

'Young-nan, I don't think destiny is almighty, and yet destiny is not punishment. I think destiny owes something to us,' I said and went another step nearer to her.

But the moment we were to touch each other, Young-nan suddenly stood up and shook her head. She said, 'It was when

I was still in the primary school. You came to see my brother and had a heated discussion with him, and there you repeated the word "owe" and I didn't know the meaning.' She laughed hysterically, but I could detect a trace of sadness in her laughter. While her laughter lasted, something that had been filling my heart for the past few weeks turned into the form of a firm resolution to reconcile myself with life, and I had received this through her, through misery and distress.

Four days later I left the hermitage. People saw me off at the gate, and Young-nan accompanied me as far as the hilly path. Sister Hejong looked at Young-nan first and then at me with a warm smile. I saw a plea in her eyes, the plea that I should look after her with all my heart. She could have led her unhappy niece into the direction of Buddhistic renunciation of worldly cares, but she trusted me and left her in my care, for which I was grateful to her. We walked for a while in silence. Words were no longer necessary to us. My heart was filled with the words I had heard from her during the past few days. She told me that she had loved me from the very beginning of my haunting her house, and she asked me if it was not natural to love a man who frequented her house, while she was motherless and extremely sensitive. Her memory of the days gone by was very good, and the way she remembered details of the past seemed to be a confession of her love to me. In my childhood I used to pronounce sand as '*molae*' instead of '*morae*' which was correct, and Young-nan noticed it and whenever she imitated my pronunciation secretly she felt her heart agitated as if she was meeting me. Though she didn't say much about her married life, she told me that she always had a guilty conscience towards her husband because she couldn't get rid of my image from her heart. In fact, I didn't need to hear about her past from her own mouth; I knew it well and I knew too that her seemingly happy and merry way of life had directly stemmed from the despair which she had wanted to hide so desperately.

Since Young-nan was childless and her step-children renounced her, she was free, which was rather fortunate for both of us. So we made an arrangement that I should go to Seoul ahead of her and she would follow me and meet me at a certain place at a certain time.

Clouds began to disperse and the sky started to show its blue colour. Azaleas along the path had lost their flowers during last night's heavy rain. The sun appeared and then disappeared, alternating light and shadow on the hill. Young-nan was in a simple and white dress, and her face was lightly made up. With her beside me, I walked along with full of hope for the future. I also thought of my student days and my youthful ideals.

The Changja Lake came into sight and at a far distance the white waves of the East Sea were visible. When we arrived under the zelkova tree we stopped by the rock and looked at the lake. A passing wind made rippling movements on the surface of the water, on which were reflected the clouds driven by the wind and the blue of the sky mostly covered by dark clouds. A patch of clouds, thick, heavy, and dark, was fixed on the surface of the lake and did not move. The sun seemed to be hidden there, for round it was a golden halo. A shower seemed imminent. Thunder rolled in a far-off place. Young-nan seemed to tremble at the sound. I called her in a rather urgent voice, 'Young-nan!'

'Yes?' She turned her head to me, shrinking visibly.

I couldn't find anything urgent to say to her, so I repeated what I had already said so many times, 'This Saturday, at two, yes?'

She just nodded.

We had to part there. I asked her to go back, but she said she would wait and see me go. I gave in and took my way. After I walked round a turn I went to a place to look back at the rock where Young-nan had been standing. As soon as I saw Young-nan again I called her name, across the lake. The sky got clear and the threat of impending shower disappeared. I took a seat along the path and waited until she would go back. But Young-nan did not move. She too sat down against the rock.

In my eyes the person and the rock melted together and became one. Then an idea occurred suddenly in my mind, and idea that she was no longer a person but a rock and she would never move from the present position and come to me. I was convinced of this. Something crumbled in my heart. The sense of emptiness which I had carried with me on my way to the hermitage returned to me.

A wind rose again, and the sound of the sea far down at the foot of the mountain became louder. I came back to myself and found it was already far into the afternoon. I looked across the lake, innumerable branches of the zelkova tree were reflecting the twilight, and the darkness was setting into the space under the tree. The rock was not visible; she was just the same dark lump as the rock. A dark rock discernible from a distance.

I stood up and resumed my walk. All of a sudden I was reminded of a remark Young-nan once made to me, 'Goodness was also punished like evil.' I stumbled over rocks and stones, but it wasn't because it was getting dark nor because I couldn't see my way.

MEETINGS AND FAREWELLS

YI SANG

Translated by Chung Chong-wha

I

I am twenty-two years old. It is March. I am coughing up blood. One day I shaved off the beard that I had so carefully groomed for six months, leaving only a little butterfly of a moustache. Then with ten packets of Chinese medicine I went to a quiet hot-spring called 'B' which had just been opened. There I would have been happy to die. But my still unflowered youth clung to the medicine. I couldn't give up life. Every night under the cold lamplight of the inn I was invariably sulky, grumbling that life was not fair to me.

On the third day, with the innkeeper as my guide, I went to a kisaeng house* where drums were heard every night, and there I met Kum-hong, a kisaeng girl.

'How old are you?'

She was small but quite conceited. While I was wondering if she were fifteen or eighteen at the most, she said, 'I'm twenty, sir.'

'Can you guess how old I am?'

'Well, forty? Or thirty-nine?'

*The Korean version of a geisha house.

I just said 'Hm' and folded my arms, pretending to be dignified. When we parted that day nothing had happened.

Next day my artist friend K. came to see me. He was on joking terms with me. He made fun of my butterfly moustache and I shaved it off. As soon as it was dark we hurried to see Kum-hong.

'I must have seen you somewhere before,' she said.

'The gentleman with the moustache last night was my father. We have the same voice, don't we?' I said, pulling her leg.

When the party was over I whispered to K., stepping into the garden, 'What do you think of her? Isn't she nice? Would you like to have her?'

'No thanks, but you go ahead, if you like.'

'Let's take her to the inn, and toss a coin to decide.'

'Good idea!'

K. slipped away, however, pretending that he was going to the toilet, so there was no need to toss the coin. That night Kum-hong confessed that she had once given birth to a baby.

'When?'

'At fifteen I was taken by a man and became a mother at sixteen.'

'A boy?'

'A girl.'

'Where is she?'

'She died round about her first birthday.'

Instead of taking medicine I spent the whole time making love to her. Though it may sound silly, the power of love stopped me coughing up blood. I didn't leave tips for Kum-hong. Why not? Because day and night either Kum-hong stayed in my room or I went to hers. Instead of giving her tips, I introduced her to Mr Woo, a playboy who had been to France to study. Kum-hong went to a 'private bath-house' with this man as I suggested. The 'private bath-house' is a rather obscene establishment, but I didn't feel upset when I saw their shoes side by side on the doorstep of the place.

I also recommended her to a lawyer C. who was staying in the room next to mine. Quite moved by my invitation, the lawyer invaded Kum-hong's room, too.

My beloved Kum-hong, however, would always stay close by me. She would show me several ten *won* notes that she had taken from Mr Woo or Lawyer C., and boast about them playfully.

Then one day I had to go back to Seoul for the first memorial day of my uncle's death. Before I left, we went to a lovely place where peach trees were in full blossom and a small stream went rippling by a pavillion, and we spent the whole day together as a farewell. At the station I put a ten-*won* note into her hand. She sobbed, saying she would use the money to get her watch back from the pawn shop.

2

By the time Kum-hong became my wife, we loved each other very much. We decided not to talk about our past. As I had no past life worth mentioning, it meant, in other words, that I promised not to question Kum-hong's past.

Though Kum-hong was only twenty, she was more mature than a woman of thirty, although she looked only sixteen to me. I for my part looked forty to her, though I was really twenty-two and acted like a boy of ten or eleven. As a couple, however, we lived very happily.

Time flew by. A year passed, and it came to August, the last of the summer and early autumn.

Kum-hong began to feel homesick for the old days, for her past life, because I slept day and night and life was not very exciting for her. She began to go out, meet interesting people and enjoy herself.

This time she did not boast of her adventures; she tried to hide them from me. This was not like her. Was there anything to conceal? She need not have kept anything from me at all. She could have been proud of her adventures, if she wanted, but kept quiet about them.

I often went out and slept at P.'s house to make Kum-hong's life easier, for which P. must have pitied me. It was not that I didn't believe in wifely virtue and fidelity, but rather I wanted to take her adultery as a sign of her wish to awaken me from my lazy and sluggish life. So keeping up a front of 'wifely virtue' was her one big mistake.

To help her feign virtue I naturally went out as often as I

could, to offer her my own room for her business. And time went by.

One day I was beaten by Kum-hong for no apparent reason. I cried in pain and left home. I was so afraid of Kum-hong that I couldn't go home for three days. When I went back she had gone away, leaving her dirty socks in a corner of the room.

It was as silly as that; and thus I became deprived of my wife. Several friends of mine came to see me with unpleasant gossip about Kum-hong's elopement, and tried to console me. But I couldn't understand what they were getting at anyway. They said that they had seen a man and Kum-hong go by bus as far as Mt Kwanak near Kwachon. The bloke must have been a real coward to run away all that way.

3

As I had temporarily been leading a life in which I refused to be a human being, my memory quickly became rusty. So in two months I completely forgot even her full name. One fine day during this period when my life stood still, Kum-hong came back to me like a returned letter. She'd had this lucky day chosen for her by a fortune teller. I was greatly surprised to see her.

Her shabby looks made me sad. I didn't scold her. On the contrary I bought some beer and fish-shaped salty crackers and comforted her. I also bought her some hot beef soup with rice in it. But she was still angry with me and denounced me, crying bitterly. I also broke down and cried.

'It's too late. It's been two months since you went away. Let's make a complete break of it.'

'Then what happens to me?'

'Get married if you find a suitable fellow.'

'Will you get married, too?'

Even on the point of farewell there must be some consolation for the person you're leaving. When she left she gave me a pillow as a gift.

A word about this pillow. It was big enough for two people. She insisted on my taking it, though I tried to refuse. I laid my head alone on it for two weeks. It was too big to make me feel comfortable. Besides, it had a peculiar smell of hair cream which certainly was not mine. The smell bothered my sleep.

One day I sent a postcard to Kum-hong. 'I'm gravely ill. Come back immediately.' Kum-hong found me in a pitiable state, a dying man – if I had been left alone a few more days I would have starved to death. She said she would roll her sleeves up and start working the very same day to feed me.

A paradise on earth! Though the day was chilly, I didn't even sneeze, and I felt so comfortable!

And it was like this for two or perhaps five months. Then one day Kum-hong suddenly went away again.

Over a month I waited for her to feel homesick. At last, tired of waiting, I sold all my household stuff and went home again after twenty-one years.

I found my parent's house in a poor state. I, Yi Sang, the faithless son, had caused the ruin of this already declining home. For two years I myself had been declining, and now I was twenty-six years old.

I am fully convinced that every woman in the world has a streak of the prostitute in her. Nevertheless, when I pay silver coins to prostitutes I never think of them as professionals. This may sound like a theory divorced from my life with Kum-Hong, but in fact it is derived from personal experience.

Writing several novels and a few lines of poetry aggravated my poor health. I had reached a point where it was impossible to go on living this way. I had to get away from this country, become an exile.

Where would I go? I boasted to every one I met that I would go to Tokyo. I told some friends that I would study electrical-engineering; to my school teacher I said that I was going to learn the art of advanced single-unit printing; to intimate friends I lied that I would master five foreign languages, and perhaps even study law. Most of them believed what I said, but a few didn't. However, these were merely Yi Sang's last desperate lies, as empty as his penniless pocket.

One day as I was drinking with, and lying to, my friends, someone shook my shoulder. It was a man known as Kin Sang.*

*Kin Sang in Japanese means Mr Kim.

'We haven't met for a long time!' he said. 'There's someone who would like to see you. Do you want to meet this person?'

'Who is it? A man or a woman?'

'It's a woman, of course, which makes it all the more fun.'

'A woman?'

'A woman who was once your wife!'

So Kum-hong had come back to Seoul! What did she want from me? I got her address from Kin Sang, but I hesitated. She was with her sister, Il-sim.

At last I made up my mind to see her and called on Il-sim.

'Your sister came back?'

'Wow, my dear brother-in-law! I thought you were long dead. What made you take so long to come to see us? Do come in, please!'

Kum-hong still looked shabby. I could read the worn-out expression on her face, the signs of struggle in life's battle.

'You bastard, I missed you and here I am. What else should I bother to come for?'

'So I've come to you like this, too.'

'They say you got married, bastard!'

'Shut up! The same stupid nonsense!'

'Not married, then?'

'Of course not.'

Suddenly the wooden pillow flew at my face. I grinned stupidly as usual.

A table was set for a drink. I drank and she drank. I sang a Youngbyun Song* and Kum-hong sang a Yukja Baiki.† The night was already deep. We talked about the evening as if it would be our last meeting. Kum-hong sang a sad song which I had never heard before, beating the table with her silver chopsticks.

> Cheating is a dream,
> Getting cheated is also a dream,
> Drifting life is a winding stream,
> Set fire to your shadowy dream!

---

*A folk song of the northwestern provinces of Korea.
†A folk song of the southwestern provinces of Korea.

PICTURE OF A SHAMAN SORCERESS

KIM DONG-NI

Translated by Chung Chong-wha

Shadowy hills lie in the distance; a dark, wide river flows in the foreground; blue stars seem to fall over the hills, over the fields, and over the dark river. The quiet late night is holding its breath. On a sandy beach by the river is pitched a big tent, in which the women are gatehred, intoxicated by the magic incantations of a sorceress. Their faces show undoubted signs of sad excitement, and of tiredness such as one feels as the dawn approaches. The sorceress, in such ecstasy that she seems to have turned into a disembodied soul, dances round, her ritual garment swirling lightly.

This picture was drawn in the very year when my father got married – it therefore goes back even before my birth. I come from what they call an old-established family, which in times past was noted for its wealth and power, especially for the patronage of calligraphy, paintings, and curios – and there were always passing scholars staying in the house as guests. The love of art and antiques was very much a part of the family tradition, handed down through generations from father to son, from son to grandson, along with the wealth.

The riches of my family disintegrated in my father's time, but at the time when the picture was drawn, my grandfather could still, as part of the family tradition, entertain passing travellers in his reception room, and poets and calligraphers were constant family guests.

It was late one spring evening, apricots were blooming in the garden, the wind had been blowing the dust around all day, when a stranger came to the house: a small man in his fifties, in a plain jacket and trousers and no coat, wearing a bamboo hat on which a silk handkerchief was tied. He was holding the rein of a donkey, on which sat a pale-looking girl of about sixteen. The relationship appeared to be that between a manservant and his master's daughter.

But the next day the man said, 'This is my daughter, sir. She is, so everybody tells me, astonishingly gifted in drawing. That is why I brought her to you, sir.'

She wore a white dress, and her face, paler than her dress, was sorrowful.

'Your name, child? Your age?'

The master of the house spoke to her, but she looked at him only once with her big eyes, without attempting to answer. The father spoke instead, 'Her name is Nang-i, sir, and she is sixteen years old.' He lowered his voice and said, 'She is a little deaf, sir.' The master of the house nodded in acknowledgement. He told the man to stay on and to ask the girl to show her talent.

Father and daughter stayed for a month or so, drawing pictures and telling their history. When they were leaving, my grandfather gave the unhappy pair some expensive silk and plenty of money for their future keep. The girl on the donkey, however, bore on her face the same distressed expression as before.

The story of the girl and the picture she left behind were handed down from my grandfather; her drawing he called 'Picture of a Sorceress'.

II

There was a small village, about two miles outside the city wall, in the suburb of Kyongju; it was sometimes called Yomin Village and sometimes Japsung Village. There was in the village a sorceress by the name of Mowha – a name given to her on account of the fact that she had come from the village of that name. Mowha's house was old and decaying on one side; green fungi grew on the roof tiles, and an offensive smell came from the rotten earth. The stone wall, which surrounded the house like an old castle, was crumbling here and there. The large vacant lot inside, which served as the garden, was always covered with green slime where, the drains being blocked, the rain water had stagnated; and goose-foot, foxtail and other nameless weeds grew up in a black tangle as tall as a man. In these were earthworms almost as big as snakes and gnarled old frogs, wriggling and waiting for the nightfall. The house indeed looked like a haunted den, deserted by human inhabitants decades or centuries ago.

In this old, decaying, haunted house lived the sorceress, Mowha, and her daughter Nang-i. The girl's father was said to be a fishmonger, who had his shop on the east-coast road, about ten miles away from Kyongju; he was said to be so fond of his daughter that he would personally bring her, in spring and autumn, nice floury kelp and clean, good quality, knotted seaweed. Except when Wug-i unexpectedly appeared or when occasional visitors came for Mowha's exorcism, the mother and daughter lived in almost total isolation.

When someone came from a distant place to ask for Mowha's exorcism, she had to go very close to the door and shout two or three times:

'Hello there, are you in, Mowha?' 'Mowha!' 'Mowha!' Concluding that there was nobody in the house, the visitor would try to open the door, putting a hand on the wooden handle, and only then would a girl open the door from the inside, without a word – she was Nang-i. Distracted in the middle of her painting she would look very frightened and turn pale.

Mowha was usually not at home. As soon as the dawn broke she went to the town and came home only when the sun touched the ridge of the western hills. Tipsy, and carrying a peach wrapped in her handkerchief, she would dance and sing on the way home:

> Daughter, daughter, my daughter of Kim's family
> My daughter, Nang-i, flower of the Undersea
>   Kingdom.
> In the palace of the Undersea Kingdom
> Bolted are all the twelve gates.

Open the gates, open the gates,
Open wide your twelve gates.

Her plaintive tone would echo through the whole village.

'Mowha, you had a drink today again,' a villager would greet her, and Mowha would turn her shoulder shyly and bow politely, saying, 'Yes, I have been to the market.'

Mowha was always at an inn when she was not called to do exorcism. She was as fond of drinking as her daughter was of peaches. In the summer, she would always bring a peach home for her daughter, 'Daughter, daughter, my daughter!' she would call on entering the house. Nang-i would run to get the peach and eat it, as in her childhood she had run to the mother's breast as soon as she came in from an outing.

According to Mowha, Nang-i was an incarnation of the Flower Goddess of the Undersea Kingdom; and she was born seven days after Mowha on her dream had eaten a peach which the Dragon God had given her. Mowha said that the Dragon God had had twelve daughters; the first was the Moon, the second the Water, the third the Cloud ... and the twelfth the Flower; it was being arranged that they should marry the twelve sons of the Mountain God – the Moon the Sun, the Water the Tree, the Cloud the Wind ... but the twelfth daughter, who was by nature flirtatious, couldn't wait her turn and eloped with the Bird who was to have been the husband of the eleventh daughter, the Fruit. As a result, the Butterfly had appealed to the gods of the Undersea and of the Mountains for their intervention. The Dragon God became very angry and decided to punish the culprits: the Flower was banished from the Undersea Kingdom and kept mute in the form of a peach flower; since then she has become the red flowers, in spring, standing along the river banks and along the hill slopes, and could neither speak nor hear the song of the Bird, though he sang his heart out on the branch of her flower tree.

Mowha often got up impulsively and ran away in the middle of her drinking bout at the village inn, or in the middle of her dancing in the company of village sorcers. When someone asked why she had behaved in such a strange way, she would say that she was only temporarily in charge of the daughter of the Undersea God; if she did not take good care of her, the God would become very angry with her.

It was not Nang-i alone who was the incarnation of a spirit in the eyes of Mowha; she called everyone an incarnation of a spirit, tree, stone or something else, and she told them to pray to the Great Bear or to the Undersea God.

Mowha was always shy in front of people, and she turned her shoulders slightly sideways as she bowed in greeting; often she trembled in fear even before children, but sometimes she would become coquettish with dogs or pigs. In her eyes everything was animated; not only human beings, pigs, cats, frogs, earthworms, fish and butterflies, but persimmon-trees, plum-trees, pokers, pitchers, steps, sandals, jujubi thorns, clouds, swallows, winds, fire, rice, kites, gourds, sties, ovens, spoons, lamps. . . . All these could, like her human neighbours, she thought, see her, call her, speak to her, hate her, envy her and get angry with her; hence she called everything 'Sir' or 'Madam'.

III

Since Wug-i had come home, the haunted house had begun to show signs of human habitation. Nang-i, who had hated to go to the kitchen, cooked rice for Wug-i from time to time. At night a milky-coloured paper lantern was quietly hung at the end of the tiled roof of the crumbling house; before it had been filled only with starlight in the darkness.

Wug-i was born illegitimately at the time when Mowha had lived in the village from which she took her name, and before she became possessed. He showed the promise of an unusual intelligence in his early childhood. he was known almost as a genius. But he came from the lowest class, and it was not easy to go to the village school. When he was eight he was sent to a temple on the recommendation of an acquaintance of Mowha's. Wug-i sent no news for nearly ten years, and then he came home suddenly one day. Wug-i, in short, was the half-brother of Nang-i, sharing the same mother. Nang-i, when she was about four or five, before she had become deaf, used to be very fond of him, calling out 'Wug-i' in a special voice. A little while after Wug-i had gone to the temple, Nang-i was ill for nearly three years and afterwards became deaf. Yet nobody knew how deaf she was. Once or twice she asked her mother

in an unclear and stammering voice. 'Wu, Wug-i, where has he
gone?'

'Gone to a temple to study.'

'Whi ... which temple?'

'Jirim Temple, a big place ...'

But this was not true. Mowha herself did not know where
Wug-i was. She simply did not wish to say that she did not
know. So she just gave a name, as it occurred to her.

When Mowha returned from the market and saw Wug-i, she
first looked frightened; she seemed on the point of running
away, twisting her shoulders. And then she suddenly opened
her two long arms and embraced him, as a mother bird
spreads her wings over her young.

'Who is this, who is this? Oh, my son, oh, my son!' She
began to sob. 'My son, my son! You've come, you've come,
have you?' Mowha broke down in tears.

'Oh, mother, mother!' Wug-i too cried for a while, resting
his left cheek on his mother's shoulder. The young man of
eighteen, who had his mother's slender waist and long neck,
looked noble and beautiful, and showed no trace of his long
wandering from one temple to another.

Only then did Nang-i seem to realize that the young man
was really Wug-i. The strange young man who came to the
house so frightened her that she was speechless, cowering in a
corner of the room. On seeing her mother cry 'Oh, my son,
oh, my son!' with Wug-i in her armms, Nang-i too became
tearful. (She in fact felt happy beyond description to see that
her mother had such a warm affection.)

However, Wug-i became a riddle, within the next few days,
to both Mowha and Nang-i. At every meal, before he went to
bed in the evening, and as soon as he woke in the morning,
Wug-i shut his eyes and moved his lips in prayer. He then
took out a small book from his vest and read it, whenever he
had time to do so. When Nang-i looked at the book with
curious eyes, Wug-i, with a smile on his beautiful face, said to
her, 'You must read this book.' He opened it in front of Nang-
i, whose reading had not progressed beyond *The Story of Sim
Chung,* and who could read Korean characters only slowly. She
looked at the book and read the *New Testament* in a clear
inscription on the cover. She had never heard of the *New
Testament.* She looked, with a puzzled expression, at Wug-i,

who again smiled broadly. He asked, 'Do you know who made man?' She of course could not hear him. Even if she understood his questions, though vaguely, through his gestures and expressions, she would never have thought about such a difficult question before.

'Then do you know what happens after you die? All these questions are answered in this book,' said Wug-i and pointed to the sky several times. Nang-i finally managed to understand one word, 'God'.

'It is God who made man. He made not only man but the universe and all creatures. When we die we all return to Him.'

Very soon Wug-i's God roused Mowha's suspicion and reaction. Two days after Wug-i had returned home, Mowha asked her son, who was on the point of praying at the breakfast table, 'Is it in the teaching of the Buddha?' Mowha truly believed that her son had studied at temples and that anything he did must be a practice of Buddhism.

'No, mother, I am not a Buddhist.'

'Not Buddhist? What else can you be then?'

'Mother, I ran away from temples, hating the ways of the Buddha.'

'You hated the ways of the Buddha? Buddhism is the greatest religion. Are you then a Taoist?'

'No, mother, I follow the ways of Christ.'

'The ways of Christ?'

'They call it Christianity in the north. It is a new religion.'

'Then you must be an Easternist!'

'No, mother, I am not an Easternist. I am a Christian.'

'Then in what you call Christianity, is there any incantation before you take a meal?'

'No, it is not an incantation. It is a prayer to God.'

'To God?' Mowha opened her eyes, big and round.

'Yes, it is God who made us, mankind.'

'Oh, you are possessed with a devil,' exclaimed Mowha, and her face turned pale. She didn't ask further.

Next day when Mowha came home from giving the 'rice and water treatment' to a person who had been possessed with a wandering devil, Wug-i asked her, 'Where have you been, mother?'

'I have been to Messenger Park's place to drive out a wandering ghost.'

After a little thought, Wug-i asked, 'When you exorcize, do the devils go away?'

'If they don't, the sick man cannot get better,' answered Mowha as if it was a nonsensical question.

She had performed hundreds of exorcisms and sorceries around Kyongju, and cured hundreds of thousands of illnesses, and there had not been a single instance of doubt or worry about the response of her Mountain Spirit to her performances. She had always regarded the 'rice and water treatment' to a wandering ghost to be as easy and as natural as giving a glass of water to a thirsty man. Mowha was not alone in thinking this way. People who had asked for Mowha's exorcism and those who were believed to be possessed with devils thought likewise. Whenever they fell ill they always thought of going to Mowha instead of going to a doctor. In their view Mowha's exorcism and incantation had a more certain effect than a doctor's acupuncture and medicine.

Wug-i lowered his head and seemed to sink into deep thought for a while. He then raised his head, looked his mother in the face, and said, 'Mother, it is a sin against God. Look here, mother, it says in verses 32 and 33 in Chapter 9 of St Matthew's Gospel:

"As they went out, behold, they brought to him a devil.
And when the devil was cast out, the dumb spoke!" '

But Mowha no longer listened to him. She got up, went to the Table of Spirits which was always kept ready in a corner of the room and began to chant:

Spirits! Spirits! East and West, South and North,
Above and Below, Heaven and Earth;
The flying creatures fly, and the crawling creatures crawl.
Life with dark hair, as brief as morning dew, as thin as thread,
Goes on as smoothly as on the main road, as smoothly as on the main road,
Embraced in the bosom of Spirits, embraced in the bosom of Spirits.
Rejecting a dirty ghost, accepting a comely one,
House Spirit offers a house, Kitchen Spirit food,
Nativity Spirit life, and the Seven Stars protection;

In the care of Mitraya this thin life goes
As smoothly as on the main road
As smoothly as on the main road.

Mowha's two eyes shone like a pair of diamonds. Her back
shook as if she was in a strong convulsion, and she rubbed her
palms together. When she finished her incantation, she picked
up the bowl of cold water from the Table of Spirits. She took
a mouthful of water, and then sprayed it on Wug-i's face and
body. She sang again:

Curse you, devil, be off
This is Peiru, the highest peak of Yingzhu
With the steepest cliff and the water of fifty fathoms.
You cannot reach here.
Sword in the right hand, fire in the left hand,
Curse you, devil, be off

Wug-i was so taken aback that he watched Mowha chant
for a while, but he soon dropped his head and prayed, and
then he went out. Mowha went on with her incantation for a
while after Wug-i had gone out, splashing water into the four
corners of the room.

IV

Wug-i decided to pay visits to the Christians of the area when
he had left his mother. He didn't come home that night.
Mowha and Nang-i waited for him, crouched dejectedly in two
corners of the room.

'Do you have the Jesus Devil's book there?' Mowha asked
Nang-i, who answered negatively by shaking her head. Nang-i
suddenly felt a pang of regret that she had not taken charge
of what Wug-i called the 'New Testament', which Mowha
referred to as the 'Jesus Devil's book'. As Mowha truly
believed that Wug-i was possessed with a devil, so Wug-i
thought Mowha and Nang-i were possessed with devils, He
believed that was why Nang-i had become a deaf mute.

'Jesus several times cured the dumb who were possessed
with devils,' Wug-i thought to himself. He made a firm resol-

ution to cure his mother and sister by praying hard to God. He remembered Mark 9, 25–29:

When Jesus saw that the people came running together, he rebuked the foul spirit, saying unto him, Thou dumb and deaf spirit, I charge thee, come out of him, and enter no more into him.

And the spirit cried, and rent him sore, and came out of him: and he was as one dead; insomuch that many said, He is dead.

But Jesus took him by the hand, and lifted him up; and he arose.

And when he came into the house, his disciples asked him privately, why could not we cast him out:

And he said unto them, this kind can come forth by nothing, but by prayer and fasting.

Wug-i thought if he prayed to God with all the sincerity he possessed he could drive the devils out from his mother and sister. He also sent letters to Minister Hyun and Elder Lee in Pyong Yang under whose care he did his study.

Dear Minister,

By the grace of the Lord I have safely come to my mother. But the words of our Lord have not reached the district, and there are many people who are possessed with devils and who worship idols. To speed His words we need a church very urgently. I am much ashamed to confess to you that my mother is possessed with a sorceress devil and my sister with a deaf and dumb spirit. I try hard to pray to our Lord, according to Mark 9, 29, but it is difficult to pray as there is nowhere I can do it. Please pray to God that we may have a church here soon.

Minister Hyun was an American missionary, who had supported Wug-i while he was studying. Wug-i had been a trainee at a Buddhist temple until he was fourteen, but he left the temple, in the summer of his fourteenth year, to go and see the capital city. He drifted as far as Pyong Yang in the autumn of the next year, and that winter he became a protégé of Minister Hyun through the introduction of Elder Lee. When

Wug-i told Minister Hyun that he wanted to go and see his mother, Mr Hyun said: 'I am going home in three years' time. If you wish I will take you to America with me.'

'Thank you, Minister. I would very much like to go with you to America.'

'Then go and see your mother and come back soon.'

The world in which his mother and sister lived, to Wug-i's surprise, was very different from what he had known with Minister Hyun and Elder Lee. In place of happy hymn-singing, the sound of organ music, the Bible-reading, gathering together and praying, and merry laughter before delicious meals, Wug-i found a forlorn stone wall which had crumbled here and there, the old tiled roof covered in green fungi, and the frogs and earthworms in tangled weeds. When he realized that his mother had been bewitched by a sorceress devil and his sister possessed with a deaf and dumb spirit, he was filled with apprehension that he might become trapped in a terrible, haunted house.

When Wug-i came home again after visiting the Christians in the area, Nang-i became strangely changed. With her slender body, with her smooth white face, as white as paper, and with her big, glossy eyes, Nang-i, without a word, without a smile, watched all day long what Wug-i did, crouched in a corner of the room. When night fell and the whitish paper lantern was hung on the eaves, Nang-i would come to Wug-i from a corner of the garden where bloodthirsty mosquitoes flew, whining, and she would hug him and touch his neck with her icy cold lips and hands. Wug-i couldn't help being startled whenever he felt her cold hand and lips on his neck and chest. Shivering, she would embrace him again and then he could not but hold her hand impulsively and walk towards the whitish paper lantern.

After Nang-i's attitude had changed, Wug-i became paler and paler. About a fortnight later Wug-i left home as suddenly as he had come. Two days after he had gone Mowha sat up in bed and drew a deep sigh. She woke up Nang-i who was lying next to her, and, in a very melancholy voice, asked, 'When is Wug-i coming back, do you know?'

When Nang-i was quiet, Mowha said angrily, 'I told you to prepare his dinner, but you haven't.'

As days went by Mowha became more and more impatient.

She would go into the kitchen and light a lantern with perilla oil. She then laid Wug-i's dinner on the kitchen floor. She began to chant:

House Spirit, our House Spirit!
Seven Stars, our Seven Stars!
Kitchen Spirit, our Kitchen Spirit!
I pray and pray to our ancestor-spirits.
Stars in the sky, pearls in the sea.
My son, as precious as gold and silver,
My child, as beautiful as jade.
Life from the Mountain Spirit,
Long life from the Nativity Spirit,
Food from the Kitchen Spirit,
Cleverness from the House Spirit.
Stars in the sky, pearls in the sea.
Nativity and Kitchen Spirits would not refuse to come.
Jesus Devil, the starved, fire devil of the far-away West.
Burning, burning, fire is burning, fire devil is burning.
From the ashes my child rises like gold and silver,
Here comes the Nativity Spirit,
Here comes the Kitchen Spirit.

Mowha rubbed her palms, bowed, danced and made coquettish gestures as if she was mad. Nang-i, while she watched, holding her breath, through a peep-hole in the door, what her mother was doing, suddenly felt a chill and her chin began to shake. She got up, as if she too had become mad, and took off her blouse. She took off her skirt too. While the mother danced in the kitchen, the daughter danced in the room, to the same rhythm, to the same melody. This scene repeated itself every night, till one morning Nang-i found herself lying stark naked.

Wug-i returned home to his mother and sister, with a smile on his face. Mowha was trying on a new pair of rubber shoes, which she would wear when she was called for an exorcism. When she saw her son had come, she clasped him to her slender waist with her long arms. She began to cry. With her arms round Wug-i's neck, she cried quietly for a long time. Her face, which was always pale, took on colour, and she behaved as normally as if she was not possessed at all.

'Mother, I want a rest,' said Wug-i, and disengaged himself

from his mother's embrace. He went in to lie down. Mowha sat down in a corner of the wooden floor with her head down. She looked bitter and dejected. After a while she too entered the room and took out Nang-i's paintings.

That night, Wug-i awakened suddenly from his sleep, feeling that something was missing from his vest where he usually carried his Bible. He heard his mother begin her incantation. He sat up, but the New Testament was no longer with him. His mother, who had been between himself and Nang-i, was not there. He trembled, seized with a terrible premonition. The murmuring sounds of the incantation, which were almost the cries of a ghost underground, became more audible. Instantly his eyes were drawn to a hole in the hatch that opened into the kitchen.

You starved, fire devil of the far-off West,
With fire in one hand and a sword in the other.
One move this way the Mountain Spirit meets you,
One move that way the Dragon Spirit meets you.
On the run north the Seven Stars meet you.
Going, going in the cloud, running, running in the wind;
Yet the Cloud Spirit is here and the Wind Spirit is there.
Outside the Undersea Palace, all the twelve gates are locked;
On knocking at the first gate the Four Devas meet you,
With their bowl-like eyes wide open,
With their iron fists raised high.
On knocking at the second gate two pairs of fire hounds meet you;
The hound spits fire-flowers, the bitch spits fire-pistils.
On knocking at the third door, two pairs of seals meet you.
The male seal barks and the fire-flowers die.
The female barks and fire-pistils die.

Mowha was dressed in white ritual clothes. She rubbed her palms, bowed her head and danced with coquettish gestures. Above the kitchen shelf was a clean light burning on a dish with perilla oil, and underneath was a table with a bowl of cold water and a dish of salt. Beside the table was the New Testament in flames. From the last red flicker of flames a line of blue smoke was rising up, and a corner of the thick cover was already reduced to ashes.

Mowha had a curious derisory smile on her lips, as if she was challenging something. She picked salt from the dish and threw it at the book, which was by now completely reduced to dark ashes.

> Jesus Devil is returning to the far-off west.
> Getting travel money from the Mountain Spirit,
> Getting shoes from the office of the War Spirit,
> Jingle, jingle, marches on, bells on his ears,
> Over the hills, across the rivers.
> When will you come back?
> With sore feet you cannot come back.
> In warm Spring months will you come back?
> With hungry stomach you cannot come back.

Mowha's voice pierced Wug-i like the fragrance of a magic drink. Wug-i could no longer bear the coquettishness in her gleaming eyes, the movements of her hands and of her ritual garment. As if waking from a nightmare he drew a long, deep breath and stood up. The next moment he instinctively rushed out of the room and kicked open the kitchen door. He tried to pick up the bowl of cold water from the table. But before his hand reached the bowl, a kitchen knife was flashing in Mowha's hand. She waved the knife between Wug-i's hand and the water bowl. She calmly began to dance, chanting:

Curse you, you devil, be off
At a close look you are the starved devil of the west far-off.
This is Peiru, the highest peak of Yingzhu
With the steepest cliff and the water of fifty fathoms
And there is a thorny blind of Kalopanax pictum.
This is not the place for you.
Sword in the right hand, fire in the left hand,
Curse you, the devil of the west, be off.

Mowha aimed her knife at Wug-i and tried to hit him across the face with it. Feeling the blade of the knife at the corner of his left ear, Wug-i dashed under Mowha's arm to the water on the table. He picked up the bowl and threw it in her face. In this chaos the light in the dish fell, and was set ablaze. In order to stop the fire spreading into the room, Wug-i jumped

95

up onto the kitchen range. Mowha, enraged by the water thrown in her face, followed him and jumped up onto the kitchen shelf as well, brandishing her knife wildly. The moment Wug-i threw himself onto the fire on the hatch and extinguished it, he felt a sharp pain in his back. No sooner did he try to turn round, covered with blood, than he was embraced by Mowha, who was grinning, showing her white teeth.

V

Wug-i, wounded on the head, on the back of the neck and on the back became seriously ill. But the bodily wounds were not the only cause. As days passed, he became thinner and thinner round the ribs, and his eyes became more hollow. Mowha devoted herself entirely to looking after Wug-i. If there was anything Wug-i wanted, she did her best to obtain it. She often made him sit up and held him to her breast. She tried medicine, exorcism and incantation, but in spite of all these, his condition did not change.

From the moment she devoted herself to Wug-i, Mowha seemed to lose her interest in sorcery. When people came to her and asked for her exorcism, she usually refused them on the excuse of her son's illness. Soon a rumour began to spread slowly that Mowha's exorcism and incantation had become less powerful than before.

Meanwhile a small church was erected in the area and a missionary arrived. And soon the result began to work as fast and powerfully as a fire in the wind. The church sent groups of evangelists to villages. The gospel finally reached Mowha's district.

'Let us give thanks to the Lord for being together with our parents, brothers and sisters. God made us. He loved us very much. We are all sinners, we are full of wickedness in our hearts, but Jesus died on the cross for us. Therefore the only way we can be saved is to believe in Him. Let us sing a hymn. Let us pray to God.'

People said that it was more fun to see an American missionary with blue eyes and a big sharp nose than to watch a monkey. 'It's free. Let's go and see,' said the villagers, and off they went in a huge crowd to the missionary. Assistant

Preacher Yang, who was the son-in-law of the grandson of the second cousin (on the mother's side) of Mr Bang, an old man in the village, and who came with the missionary, sent his wife to every house. Mrs Yang said, 'To believe in a sorceress and a blind fortune-teller is a great sin to our Father, who is holy, who is absolute and one. What can a sorceress do? Look, she only bows and prays to dead, rotten trees, or to Maitrayas who can neither hear nor see. What power does a blind fortune-teller have? Look, how can he ever save people while he himself cannot see and has to rely on a stick? It is only our Father who can do all things, our Lord who is absolute and one. He made us. And our Father said that we should not have another god...' At the same time the stories of Jesus spread around; how he, the only son of our Father, the Lord, healed the people who had been possessed with devils, the lepers, the cripples, the dumb and the deaf; how Jesus was nailed to death on the cross; how he was resurrected three days after his death; and how he ascended to heaven afterwards.

Mowha laughed at them, and said, 'Those spiteful devils.' But their accusations against her and their curses on her seemed to hurt her terribly. She beat big and small gongs and chanted:

Curse you, you devil, be off
You starved devil, you beggar of the worst famine year,
Don't you see Mowha?
If you stay here, all your children and grandchildren
Will be thrown into
The water fifty fathoms deep; Kalopanax pictum; an iron
    cauldron; white horse skin;
To be starved to death;
To be locked away, never to see the world again
To be locked away, never to see the sun again.
Curse you, you devil, be off
To the far-off West,
With fire on the tail
With bells on the ears,
Jingle, jangle, jingle, jangle.
Be off in a flash.

However, the 'Jesus Devil' not only did not go away, but his followers even increased. What is more, some of Mowha's previous customers became possessed with Jesus Devils. One day an evangelist came from Seoul. He was reputed to have the power of curing cripples by his prayers, and huge crowds gathered at his meetings. When he put his hand on the head of a patient and prayed, saying: 'This sinner suffers from her own sins', a woman who had suffered from irregular periods or from womb discharges was forgiven her sins and cured of her illness. He was also reputed to open the blind man's eyes, to make the cripple walk, to make the deaf hear, the dumb speak, the paralysed and the epileptic be free of their sins, according to how much they believed in God. At the evangelical meetings women competed every day to leave their silver and gold rings on the platform. Contributions poured in. In the end they thought that Mowha's sorcery was nothing compared with what the evangelist could do.

'Yanks brought in magicians,' said Mowha with a grimace. Mowha firmly believed that the act of driving devils out from the possessed by sorcery and incantation was the privilege and power which her Spirits had given to her alone. And her Spirits were what the Christians most hated: the dead trees, Maitrayas, the mountains, and the water.

'To believe in a sorcerer and a blind fortune-teller is a great sin to our Father who is holy, who is absolute and one,' shouted the 'Jesus Devils', blowing trumpets and beating drums, to which Mowha counter-attacked, striking big and small gongs, all by herself, crying, 'With fire on the tail, with bells on the ears, jingle, jangle, jingle, jangle, be off, you devils, to the far-off West.'

VI

Wug-i's illness became noticeably worse as autumn turned to winter. Often Mowha chided her son in a choking, pathetic voice, 'My boy, my boy, what has happened to you? What is all this after you have come such a long way to see your Mother?' She would hold Wug-i's hands and shed tears.

'Mother, don't worry so much. When I am dead, I will be returning to our Father,' Wug-i would answer in a quiet voice. When asked if he wanted anything, he would just turn his head away without a word. But when his mother was out and Nang-i was left alone with him, Wug-i would hold her hand and say, 'I wish I could have a Bible.'

Next spring, Minister Hyun whom Wug-i had waited for with such a longing came to see him from Pyong Yang. That was just three days before Wug-i died. He came to the house with Mr. Yang. As soon as he was led into the garden, the ruin and the offensive smell from the mud made him grimace. He asked Mr. Yang, 'Does Wug-i really live in a place like this?'

When Wug-i saw them, he called 'Minister Hyun!' twice, with sparkling eyes. Minister Hyun, without a word, held Wug-i's thin hand, and then his face suddenly flushed, puckering around his eyes. He shut his eyes for a while, as though trying to suppress his feelings.

Mr Yang spoke, as if he wanted to break the strain of the silence, 'It is to this young man's credit that we have a church in Kyongju so soon.' As he explained, it was Wug-i who had sent a petition to Minister Hyun in Pyong Yang, who had subsequently sent a letter to the Council of Elders in Taegu. Wug-i, with the support of Christians in the Kyongju area, had come into contact with the Taegu Council of Elders, which in turn pressed on with the building of the church.

When Minister Hyun promised to come again with a doctor, Wug-i asked, 'Please, Minister, buy me a Bible.'

'Keep this for a while,' said the Minister Hyun and took out his own Bible from his bag and handed it to him. Wug-i took it to his heart and shut his eyes. Tears trickled down his face.

VII

There was no change in Mowha's house; weeds grew, and old frogs and earthworms crawled around, as usual. Mowha had refused to accept any requests for exorcism; she stayed at home in the crumbling old house, beating big and small gongs. People said that Mowha had gone mad. She hung pieces of cloth in various colours on the kitchen ceiling. She also put out a flag decorated with Nang-i's drawings. She did not eat, her lips grew ashen and her eyes became shiny with a strange glow.

Jesus Devil is returning to the far-off West,
With fire on the tail,
With bells on the ears,
Jingle, jangle, jingle, jangle.
Curse you devil, be off quick!
If you delay, your children will be thrown into the
Water fifty fathoms deep,
The thorny Kalopanax pictum,
Iron cauldron and the white horse skin.
Curse you, you devil, be off.

She sang the same incantation every day, and beat small and big gongs. When a neighbour paid a visit with some rice drinks and said, 'You must be missing your son very much,' she would answer, with a deep sigh, 'My son has been taken by the Jesus Devil.'

'When are we going to see Mowha's exorcism again? She used to be very good at it.' People would say, feeling sorry for her. They thought she had gone completely mad.

Then a rumour spread that Mowha was going to perform her last exorcism. The daughter-in-law of a rich man in town had thrown herself into a deep river, called Yekiso. The rumour had it that Mowha had agreed to the sorcery at the price of two sets of silk clothes from the rich man. It was also said that at the same time she was going to make Nang-i speak, and that she had boasted, 'We will see which is real, the Jesus Devil or the Mountain Spirit!' People, full of expectation and curiosity, came a long way to Mowha's exorcism across the hills and rivers.

The scene of the exorcism was a sandy beach, north west of which the dark blue river flowed quietly and deeply, holding secrets and resentments. The river, as deep as the whole length of a silk thread on a bobbin would reach, was reputed to lure a human being to commit suicide each year. On the beach, people, under canopies or straw mats, sold and bought rice-cake, rice drink, and steamed rice. In the middle of the crowd was pitched a big tent, under which the exorcism was in progress. Silk-thread lanterns in five colours, blue, red, green, white and yellow, were hung under the tent like flowers. There was a table of food for the Master Spirit, with rice-cake in a big pot, rice drink in a jug, and roast pig; a second table for

Sakraderanam Indra, with a pile of rice, bundles of threads, a skewer of dried persimmon and some bean curd; a third table for Maitraya, with threads in three different colours, white rice-cake mixed with fruits, vegetables, soup, dried fish, and fried rice-cake; a fourth table for the Mountain Spirit, with twelve different vegetables from the mountains; a fifth table for the Sea Spirit, with twelve different kinds of sea food; a sixth table for the Street Spirit, with a dish of every imaginable food; and a table for Mowha herself, with just a bowl of cold water. There were many other big and small tables for other spirits.

Mowha looked unusually dignified and calm, considering that she had lost her son recently, and that she had been so mercilessly abused and jeered at by the Christians. Her face almost recalled the days when she used to go to the mountains on moonlit nights for prayer. She did not behave in her former coquettish and boisterous manner. She looked at the tables of food for various spirits, and she did not look happy. On the contrary she said almost audibly, with a contemptuous grin, 'Dirty bitches! They only care for the spirits' tables.'

People began to whisper that Mowha was going to be possessed with a new spirit. A woman said, 'She is possessed with the spirit of Mrs Kim who died.' Other women agreed, 'Yes, she is possessed with Mrs Kim's spirit. Look at her face, so dignified and cool. Mowha was not as pretty as that before. She has become the replica of Mrs Kim.' The whisper spread among the crowd. Some people began to say that Nang-i was going to speak after this exorcism. They also remarked that Nang-i was pregnant by some unknown man. All the women felt that the night's sorcery would bring answers to everything.

Mowha narrated in her incantation the personal history of Mrs Kim from her birth to her death in the water. And then she began to dance to the music of flute, fife, and fiddle. Her voice was sorrowful. Her movements were almost the music itself, as if her flesh and bones had disappeared. The female spectators, as if drunken or enchanted, drew their breath in and out as Mowha's garment fluttered. The movements of the garment seemed to have become one with Mowha's breathing. Mowha, possessed by the spirit of Mrs Kim, in an exalted trance seemed to swallow all the stars in the sky.

It was about midnight. People began to whisper that they

had failed to catch the spirit of Mrs Kim. Sorcerers and junior sorceresses tried several times to fish up the hair of the dead person with a rice bowl at the end of an invocation rod in the water. They said that the late Mrs Kim was not responding to Mowha's invocation.

'We haven't got her spirit yet. What shall we do?' A junior sorceress with an anxious face whispered to Mowha, who, unhesitatingly, as if it were a matter of course, went into the water with an invocation rod. Sorcerers with invocation rope followed the movements of Mowha's rod, and put the rice bowl into the water several times.

> Rise up, rise up, the spirit of Mrs Kim,
> Thirty-two years of age.
> Born with the Horse Star,
> Blessed by Seven Stars.

Mowha called the spirit of the dead woman in a truly sad voice, while she moved her rod here and there in the water.

> Grown up like a flower,
> Kept like a jewel.
> Both parents still alive,
> Young children in bed.
> Had the Sea Spirit deserted you
> When you jumped into the dark water?
> Your skirt floats.
> Are you now on a lotus boat?
> Your long dark hair is let loose.
> Have you become a water ghost?

Mowha walked farther and farther into the river, following her rod. Her clothes were soaked in the water, while some twisted tightly round her body, some floating on the water surface. The dark water reached her waist, and then her breast. Still she went farther. Her voice became distant, and her incantation sounded senseless.

Fare you well, fare you well.
Call me, call me to you, dear Sister.
In spring when peaches are out along this river,

My dear Nang-i, in your mourning white dress, remember me well.
At the first branch, ask for my well-being.
At the second bran. . . .

Before Mowha finished her incantation, she had sunk into the water, her voice with her. At first one could see her garment, but soon it disappeared. There was only her rod floating around on the surface of the water, and then it too was swept away downstream.

About ten days later a small man came with a donkey from his fish shop near the East Coast. Nang-i with her big eyes, was ill in bed. The man fed Nang-i with rice gruel.

'Father,' Nang-i called almost audibly, as if Mowha's last sorcery had brought the prophesied result.

When another ten days passed the man said to her. 'Get on this,' pointing to the donkey with his hand. Nang-i, without a word, obeyed her father. After they left, no one came to the house. Only mosquitoes flew wildly in the night, whining among the tall weeds.

THE WINGS

YI SANG

Translated by Moon Hi-kyung

Have you ever heard of 'a genius who had been stuffed and preserved'? I feel a pleasure. At this moment. I can even find some pleasure in making love.

Only when the body is so weary as to be limp does the spirit become as clear as a silver coin. When nicotine seeps into my worm-ridden belly, a virgin sheet of paper is inevitably spread out in my head and on that paper I lay out wit and paradox, as if I were arranging stone pieces on the Go table. It's a malady of common sense, which is to be abominated.

I am also planning a life with a woman. I am a person who has become unfamiliar with the art of love, someone who has caught a glimpse of the very summit of human intellect; in other words, a kind of mentally excitable person. What I mean is that I am planning a life which will accept only a half of this woman – which is in fact the half of everything. I will put only one foot in this life and my two halves will face each other like the two suns and giggle. All the activities of life seem unbearably dull to me and I have renounced them. Good-bye!

Good-bye! I think it would not be a bad idea if you occasionally put into practice the irony of greedily swallowing the food that you like least ... with wit and paradox.

Sometimes, it is worth trying to counterfeit yourself. Your work will be simple and convenient as well as lofty and sublime among the ready-made products that you have never seen before.

Bring down the nineteenth century, if possible. The spirit of Dostoevsky can easily seem a waste. Someone like Hugo a piece of French bread and this seems an apt expression. But should you be taken in by life or its model because of mere details? Don't look at disasters. I earnestly beg you. . . . (When the tape snaps, it bleeds. I believe the wound will heal in good time. Good-bye!)

Emotion is a certain pose. (I am not sure whether I am merely pointing to the element of that pose or not.) When the pose becomes so refined as to turn rigid, then emotion ceases to flow.

I looked back on my astonishing development and have determined the way I would look at the world. The queen bee and the widow – among all the women in the world, is there any who is not by nature a widow? What I mean is that would it be an insult to women to argue that in her daily life every woman is a widow? Good-bye!

The layout of Number 33 was not unlike that of a brothel. Eighteen lodgers lived in this one house, which had a long row of identical doors and fireplaces. The people who occupied the rooms were all young like blossoming flowers. The sun never shone into the house. It was because everyone ignored the sun. They hung up their quilts and mattresses on a wire line under the pretext of airing them, and thus blocking out the sun, they slept all day long in their darkened rooms. Didn't they ever sleep at night? There was no way of finding out. As I myself slept night and day, I could never find out. In the afternoon a deadly quiet hung about Number 33.

But the house was quiet only during the day. When it became dark, the lodgers took their quilts down from the line and Number 33 became brighter than the day. It became busy. Several different kinds of smell would begin to waft about –

the smell of grilled herring, of perfumes, of rice cooking and of soap.

But before these smells could assail the nostrils, the nameplates on the front gate would begin to swing. The house did possess a two-pillared front gate, although it was a few yards from the rooms. The gate, however, was always left wide open and had now become part of the public road. All kinds of vendors came in and out all day long and the lodgers bought their beancurd not at the gate but from their rooms. It was entirely meaningless to put up nameplates on such a gate, so there grew a custom of putting them up over the sliding doors of the rooms, next to the tablets bearing words such as 'The House of Hundred Patience' or 'The House of Good Fortune'. A card bearing my, no my wife's name, which hung over the door on one side, also followed this custom.

I did not mix with the other lodgers. In fact, I was not even on nodding terms with anyone. I did not want to speak to anyone except to my wife. This was because I thought it would be embarrassing for my wife if I spoke to or became friendly with anyone in the house. This shows how much I cherished my wife.

I cherished my wife because I have come to learn that of the eighteen people living in the house my wife was the smallest and the most beautiful, just as her name card was more beautiful than those of others. Among these eighteen lodgers, all of whom were like flowers in full bloom, my wife was a particularly radiant blossom, which dazzled the eye in this shady spot beneath the roof where no sun ever came in. And I, who guarded this blossom – no, who rather depended on this blossom for a living – could only be called an indescribable nuisance.

My room – not my house for I had no house – pleased me a great deal. The temperature of the room suited my body temperature perfectly and the room had just the right degree of dimness to be soothing to the eyes. I wished for neither a warmer nor a colder room. Nor did I wish for a brighter or cosier one. The room seemed to be keeping everything just as it is purely for my sake and my feeling for the room was one of gratitude. I felt as if I were born for this room and this thought gave me a pleasure.

But this did not mean that I measured my happiness or unhappiness in any way. What I mean is that there was no need for me to think of myself as being neither happy nor unhappy. Everything was fine as long as I could pass my days without a purpose and in complete idleness.

Lolling about in this room, which fitted both my mind and body tightly like a well-fitting suit, was the most comfortable and idle, in other words the most absolute state to be in, a state which took no account of such worldly matters as happiness or unhappiness. This was the state I loved to be in.

This room, which was so absolute to me, was, to be precise, the seventh from the front gate. That seven was a lucky number held some meaning for me, for I loved number seven like a medal. But who could ever know that this room was divided in the middle by a sliding door and that this partition was the symbol of my destiny?

The sun came into the lower part of the room. In the morning the sun would light up a patch of floor about the size of a scarf and in the afternoon the patch would shrink to the size of a handkerchief before it vanished. I needn't mention that the upper half of the room where the sun never came in was my half of the room. I no longer remember which of us, my wife or I, had decided that I should take the sunless half, but I have no complaints against my wife.

Whenever my wife went out, I would quickly go into her part of the room and open the window which faced east. The sunlight came in through the window and the bottles on her dressing table, becoming multi-coloured, glittered brilliantly. Watching these shining objects was my favourite pastime. I would take out a small magnifying glass and start burning a sheet of white tissue paper, which was reserved for my wife's sole use. The magnifying glass would refract the parallel rays and draw them together into a point on the paper, which, becoming hotter and hotter, would begin to burn. A thin whisp of smoke would rise from the burning point and eventually a hole would appear. I found this brief anxious moment painfully exciting.

When I was tired of playing this game, I played various games with my wife's hand-mirror. A mirror is a useful object

107

only when one looks into it. At other times, it is no more than a toy.

I would soon get weary of this, too. Then I would jump from a physical amusement to a mental one. I would throw the mirror down and approach my wife's dressing table and start inspecting various bottles which were neatly arranged in a row. I found these bottles more attractive than anything in the world. I would select one and carefully unscrew the cap and putting it against my nose, sniff gently. As its exotic and sensual scent penetrated my lungs, I would feel my eyes closing gently. Without any doubt, it was a fragment of my wife's odour. I would screw the cap back on and think. From which part of her body did I smell this? I was not sure. Why? Because her odour must be a mixture of all the different smells contained in these bottles.

My wife's half of the room was always gaudy, unlike my half of the room which was so bare as not to have a single nail on the wall. Along the walls in her room were lines of hooks on which were hung bright coloured skirts and blouses. The patterns on her clothes were pretty to look at. I imagined over and over again these skirts wrapped around my wife's body and the various postures her body could take. In such moments, I was not particularly dignified.

I had few clothes. My wife didn't give me many clothes. A corduroy suit that I had on served as my night-wear as well as day- and fine-wear. I had a round-neck sweater which I wore all year round. All my clothes were dark. The reason for this, I think, was to minimize washing and yet keep me looking fairly presentable. Wearing a baggy pair of shorts with rubber bands around the waist and the legs, I amused myself quietly.

A spot of sunshine the size of a handkerchief disappeared but my wife was still not home. Even these games tired me out and feeling I should be back in my room before she returned, I hurried back to my side of the room. It was dark. I pulled the quilt over me and took an afternoon nap. My quilt and mattress, which had not been put away once, were welcome to me, as if they were part of my body. Sometimes sleep came easily, but at other times, my whole body felt stiff and I could not sleep at all. When that happened, I would choose a topic, any topic, and start studying it. Under my clammy quilt, I had invented ever so many things and written ever so many theses. I had also written many poems. But as soon as I fell asleep, they seemed to dissolve into nothingness in the close air of the room, just like soap bubbles in the water. When I woke up, I was just a bundle of nerves, no more than a pillow stuffed full of cotton shreds or buckwheat chaff.

Because I spent so much time in bed, I disliked bedbugs more than anything in the world. But my room was always full of bedbugs, even in winter. If ever I had a source of anxiety, it was my hatred of these bedbugs. I would scratch the bites until they bled. They felt sore. I cannot deny, however, that they gave me a dull pleasure of some sort and I fell into a sound sleep.

Though I led a life of contemplation under the quilt, I never thought of anything positive. There was absolutely no need for me to do that, for if it ever happened that I thought of something positive to do, I would have had to consult my wife and my wife would undoubtedly have rebuked me. I was not afraid of her rebukes but I found them bothersome. Rather than working and becoming a socially responsible person, rather than listening to my wife's lectures, I wanted to be as idle as the idlest animal on earth. I wanted to cast off as much as possible the meaningless mask of humanity.

I was shy of human society. I was shy of life. Everything was strange and unfamiliar to me.

My wife washed her face twice a day. I didn't even wash once. I usually went to the lavatory at about three or four in the morning. When the moon shone brightly, I would stand in the yard for a while before returning to my room. The life I led made it possible for me to avoid ever coming across any of the eighteen lodgers of the house. Yet I knew the faces of all the pretty young women in the house. None outdid my wife in beauty.

My wife's first wash, which took place at about eleven in the morning, was a simple business. Much more time and care were bestowed upon her second wash at about seven in the evening. Also, she wore cleaner and prettier clothes in the evening. She went out during the day as well as in the evening.

Did she have a job? I had no means of finding out what her

job was. If she did not work, she had no reason to go out, like
me who had no job. My wife not only went out but she also
entertained guests in her room. On such days, I had to keep
to my side of the room all day long. I could not sniff her
bottles nor play with them. On those days, I became con-
sciously depressed. Then my wife gave me some money, usually
a fifty-pence silver. That pleased me. But not knowing what to
do with it, I usually left it in a corner and it became a considerable sum. Seeing this one day, my wife went out and bought
me a savings bank, which looked more like a safe. I dropped
the silver coins one by one into the bank and my wife kept the
key. I remember putting a few more coins in it but I was lazy.
Sometime later I saw sticking out from behind my wife's head
a hair ornament. Did it mean that my bank had become
lighter? I ended up by refusing to touch the savings bank which
lay over where I slept. I was too lazy even to be bothered by
such a thing.

On a night when my wife entertained a guest, I found it
difficult to fall asleep as it was on a rainy night, however
deeply I might burrow under the quilt. On such a night I
speculated profoundly on how my wife came by her money
and why she had so much of it. Her guest was probably not
aware that I was at the other side of the door, for he made
jokes which even I would have found difficult to utter in her
presence without a feeling of shame. One or two of the guests
seemed relatively gentlemanly, for they always left before midnight. A few of them seemed even quite cultured and they
usually had their dinner ordered from somewhere. That was
probably how they kept strong and healthy.

I embarked on the business of finding out what my wife's job
was. But because of my narrow vision and limited knowledge,
it was not easy. Perhaps I will never learn what she does!

My wife only wore brand new socks. She also cooked.
Though I had never seen her cook, she never failed to bring
me a tray in my room when the meal time came around. Since
there is no one else beside my wife and myself, it can only be
my wife who must have personally prepared the meals.

But my wife never once invited me to her room.

I always ate alone in the upper room and slept alone. The
food was tasteless and the dishes were poorly done. Though I

ate what was put before me without any complaint, like a hen or a dog, I was not entirely without resentment. I became paler and lost much weight. I grew visibly weaker every day. Bones began to stick out here and there from malnutrition. I tossed and turned in bed every night because bones stuck into me if I lay on one side for long.

For these reasons I sought to discover the source of my wife's income and attempted lightly to find out through the gap in the partition what she was eating at the other side. I could not sleep well.

I discovered it. I realized that my wife's money was left by those guests, foolish as they appeared to me, who came to see her for some unknown reason. It seemed that their leaving her money and my wife taking it was a question of courtesy which was quite beyond my understanding.

Could it be from mere politeness? Or was it in payment of something, some compensation? Did my wife appear as an object of pity, which required their sympathy?

When these thoughts occurred to me, my head whirled in confusion. The only conclusion that I came to before I fell asleep was that it was all very unpleasant. But I never once asked my wife what it was all about. It was much too bothersome; besides, when I woke again, I usually forgot about it.

After the departure of the guest or after returning home, my wife would change into something comfortable and come and see me in my room. She would pull back the quilt which I had pulled over me and would try to console me with a few gay words. I would gaze at her beautiful face with a smile which was neither mocking nor bitter nor hearty. She would smile silently. But I did not miss a shadow of sadness clouding over her face.

My wife probably knew very well that I was hungry. But she never gave me what was left over from her table. Without a doubt, it was because she had a deep respect for me. Though I was hungry, I liked being strong-minded. My wife's chattering words left me unmoved. Only a piece of silver shone in the electric light.

I wondered how many silver coins were in the savings bank. But I did not even lift it once to feel how heavy it was. Without any desire, without a wish even, I merely continued to drop silver pieces through the button-hole-like slit.

Just as it was impossible to answer the question why my wife's guests gave her money, so it was impossible to say why my wife gave me money. Though I did not dislike my wife giving me money, the only pleasure I got from it was in the brief sensation of holding the coins between my fingers before they disappeared into the bank. Beyond that, the money had no other charm for me.

One day I took the bank and threw it down the toilet. I had no idea how much money it contained. All I knew was that there was quite a lot of silver pieces in it.

When the thought occurred to me that I was living on the earth and that the earth was speeding through the empty space in the speed of a lightning, I was suddenly overwhelmed by a sense of futility. I felt that I would get dizzy on this fast-moving planet and wanted to get off it as soon as possible.

After this thought had occurred to me in bed, I lost even the desire to drop silver coins into the savings bank. I was hoping that my wife would put them in herself. Since it was my wife who needed the bank and money and since it had no meaning at all for me from the beginning, I wanted her to take it to her room. But she did not take it. I even thought of taking it to her room myself, but lately I had no chance of going into her room as she had many guests. There was nothing I could do but to throw it into the toilet.

I waited with a sad heart for my wife to reproach me. But she not only kept absolutely silent on the subject but continued to leave me silver pieces. Again, a considerable sum gathered in a pile above where I lay.

Lying in bed I began once again to give deep thoughts to the idea that pleasure alone and no other reason was behind her guests' giving her money or her giving me money. If it is a pleasure, what kind of pleasure could it be? I continued to give serious thoughts to this question. But it was impossible to find an answer with an inquiry conducted in bed. Pleasure – pleasure – the question raised in me an unexpected interest.

It was obvious that my wife kept me in a state of virtual imprisonment. I had no complaints. Yet I longed to see whether a thing called pleasure really existed or not.

While my wife was out at night, I took advantage of the situation and went out. In the street I changed the coins, which

I had remembered to bring with me, into bank notes. The sum amounted to as much as five *won*. I pushed the notes into my pocket and started to wander about the streets in order to forget the reason for my being out on the street. Because I had not been out for a long time, it excited my senses to an astonishing degree. I became exhausted in no time. But I continued to wander about aimlessly without knowing why I was doing this until it was quite late. Of course I did not spend a penny. I could not pluck up enough courage to spend it. It seemed to me that I had completely lost the ability to spend money.

As was expected, I could not endure the weariness of it any longer. I barely managed to find my way home. Because I had to pass through my wife's room in order to reach mine, I stood awkwardly before her door, coughing loudly, worried lest she should be entertaining a guest. Suddenly the door slammed open with violence and my wife's face appeared; behind her the face of an unknown man looked out. I hesitated, taken aback by the sudden flash of light which dazzled my eyes.

It was not that I failed to see the expression in my wife's eyes. But I had no choice but to ignore it. Why? Because I had to go through her room.

I pulled the quilt over my head. My legs ached unbearably. My heart beat loudly and I felt that I was about to faint. Although I did not realize it while I was walking, I was out of breath. My back was wet with cold sweat. I began to regret going out. I longed to forget this tiredness and go to sleep. I wanted to have a long sound sleep.

I lay on the side for a while and slowly the heartbeat regained its regularity. It was a relief. I moved and lay on my back and stretched my legs.

But once again my heart started to beat loudly. From the other side of the partition came the sound of my wife and the man whispering together so softly that it was almost inaudible. I opened my eyes wide to make my ears more alert and held my breath. But already my wife and the man seemed to have got up from their seats and I heard the sound of someone putting on his coat and hat. This was followed by the sound of the door sliding open and of heels; then with a thump someone was stepping down to the yard. A few steps were heard and even as I was waiting to hear the soft steps of my wife's rubber shoes, the two had disappeared in the direction of the front gate.

I had never seen my wife behaving like this before. My wife never whispered with anyone in her life. Although I sometimes missed a few words uttered by her guests, whose tongues seemed to have become stiff with drink, I never missed anything my wife said in her neither high nor low voice as I lay listening in bed. Occasionally she said something which irritated me but she said it so naturally that it set my mind at ease.

I thought she probably had a good reason for behaving differently and though I was a little hurt, I felt so exhausted that I resolved firmly to suspend all thinking for the night at least and waited for sleep to come. But sleep did not come soon. Nor did my wife, who had gone to see him off at the front gate. Without my knowing it, I was fast asleep. In my dream, I was still wandering about, confused, in some strange unfamiliar streets.

I was violently shaken awake. It was my wife who had returned to the room after seeing her guest off at the gate. I opened my eyes wide and stared at her face. There was no smile on her face. I rubbed my eyes and looked at her face searchingly. Her eyes were narrow with anger and her thin lips trembled with fury. It looked as if it would be difficult to mollify her. I closed my eyes. I was waiting for a thunderbolt to fall on me. She breathed rapidly, there followed the swish of her skirt; the door slid open and she went out. I lay on my stomach and pulled the quilt over my head. In this position, though hungry, I once again wished that I had not gone out.

And I apologised to my wife. I wanted to say to her that it was all a misunderstanding. I had mistakenly thought that the night was far advanced. It did not occur to me, even in my dream, that it was before midnight. I was too tired. It was a mistake to have walked so much when I was not used to it. That was the only wrong I had done, if I had done any wrong at all. And why did I go out in the first place?

It was because I wanted to give away the five *won* that had accumulated by itself to someone, to anybody. If that was wrong, I will accept it as such. Was I not repentant?

If I had been able to spend the money, I would not have

returned home before midnight. The streets, however, were too noisy and there were too many people. I was too confused to pick out anyone to give the money away and meanwhile I had utterly exhausted myself.

I wanted above all to rest. I wanted to lie down. I had no choice but to return home. To me it had seemed as if the night was fairly advanced and it was unfortunate that it should have been before midnight. I was sorry. I was prepared to apologise fully. But what would be the good of apologising if I could not get my wife to forgive me? It was a wretched situation.

I spent about an hour in this state of anxiety. Then unable to bear it any longer, I flung away the quilt and stumbled into my wife's room. I was almost unconscious. The only thing I remember is taking the five *won* notes from my pocket and thrusting them into my wife's hand before I fell on her bed.

When I woke up next morning, I was in my wife's room, in her bed. It was the first time we slept in the same room since we moved to Number 33.

From the window I could see the sun high in the sky. My wife was no longer at my side. She was already out. She may even have gone out at night while I was unconscious. I did not want to investigate this matter. I felt stiff all over and I felt too weak to lift a finger. A patch of light, smaller than a book, dazzled my eyes. In that small patch of light, innumerable dust particles were whirling about like micro-organisms and I felt that they were blocking up my nose. I closed my eyes again and pulled the cover over my head and tried to go to sleep again. But the smell of my wife's body which tickled my nose was quite provocative. Twisting my body about, I searched restlessly for various different smells from the cosmetic bottles on her dressing table that I used to sniff at. It kept me awake but I could do nothing about it.

Unable to bear it any longer, I kicked the cover away and went into my room where I found a dinner tray. The food had gone cold. My wife must have left it there. I was hungry. I took a mouthful but it tasted like cold ashes. I put the spoon down and crawled under the quilt. My mattress and quilt, which had been left unused for the night, welcomed me as always. I pulled the quilt over me and this time fell fast asleep.

The electric lights had come on when I woke up from my sleep. There was no sign of my wife. Perhaps she had come in and gone out again? I had no way of knowing. What use was there in thinking about such a thing?

My head felt clearer. I thought of what happened the night before. No word could express the pleasurable sensation I had felt when I put the five *won* notes into my wife's hand. Feeling that I had at last discovered the secret of pleasure, the reason why my wife's guests gave her money and why she gave me money, I was overjoyed. I smiled inwardly to myself. I thought I was a fool not to have discovered such a pleasure until now. My shoulders danced.

I wanted to go out again in the evening. But I had no money. I regretted having given my wife all the money. I also regretted having thrown the savings bank down the toilet. Foolishly disappointed, I put my hand from habit into my pocket where the money had been. Something unexpectedly came to my hand. There was two *won*. As long as there was some money, the amount did not matter. I was thankful to have whatever was there.

I felt stronger. I put on my worn-out corduroy jacket, the one and only jacket that I had, and forgetting my hunger and the indignity of it, flew out of the house. As I was leaving the house, I was full of impatience, wishing fervently that time would fly and midnight flash by. Although it was a pleasure to give my wife some money and sleep in her room, to return before midnight and lay myself open to her anger was a matter of not a little terror. Looking at the street clocks constantly, I wandered about the streets aimlessly. But I did not feel tired at all that evening. I was only anxious that time seemed to be dragging.

I took my way home after I had made certain by the clock at Kyungsung Railway Station that it was past midnight. At the front gate, I encountered my wife talking to a man. Pretending not to notice, I walked past them and went into the room. My wife followed me in. She started to sweep the room, a thing she had never done before. As soon as I heard my wife laying herself down, I stepped into her room and gave her the two *won* that I had. As if she found it odd that I should be bringing the money back without spending it, she glanced at me side ways several times and let me sleep by her without a word. I did not want to exchange this joy with anything on earth. I slept well.

When I woke up next morning, again there was no sign of my wife. I went to my room and slept soundly again. When my wife shook me awake, it was after the lights had been turned on. She asked me into her room. This was also something new. She pulled at my arm, a smile constantly playing over her face. This strange behaviour of my wife's gave me a vague sense of fear, lest a conspiracy lay hidden behind it.

My wife dragged me into her room. A table was neatly set for two people. I recalled that I had not eaten anything for two days. I had even forgotten hunger in my bewilderment.

I thought to myself. I thought that I would have no regrets even if a thunderbolt should descend on me the moment this last supper came to an end. In truth, I had been finding human society unbearably dull. Everything was bothersome and troublesome. But in unexpected disasters could be found some pleasure. I sat at ease and ate this strange dinner with my wife in silence. As a couple we never talked to each other. After dinner, I got up in silence and went to my room. I leaned against the wall and smoked a cigarette, waiting for the thunderbolt to fall, if it would.

Five minutes – ten minutes – No thunderbolt fell. Tension relaxed. Already I was thinking about going out at night. I was wishing for some money.

But I had no money. Even if I went out, what pleasure would there be for me? Everything looked bleak. In a fit of rage, I pulled the cover over my head and rolled on the mattress. I felt like vomiting up the dinner I had just eaten. I felt nauseous. I was full of sorrow and resentment that money did not just come pouring down from the sky. I think I even cried a little under my quilt, asking myself why I had no money.

Then my wife came into my room again. In amazement and waiting for the thunderbolt to finally fall on me, I lay prostrate like a frog, hardly daring to breathe. But words that came from my wife were tender. They were affectionate. She said she knew why I was crying. It was because I had no money, she said. I was astonished. That she could read so clearly what was going on in my mind was a cause of some dread, but her tender words raised in me a hope that she would perhaps give me some money. Oh, what a joy it would be if she were to do that! I lay all wrapped up in my quilt, waiting for what she would do next, not daring to raise my head. Then she said, 'Here,' and from the noise of something soft being dropped lightly above my head, I felt sure that it was a note. She then whispered softly in my ear that it would be all right if I returned home even later than I did the night before. To me there was no difficulty in that. I was glad and only too grateful for the money.

Any way, I went out. I am a bit blind at night. I decided to wander about the streets which were only lit brightly. I then went to a tearoom, which was just by the first and second class waiting room in Kyungsung Station. This was a big discovery for me. First, nobody that I knew ever used it. Even if they came in, they soon left. I made up my mind to come here every day to pass my time.

What pleased me the most about the place was the thought that no clock would be more accurate than the one here at the station. To trust an inaccurate clock and find that I have reached home before it was midnight would have been a disaster for me.

I sat in a box seat opposite an empty seat and drank some hot coffee. Travellers too probably find some pleasure in a cup of coffee, in spite of their hurry. They empty their cups quickly, their eyes wandering aimlessly over the wall as if in deep thought, and then they hurry out. It was all very melancholy. But the melancholy atmosphere of the tearoom touched me more deeply and pleased me more than the gay and noisy atmosphere of other tearooms on the street. The occasional sound of a train whistling – now sharp, now powerful – felt closer to me than the music of Mozart. I read the names of few dishes on the menu over and over again. They seemed to be from some dim and remote past, like the names of my childhood friends.

While I was sitting there letting my thoughts wander, the room became almost empty of people. The waiters were removing the covers and it was probably getting late. Muttering to myself that it must be some minutes past eleven and that even this place could not afford me a permanent refuge, I left the tearoom, worrying about where to spend the remaining hours before midnight. It was raining. Heavy drops were about to fall on me, who had neither an umbrella nor a raincoat. I could not linger about the railway station any longer in such a peculiar manner, so I decided to leave the station, regardless of the weather.

It was unbearably chilly outside. The corduroy suit soon got wet through and I got soaked to the skin. I had determined to wander about the streets even in the rain until it was time for me to return home, but it was not possible to endure the cold any longer. My whole body trembled and my teeth chattered uncontrollably.

Walking back fast, I asked myself whether my wife would be entertaining even on such a night and told myself that she would not be. I must hurry home, I thought. If unfortunately she has a guest, I will explain. When she hears me and sees the rain, then she will understand.

I hastened home. My wife had a guest. Being too cold and wet and bewildered, I lost my head and forgot to knock. And I witnessed something which my wife would not have liked me to have seen. In big strides I went across my wife's room into mine. I pulled off the wet clothes and got under the quilt. I was trembling violently and it was getting worse. I felt that the earth was gaping under me. I lost consciousness.

When I woke up next morning, my wife was sitting beside me with quite a concerned look on her face. I had caught a flu. I kept feeling cold and my head ached. There was a bitter taste in my mouth and my limbs felt heavy. My wife felt my brow and said I had to take something. The touch of my wife's hand felt cold like ice and from this I gathered that I was running a high temperature. I was thinking that I needed to take something to bring down the temperature when my wife returned with a glass of warm water and four white tablets. I would feel better if I took them and had a good sleep, she said. I took the tablets without a word. They had a slightly bitter taste to them and I thought they were aspirins. I lay down again and fell into a deep sleep.

I lay ill for several days with a runny nose and during this time, I continued to take the tablets. After a while, I got better. But the bitter taste in my mouth remained.

Slowly the desire to go out again rose in me. But my wife told me to stay home. She said I should continue to take those tablets and lie quietly at home. My going out had only resulted in my catching a cold and had caused her nothing but trouble, she added. It was true. I promised not to go out and thought I would stay home and take care of myself.

I slept all day long and all night long. I felt unusually sleepy and I believed firmly that it was a sign of my recovery.

I must have spent about a month in this manner. My hair and beard grew uncomfortably long and wild, so I wanted to go and look at myself in the mirror. While my wife was out, I went into her room and sat before her mirror. I looked terrible. My hair and beard had grown wild. I decided to pay a visit to the barber and, since I was in her room, thought I would take a sniff at her bottles. From the scents that I had forgotten for a while came the smell of her body which clung to me tightly. I called my wife's name silently to myself – Eun-Shim!

I also toyed with the magnifying glass and the mirror. The sun which shone through the window felt wonderfully warm. Come to think of it, was it not May already?

I stretched myself luxuriously and lay down, resting my head on my wife's pillow. I wanted to boast to God of such comfortable and pleasant hours. I do not have dealings with anyone in this world, so I feel that God can neither reward nor punish me in any way.

But the next moment, a strange, a truly strange sight caught my eyes. It was a packet of sleeping pills called Adalin. I discovered it under my wife's dressing table and thought it looked like a packet of aspirin. I opened the packet. Four tablets were missing.

I remembered taking four tablets of aspirin that morning. And I had slept as I had done yesterday and the day before – I just could not keep awake. Although I was well again, my wife continued to give me aspirin. Once fire had broken out in one of the neighbouring houses while I was fast asleep: I knew nothing about it. That was how deeply I slept. I had been taking Adalin for a month, believing it to be aspirin. It was rather too much.

I suddenly felt dizzy and almost fainted. I pushed the Adalin packet into my pocket and left the house. I made my way towards a hill. I wanted to get away from the human society. I made an effort not to think about my wife. It was because I did not want to faint on the street. I wanted to find a sunny spot where I could slowly and seriously think about my wife. I concentrated my mind only on things like a small brook, pins, golden bell trees that I had never seen before, skylarks and a story of stones hatching little stones. I thought of these things and I fortunately did not faint.

I found a bench. I sat on it stiffly and gave deep thoughts to aspirin and Adalin. But I felt too bewildered to think systematically. In less than five minutes, I had had enough and I suddenly became annoyed. I pulled the Adalin packet out of my pocket and angrily chewed up the remaining six tablets. They tasted peculiar. I then stretched myself out on the bench. What made me do that? I had no idea except that I wanted to do it. I fell into a deep sleep. There whispered in my ear, as if from somewhere remote, the soft sound of a running brook.

It was light when I woke up. It seemed that I had slept a whole day and night. The landscape looked – jaundiced. The thought of Adalin and aspirin suddenly flashed across my mind. Aspirin, Adalin, aspirin, Adalin, Marx, Malthus, Malthurus, aspirin, Adalin.

For a whole month, my wife had been deceiving me, giving me Adalin instead of aspirin. The fact that a packet of Adalin had been discovered in her room was a clear proof of her deceit.

Why did my wife have to make me sleep day and night?

What did she do while I was thus asleep?

Did she want to kill me off slowly?

But on second thought, perhaps it *was* aspirin that I had been taking. Maybe my wife had a worry which kept her from sleeping and maybe it was she who actually took Adalin. If this were the case, then I have wronged her. I was sorry that I should have entertained such a terrible suspicion about her.

So I hurried down the hill. My legs wobbled and I felt dizzy, but I managed to reach home. It was almost eight o'clock.

I wanted to confess to my wife all the wicked thoughts I had had and beg her pardon. In my anxious haste, I forgot what I should say to her.

Then a most terrible thing happened. I saw with my own eyes something that I should never have seen. Without thinking, I slammed the door shut and to calm a fit of giddiness that suddenly overcame me, stood leaning against the pillar with my eyes closed and my head bent. The next minute the door slammed open and my wife, the buttons of her blouse undone, leapt out of the room and took me by the collar. My head spun and I fell to the floor. My wife fell upon me and started biting and tearing at me. It really hurt. I had no will nor strength to resist and merely lay there waiting for what was to come, when some man seemed to emerge from the room and carried her back into the room. The way my wife let him thus carry her into the room without a single word of protest was hateful to me. I hated her.

My wife screamed at me, her shrill voice accusing me of spending the nights thieving and philandering. It was too unjust and I was too amazed even to answer her back.

I wanted to scream back at her, asking her whether it was not she who had been trying to murder me. But I was not sure what would happen if I uttered such an accusation without a clear proof. Although it was unjust, it occurred to me that the best thing would be to remain quiet and from some strange motive, I got up and took out a few coins from my pocket. Then quietly sliding the door open, I pushed the money into the room and ran away as fast as I could.

I was almost run over by a car several times before I reached Kyongsung Railway Station. I sat opposite an empty seat and wanted to drink something to wash away this bitter taste in my mouth.

Coffee – That was lovely! Then I realized that I did not have a penny on me. All was confusion again. I lingered hesitantly without knowing what to do ... pacing up and down the tearoom like a man out of his wits.

I could not remember where I had been wandering. All I knew was that when I found myself at the roof of Mitsukoshi Department building, it was almost noon. I sat down and looked back on the twenty-six years that I had lived through and in the dimness of my memory, there rose before me no definite title to put above these years.

I then questioned myself, asked myself whether I wanted anything from life? Something or nothing – I did not want to answer such a question. Even to feel that I existed was a difficulty.

I found myself bending over a bowl of goldfish and gazing into it intently. The goldfish looked really handsome – both the big ones and the small ones looked equally handsome. It was May and the sun was casting big shadows of goldfish at the bottom of the bowl. The movement of their fins seemed to be imitating a handkerchief being waved softly in the air. I stood there, counting the number of fins. I was in no hurry to straighten my back, which felt warm.

I gazed down at the joyous street. There life of weariness and fatigue were swaying slowly like the fins. It was caught in some invisible web and could not shake itself free. I thought to myself that I had no choice but to let my exhausted body, which was faint from hunger, mingle in this joyous street.

As I began to walk down towards the street, I suddenly thought again. Where are my steps leading me?

There fell before me, like a thunderbolt from the sky, the vision of my wife's face. Aspirin and Adalin.

There must have been some misunderstanding. My wife could not have been giving me Adalin instead of aspirin. I could not believe it. She had no reason. Then did I really spend my nights womanizing and thieving as she said? But no. I was certain that I did not.

As a couple we were a lame couple, fated to be incompatible. There was no need for me to ascribe any logic to my wife's actions nor try to change anything. Whether it was truth or misunderstanding, we needed only to limp our way endlessly through the world.

Still, it was somewhat difficult for me to make up my mind whether I should retrace my steps to my wife or not. If not, where should I go?

At that moment, the siren blew. Suddenly people seemed to spread their wings and beat them like cocks, and all the glass, steel, marble, notes and ink seemed to bubble over into a moment which was dazzling in splendour itself. It was noon.

All of a sudden my armpits felt itchy. Ah! It was where my artificial wings had once been, the wings that I no longer have. There flashed across my head the vision of endless empty pages being flicked over like the leaves of a dictionary, the empty pages from which hope and ambition had been erased.

I stopped and wanted to cry out loud just this once!

Oh, Wings, sprout once more!

Let's fly. Let's fly again. Oh, let's fly just once more!

THE NIGHT OUTING

KIM SUNG-OK

Translated by Eugene Chung

Hyunju could feel the man's eyes clinging to her. She didn't even need to check; it would be without doubt some man, drunk and a stranger to her. Without even turning around to look, Hyunju could sense that the man was walking towards her. He blocked her way and opened the conversation:

'Excuse me, but where do you live?'

As he spoke, his breath gave off the sweetish smell of booze. The knot of his tie had been loosened and the top button of his shirt was undone, and Hyunju could see his throat revealed by the bright beam of the headlights from cars. It was like the skin of a rooster, plucked and dyed bright red. His prominent larynx was making little quivering movements and bobbed up once and came down again. He must have swallowed his spit. Or swallowed something he was going to say. Whatever it might have been, he was unmistakably nervous. Perhaps it was the way that Hyunju stood stock-still and expressionless, staring hawklike at his throat that unnerved him.

'Excuse me, but where to you live? I thought perhaps if we are heading in the same direction we could share a taxi.' From the way he started making excuses it seemed that he was preparing to beat a hasty retreat.

'As you see, at this hour one must be prepared to share a ride in order to catch a taxi. . . .'

Instead of looking at the road which the man was pointing to with exaggerated motions of his hand, Hyunju looked at the manila envelope that he held in his hand. It was full of creases as if it had been used to sit on at the bar. His ruddy throat, with the pores showing in little bumps like the skin of a plucked chicken, the common brown manila envelope full of creases, the sweetish smell of booze, his loosened tie, and his face, which sat on top of all that: that face which she was trying desperately not to look at, was rapidly breathing in and out in nervous gasps. His tone of voice was already different from when he had boldly blocked her way with a confident, 'Excuse me, but where do you live?'

A greenhorn. Finally he must have plucked up enough courage, with some help from the booze he had taken. At this hour with the curfew not far away, he must have seen countless drunk men by the bus stops around Chongno or Ulchiro or Myungdong accosting the nearest woman in a blind rush for a chance encounter. And so he had tried to ape them. Not to even think of trying because the woman might shun him and curse him in a taut and desperate voice, now that was really nothing at all. If some woman did nothing more than walk past some man, then what was the difference between this hour and any other hour at the bus station!

Also Hyunju knew that what lay behind the pretence of a malicious jest, was the desire to flee from your daytime existence, from this city, from your carefully planned out life, from your own self that you knew so well it disgusted you. She knew it as well – that there were those who could flee, and those who wanted to but didn't. That throat like the skin of a chicken, the creased large-size envelope and the voice now starting to tremble nervously under her unflinching silence. This one will never be able to escape. There would be no other way but to let him return to his home, to his daily life by a 'shared taxi ride' as he had said, which cost a hundred *won* per head. Let him return, since that is what he wants.

'I'm sorry but my house is right around here.' She lied quietly, and still she did not even bother to look at his face.

'Oh, is that so, I thought – . I'm so sorry.'

The man staggered as if he could hardly control his body, pretending to be drunker than he actually was, and disappeared into the crowd.

125

Before he disappeared, without meaning to do so she caught a glimpse of his face. Without being especially striking, it was a sympathetic face. Above all it was a much younger face than she had imagined. Perhaps twenty-seven or twenty-eight?

Suddenly an unwanted feeling of loneliness welled up inside her. She felt it even though the cause had outwardly little to do with her. She had felt like that when she had once seen a newsreel at a cinema. Soldiers off to the war in Vietnam were crowded on the deck of a troop carrier. Every soldier wore a wreath around his neck and was smiling and endlessly waving towards the people standing on the quay. Hyunju was shocked to see that they were young enough for their faces to seem still boyish. And seeing so many faces at once she could pick out a special characteristic of the so-called Korean face. Since their faces were not old ones, each with its own character moulded, whether they liked it or not, by the lives they had led, but the young faces of those now about to embark on their own lives for the first time, what she had noticed was almost certainly to be true. What she concluded was that the role of a soldier didn't suit Korean men at all. Was it because of the American-style uniform? As she was watching the newsreel, she decided that as soon as she arrived home she would have a go at designing a uniform in which a Korean man would look soldierly. At the same time she concluded that such a design would be impossible. Suddenly the camera closed up on a soldier who, like the others was wearing a wreathe on his neck and was waving. She couldn't tell why the cameraman had chosen that youth, but as she watched the screen she bit her lip because of the emotion welling up inside her. It was his face which best displayed that characteristic. A flattish forehead, thick eyebrows, smallish eyes, an oval face with slightly prominent cheekbones. . . . She didn't want to send him off on the troop carrier. She almost stretched out her arms towards the screen. But the picture on the screen changed, and the troop carrier grew further away from the sea of fluttering national flags.

Then, as if exhausted she felt quite empty and she felt a slow wave of loneliness coming over her.

As she walked through the people running hither and thither in order not to miss the last bus she thought it a great relief that she had promised to herself insofar as it was possible not to look at the faces of the man who stopped her.

The reason for her promise was quite different from the effect it had on people. In other words, the reason why she tried so hard not to look at the faces of those who accosted her in the night streets was to bolster their courage. She thought, if I were a man, and were to stop a passing woman half in jest, half in earnest, on the night streets and that woman could not even look me in the face but just stood there silently, then I would be greatly emboldened and would even perhaps feel a great sense of elation to find that the jest was now quite serious. If she were a man, she wouldn't waste any more words and grasp the woman by the wrist and would drag her off.

But always her silence and her indifference would only result in the man shaking from fright and anxiety. Even the most arrogant one she had met had slowly backed off, saying 'I've never seen such a . . . Must be deaf.'

Hyunju didn't complain about this. Which was not at all what she expected. Rather she was happy because she could save on a lot of things a lot of time, a lot of words, and above all the effort spent on finding out whether the man who struck a conversation with her was what she needed.

She now had another reason for being happy. Her loneliness which had spread like a drop of ink in a bowl of water and had now reached even to her toes, might have seized her from his very first words, had she seen his face from the start. Then she might even have thrust out her arm for him to take, as she had almost flung out her arms towards the screen at the cinema. Really she might have done such a thing.

Recently she had become unsure of what she wanted.

That her desire was reckless and unreasonable and antisocial she knew from the very beginning when it had first budded in her. But from the incident that had awakened her desire, and the knowledge that whatever people's dark desires might be, there glittered a streak of bright light from each one, she had dared climb stealthily over the fence beyond which lay all that seemed reckless and antisocial and unreasonable. At some time, in some place, for some people, that desire need not be reckless, not antisocial nor unreasonable. For instance, she thought of a convict wanting to escape from prison. He discovers by accident a flaw in the barbed wire fence. Upon discovering it he realizes at last that he had always wanted to escape, and he makes plans for his escape. On some moonless night, for which he had scheduled his escape, he crosses the barbed wire fence. From some point of view, his action would certainly be reckless and unreasonable and antisocial, but even so you couldn't completely deny him his wish.

It was on some day in early August that Hyunju discovered the flaw in her own fence. And although it was now a thing of the past that she could in no way undo, she found it harder to believe as time went by that it had happened in broad daylight. But of course it had been in broad daylight . . . around three o'clock in a long August afternoon.

She had been slowly going up the stairs of a footbridge in front of Shinsegge Department Store. She was not wearing her bank uniform, but a one-piece dress patterned with pink leaves. She was in the middle of a week's holiday she had earned. It was the last day of the holiday and she had got off the inter-city coach a few hours ago, having spent her holiday at her home town with her mother.

She had had so many plans for the holiday ahead of her but she had not been able to carry out a single one, and she ended up spending it in a place that had nothing to do with her original plan. She decided out of duty to spend the holidays with her mother, who lived in her hometown in the country and whom she had not seen for a long time. And so she went to stay with her. Mother and daughter spent the first day in a happy daze because of the reunion. The next day was spent quietly discussing various matters about the house. The next day mother started nagging in her own inimicable and irreproachable way, and on the third day the daughter grew irritable in her old inimicable way.

On the last day they had a big row. At dawn next day, before the daughter set off for the bus station, they had quietly made peace and when the daughter boarded the bus the mother clung to the window sobbing with the sorrow of parting, and the daughter's eyes too were bright with tears. That was all that had happened on her holiday.

As she was going up the crowded footbridge she was examining her toes which poked out of the leather thongs in a neat row. They were so dirty from the sweat and dust that she felt quite ashamed. She felt as if they were the only parts of her which did not belong to her. No, she felt as they were the only parts of her which really belonged to her.

A little while before mounting the stairs she had told her husband that she had returned from the trip. He worked at the same bank as her, but no one at the bank knew that they were husband and wife. They had got to know each other at the bank and had fallen in love and got married. But they had had no wedding, and they tried to hide from people the fact of their marriage. At work they acted as if they were complete strangers, and when they spoke to each other they addressed with blank faces as 'Mr Park' and 'Miss Lee'. Their little charade had gone undetected for two years. Now they weren't even aware that they were playing a game and the habit of taking care not to let people catch on to their relationship was now engrained in them. Of course it is a risky habit. It was not the husband but Hyunju who had first suggested the idea.

Her bank did not employ married women. If a woman got married she either had to quit her job or find work at another place which did employ married women. But Hyunju was not sure she could do either of those things. She was seized by the fear that her husband's meagre wages would not suffice to supply them with life's commonplace happiness, and she did not wish to lose the chance of saving a little money. At first her husband clung to his male pride, but when he saw how desperate her appeal was, his hurt pride was placated and he gave way to her demands. Of course, they meant to send off proper invitation cards like everyone else and have a wedding with the bank manager as the master of ceremony one day. Then Hyunju would gladly resign from the office with her pension and she would no longer make her husband use a contraceptive, and she would say to her husband, who would then be the head of a department, 'Tell everyone who works under you to come and have supper at our house today.' It was a lonely dream which would more than compensate for their little charade which had become an uneasy habit.

But why did they look so dirty. She was going up the stairs. Had the time come for her to leave her job?

'It's me. I arrived in the morning. I tried to wait until you came home, but I missed you. . . . Is there someone next to you?'

'Yes.' Her husband's reply was short and expressionless.

'Oh, I see. Then I will see you later. I'll come home after doing some shopping first. You will be coming home early, won't you?'

'Of course.'

'I'll hang up now.'

'Me too.'

She could still hear the distinct metallic whine of the receiver. Someone accidentally scraped her temple with the sharp point of a parasol as she went down and went off as if nothing had happened. She could see a couple of pigeons escaping the hot sun under the shadow of the dome of the Bank of Korea building. It was when she was mounting the last step. She felt the strong grip of a strange man around her elbow.

It was someone she could never remember having seen before. No, perhaps she might have seen him before. Perhaps in a crowded bus or at the counter at the bank or in the lobby of a cinema or in a narrow market lane, or. . . . It was a face she might well have seen at that kind of place and have not the distinct recollection of seeing. The man was rather fat and his face, tanned brown by the sun, was sweating profusely. About thirty-four or thirty-five? He was not ugly.

'What do you want?'

She tried to free her hand from his grip. Her arm chafed because of the sweat-soaked man's hand. But he did not let her go.

'I have something to quietly say to you. Don't say anything and please follow me.'

So saying, he slid his hand down her arm and grabbed her wrist. He went down the stairs that she had just climbed, and she could do nothing but let herself be dragged tottering down the stairs. It was not because she had been fooled by his urgent tone but because she was choking with fear. There must be some misunderstanding. I hope I can clear it up . . .

'Why are you doing this? Really . . .'

'It won't take long.'

'Where are we going?'

'Just around there.'

'Let me go, I won't run away. Do you know me?'

'No.'

The man did not let her go, and he did not even turn to look at her. Except when he had grabbed her elbow and spoken to her at the over-pass he had not looked at her. She was drowning with terror and anxiety and she felt quite out of breath. She tried wriggling but there was no path out of her swamp in which she was sinking. Her head was swollen with hot mud. At last she thought: finally the whistle has been blown on my little game. My game is up. I have been arrested for having tricked them. Will they torture me? No, I must confess before they torture me. No, I needn't do that. We never had a wedding and we won't have one. Then I won't have anything to confess.

They went inside the department store and crossed the street. In the middle of the street, while they stopped so let some cars pass by, the man muttered suddenly, 'It's very hot, isn't it?' He seemed to be muttering to himself rather than talking to her. Rather he talked through his hands that held her wrist. His hands which she was trying to slip out of, and which would not let her go were grasping her with a kind of slippery friction and when she noticed what they were doing she mistakenly thought he was caressing her. He had made a sort of ring by putting his thumb against the four fingers. It was as if her slender wrist were trapped inside that ring. The ring was loose enough for her to move her wrist freely, but she could not slip out of it. She liked his delicately chiselled hand. Was it because she felt at ease within her terror? She decided to free her wrist. As she did so, the ring shrank and tightened on her wrist which now stopped moving as far as it could without hurting her. She felt she could hear the rough breath of life from the gap, slippery with sweat, between her hand and his. It throbbed like a drum and fluttered in laboured beats like the gills of a fish out of water. It was as if a new life which was neither the man's nor her own, had been born in the gap between their sweat-drenched hands; then her fear and confusion shook her with unspeakable force.

'What, what is it you want of me?'

'What? You are mistaken, I have something to say to you.' He spoke calmly in a low voice.

Hyunju had thought that their destination would be a nearby

tearoom or at worst a police station and when he dragged her into a two-storey building, newly decorated, without a word of explanation, and without once looking back at her, she was so surprised that her jaw just trembled and she could not say a word. It was a hotel.

'Now, stop crying. Now you can go and tell the police that you have been raped. You see, I am not afraid of going to prison. Your arm looked so smooth. I wanted to grasp it in my hand and touch it. What would have happened if I had just passed you by? Nothing would have happened. Are you also one of those women who think that it would be better if nothing had happened? It's such a hot day, isn't it. Stop weeping, if you weep in the summer they say you catch a cold.'

That was the gist of what the man had said.

Immediately after that incident, she wanted to see it as a mere piece of bad luck. She tried to think of it as a spark which flew when her sense of guilt collided with the immoral desire of a ruffian, and she tried to think that she could in no way be held responsible for that incident. She felt guilty towards her husband that the body of a man who was not her husband had touched hers, but to confess what had happened and to beg his forgiveness – she did not in the least want to do that kind of thing. All she wanted was to forget it as soon as possible.

But as time went by, the marks left by the incident became more distinct. In the same way that a wound which had been a mess of blood and pus would after a long while heal into a whitish scar; the incident had taken root inside her.

She thought that if there were someone to be held responsible for that incident it would not be the ruffian but her husband and herself. Not only that, she now thought that it was impossible to tell whether it had been her hand or the ruffian's that had been grabbed on that day at the overpass. She saw her uncleanness and she wished to flee from that place and everything that was there. Someone was passing her by. She grasped his wrist and begged him to take her somewhere other than 'here'. He took her – to somewhere other than 'here'. It was not any better but at least she was sure it was not 'here'. That was what had really happened, her heart told her.

She ended up thinking that she must have clung to him. It seemed to her that he had behaved in a most stalwart fashion. And the way he had broken her unwilling resistance! Sweat, yes. Was not the sweat which had bathed her whole body without rest the bitter tears of defeat shed by the place she was running away from?

But her life on the surface continued as it always had done. She arrived at work usually twenty minutes after her husband. At work they avoided each other and when they did speak to each other they addressed each other as 'Mr Park' and 'Miss Lee'. When the day's work was over her husband left the office in the company of other employees and she also left the office together with her fellow employees. After that they were left with almost no time for each other at home.

Late one night, she had walked to Myung-dong and boarded a bus after having seen the last show at the Chung-ang Cinema. It was the hour when bar girls went tottering home, drunk. Hyunju, who had already taken a seat, was looking out at the street scene through the window while the bus was idling. The street at this hour seemed somehow rather out of the ordinary to her. The street was next to the bank where she worked so it was familiar to her during the daytime or in the early evening. But why did it look so unfamiliar at this hour? It was not only because of the people hurrying hither and thither anxiously in order to catch the last bus. Nor was it solely because the shops in Myung-dong had all turned their lights out and pulled their shutters down. Nor was it solely because of the bar girls bedecked in childish splendour swearing in high-pitched voices as they got on the bus. From which part of the street came the sound of panting breath that filled her ears? Was someone calling her? Why was it that she heard in this street the rough winds of terror and confusion?

At last she could tell where those sounds were coming from. Here and there on the street she could see men blocking the way of passing women. She realized that she had been watching them all along.

Some of the women followed the men who accosted them and some didn't. She could guess from their attire that they were mostly bar girls. Of course she couldn't tell whether the girls who did follow the men thought nothing of what they did because of the nature of their work. But when she became aware of them as she sat looking through the bus window she could not but be shocked at the fact that there were so many women who held themselves in such low regard.

As the bus raced on, she thought about them. Where did they go once they were over the fence? What sort of place did they end up in? Would the sentry fire upon them as they climbed over the fence? Would they be pursued by the sound of panting guard dogs? Would they be relentlessly harried by the round beam of a search-light? She wanted to pray for their safe escape.

Thereafter, she would be struck from time to time by a desperate urge to climb over that fence that she had once climbed over by chance on a hot August day. At last she ventured out into the streets one night, having deliberately chosen the hour when the bars would be closing down.

She walked slowly occasionally bumping into people's shoulders. About an hour later the city closed down. Cars were rushing at fearful speed. Pedestrians were walking briskly and her slow walk caught the eye. This was what she was counting on.

It was a cold night, and though she felt it was still autumn the temperature had dropped to below zero. A man was seen squatting in the shade of an alley way next to Chong-no Department Store vomiting noisily. Every time he wrenched his body in agony the hem of his coat, which looked as if had come straight from the cleaner's that morning, trailed on the ground. His hair, which had been greased and neatly combed, shone like steel wires from the light of the street lamp. Another man who was dressed almost identically was sniggering and pounding the first man's back with his fist. The one who was vomiting put one hand over his shoulder and shook it, saying, 'You bastard, that hurts, that hurts, you fucking bastard.'

She averted her eyes and walked past them. An unspeakable hatred for them boiled up inside her. She knew who she hated: she could not tell the difference between them and her husband. Was it because of the way they were dressed? Was it because the office workers whom you could see wherever you went in the central area of the city all wore almost exactly the same clothes, that she had confused for an instant those men with her husband? She hated those men. The one who sniggered as he pounded his friend's back, not out of a desire to stop his friend's vomiting, but because he took pleasure in beating him. And the other, who despite his smart clothes, swore like some street tough. And as she hated them, had not her hatred turned towards her husband as well? People who could behave as childishly as those two would be well capable of concealing their marriage to their colleagues and still keep a poker face.

That night she saw lots of men squatting and being sick. Then she finally got what she wanted.

'Where are you going?'

A man walked up to her. She stopped walking. She suppressed her desire to turn around and look at him in the face and kept her eyes glued to the ground. He put his hand on her shoulder and said: 'I'm thinking of going somewhere for a cup of coffee. Wouldn't you like to join me?'

Hyunju stood still, waiting for the familiar terror and confusion to seize her.

'There should still be a tearoom somewhere which hasn't closed yet. Let's go.'

He lightly pushed her shoulder as if his mind was firmly made up. But she didn't budge an inch. His hand was too weak.

'Huh, must be a stone buddha. Well then, I'll go alone. Mmm ... I'll bet that coffee will be delicious.' He slowly backed off.

At last she realized that the man had taken fright at her silence. She felt very unhappy that the man had tried to dismiss what he had done as a joke. It was only after the man had gone that she realized that what she had been waiting for was not only the fear and the confusion, but for a strong male hand to drag her along. It was natural that she had not been overwhelmed by terror and confusion, because it would only happen after the man has roughly seized her wrist. She dearly missed the man who had assaulted her last summer. In the end she took a taxi and went home.

Her walks always ended in this manner. Slowly she realized that in almost every man, there was a condition attached to his desire for escape. In other words none of them seemed to want to leave 'here' forever. They would step outside the fence, but when morning came they would rush back to their places again. No, it wasn't even that. They were inside the fence, running their fingers over it and thinking the same thoughts over and over again.

She suddenly realized that her desire would always be satisfied when they boldly satisfied their own desires. For how could she confess her uncleanness if they did not stir terror and confusion in her!

She walked. And walked. And walked. But there was no one who said, 'You see, I am not afraid of going to jail.' And she would have to take a taxi home for fear of the impending curfew.

One day, while at work she turned towards her husband and without thinking called him 'Darling!' as she always did at home. It was only when she saw her husband's face go bright red and the employees about him burst out laughing that she realized her mistake. She had never before made such a mistake. Her husband had quickly turned things into a jest saying, 'What! Am I your husband, Miss Lee?', but it had been a great shock to her. The game is up now, and she stubbornly thought that the time had come for the masks to come down.

One night she met quite a different sort of man from those she was used to. Anyhow he roughly seized her hand and dragged her with him. When they were in sight of a hotel tucked inside an alley that seemed to be their destination Hyunju could feel the terror and confusion that she had been awaiting rise up in her like steam. They arrived at the hotel porch and she saw him turn around and look at her. It felt as if he was trying to ask her, 'Will it really be all right?' Then her fear and confusion vanished and all that was left in its place was loathing for the man. She tore herself away from his grasp and ran out of the alley. She took a taxi and went home. Inside the taxi she realized the significance of the man in August who avoided looking at her in the face until they were inside the hotel. It was very important. It was then that she realized that her desire would not be easily satisfied. She didn't believe there were a lot of men like that man in August.

And so recently she was unsure of what she wanted, and she wondered if it were not possible to be led off by a man without the terror and the confusion. Like those prostitutes. No, like those masses without a desperate need for prayer.

But what she was most afraid of was that her desire would be wrapped up in such empty ceremony. She knew vaguely that if she did what she did without the terror and the confusion, what would eventually be left would be empty ceremony, and this would surely lead her to a moral downfall.

But what she wanted was not her downfall but her salvation. She wanted to be freed from her circle of deceit. But as her walks became more frequent, the temptation to replace desire with ceremony grew. And she was afraid of the temptation, because it came from within her. Like that man's face for instance. No, it wasn't because his face was young and sympathetic, but because of the loneliness which welled up inside her when she saw his face. It was that temptation to fling out her arms towards the screen. It was the sorrow she felt for her people who died bedecked with wreathes, smiling and waving their hands. A man blocked her way and opened the conversation. 'Excuse me, where do you live?'

Part 2

'THE CRAG' AND OTHER STORIES

THE RED HILLS: A DOCTOR'S DIARY

KIM DONG-IN

Translated by W. E. Skillend

It was when I made a journey through Manchuria. I had
wanted to look at the customs there, and at the same time to
make some investigation of the spread of diseases amongst
people who had not yet received the baptism of civilization. I
had set aside a year for this, and gone right into the wilds.
I shall try to record here what I saw in a tiny village which I
shall call 'Xx'.

It was a small village of a couple of dozen households, where
all the inhabitants were Korean tenant farmers. It did not even
have a name, and was set in the middle of the vast Manchurian
plain. Look where one might, there was not a single hill to be
seen.

I had been round all the villages of Manchuria on a mule,
with one Mongolian with me as an attendant, and when I
reached Xx, autumn had already gone, and the furious winter
had arrived.

There was nowhere in Manchuria without Koreans, but I
was glad to come upon such a remote place where the whole
community was made up of Koreans only. Moreover, the
people there were only tenants. But they were comparatively
gentle, honest and sturdy, yet at the same time all at least
partly educated. Manchuria was bleak, and Manchurians and
Koreans alike led a bleak life there, as I had seen in my travels

141

over nearly a year. Now I had come upon this comparatively peaceful community. I might have been glad even if it had been a community of foreigners, but to find that they were all my own people! For a fortnight or so I visited the houses every day, and spent the days chatting, revelling idly in the feeling of peace which I had not experienced for so long.

It was here that I saw a person called Chung Ikho, who had the nickname 'Wildcat'.

No one in Xx knew where he came from. His accent seemed to be that of the home counties around Seoul, but at times, when he chattered rapidly, one could detect a southern accent too, and then, when he was in a mood to fight, one could detect a northwestern accent as well. So there was no guessing where the came from by his accent. He knew some simple words of proper Japanese, and a few Chinese characters. Of course he could speak Chinese fairly well, and he could say some simple Russian phrases. This suggested that he had scraped a living in many places, but no one knew his background for certain.

He had apparently drifted into Xx empty-handed, like a neighbour dropping in, about a year before I had got there. In looks, he had a face like a rat, and sharp teeth. His eyes always had a crafty and baneful appearance, and in his bulbous nose the nostril hairs grew so long that they even stuck out and could be seen. He was a short man, but nimbly made. One could put his age at anywhere between 25 and 40. Whichever way one looked at him, his body and face gave one a feeling that he was a repellent fellow, hated by everyone.

Admittedly he was said to have some gifts: to be a habitual gambler; and to love fighting, picking quarrels, brandishing a knife; and being rough with the girls.

His looks told that he was the sort of man who was hated by everyone, and his whole behaviour in the village had been so repulsive that there was no one there at all who welcomed him. All the people avoided him. He had no house, but if he went to somebody else's house for a bed for the night, the man of that house would just have the bedding ready for him to sleep, and insist on making off to another room. So Ikho would sleep on until broad daylight the next day, and then, taking his time about getting up, just as if he were in his own house, would order breakfast and leave without a single word of thanks. And if anyone should not accede to his demands, he would start a quarrel and a fight, always with a knife.

From the time he had come into the community, the girls and young women had been uneasy about going out and about. Several had unwisely gone out and got into trouble.

'Wildcat': goodness knows who gave him that nickname. It just happened that no one called him Ikho, only Wildcat.

'Whose house did Wildcat stay at?'

'Mr Kim's.'

'Any mention of more trouble?'

'Luckily not, I believe.'

Instead of 'good mornings', they asked what Wildcat had been up to.

Wildcat was a huge cancer in the community. Because of Wildcat, even at times when they were most short of people for the fields, several young men had to stay in the village to protect their young women. Because of Wildcat, even on the hottest summer evenings the women and children could not step outside and get a breath of fresh air easily. Because of Wildcat, the community had to have someone up all night to protect the chicken coops and pigsties.

There were several meetings of the elders and youngsters to discuss the expulsion of Wildcat from the community. Of course there was agreement, but there was no one who would take the first step to expel him.

'If you'll take the first step, I'll be responsible afterwards.'

'Don't worry about afterwards, you speak to him first.'

Each one of them avoided being the first to tackle Wildcat. In spite of the council's agreement, Wildcat stayed on in the community as if nothing had happened.

'Has their girl cooked my breakfast?'

'Has their boy got my bedding ready?'

Wildcat moved from house to house just as if everyone in the community was his relative.

If anyone died in Xx, instead of condolences, no one ever forgot to say, 'and it wasn't Wildcat who died.' If anyone fell ill, they said, 'Ay, let Wildcat catch it from him.' A cancer: no one felt any sympathy or love for Wildcat.

Wildcat himself was a man who could do without sympathy or love. However anyone treated him, it meant nothing to him. If he could see that he was being given a cold reception, he would pick a quarrel and even wave a knife, but whatever was said behind his back and even if it came to his ears, it meant nothing to him.

'Hm!': that one word was his main philosophy in life.

He often used to go to the Manchurians' haunts in the next village to gamble. Sometimes he got beaten up and a back covered in blood, but he never complained about it. Even if he had, no one would have listened to him. However badly he had been beaten up, he would bathe his wounds in a spring, limp out, and the next day he would be out and about again the same as ever.

It was the day before I left the village. An elder, Mr Song, loaded that year's harvest on a donkey and went off to the village where the Manchurian landlord lived. He came back a corpse. He was beaten up because his harvest was said to be no good, and his broken, bent body was tied on the donkey's back. He just made it home, and as his shocked family took his body down off the donkey, he breathed his last breath.

The youths of the community were all outraged over the brutal murder of Mr Song. They shouted for revenge, and each seemed ready to set out that very moment. But that was all. No one could be found to take the lead. Perhaps, if there had been anyone to do so at that time, they would have raced of to the landlord straightaway. But no one could be found. Each one looked to the next man.

They stamped their feet. They shouted. They pleaded the agony of the ill-treated, and they went. But that was all. Perhaps they hesitated to throw away their own livelihood by turning on their landlord when it was somebody else's affair, but no one was found brave enough to step out in front.

In my professional capacity as a medical doctor, I examined Mr Song's body. On my way back, I met Wildcat. He was a short man, and I looked down at him. Wildcat looked up at me.

'Miserable man! Leech of a man! Worthless man! Weevil! Parasite!' I said to him. 'D'you know Mr Song's dead?'

Wildcat had been looking up into my face, but at these words he lowered his head. Then, as I went to walk off, there flashed momentarily on Wildcat's face a pathetic expression which I could not miss.

I could not get to sleep that night for thinking of the pitiful state of people who were being ill-treated a thousand miles away from the homes they had left. I could not prevent myself weeping for thinking of us Koreans, with nowhere to plead our anguish.

It was next morning. I got up at the sound of someone coming to wake me – it was a reflex action. Apparently Wildcat had died, covered in blood, just outside the village. I frowned at the word 'Wildcat'. However, I was a doctor, so I picked up my bag at once, and ran to where Wildcat had fallen. Several people had gathered for Mr Song's funeral, and they ran after me.

I saw him. Wildcat was bent at the waist, in the shape of the first letter of the Korean alphabet, like a figure seven. He had fallen on a furrow in a field. I ran to him and looked. He was still slightly warm.

'Ikho! Ikho!'

But he did not regain consciousness. I gave him some emergency treatment. His limbs jerked terrifyingly. After a while his eyes flickered open.

'Ikho, are you conscious?'

He looked up at my face for a while. His pupils moved.

'Doctor, I went.'

'Where?'

'To his landlord's house.'

I was astonished. I forced my eyes shut, or else would have wept. I grasped Ikho's hand, which was already growing cold. There was a short silence, then a terrible incessant jerking in his limbs. It was the death throes. A tiny sound, barely audible, left his lips again.

'Doctor!'

'Yes.'

'I want to see, I want to see ...'

'What?'

His lips moved, but no words left them. He looked as if he did not have strength enough. After a little while his mouth moved again. Some sound left his lips.

'What?'

'I want to see – the red hills – n' white clothes.'

Facing death, he must have thought of his homeland and his own people. I had closed my eyes tight, but now I opened them gently. Just then Wildcat's eyes flickered open again. He was trying to raise his hand, but it was already broken and would not rise. He tried to turn his head, but he did not have the strength. He gathered his last ounce of energy onto the tip of his tongue and opened his mouth.

'Doctor!'

'Yes.'

'Those – those – '

'What?'

'The red hills over there – and the white clothes – Doctor, there they are!'

I looked round. But there was only the vast Manchurian plain unfolding.

'Doctor, please sing me a song. Last wish – give me a song. The East Sea and Mount Paekdu may drain and wear away...!'

I nodded and closed my eyes. Then I opened my mouth. The song flowed from my lips. I sang gently: 'The East Sea and Mount Paekdu...' Following my gentle singing the solemn chorus rose from the lips of the others standing around.

'Rose that dies not, lands that end not,
Splendid rivers and hills...'

In one corner of the vast wintry Manchurian plain, the solemn song gradually grew to full dignity, consolation for the dying weevil, Ikho. Ikho's body steadily grew cold.

SNOW

HWANG SUN-WON

Translated by W. E. Skillend

From nightfall it began to snow. At first there was just a sprinkling, like white ash, outside when I opened the door, but suddenly it started to snow with flakes as big as magnolia petals. When the neighbours shivered as they stepped into our house, the snow glided down on their backs.

That night I went down again to 'Six-Fingers' Grandfather's shack. Since I had returned in autumn the previous year to what was after all my home, it had become a habit with me during the two winters to drop in at this shack whenever I had a free evening.

Everyone who assembled there was very well known to me since childhood, except for a man they called 'Sambong's Father'. He had moved here some time ago from somewhere in Hamkyong Province.

We sat there together, but had nothing particularly remarkable to talk about. At that time of year, we usually discussed the quota for taxation. We talked about everyone else's worries as if they were our own, and our own worries as if they were everyone else's.

As I stirred up the dying embers in the brazier, I sought in the conversation of these familiar people for something of the spirit of my farmer grandfather of half-farmer father, that might still be in some hidden depth of myself. My head sank

147

forward as I stared into the embers, reflecting on my own life and the lives of the people of my home village.

Outside it was still snowing solidly. Someone opened the door and shut it again, saying that it must be a foot deep by now. The conversation went on – there had been a lot of rain this May, and now the snow had come so early; in the sharp spell last year the wheat and barley had frozen; but it looked as if the wheat and barley would be all right this year, with so much snow coming.... Someone got round to asking Sambong's father whether the snow over his way was as terrible as ours. He joined in the conversation with his Hamkyong accent, and said it was.

It is true that the snow over Samsu and Kapsan way is terrible, and one hears all kinds of strange stories about it....

In the winter every household ties a rope connecting the house to the privy, and when the snow piles up, the only way to get to the privy is to make a tunnel by shaking the rope.

Or, if anyone loses a shoe walking in the snow, it is quite possible, that he would find it after the next spring thaw, hanging on a branch of a pine tree....

And once a village is caught in a really heavy snowfall, communications with the outside world are often likely to be completely cut until the thaw the next year.

Once there was a house, he said, in an isolated valley, where the food was running out, and the husband went to get some more. While he was away, a heavy snowfall started. That same evening a traveller who was passing by was forced to shelter there.

The woman of the house filled the kitchen with wood. She even dragged it into the living-room, and piled it up in there, leaving space only for one rush mat on the warmest spot of the heated floor. Then she brought in a jar with holes in the bottom, and set it in a bowl. Into this she emptied a gourdful of beans, of which she had no more than a couple of bushels left, and poured water on them. This was for her to grow bean sprouts.

The snow continued for several months, so it became impossible to go in and out. The lady and the traveller passed the whole of that winter drinking soup of soya sauce and water with a few threads of been sprouts.

Spring came. The snow had melted and the roads appeared

again before the traveller could leave and go on his way. He went, and at the end of the day arrived at an inn. It happened to be the very place where the husband, who had gone away to get food months previously, had stopped. The husband too had been caught by the snow, and was only now on his way home.

The two of them slept in the same room, and, as they chatted, the husband realized that the house where this traveller told him he had spent winter was his own house. So he asked whether the woman in the house had not starved to death. The traveller told him how they had passed the entire winter together on bean sprouts.

The husband listened attentively, thanked him very much, and said that the woman was his wife. He was full of appreciation. So the next morning they shared their wine, and gave each other a cordial 'Take care of yourself' before parting.

Outside the heavy snow was still falling. The people in the shack stopped talking for a while and sat silently. They continued to see a ray of hope at least in the meagre returns likely in next year's farming, but somehow they had to get through the winter without disaster. They seemed sunk in thought.

I stirred up the embers a couple of times. They were dying right away.

DOGS IN THE VILLAGE BEYOND HILLS

HWANG SUN-WON

Translated by Bob Donaldson

One had to go through passes everywhere on the road. Only the south had really long and deep valleys, but since there were hills in every direction, one had to go through passes. So the placed was called 'the village beyond hills'.

From early spring to late autumn people on the move clogged the road to the northwest that passed through the village. Naturally, they would stop to rest their tired legs by the well next to the hut at the foot of the west mountain. It appeared that most of the families weren't what you could call small. There was the occasional young couple who looked like man and wife, but most of the people that went through the village were in large families. The younger ones carried tattered bundles, and the old people held the children's hands as they shuffled along. And the women carried various things on their backs and heads.

As soon as they reached the well, they slaked their long-standing thirst in the shade of the weeping willows. They formed a line and all passed by the well to drink, then they went round again: the playful children and even nursing babies drank the water. Rather than tiring of mother's milk, the babies appeared to think the water was just better. Next the travellers splashed the cold water over their blistered and scorched feet. This time too they formed a line and took turns.

After the adults were through, the children used to go back, draw more water from the well and splash their feet some more. But when they left, they hobbled as before, disappearing through the mountain pass to the north. A group that arrived towards evening could stay overnight, too. When that happened, they naturally went into the old gristmill. As soon as they were settled there, the women pulled out the gourd dippers they were carrying and went out to beg for rice. The first place they went to was the foot of the east mountain, where sat two tile-roof houses facing each other. The little children usually stuck close by, following their mothers. If some rice dripped into the gourd the kids would dive for it and fiercely gulp it down. Now and then the mothers would gentle scold the children, saying, 'The adults have to eat too, don't they?' Even so, when they emerged from the tile-roof houses, the gourds were often empty. Next morning in the darkness before the eastern sky turned grey, these travellers would disappear, wending their way to the north.

In the spring one year, in the mill next to Kannan's house at the foot of the west mountain, a dog, unaware of when the last batch of grain was milled, was licking a winnower covered with dust, not chaff. The dog looked like it had once had beautiful and luxuriant white fur, but now the yellow dust had changed it to a dirty yellow, and it appeared quite hungry. Stuck close to its hind legs, the dog's belly pulsed with each breath. The dog had probably come from quite a long way.

And there was something else: a cord of some sort around its neck. A rope that seemed to say the dog had come far. Perhaps this dog's master was one of the travellers who passed through heading northwest; many of them had dogs like this trailing along, with similar cords around their necks. When the master first packed up all the unnecessary furniture and things that couldn't be taken on such a long trip, the dog was probably included and sold with everything else to defray travel expenses; but when the stuff to take was packed up, the dog must have followed, like a lamb thinking itself one of the family – so the family brought it along. Undoubtedly the children had teased and disputed till the dog was taken along to their destination – that was certain. So the dog was brought along, but on the way from Cholla Province or Kyoung-sang

151

Province or wherever through Pyoung-an Province, the dog was perhaps left tied to a tree when even the bean cakes ran out and the travellers were going hungry; there probably wasn't enough food for the dog too. The travellers were hoping that someone who could feed it would come along and untie the dog, evidently. So maybe the dog, in yelping and straining against the rope in hopes of following its master, broke free and took off before anyone found it. And so in wandering in search of its master, it came to this 'village beyond hills'.

Maybe the travellers through the northwest pass realized while coming through that they couldn't take the dog all the way to their destination and sold it somewhere. Maybe the dog was left with a request to raise it well at someone's home in payment for a meal. And maybe the dog didn't forget its old master and in following him wandered into this village. Besides, the yellow dust that covered the dog somehow had a different tinge from the yellowish earth of Pyoung-an Province.

The dog seemed to realize that no matter now much it licked the bottom of the winnower, it would find only dust. The millstone attracted its nose, and as it walked over, one of its hind legs limped, as if the dog really had come from far away.

The dog licked the millstone vigorously, but there too was only dust. Even so, the dog kept licking for a moment; but then it stopped, proceeded to follow its nose around here and there for a bit, and finally emerged from the mill, all the while wondering whether it had been left behind one night after a master's troubled dreams, whether the travellers who'd stopped at the mill had left it by the road in hopes of leaving their desperate circumstances there too, whether its master was concerned about it. The dog left the mill and went through a hole in a latticed door at Kannan's house, next house over. There, the resident yellow dog, resting on the floor of the mud-walled room, raised its head, got up, and approached with a strange look. The new dog, thinking it was about to be chased out, slapped its tail down towards its belly and fled.

There was a kitchen garden at the edge of this village of crab-shell crusty and poor villagers. While passing it, the new dog realized the yellow dog wasn't following, and kept limping along at about half-pace. At the end of the garden was a rough and uneven field. At the end of the field there was only gravel in a ditch, bone-dry during droughts, but now there were little pools of standing water, stagnating. The new dog quickly lapped up the stagnant water.

Straight across the ditch was a sloping hill, and on the inner part of the hill sat the houses of the village chief and his relatives, on a small parcel of turf. And there was a mill, which during the winter was used only by these two households. The new dog headed for this mill, just limping along. But here there was rice chaff mixed with the dust. The dog moved about, busily licking the bottom of the winnower. Its emaciated stomach throbbed even more busily.

As the new dog was licking the bottom of the winnower, the village warden's black dog across the way took notice and trotted over. It stopped outside the mill a moment, then continued coming, ruffling its fur, gnashing its teeth and snarling; the new dog growled back, as if it had been bitten, but didn't stop licking the winnower. At that point, the black dog decided the new dog wasn't hostile, and stealthily approached it to take a sniff.

The black dog recognized that the new dog was a bitch, and was so relieved that he shook a little, all the way to his tail. The new dog trembled a bit too, with the black dog so close, but continued to lick the winnower as before. After the new dog had licked off both the winnower and the millstone, she even took a stroll to the outhouse, then came back and lay down beneath the winnower. She began blinking her eyes, as if trying to keep them closed. The blinking finally stopped and the eyes closed tight. The black dog sat down a little ways away and kept watch.

It was evening of the same day. A woman's voice called, 'Hey, hey,' from the senior village warden's house; she was calling a dog. The black dog took off for the house. The new dog got up and began licking the same places as before, then started limping towards the warden's house, as if she sensed something. Inside the main gate, the black dog was hastily slurping up some rice from a trough that stood just outside the kitchen door. The new dog unconsciously put its tail between its legs and tremblingly approached. But scarcely had the new dog drawn near when the black dog ruffled its thick fur, bared its teeth and began to growl. The new dog stopped, watched the trough momentarily, then sat down as if to wait.

The black dog appeared to have finished, and his long tongue traced all sorts of patterns over his lips as he licked them clean; he then left the trough. The new dog arose, wandered over to the trough, mouth first. There was rice left underneath, and lots of grain scattered around the trough. The new dog lapped these up hurriedly, and her body shook a little. After licking everywhere several times till there was no place left to lick, the new dog left the trough, passed by the spot where the black dog kept watch, and emerged from the house.

When the new dog went back to the mill later, another dog was blocking the door. It was the assistant warden's black and white dog. Frightened, the new dog couldn't help shrinking back. The black and white dog took a sniff at the new dog, and turned his nose as if he caught an unusual scent. The new dog began licking the moisture from the black and white dog's mouth; he'd just eaten. Properly annoyed, the black and white dog headed for his own house, with the new dog following closely. The black and white dog went inside, found a spot and lay down. The new dog went straight to the kitchen door.

Around the kitchen entrance, just like the warden's house, rice lay on the ground, the grains scattered widely. The new dog licked these up quickly, then left and headed for the bottom of the winnower in the mill.

That night a dreary rain began falling , and continued for two days. As soon as the weather cleared up a bit, the new dog ventured out; things looked better than the previous day, but the new dog couldn't tell if anyone in either house had provided for the dogs or not. At first, after several visits, the area around the trough was all wet, and no one had set out breakfast. Then breakfast starting coming out again, but the new dog had to wait for the resident animal to leave the trough first. So after the house dog had finished eating, the new dog finished licking the trough and went back and lay down underneath the winnower in the mill. During the day the new dog would come out and lap up some rainwater, then crawl back under again.

In the evening the rain stopped, and the new dog made its rounds as before between the two houses, eating the leftover rice. On this particular day there was lots left, as if the black and white dog had lost his appetite.

The next morning brought a bright and clear spring day. The new dog was up at the crack of dawn, visiting the two houses and eating the rice in the troughs – but this day she hardly limped at all. She went into the mill, found a sunny spot, and began to soak up the rays.

There was some noise like someone was coming, and the farmhand who worked for the warden appeared, carrying a bag of rice; he was coming from a late breakfast. Inside the mill, he let down the bag with a thud, turned and stopped. He was followed by Kannan's mother carrying a winnow, and by Kannan's grandmother carrying a net on her head. Kannan's grandfather had worked for the warden before as a farmhand, but now that he was working for two households, he was thinking of quitting work and just watching instead. The mother swept the millstone off with a broom and the farmhand hefted the bag of rice again and came forward, with one hand clasped shut.

A hard dry smell slowly emanated from the rice sack as it sprawled on the ground. The new dog started for it, smelling something like rice. But the farmhand didn't see things from the dog's point of view, though, and so, preoccupied, he shoved the dog inside with his foot and an exclamation: 'bothersome dog!' It wasn't a real strong push, but the farmhand's leg was firm and tough, and the new dog raised a yelp and scrambled off to the side, then settled down again in the same sunbathing spot. When the first batch of rice was nearly hulled, the assistant warden came in. He was rather dumpy, with hair cut very close. But his skin colour was quite good, and though he was forty years old there was no way he looked it. He came into the mill and, sounding firm and masculine, said 'Well dried?' But he wasn't talking to anyone in particular, nor did he wait for an answer. 'Don't crack the grains.' Grandma, who'd followed the cow in, scooped up a handful of rice from the millstone and held it close to her eyes to see how well it was hulled, then poured it back without a word. The rice was well-hulled, it seemed. The assistant warden walked about a bit, and discovered the new dog. 'Whose dog is this?' But before the grandmother and the mother turned their heads in his direction, the assistant warden's kick found the dog's middle. The dog let out a yelp at this unexpected blow, and disappeared outside. But shortly thereafter, the dog looked back at the mill; the farmhand, the grandma and the mother were all muttering things like 'Whose dog is it? It's not my concern.' And when the dog saw the assistant warden facing her direction and then bending down to pick up a stone, she ran off with every bit of strength she had. As she started down the hill, a stone flew past, as expected, and landed to the side.

The dog crossed the ditch, by now somewhat filled with rainwater, and ran till she'd passed the sod of the broken-up field that Kim Sondal's men worked. Luckily, her feet were the only things that didn't wobble. When she came to the mill at the foot of the west mountain, she went in and laid underneath the winnower; again, there was only dust there. But soon after she came out again and started for the warden's mill. As she went up the sloping hill, no warden was in sight by the mill; relieved, the new dog turned her feet in that direction. But the second her eyes rested on the farmhand at the bellows, she stopped, looked for a moment, then turned and went back the way she came.

As day waned, the new dog saw the grandmother and the mother fix the latticed fence, and then they headed in her direction. Before they went into the house, they looked for a moment towards the new dog. The dog rose, wondering what the women were thinking about, and started to move away, but the women just went into the house and took no notice of the dog.

The new dog headed for the village warden's mill. It had been swept once, but there was still a lot of rice chaff scattered about, and a lot was stuck to the pillars and such. The dog began at the bottom of the winnower and licked vigorously.

That day at early evening, the new dog stood just inside the village warden's gate and watched the black dog, now almost finishing off the trough, when the door opened and the village warden came out. He was pudgy like the assistant warden, with hair cut short. His skin colour was very good too, so he looked quite young. At a quick first glance, one would be inclined to think the two wardens were twins, so similar were they. They weren't, of course, but many times people mistook one of them for the other.

As the chief stepped down into the yard, he discovered the new dog, evidently preoccupied; he hadn't seen it before, and stamped his foot, exclaiming, 'wretched dog!' Even his voice was as hard as the assistant warden's. The new dog, caught totally by surprise, disappeared through the dog hole in the gate. The warden stood in the gateway, and the assistant warden, who'd just finished dinner, came out. He saw the new dog, and thought that it was perhaps the same one he'd chased from the mill that morning. Seeing that the same dog was chased away by his brother, suddenly he thought 'this dog might be crazy'. So he raised a cry: 'Grab the mad dog!' As the new dog ran by with its tail between its legs next and its stomach raised up, unfamiliar to the village, the warden too thought 'maybe this dog is crazy!; he flew through the gate, wondering if the dog had been caught. He found a suitable club, came out, saw the dog and began beating it, all the while yelling 'mad dog! mad dog!' When the wardens got to the hill, the dog was already scampering across the rough field, but Kim Sondal* was in the field till late, heard the cries about a mad dog, and looked around. Ah, he thought, here's the mad dog; he grabbed a shovel, and took it to the dog's rear. The two wardens no longer thought of beating up the dog, they just stood there and yelled 'mad dog! mad dog!' by turns. And Kim Sondal continued to beat the dog, bracing himself to apply more vigour as he heard the two wardens yelling, wishing that someone would come from the village at the foot of the west mountain and help beat and capture the dog. The shouting continued even after the dog had disappeared into the shacks at the foot of the west mountain, and even after Kim Sondal's back couldn't be seen anymore, running in that singular fashion after the dog.

When the warden brothers' loud yelling stopped and evening became quieter, the sound of commotion from the people living at the foot of the west mountain was heard so clearly that you could grasp it; a thin fog began to rise slowly and it was followed by some of the people, with Kim Sondal before them. At first it was evident that he hadn't caught the mad dog. He crossed the garden, but before he got to the rough field, the assistant warden started towards him and called out, 'What happened?' His voice, though amazed, seemed far too loud on this calm night; it spread out like a shriek in the night

---

*Sondal = a title given to a man of letters in the Chosun Dynasty, but now obsolete. It is equivalent to 'Mr'.

air. There was no answer. The warden, a bit chagrined, repeated the yell: 'Well, what happened?'

'I lost it. That damn dog was just too fast. It took off up the mountain.'

What sort of harmony was this? Kim Sondal's voice sounded at once like it was coming from beneath their very feet, and at the same time sounded like it came from far away. Such was the deep calm of the night in the mountain valleys.

'No matter how fast the thing is, you should have caught it! But maybe it was too scary for you, eh? Scared of a little puppy. . . .' It was the warden's voice. Kim Sondal, as if to say that sometimes there was room for caution, didn't answer the warden, who was a habitual joker; he just went off into the fog to the field he was working before to find his weeding hoe.

After it got dark, a few people were sitting around the courtyard at Chason's house, since it was early in the season, talking about farming affairs and how they'd have cause for concern till the new barley ripened, and towards the end of the conversation someone brought up the mad dog. Kim Sondal said that the other night as he was returning from the village to the south and crossing one of the mountain passes, he heard a really strange-sounding dog far away, and he was a bit scared. He said that the dog sounded like it had some disease, or like someone had tried to drag it around by the throat. But the strange thing was that if someone was trying to drag the dog around by a rope, the sound wouldn't come from one spot like it was doing. Kim Sondal said he didn't know but that it might have been that damn mad dog.

If one is really good, he can really pull the wool over people's eyes in a funny way; the people in the village knew that whenever Kim Sondal's name was mentioned, or something was ascribed to him, it was tough to distinguish fact from fancy, and the people in the surrounding areas knew this too. But Chason's father, during the account of the dog being dragged around by a rope although the sound of it came from one place, spat some tobacco on the ground as if he had something to say: 'Maybe it was a dog belonging to one of the travellers that passed through the northwest pass a few days ago, eh?'

Or maybe one of the travellers just tied it to a tree and that drove it a little crazy till it broke free and came to the village.

Chason's father continued. 'An animal goes crazy if it starves for a while; Kim Sondal, what you heard was probably just as tied-up dog that's starving and a little bit crazed.'

But Kannan's grandfather, who was there, and though he thought Chason's father was probably right, thought of something his wife had told him a little while before. He recalled that she'd seen the new dog in the mill, or in the other mill when she came out after hulling the rice, and it didn't seem like a mad dog at all. But the grandfather hadn't seen it, so he couldn't really say whether it was crazy or not. It was clear that whether the dog was mad or not, it was probably going to come back to the village. Chason's father said that since the dog would probably be back, everyone should be extra careful.

At that same moment, however, the new dog had come down from the west mountain and crossed the rough field, and was trotting around in the dark among the houses. Since it was dark, the dog was careful as she trotted. As the dog headed up the hill road, she stopped and looked towards the two warden's houses, then proceeded with great caution to the senior warden's house. The new dog slipped in through the hole in the hedges, and since by now the black dog was familiar with her, he made no noise. The new dog went right over to the trough and began to lick. The black and white dog at the assistant warden's house too had become very familiar with the new dog, and so she went right in there as well and started licking the trough.

The new dog left the assistant warden's house and headed for the warden's mill, where she lapped up some water in the same place as during the daytime. But she didn't stay there at the mill to sleep, she went back down the west mountain.

The next morning, Kannan's grandfather got up early as usual and opened the lattice door – and discovered the new dog under the winnower. He turned back inside, picked up an A-frame support pole, hid it behind his back, and came out, thinking 'If it's really a mad dog, one blow will kill it.' The new dog heard the sound of someone approaching and got up; down went the tail between the legs, automatically. That wasn't a very pleasant thing. Kannan's grandfather stood for a moment and glared at the new dog, the pole crunching slightly as he grasped it tightly. But there was no frothing at the mouth, no saliva dripping as sick dogs have, and it seemed that even if the dog was mad, the madness hadn't reached a serious stage yet. Grandfather looked at the dog's eyes. The new dog, too, looked at the grandfather, wondering if this person was going to beat her or what. If the dog was crazy, the eyes would be blood-red, or the pupils would have a sort of blue fire in them, but this dog wasn't that way at all. There was just a little sticky stuff in the corner of two normal, frightened eyes. And in the dog's eyes, this person was immense, with a dark face covered almost entirely by a grizzly beard, with sinister and glaring eyes that likewise had that little touch of sticky stuff in them and skin at the corners spread out like the ribs of a fan; but the dog sensed that this person wasn't going to beat hell – the eyes told her so – and she raised her lowered tail just a little bit. This was no mad dog. At least it wasn't completely mad yet. Kannan's grandfather relaxed the hand that had concealed the pole. But as soon as the dog saw the pole the grandfather had been hiding, she started: down went the tail again, and zip, she dashed past the grandfather and was gone. The yellow dog in the courtyard saw the back end of the new dog and started to go after her. The grandfather knew at a glance that if the dog was crazy the yellow dog would probably bite her, so he called the yellow dog back. But the yellow dog had already taken off after the new dog. The new dog kept her tail down, but the yellow dog was familiar to her, and he touched his nose to hers; she responded in kind, and her tail started to go back up. Once again the grandfather said, 'This is no mad dog.'

The new dog went on up the hill towards the two warden's houses, as if she were waiting for them to go out of their houses. After breakfast the two wardens left for the rain-watered field where they were breaking ground for new farmland in the lower part of the valley. Chason's family farmed on the upper fields which the senior warden owned, while Kannan's family farmed the assistant warden's field near the lower wells; they were working that day to make the field's more arable. From the first thaw, in fact, Chason's and Kannan's families had all been out working in these new fields whether they liked it or not.

After the two wardens had left to supervise the field work, the new dog waited a bit and then entered the houses very guardedly and licked the troughs. Then she went to the mill and licked up all the new chaff along with the dust. She went into the back room too, then headed out and up the mountain, stopping to rest underneath a tree. Day waned, and after evening fell, the night grew very dark; the new dog came back down and after going into each of the houses again, came back to the mill at the foot of the mountain, drinking a little of the stagnant ditch water along the way.

Every morning Kannan's grandfather used to open the lattice door, but the new dog was always up earlier and had already left the mill: all he saw was her tail as she crossed the rough field outside.

One night, as the new dog was licking the trough out, the door opened and the senior warden came out.

The warden stepped softly, picked up a stick in front of the storeroom door, and stealthily crept up behind the new dog. The dog stayed put, unable to take her tongue from the trough, as if she didn't know what the warden was doing. She knew he was there, though, and suddenly ran past him for the door. Just then, the warden saw a strange blue light right at the spot where the dog's eyes were. The thought that 'this dog is really crazy' flitted through his mind, but for some reason he couldn't raise a yell. But when the dog disappeared through the hole in the hedges, the warden yelled 'grab the mad dog!' and ran after her. Though it was dark, he could tell that the dog was scampering towards the hills to the rear. The warden kept yelling 'grab the mad dog!' and kept following. But he was a little scared to approach too close. But his cries of 'get the mad dog' became louder. The dog ran up the hill and out of sight, and after the warden yelled a few more times, the assistant warden and his wife came running out. The warden was thinking, though, of the other day when he was scornful of Kim Sondal for not catching the dog because it was 'too scary'; he grew a little upset at not having fractured the dog with one stroke in the yard just now, and then he really got angry at himself for being scared and not giving chase when he probably could have. He approached his brother and his brother's wife and breathlessly called out 'Why aren't you catching the mad dog?'

The next morning before the senior warden left to supervise the new field's cultivation, he chatted with every person he met as they came home from the village below the hill. 'That

161

dog is really mad; there was a blue fire in its eyes last night and I barely beat it away from me. So if anyone ever catches a glimpse of it, you must kill it on the spot, no matter what you have to do.' The villagers, having heard the chief's cries the night before, knew that he'd been chasing the dog that had come back, but if it really had a deep blue fire in its eyes and had taken to attacking people, all were agreed that the dog would have to be disposed of on sight.

The new dog was extra-careful from this point on, staying away from not only the village wardens but making sure no one saw it at all. One night soon after, Kannan's grandmother came in from the outhouse and said the mad dog was back in the village, with the blue fiery eyes and everything. Grandmother had thought the dog was all right from the first time it'd been chased out of the village as crazy, but this time she saw some blue fire and said the dog really was mad; grandfather merely replied that, dog or man, when starving or taken with a disease, eyes got that way, and they didn't know for sure whether the dog was really crazy anyway. 'The dog's just hanging around, there's nothing to be scared of.' But just then grandfather realized that maybe the dog was there to eat up some of his valuable fertilizer, and he dashed out of the room, grabbed a stick, and headed for the outhouse. Crying 'damn dog!' the grandfather swung the stick and struck one of the outhouse pillars. The blue fire turned, and something whitish slipped through the lattice door. After this happened, no one saw even the shadow of the new dog.

Later on, when the first days of summer came, and after the two wardens finished the new field and had got the rice planted, a rumour started making the rounds. Seems that while Kim Sondal was weeding the rough field, he stopped for a rest and a smoke, and while resting he saw something flitting about among the trees on the mountain behind the senior warden's. Kim was sure it was the mad dog. But the dog wasn't alone – there were others following it, none other than the senior warden's black dog, the assistant warden's black and white dog, and one other. As a matter of fact, the two wardens' dogs hadn't been home for a couple of days, so Kim Sondal's story was probably right. The two wardens inferred that the damn mad dog had been making their dogs crazy from the first, and they were a little frightened. Kannan's grandfather had forbidden any discussion so the few in the village who claimed to have heard growling and barking that day and the day before from the west mountain. Some said they heard it at night as well as during the day. The wardens were upset and realized their mistake in not running after the dog and killing it.

On the third day, the wardens' dogs returned, in orderly fashion. Kannan's dog came back too. Each dog entered its house, found a shady spot, lay down, opened its mouth and let its dripping tongue hang out, began to pant, closed its eyes and fell asleep. All seem to have been exhausted during those two days. That same third day when the wardens were coming in from inspecting the newly ploughed and planted field, the farmhand informed them that dogs had returned. The warders replied, 'Okay, good; grab 'em and take care of it,' then followed the farmhand and Kannan's grandfather into the house. Kannan's grandfather approached the black dog bare-handed. The senior warden's party watched and stood way back, thinking, 'Boy, is he in for some trouble?' The grandfather stroked the black dog's head, and the dog, pleased with the attention, closed his eyes and wagged his tail, sweeping the ground like a broom. The grandfather accosted the warden: 'What's this about a mad dog, eh?' But he replied, 'We're lucky it's not totally mad yet. It's obvious the dog's going crazy, look at how its eyes stay shut and how it drools. We ought to dispose of it before it's gone totally crazy.' The farmhand said 'A mad dog won't eat, right? Let's give it something and see.' So he went to the kitchen and brought out some rice with a bit of water. But the black dog just shut his eyes again after inspecting the bowl in front of him, as if it had a strange smell. The senior warden exclaimed, 'So, you see!', but the grandfather said the dog was sleeping because he'd been out doing what male dogs tend to do. The senior chief jumped up: 'You mean with the mad dog? That's even worse! Quick, let's set some traps!' Then, as if to himself: 'The first of summer is only a few days away, the festival should be pretty good.'

There was nothing the grandfather could do. The farmhand had already set a snare for the dog's neck, so he took a rope from the farmhand and tied it around the black dog's neck. The farmhand held the other end, then suddenly jerked the rope and dragged the dog to the gate, tied the rope to the bottom of the gate post and pulled it tight.

The dog, caught by surprise, yelped and jumped, but to no avail. At the sound of the barks, some other dogs came from the west mountain to where the black and white dog could see them, and began to bark too. Blue fire sprang up in the black dog's eyes, and he vainly clawed at the ground and the gate post. The senior warden had watched this sort of thing before, but when he saw the fire in the dog's eyes, he thought again that this dog was obviously crazy. The black dog excreted, gave one final spasm, and then hung limp. Next at the assistant warden's, the black and white dog was sneaking across the yard softly as if it sensed what was going to happen. But it was caught by both the paw and neck in a snare. The farmhand grabbed and pulled the rope with a bit more agility this time, and the black and white dog died on the spot.

There was a big cauldron beneath the chestnut tree behind the senior warden's house for boiling the water to cook up the dogs. The wardens had been discussing something, called the farmhand over, and told him to go to 'Hanging-Rock Village' and fetch back the village warden and Pak Choshi.*

When the two dogs were bubbling away in the beanpaste soup, the immaculately groomed and pomaded village warden from 'Hanging-Rock Village' came carrying two *dois** of *soju* on the farmhand's shoulders. With him was the fatty Pak Ch o-shi wearing a horsehair hat, his ramie-cloth summer suit which looked like dragonfly wings. The drinking started with a side dish of well-done dog gut. As the cups were passed around, the senior warden doffed his jacket and said, 'All right, off with the shirts. Let's have some fun here.' Both senior and assistant wardens decided not to say anything about the mad dogs that made up the meal. It probably would have made their guests lose their appetite and spoiled all the fun. The 'Hanging-Rock Village' warden took off his shirt and said, 'A nice First-of-summer party.' The assistant warden took off his shirt too. Only Pak Choshi was left with his shirt on. Not only had he never taken his shirt off at a drinking session, since

---

*Choshi: a title, now obsolete, given to a scholar who passed the first part of National Civil Service Examination in the Choshi Dynasty.
doil = unit of measure.

everyone knew that he thought it a breach of etiquette to leave the house without a long coat on, even for short trips, no one asked him to remove his shirt. 'Shall we do this again over at our place during the summer?' asked the visiting warden, looking like he thought it would be appropriate, and glancing at Pak, who nodded his head in agreement. The visiting warden kept his eyes on Pak and said, 'Kil-son has a dog, right? He wants to sell it, he's short of cash since he got that food poisoning from those vegetables; we could get the dog real cheap. The dog's been starved, but it's a big dog.' Pak continued to agree with everything the warden said, and nodded his head once again.

The meat of forelegs was brought and the meat of hind legs. Kannan's grandfather busily picked apart the pieces to replenish the food served with the drinks. And the shadows of the first night of summer swiftly and suddenly grew longer, then spread; at the drinking party, one batch of booze had disappeared down the men's throats, and new bottles came in. All the revellers got properly sotted.

A very drunk senior warden now proceeded to reveal that the dogs caught that day were mad, and since mad dog meat would prove a great tonic, he hoped his guests would like it and eat a lot. The visiting warden replied, 'Great ... just a tonic? I thought it was so tasty, now I know why. Let's eat till everyone's navel turns bright red,' and loosened his belt till his belly was exposed.

The assistant warden kept stroking his close-cropped hair back, as usual, and he asked the visiting warden and Pak Choshi to get a puppy dog for him. The Hanging Rock Warden replied that he could, that in the village where his in-laws lived a dog had just had puppies, so not to worry, because the pick of the litter was really a good one. Here the assistant warden said to be sure and get him one, so he could raise and eat that one too. Pak said 'good idea', and softly chuckled to himself and nodded his head. His back was sweating and the sweat was slowly soaking through the white ramie-cloth shirt. The bare torsos of the others shone with dog-oily sweat, and soon the party was swallowed up in the evening shadows. The farmhand brought out an oil lamp and hung it on the chestnut tree. The Hanging Rock Wardens pomaded head and the lustrous sweat shone in the lamplight. The listless eyes of the men in the circle, the exchanged cups, the broken pieces of meat, the slaps at the mosquitos that landed on chest and neck, all made the group look just like a herd of animals sitting together. The 'Hanging-Rock Village' warden wanted to sing and, stiff-tongued, began a fragment of a song. The assistant warden thought the fellow's voice was quite good. Pak sat silently, beating time against his knee. The dim lantern light on this first night of summer made the group look like bawling animals.

While the men were gathered around Chason's yard at the foot of the west mountain, Kim Sondal said that, no joke, he thought he could hear the dog's barking plea not to be killed while he ate the meat, and everybody laughed. He also commented that what the Hanging Rock Village warden and the assistant warden said were all the black one's voice and the black and white one's voice, and everybody laughed again. Kim Sondal and the others in the village wished to have the taste of the meat, no matter how unsavoury it was. Till late that night the oil lamp hung from the chestnut tree, like the eye of a wild animal.

The next day the two village wardens came to the foot of the west mountain, and said that he knew there was one other dog that had followed the mad one, and it should be disposed of immediately. He firmly declared that if the owner didn't obey his order, the person should be ready to leave the village. Of course Kannan's grandfather just left his yellow dog alone. Five days, then ten passed, and it didn't go mad. The people at the foot of the mountain swept the dust from the long-unused mill and started hulling barley. And the new dog used to come in at night and lick up all the grains left after sweeping. Compared to the previous time, this was like a cornucopia, a wind-fall; the ongoing grinding of barley with the chaff all over was just too wonderful for words.

Two months passed, and the yellow dog was normal as ever. The people at the foot of the mountain began to harvest the millet. For poor people, the day they can eat millet rice is a big occasion. How else could they get that nice nutty taste? And there's an old saying they thought of that made the stuff worth eating: If a young girl ate millet rice and radish kimchi, her bosom would expand.

Of late the new dog had been slipping in at night to eat and to sleep too in the mill. No one had seen her for a long time and she was pretty relieved. But she didn't forget to rise very early each morning and head for the mountain, so even Kannan's grandfather wouldn't see her.

One day, a rumour started that the mad dog was back and was sleeping in the mill at the foot of the mountain. Chason's father said he saw her. Early one morning, as he was going to the mountain, while breaking apart a bamboo pole for his oxcart, something came out of the mill; he'd looked carefully, and found it was the same mad dog. Everyone believed him; Chason's father's night vision was excellent. The warden brothers heard about this and came to the village. They wanted to dispose of the dog that night (they didn't say it was mad – they knew that if it was, it wouldn't have continued to eat, but would have bitten its own leg or something and died long ago). And if it had puppies, they were probably the offspring of a jackal, so since the meat was healthy, the wardens wanted to trap the dog, keep the pups, and give the meat to the villagers.

While waiting for night to fall, the two wardens went to Chason's house in the village where everybody had gathered in the courtyard, and made sure everyone had a stick or club. Kannan's grandfather was one of the group. Of course, he knew the new dog hadn't changed, but if it had come to the mill next door to sleep, then naturally it would have gotten into his valuable fertilizer, so he joined in with the group to beat and capture the dog, since he knew he couldn't drive it out of his storeroom himself. The villagers welcomed the occasion to have the taste of dog meat, however unsavoury it might be.

Night grew deeper, and Chason's father, on watch, called out that the dog was approaching the mill. The villagers could almost taste the unsavoury meat in their mouth, with hushed steps they moved towards the mill. The two wardens removed themselves away from the group and watched what was happening in the mill.

The villagers surrounded the two exposed walls of the mill, looked inside, and found the dog moving around, as they thought. The dog looked white, even in the dark room. For sure it was the new dog. The villagers crowded together, step by step. While retreating the light shone on one part in the eyes of the mountain dog. The villagers gave it all they had with their clubs, even Kannan's grandfather mustered all his strength. The circle tightened. The blue fire in the dog's eyes shone, and the dog wheeled about quickly, looking for an escape. There was something strange about the blue fire, though; Kannan's grandfather realized that it wasn't a single body that generated it, but it was a combined thing; it looked like a combination of the dog's eyes and the fire from the puppies inside her, all put together. Kannan's grandfather thought for second . . . if the dog really going to have puppies?

Just then someone shouted 'strike!' and the next few moments were ones of much confusion as all around the grandfather struck out at the dog. At the same time the grandfather felt a quick blaze past his leg. Someone then yelled 'Who broke the circle? Who did it? Who was it?' Amid the uproar, the warden's farmhand's face rose up under the grandfather's chin, looked at him and said 'It was you!' The senior warden, curious as to what happened, called out in the dark 'Well, what's going on?'

'We lost it.'

At the farmhand's response both wardens set up a yell.

'You *lost* it?'

The senior warden's voice started moving towards the mill; he was losing his temper and yelling 'Who's the idiot that let it out?' Kannan's grandfather left and went inside his house next door. In a moment the senior warden's voice was heard inside the house. 'Damn you to hell, you old goat! Why don't you just die?'

About one month later, when everyone was preparing to gather firewood for the winter, Kannan's grandfather decided to go to the fox ravine to gather wood which was rather dangerous and thus avoided by woodgatherers generally, because he knew that there would be a lot of wood there. Coming home with a load of wood, he was just looking around when he spied something that looked like baby animals lying in a group down a ravine. Were they tiger cubs, he thought, and when he looked closer, he found they were puppies, and they were asleep. And the new dog was standing by, keeping watch, looking nothing but skin and bones.

The grandfather moved close to the puppies, and was suddenly surprised. The puppies were a blend of the black dog, the yellow dog, and the black and white dog. But just then the grandfather realized what had happened, and that there was nothing unusual about this. A smile welled up inside the grizzled bushy-whiskered fellow, normally so fierce-looking. After he left the ravine, the grandfather told no one about what had happened to him that day, not even his family.

This is a story that I heard during my second or third year of middle school during summer vacation at my mother's family's house in the village beyond hills, as Kannan's grandfather, Kim Sondal and Chason's father rested from their work and gathered under the weeping willow by the well; they talked about this and that, and this story came in the end. Kannan's grandfather said that this happened years ago, and he put in commentaries as he went along, stopped and corrected himself, and added supplements and important circumstances during the course of the story.

After Kannan's grandfather discovered the puppies in the ravine, he was even more careful not to let anyone know where he went to gather firewood; he enjoyed going up to the mountain and seeing the puppies. Sometimes he would hide some leftover barley from his wife and take it to the puppies, even though it was food for people. And once he came back from the mountain carrying one of the puppies, telling his family that it was one he had been given by someone he knew. He gave one to Kop-dan's house, having 'just being given'. And whenever he went up to the ravine, he brought a pup back; the next one he gave to someone in the west part of the village. In this way he finally brought down all five puppies to new homes.

After grandfather finished his story, he said that the dog in his house right then was a great granddaughter of the new dog, and since the pick of that first litter was so healthy, that just about every dog in the village beyond hills, if they weren't a great grandson, was a great, great grandson. He said that even the houses of the warden brothers had dogs now that were great, great grandsons of the new dog. As he mentioned that, a smile grew on the face of the bushy-whiskered grizzly-legged man. But when I asked what happened to the new dog, the smile instantly vanished. He said that they thought a hunter came along in the first part of the winter that year and shot the new dog, at least that was the rumour, anyway, no one

169

ever saw the new dog again. Well, I said, I guess I asked a useless question.

SPRING, SPRING

KIM YUJONG

Translated by W. E. Skillend

I call him my father-in-law, and keep telling him that it's about time. It's an effort for me to do this, so I have to rub the back of my head for help. We're old enough now, I tell him, so won't he let us get married? But his answer's always the same: 'What d'you mean, boy, married? You've got to be grown up for a thing like that.'

Actually, when he says 'You've got to be grown up', he doesn't mean me, but his little Chomsun, who's to be my wife. It's three years and a full seven months since I came here to work, without getting a penny for it. Yet he keeps saying that she's not big enough, so that I wonder whether his little girl will ever be big enough. If he said that I had to work better or eat less (he's always worrying about me eating a lot), I'd have plenty to say, but at this, when he says that Chomsun's still a child and has got to grow up a bit, I'm silenced. I don't know what to make of it.

So I've begun to realize that the arrangement I've made is no good. If it was two years, then it'd be two years, if three, then three. Of course I'd have to work, but just for a fixed term. But when he just gets awkward and says that he'll let us get married when his daughter's grown up, who'll be able to tell when that little girl of his is big enough, without keeping watch on her all the time? Then again, I thought 'big' meant only full height, but mightn't there be, for all anyone knows, some people whose bodies just spread sideways from a fixed height? I just hope that the old man will be reasonable when the time comes, and I keep my nose to the grindstone without grumbling. Then, you see, he'll understand everything and say: 'All right, you've done plenty of work. That's enough. Get married!' If he'd only set up home for me too, wouldn't I be pleased! But he pretends to have forgotten, and gets into a terrible state in case he lets any words like that slip out. It's all very well being called a future 'son-in-law' and living in, but I don't relish the work, and its not much of a life, you know. Haven't I been a fool not to realize this, and just wait doggedly for a Chomsun to grow up?

Once I felt so fed up that I thought of dashing in with a ruler and measuring her up, but the old man said that men and women mustn't mix, so I can't even have a word with her face to face. If we do happen to bump into each other on the path to the well, I do try to measure her up just by eye. Every time that happens, I go off muttering 'Flaming titch!', and spit into the paddy. You see, it doesn't matter how carefully I look her over, she always looks just about titchy enough to fit under my armpit – though I'm a bit taller than most. For quite a time I beat my brains out wondering why the dogs and pigs should persist in growing while a human being refused to grow like this. Then I realized that it was because she carried the pitcher on her head so much that she was stunted. So now I draw water for her secretly. I do more. When I go wood-cutting, I put a stone on top of the cairn, and more than once I've prayed:

'Please make Chomsun a bit taller. Because if you do, I'll put some of our nice sticky rice-cake out for you next time.' But she's made small, and it's no use. And though I quarrelled with her father yesterday, it certainly wasn't because I hate him.

While I was planting, I had a quiet thinking, and felt fed up again. When these rice-plants have grown, Chomsun might eat the rice and grow a bit bigger, for all I know. But then again, that mightn't happen, so what am I doing planting them? I haven't the slightest wish to go on planting year after year to fill my father-in-law's sagging belly. (Of course he doesn't admit that he eats too much, and says how he gets chills on his stomach.)

I got a terrible pain in my belly. I stopped planting and just crawled up onto the bank of the paddy, rubbing it. I was carrying the plants on a winnow tucked under my arm, and I just dumped it down on the ground. Then I dumped myself down too. Because, however urgent the work is, if I have a belly-ache, that's the only thing that matters. Who can work if he's ill? I plucked a handful of fresh green grass and rubbed hard at the leeches on my legs.

I looked up at the old man's face. He was scowling at me with a strange look in his eyes:

'Hey, you, boy! What's all this about this time, eh?'

'I've got a bit of a belly-ache.'

My sneaking off to lie down on the grass nettled him. He splashed up onto the bank, caught hold of me, and then what did he do but grab me by the throat and hit me on the face?

'Blast you, are you trying to ruin me, stopping work? I ought to smash your head in.'

When the old man gets nettled, he lashes out something terrible. Could there be another bloody father-in-law like him, with his 'Hey, you, boy' and his 'Blast you' to his son-in-law? To tell the truth, he's the same with everyone in the village. Anyone he's not swearing at says it's a sign of bad luck. Even the tiniest children, when they're sure his back's turned, point at him and call him 'Swear-pill'. (His name's really Pongpil.) No one loves him. Really nobody loves him, not so much because of his swearing, but because he's the bailiff of Square Pac, the local landowner. Of course, a man's got to be good at swearing, good at bashing people and look like a mongrel, to be employed as a bailiff, and that's just what the old man is like. If he's not sent a chicken or something, or doesn't get help with his ploughing, you can be sure that your land will be taken back in the autumn. Then those pests who've been buzzing around, giving him money and standing him drinks all the time, sneak in and clap their hands on that land. Next thing you find a bloody big-eyed ox comes plodding along, all by itself, into my father-in-law's cow-shed. It's marvellous the way all the locals go on kow-towing to him, while he goes on swearing at them.

But he's hardly in a position to swear at me. He hit me on

173

the cheek without thinking what he was doing, but afterwards he realized. He swallowed his spit in bitter silence. I knew very well what he was thinking. It won't be long before it's our busiest time, with the rushes to be cut and the seedlings to be transplanted. If I don't work, and just up and go home, that'll finish him.

It was just about this time last year too that he went a bit too far. He called me a bloody lazy-bones for sleeping in, picked up a stone, and threw it at me. He really hurt my ankle. I groaned with pain for three or four days, and in the end he was just about in tears, wasn't he?

'That's enough, lad. Get up and do a bit of work. You've got to, so that you can get married in the autumn, if it's a good harvest, haven't you?' That opened my ears quickly enough, and that very day I got up. I ploughed all by myself as much as would take anyone else two days. Even the old man's eyes were round with astonishment. Isn't it right that he should have really let us get married last autumn? I stack the sacks of rice away neatly, but there's no talk of anything else. He points his pipe at Chomsun as she comes in with the pitcher on her head.

'Shut up!' he says. 'She's got to grow up first. What are you talking about, marriage for that bit of a kid?'

I turn red, but that's all he says. I was so mad that I could just about have tossed my bloody father-in-law out onto the step and scrammed off home, but I took a tight hold of myself. The truth is that I daren't just go home in the position I'm in. I left to get married, so they'd point at me and ask was I such a fool that I'd got chased straight back.

Anyway, yesterday I saw that the wind had gone right out of him, so I got up from the bank and stood up to him. 'I'm going,' I told him. 'You'll give me all my back-pay, I suppose.'

'You came as a son-in-law, not a hired hand.'

'Well, then, shouldn't you let us get married good and quick? You've just got me working for my keep night and day, that's all you've done.'

'Yes, but it's not my fault the kid's not growing up.'

He gets out of it again by just filling his pipe and going on and on with the same old story. Whenever I press him, it's always me that comes off worst.

'Not this time,' I said, pulling him by the sleeve, 'We're going off to the prefect to get an order.'

'Damn you, what way's this to treat your elder?'

He can shout as much as he likes that he's determined not to go, but his strength's no match for mine. What right has he got to keep me working, not giving me his daughter, and then on top of everything, actually raining blows on me?

Yet honestly it's not that I hate the old man really.

Now, the day before, wasn't I up on the new burnt-off land on the hill opposite Bird Pass, ploughing all by myself? Every time I turn round at the edge of the field, the disturbing, rich, strong smell of the flowers tickles my nose. The bees keep buzzing round my head. It's a little corner where there's nothing to be heard but a brook among the rocks. The spring sunshine makes me feel that I'm dreaming, all warm and cosy, in bed. I felt like idling, though I've never been ill from over-work before, and my heart was pounding as if I was sickening for something.

Usually I sing as I work the ox: 'Eh, up, my beauty, my beau-oo-oo-ty!' but, I don't know why, I hadn't ploughed half the field before I felt whacked. I just kept on getting cross. I beat the ox uselessly and hard: 'Anya! Anya! You perishing bastard of an ox!' (It was the old man's ox, of course.) 'I'll break your legs for you!'

But it really wasn't because of Anya that I felt like this. All my pent-up rage broke out when I saw Chomsun, the titch, coming up with my lunch on her head.

Chomsun doesn't make such a terribly pretty little girl, I know, but she's not just something you'd give the dog to eat either. She's got a good plain face, just right for my wife. She's ten years younger than me, so that makes her fifteen this year, though she looks two years younger than she is. Most people grow tall in proportion, but I can't help seeing this stumpy thing as a honeydew melon. Because of all the melons the honeydew is the tastiest and the prettiest, I mean. It's nice the way her huge round eyes are frank and friendly, and the way her mouth, though it splits her face, is big enough to take a proper spoonful of food. Damn it, if you can eat plenty, that's luck enough, isn't it? Yet, if she has a fault, it's that she often swings her body about too much. (Her old man says that it is thoughtless the way she bounces around.) So, when she brings me my meal, she often throws it onto the grass and gives me mud-splashed rice to eat. I suppose I could think it was rice with sesame seeds in it. If I don't eat it, it will make her feel that she has failed, so I sit and chew it, wondering whether what I'm chewing is rice or stones.

But this day, I don't know why, she placed some perfect rice down neatly at the end of the field. Then, because of the rule about men and women keeping apart, she moved away a little and squatted down with her back to me, waiting for the dishes.

When I had finished eating, she came to tidy up, and didn't I get a shock! As she bent over, putting the bowls on the tray, she grumbled to herself, or perhaps meaning me to hear: 'Is it going to be nothing but work, night and day?' She had been so careful to keep the rules about not mixing that I was quite flummoxed what she could mean by talking like this. Still, I thought it'd be a good chance, so I said to myself, speaking into the air:

'So what?'

'You should tell him to let you get married, that's what,' she shot back at me, and ran away to the hill, blushing all over her face. I gazed at her back for a while, not understanding what had brought all this on.

In the spring, the sap rises in all the trees and plants, and the buds burst out. Perhaps the same thing could happen with people too, I thought, and was not sorry that Chomsun seemed to have grown up suddenly – inside – within a few days.

If he still brazenly says that she's a child. . . .

When we went to see the prefect, he was pouring swill into the pigsty, which is outside a gate in his fence. He believes that anyone who's been to the capital for a bit should behave like a gentleman, so he's got his moustache trained out to points on both sides (at a quick glance it looks like the tail of a swallow sitting on a roof), and he's got a habit of stroking it as he gives a genteel little cough.

He looked at us with a vaguely puzzled interest, as if he already knew all about it.

'What are you doing here when you should be working?' he asked, raising his hand and giving his quick cough.

'Your honour, I agreed in the first place with my father-in-law . . .'

I had pushed my father-in-law, who was going into the attack first, behind me, and rushed in recklessly, but then I stopped and thought. I corrected my opening words to:

'No, er, this gentleman, my father-in-law, in the first place . . .'

The old man likes me to call him 'father-in-law, sir', and to refer to him as 'this gentleman, my father-in-law', and if we are out and I call him just 'father-in-law', he does get incredibly angry. He asks me whether I think a snake likes to be called a snake, that's how insulted he feels. He's always keeping a close eye on me to make sure that I say 'the gentleman who is my father-in-law' and 'the lady who is my mother-in-law' when anyone else can hear. And I keep forgetting. This time, too, with him beside me, I had just called him 'my father-in-law', and had only realized it when he stamped hard on my foot and glared at me.

The prefect listened to my story and looked very sympathetic. Well, it was not only him, anyone would be the same. He picked his nose with his little finger nail, which he grew long, and flicked away the snot.

'Now, Pongpil, you should let them get married soon, that's all the boy wants.'

It was what I'd guessed he'd say, but the old man glares at him and stabs at him with one finger.

'What d'you mean, get married? Shouldn't that kid grow up first?' That's all he says, and he stands there, champing and smacking his lips.

'That's true, too.'

'For nearly four years you've said she's not grown up. When will she be big enough? Drop the whole idea and give me my back pay.'

'Did I tell her not to grow, damn you? What d'you expect me to do about it?'

'The lady who is my mother-in-law is only the size of a sparrow, so how did she have children?' (In fact the old woman is shorter than Chomsun by the length of an ear.)

The old man gave a chuckle at these words, at least he tried to, but looked as if he'd bitten on a stone. Pretending to blow his nose, he gave me a sly dig, a really hard blow in my ribs with his elbow. What a filthy trick! So I pretended to swipe a fly off my calf. I bent down and gave his backside a shove with my shoulder. He crunched forward, looking as if he was going to topple through the fence gate, but he straightened up

177

and shot a terrible look at me. He wanted to swear at me, but stood there, not daring to in front of someone else. His rage was awful to see.

Anyway, except for this, I hadn't got anything particularly startling out of it, so I went back to the paddy to plant the seedlings. I'll tell you why. It was after my father-in-law had whispered something in his ear and gone off that the prefect took me quietly aside and spoke to me. (My friend Mungtae says that he had been persuaded because he rents two paddies from the old man, but I don't think so.)

'What you say's quite right. you're quite grown up, and it's not wrong of you to say that the matter of a son is urgent. However, if you say that you're not going to work, or that you're running off home at the busiest time of the year for farming, you could be sent to gaol for the crime of damages!' (This made me take notice.) 'Did you see that recently someone was sent to gaol for having started a fire up on the hill at Ginseng Field? At a time like this, when you can be sent to prison for starting a fire on a hill, what a much more serious crime it is to spoil somebody else's farming! Furthermore, you spoke of going to court.' (I had said that I would go to court to get my back pay.) 'But if you did do that, you'd only get blamed for another crime. And the same about getting married. In law, there's such a thing as "coming of age". You've got to be twenty-one before you can get married. Of course, you're worrying that it's late for you to have a son, but if we take Chomsun, she's only fifteen, isn't she? However, the gentleman, your father-in-law, was good enough to say just now that he'll let you marry this autumn, even if it means putting everything else aside. So, are you grateful? Then get along and get the seedlings planted, or whatever it was you were doing. No more grumbling now. Off with you!'

So I got through to this morning without another word of protest. When I think now of how the old man and I quarrelled, I can only say that it was completely unexpected.

For my father-in-law's part, lately he has been wanting to impress the tenants. 'If you've got money,' he says, 'you're a gentleman. There is nothing strange about that, is there?' You should see him, the way he sticks out his bulging belly and swaggers around. He may have hit me before, but he's got enough sense not to destroy the family fortune that he's built up so carefully by using land that belongs to others. And for my side of the argument, haven't I got to make sure that he approves of me for me to marry Chomsun?

Well, to come to the point, it was a terrible mistake to stroll down to Mungtae's house last night. He must have learned somehow about the way my father-in-law and I had quarrelled in front of the prefect during the day, because he never stopped teasing me.

'You took all that and did nothing about it?'

'What could I have done?'

'Good God, you could have pushed the damn fellow into the paddy, that's what!'

He became so terribly angry for me that, in shaking his fist, he struck the bowl of the oil lamp. Then, he's such a bloody quick-tempered fellow that having done that, he kept getting on at me that I should pay for the paraffin. I sat there in dumbfounded obedience, while he went chattering on without stopping.

'Are you going to keep working for him night and day? Yongduk got married after he'd lived in for a year. You've lived in for about four years. Have you got to live in longer? D'you know you're the third candidate for son-in-law? Yes, the third! Working for somebody else, you make me mad, you idiot. Go and drown yourself in the well!'

Later he even told me to slit my throat with my finger nails. He didn't care what he said to me, just as if I were his son, in fact. He said all sorts of things. I couldn't put every word of it down here, but this was the gist:

The old man had had three daughters, and the eldest one was married the year before last. To tell the truth, she didn't go to her in-laws' house in the usual way, but for that daughter too he had a son-in-law-to-be living in for a while and then sent him away. Anyway, the way he brought in one son-in-law after another for ten years – from the year she was nine until she was eighteen – he was notorious in the village as 'the man who was well off for sons-in-law'. But ten of the beggars was a bit much. Because the old man had no sons, only daughters, until he got a 'resident' son-in-law for his next daughter, he had to have someone working for his keep. Of course it would have been all right to hire a hand, but that takes money, so he had a succession of prospective sons-in-law living in, while he selected one who worked well. On the other hand, they had to take a lot of abuse, and were worked terribly hard for their keep too, so I suppose they got so fed up to the guts that they ran away. Chomsun is the second daughter, and, as for me, I'm the third man living in as her prospective husband. A fourth bloke could come in after me, but I'm a good worker, and a bit of a simple fellow, so my father-in-law's got a tight hold of me, and isn't going to let me go. The third daughter's five at the moment, and since she would have to be at least nine before she could have a prospective husband living in, I'll have to go on being worked to death for that long.

I kept on making pretty meaningless noises, but Mungtae took no notice. He'd once got some land, but had lost it again, and since then he only had to see the old man to growl senselessly, like a dog that can't get at a bone. Anyway, there was no reason for that to have happened, if he'd given Chomsun's father the top hat his family prized when he asked him for it. (It was supposed to have been worn by a mayor, but it was moth-eaten and battered.)

I took what Mungtae had to say with a pinch of salt. If I hadn't, I've have come home last night and quarrelled with my father-in-law. Then there would definitely have been trouble, wouldn't there? If we'd quarrelled then, you see, the only one who'd have come out of it badly would have been the old man, because even his daughter didn't love him any more.

I'm telling you the truth when I say that until Chomsun brought me my breakfast this morning, I was thinking only of how much food she would be giving me. Then there it all was on the tray – stew with bean-paste, a saucer of soy-sauce, a bowl of millet, and, piled up higher than the millet, a dish of wild greens. The wild greens were picked and prepared by Chomsun in her spare time, so I could eat as much as I fancied – two bowls, or even four – but the rice or millet, the old man tells her not to give me more than one bowlful, so I can't have any more. Anyway, as Chomsun put the tray down in front of me, she muttered to herself, grumbling in the same funny way that she had on the hill yesterday:

'So you've been to the village head, have you? Just been and that's all?'

I realized that I'd been a bit stupid, not having taken any

stronger action. That's what I thought to myself. I turned away from her and addressed the wall:

'I got a "no", so what d'you suggest I do about it?'

'You could have grabbed him by the beard, that's what, you idiot!'

Her face went red with anger, and looked all distorted as she dribbled and swallowed. Though there was no one there to see then, if there had been, they would have said that my face was as pitiful as that of a baby stork that had lost its mother. I doubt if there has ever been such unhappiness as I felt then. It doesn't matter how much anyone else tells me that I'm stupid, but if Chomsun, who's to be my future wife, looks on me as an idiot, I've got a bleak future.

After breakfast I put the A-frame on my back and set out for work, but then I threw it off again and lay down on the straw mats in the yard outside the house. Even death would be no worse than this, I thought. If I don't work, my father-in-law, who's too old himself to work, would end up not being able to reap his harvest.

He saw me as he came out of the front door, with his hands clasped behind his back and belching like a pig.

'Damn you, are you at it again?'

'I've got stomach cramps. Ooh, my belly!'

'You had a good meal to stuff you, what d'you mean, stomach cramps? You ruin anyone's farming and you go to gaol, remember?'

'I don't mind that. Ooh, my belly!'

I really thought that I didn't mind going to gaol for not working. In future, if I had any sons, they'd hear me being called 'idiot' over and over again, so I wanted to get it settled today, even if it killed me.

When I didn't get up even after he told me to, I could see the fury in his eyes. He strode over and came at me with the stick off the A-frame. Then he stuck the stick hard into the small of my back and turned me over and over, just as if he was flicking a stone over. My belly was packed hard with all the food I'd eaten, and every time he did that, I was in agony with a dislocated stomach. Still I didn't get up, so next he stabbed my belly from above with the stick and kicked my ribs with his foot. He did that because he was vicious by nature, but I'd provoked him equally viciously. I shut my eyes tight with the pain, and lay there, thinking what fun it was to let him do what he liked. But when he beat and thrashed me, I got up without realizing what I was doing and grabbed his beard.

No, it wasn't that I'd got angry. It was because I'd just seen Chomsun peeping secretly at what we were doing through a hole in the fence behind the kitchen. As if it wasn't bad enough that I'd been called an idiot without being able to say a single word, if she saw me being whipped as well without protest, wouldn't she take me for a real idiot? Then again, it was all right for me to give him a good hiding, because this bloody father-in-law was nothing at all, and Chomsun hated him too. That was the way I sized up the situation anyway when I grabbed his beard, and since it was what Chomsun wanted, I guessed she would be very happy this time.

'I'm going to pull it off,' I screamed, loud enough for her to hear me over there.

The old man blazed with anger, and, as I grasped him, he beat my shoulders with the stick. I went all dizzy. When I lifted my head again, it was my turn to be blazing with anger. You bastard of a father-in-law, I thought. My eyes flashed, and I pushed him and tossed him over down the bank where the bottom field was. A moment later he crawled up, panting with the effort it took, but I quickly pushed him and tossed him down again.

When he crawled up, I forced him down, and when I forced him down, he crawled up. This happened four or five times, and every time I shouted at him, 'Why d'you just keep me slaving away and not let us get married?'

Anyway, if he'd cleared the air by saying, 'All right, I'll let you get married tomorrow if you want,' I'd have stopped being angry at once, perhaps. If I had anyway, I wouldn't have hit him, and wouldn't have been branded later as the one who had struck his father-in-law. I could have gone on and on.

But then he crawled up, panting, with his eyes fixed on the crotch of my trousers. He made a quick grab, and hung on. I screamed, and the whole world seemed to be spinning round.

'Sir! Father-in-law, sir!'

'Blast you, boy, go on, kill me!'

'Ooh, aah, dear sir, spare me dear sir!'

I flapped my arms about, and the sweat poured from my

forehead. I felt sure that I was about to die. Still he didn't let
go, and I was forced down to the ground. I'd almost fainted
when he let go. Filthy! Filthy! Is this my father-in-law? For a
moment I couldn't get up, and floundered around. However,
when I lifted my face, I couldn't see anything. I groped along,
every limb trembling. In my turn, I caught hold of the crotch
of his trousers tightly.

All I knew was that he was my enemy. I never relaxed my
grip on him.

'Ooh, aah, blast you, let go! Let go!'

He flailed about and screamed continuously, like a hen
caught by a kite. Why should I let go? I'm going to teach him
a hard lesson while I'm about it, I thought, as I pulled even
more viciously. He fell to the ground, and, realizing that tears
were welling up in his eyes, he grew afraid to.

'Dear sir, let go! Let go! Let go! Let go!'

Still it didn't work.

'Hey, Chomsun, Chomsun!'

Chomsun and her mother had stayed inside, but this shout
brought them rushing out. I'd expected that my mother-in-law
would stick up for her husband, but that Chomsun would make
up her mind to take my side. What was she thinking of? Even
now I can't understand why, but after telling me herself to
teach her father a lesson, now she rushed up and twisted my
ear back to yell into it:

'You bastard! You perisher, killing my father!'

That broke my spirit completely. I ended up senseless. My
mother-in-law attacked me too, and twisted the other ear back
and yelled into it. I was helpless. The old man picked up the
stick and gave a vicious downward blow, but I deliberately
didn't try to avoid it. I gazed blankly into Chomsun's face. I
just couldn't understand her, however hard I tried.

But I know what I'd done wrong, of course. I'd made my
father-in-law beg me for mercy.

This was the reason why I got whipped until my head split,
but this was a point on which my father-in-law was conspicu-
ously good. Any ordinary man would perhaps have given me
my back pay, but would have sent me packing. No one else
but him would have wiped my broken head himself with a bit
of cotton wool, put a packet of cigarette's in my pocket, slapped me on the back, and said: 'I'll let you get married this

autumn without fail. Don't say anything, but go and get on with ploughing the field for the beans, in the valley at the back.'

I felt so grateful to my father-in-law that I almost cried without realizing it. I'd expected to be leaving Chomsun and be chucked out, and was surprised by what he said.

'Father-in-law, sir, I'll never do such a thing again,' I swore, and rapidly put the A-frame on my back and set out for my place of work.

THE BUCKWHEAT SEASON

YI HYO-SUK

Translated by Shin Hyun-song

Summer markets were doomed to listlessness right from the start, so that although the sun was still halfway up the sky, the market-place was lonely and desolate. And the fierce rays of the sun, stabbing through the cloth canopies, were burning the shoppers' backs.

Already, half the villagers who'd come to the market had gone back home. The woodchoppers, with only sluggish business, were wandering around the market-place. But they couldn't be expected to stand about for ever, watching people who were satisfied to buy just a couple of bottles of paraffin and a few fish.

The swarms of flies and bands of young louts were all irritating. Finally, Huh Saengwon,* the left-handed drapery pedlar with the pock-marked face, turned to his colleague and friend Cho Sondal.

'Shall we call it a day?'

'Good idea. I ask you, when did we ever have a good day's trading her at Bongpyong market? We'll have to hope we make a bit of money at the market at Daehwa tomorrow.'

---

*The terms 'Saengwon', 'Sondal', and 'Chomji' were all titles given to men of letters in the Chosun dynasty of Korea, although in popular usage they subsequently took on the general meaning of 'Mr'. These terms are very rarely found in Korea today.

185

'That means walking all night.'

'Well, there's going to be a moon, isn't there?'

Seeing Cho Sondal count the day's taking, jangling the money as he did, Huh Saengwon took down the canopy and gathered in his wares that lay displayed in front of him. The rolls of cotton and silk filled both wicker chests to the top. Odds and ends of cloth were left strewn untidily over the surface of the straw mat.

Other pedlars were also starting to take down their canopies, and the shrewd ones were already leaving. The fishmonger, the tinker, the toffeeman, the ginger merchant ... they had all disappeared. Tomorrow there were markets at Jinbu and Daehwa, and if they wanted to be at one of those, they would have to trek across twenty-five, thirty kilometres, all through the night.

The market-place was in a shambles, like the house of someone who has just had a feast, and the inns exploded with the sound of bickering and fighting. Mixed with the sound of a drunkard's swearing, came the shrill voice of a young woman cursing. It was what people had come to expect at the end of a market day.

'Saengwon, don't try to hide it from me. I know what you're thinking. You know what I mean, I mean you and the woman at the Chungju inn.'

Sondal said this to his friend as if he had been reminded by the woman's shouting, and grinned.

'No, I haven't got a chance. How do you expect me to beat all that competition from the younger men? Not a chance in hell.'

'Don't count yourself out yet. Most of them just go weak in the legs when they're with her; but I'll have to admit, that Dong-i has got her completely under his thumb.'

'That green-horn? He must have bribed her into it with trinkets. And to think I took him for an honest, hard-working boy!'

'Well, there's no knowing, I suppose. But come on, let's not stand around here. I'll treat you to a few drinks.'

Huh Saengwon didn't really feel like going, but he followed just the same.

Women had very little part in Huh Saengwon's life. He didn't have the courage to lift up his pock-marked face, and no one ever expressed any affection for him. His whole life had been a distorted and barren task. At the mere mention of the Chungju woman, he would go red in the face and his legs would turn to jelly.

When he came face to face with Dong-i at the inn, he could not help losing his temper. Saengwon couldn't bear watching him womanize, and doing it with some skill, his flushed face propped above the table. Saengwon burst out and told him how absurd he looked; how disgraceful he was, a green-horn, still wet behind the ears, drinking himself stupid from the early afternoon and going around whoring, giving honest pedlars a bad name. How dare he call himself one of them! As soon as they met Saengwon began telling him off.

When Dong-i turned and looked at him with bloodshot eyes and a face which said 'mind your own business', Saengwon couldn't hold back his anger and help hitting him in the face. Dong-i himself got angry and sprang to his feet, but Saengwon did not back down, and said everything he had to say – how Dong-i's parents must really be pleased to see him now, drinking and carrying on with women, and that being a pedlar called for a solid and frugal life, instead of living the way he did. He shouted at him to get out and never come back.

Despite this abuse, Dong-i did as he was told and walked out of the place without a word. Seeing this unexpected submission, Saengwon began to feel rather sorry for him and regretted having gone as far as he had, especially when they hardly knew each other.

The Chungju woman wasn't too pleased with the incident. Pouting, she complained that there was no need for all the insults and roughing up, if only because Dong-i was younger than him. She spoke curtly and slapped the dishes down. Cho Sondal cut in tactfully at this point, saying that kind of lesson would do the young people good.

'You've fallen for him, haven't you? Do you know, it's a crime to corrupt young men!' Huh lashed out at the Chungju woman. He caused quite a fuss as he got his nerve. And without knowing why, he suddenly wanted to drown himself in drink. He accepted every glass he was offered and poured it down his throat. As he became tipsy, he forgot to worry about women, and instead became anxious about what had happened to Dong-i.

'What was I going to do after I'd taken away his woman, especially in my position . . .'

He even cursed himself for being so damn stupid. So when Dong-i came running in, hardly able to breathe from excitement, Saengwon put down his glass at once and followed him out of the inn at a run.

'Saengwon, your donkey, it's ripped its harness and all hell's broken loose!'

'Must be those bloody hooligans at it again!'

Of course he was concerned for his animal, but more than that, he was moved by the fact that Dong-i took the trouble to come and tell him. As he ran down to the market-place, his eyes felt hot.

'What can you do with those rowdy yobs.'

'I'll see to it that anyone who roughed up my donkey won't get away with it!'

He had spent half his life, twenty years, with the animal, sleeping in the same inn, soaking in the same light of the moon as they tramped about from market to market, and those twenty years had made them age in the same way.

The dishevelled mane of the ass was like that of its master, and like its master, it had wet, sticky eyes. Its tail, cut short into the shape of a broom, swished about in vain as it tried to chase away the flies gathering around its rear. The hooves, worn to the quick, had been trimmed many times and re-shod with iron; but with no hope of ever growing again, the hooves bled through the gaps in the worn-out horseshoes.

The donkey recognized its master by smell and greeted him noisily, as if it had at last found someone to complain to. When he stroked and patted the back of its neck, as he would comfort a child, the animal twitched its nostrils and snorted. Mucus from its nose sprayed out.

Huh Saengwon had been through a lot for this animal over the many years that they'd been together. It looked as though the hoodlums had been vicious, for the donkey was quivering, and had worked itself up into quite a state, sweating heavily.

The bridle had come off and the saddle lay fallen on the

ground. Huh Saengwon stood there damning and cursing, but most of the hoodlums had already disappeared, and the few who remained behind seemed to get a little scared and started drifting away.

'It's not our doing. The stupid animal's gone all crazy because of the mare!' one little runny-nosed youngster shouted at him from a distance.

'Why that little devil! Listen to him!'

'When Kim Chomji's donkey left, your animal started kicking up dirt and foaming at the mouth and jumping about like a mad bull. We were only standing around watching. See for yourself. Look at the thing under its belly!' the little squirt shouted cheekily, and cackled with laughter.

Saengwon couldn't help blushing, and had to move in front of the donkey's belly to hide it.

'Ha! That randy old ass!'

At the chuckling and giggling Saengwon winced, and in the end, unable to hold back his anger, he ran after the youngsters with his whip.

'Ha! Catch us if you can, you left-handed cripple!'

No matter how hard he tried, there was no chance of catching the brats darting away. He couldn't get his hands on any of them, and finally threw down the whip. The alcohol was going to his head, and he felt hot and breathless.

'Oh, leave them alone and let's get out of here,' Dong-i said. 'There'll be no end to it if you get mixed up with them. Hooligans at the market-place are worse than the adults.'

Cho Sondal and Dong-i each saddled his donkey and started loading. The sun had already moved closer to the western hills.

In the twenty years that he had been going round the markets selling cloth, Saengwon would rarely miss the market at Bongpyong. He sometimes roved around Chungju, Jechun and other neighbouring counties, and even as far as the southern provinces, but apart from going to Kangneung to get his wares, he did not, as a rule, wander outside the county of Bongpyong.

As the markets opened every five days, he moved from village to village, more regular than the phases of the moon. He often spoke with pride of his home county, Chongju, but that did not mean he ever went back there to enjoy being where he had come from. He felt most at home among mountains and lakes. When, after trudging half the day, he approached the village where a market was to stand – especially when it was just getting dark and lamps flickered in the distance – and the scruffy donkey gave out a mighty bray, he would always get into the same animated mood, his heart beating faster.

Long ago when he was young, he had saved up his money for the future. But one year, during the Lunar Mid-July Buddhist Festival, he spent his money like water and got involved in gambling. It wasn't long before he lost everything he had. In fact his money only lasted three days. He had nearly reached the point of having to sell his donkey, but couldn't bring himself to do it because he was so fond of the animal. In consequence, he had no choice but to go back and start wandering around the markets again.

When he had sneaked out of the village with his animal, he stood and wept by the roadside, stroking its back and saying how glad he was not to have lost it. As his debts grew, his hopes of ever saving up again were smashed for good, and the best he could manage was to avoid being starved to death, and not by such a big margin either.

Even though he had thrown his money about like water, he had never been able to win over or master even one woman. Women were cold and heartless creatures. He grew sad when he realized that perhaps fate had prepared a road for him far, far away from the solace of any woman. The only being he ever felt close to was his donkey.

But despite all this, there was no way he could forget one very special incident. There had been nothing like it before and nothing since. It had happened at the time when he first started coming to Bongpyong market, and whenever he turned it over in his mind, all life was worth living again.

'It was a moonlit night, and how it ever happened, I don't know.'

Huh Saengwon was going to tell that story again tonight. Cho Sondal, ever since the day he had called himself Saengwon's friend, had heard the story countless times, but wasn't really in a position to let him know how weary he was of it. In any case, Saengwon would always pretend not to notice his friend's boredom and have his way, repeating the story as often as he pleased.

'A moonlit night is the right time to tell a story like that.'

Sondal turned his head and looked aside; of course it was not because he was touched, but because he was deeply moved by the beauty of the moonlight. Although the moon wasn't quite full, it was pouring down its soft silvery light.

It was a thirty-kilometre trek to Daehwa. They would have to climb over two hills, ford one stream, trudge across wide plains, and thread their way through hilly paths.

The road here clung to the side of a hill, and the hour, now past midnight, had made everything silent and still. In the emptiness, the moon was breathing like some living beast, and the sound of its breathing travelled through the air, and it seemed as if the sound itself could be caught by stretching out one hand and grasping it.

The bean plants and the maize were being drenched in moonbeams. Buckwheat grew thick in the fields on the hillside, and its flowers, just beginning to peep out, were like grains of salt scattered over the ground. Sondal felt he would suffocate under the softness of the moon. The purple tinted air somehow seemed so delicate, and the steps of the donkey were cool and satisfying.

As the road was narrow, the three men and their animals stretched out in a long line. The tuneful ringing of the bells diffused sweetly over the buckwheat fields. To Dong-i, bringing up the rear, the sound of Saengwon talking at the front couldn't be heard all that clearly, but he himself was given over to his own satisfaction and contentment at the freshness and mildness of the night.

'It was a night just like this one, before a market. Well, as the bare earthen room of the inn was so hot and all, I got up and went down to the stream to have a bath. Bongpyong was just as it is now. It was all buckwheat wherever you looked, on the banks of the stream and everywhere, it was all covered with white blossoms. I could have taken off my clothes on the pebbles by the stream, but because the moon was so bright I went in to the water mill. Well, what do you think? By some chance, I bumped into Mr Sung's daughter. At the time, she was the most beautiful young girl in the whole of Bongpyong. It must have been in our stars that we met like that.'

Sondal replied that it must have been, and took a long drag from his cigarette, as if he were trying to economize on his words. The mellow purple-tinted smoke spread out into the night and dissolved, became invisible.

'Of course she wasn't there waiting for me, but that's not to say that there was anyone special she was waiting for either; she was crying, of all things. I knew a bit about the money problems her family had, and in fact they were just about to run off because of their debts. With all this going on in her own house, how much do you think that poor girl must have suffered? They wanted to marry her off to a suitable young man, but she was going to resist with her life.'

There was a pause, and then Saengwon went on: 'But one thing about girls, when they start crying there is nothing which tugs at your heart with more appeal ... nothing. At first she seemed a little startled. But she had so many worries, she let down her guard after a bit, as happens in these situations, and we got to talking. Yes, the more I think about it, the more strange it seems. It was an extraordinary night ... fabulous.'

'Wasn't it the day after that they disappeared?'

'By the time the next market was due to come round, the whole family had vanished into thin air. The market buzzed with gossip about their disappearance, and they all speculated that the most likely thing to happen to the girl was that she'd been sold to a drinking tavern. Just imagine how many times I searched around Jechun market, but she'd disappeared like a bubble on the water. So that first night with her was my last. Ever since then I've held Bongpyong dear in my heart, and the memory of that place has never left me.'

'You were really blessed to have something as wonderful as that happen to you. Think about the ordinary run-of-the-mill bloke, breeding troublesome kids. And what about the worries piling up? I shiver even to think about it. But on the other hand, I can't really grow old and die a travelling pedlar. I'm going to give this up in the autumn and set up a small shop at Daehwa or thereabouts, and bring all my family to live with me. You can't slog on all your life as if you'll stay young for ever.'

'If I met up with a girl I once knew, we might settle down together, but right now, I want to walk along this road and look at that moon and carry on this kind of life till the day I drop dead.'

They came off the hilly path and onto the main road. Dong-i moved up to the front with the others, and the donkeys walked side by side.

'You know, you're a young man and in the prime of your life. I'm sorry about what happened at the inn today. It was my fault. I hope you won't hold that against me.'

'No, of course not. I'm the one who should be ashamed of himself. Chasing women isn't the right thing for someone in my position. Really, all I ever think about is my mother.'

Dong-i's voice had become more relaxed after hearing Saengwon tell his story.

'At the inn, I was really hurt when you mentioned my mother and father, because I have no father. My mother is the only blood relative I have in the whole world.'

'Why? Did he die?'

'No, he wasn't there from the beginning.'

As Saengwon and Sondal laughed and chuckled, Dong-i blushed but had to stand by what he had said.

'I was too embarrassed to tell you, but it's true. Mother gave birth to a premature child out of wedlock at Jechun, and not surprisingly was kicked out of her house. So I've lived my life never having seen my father's face, nor knowing where he came from.'

Because they found themselves at the foot of a hill, the three of them got off their donkeys. The ridge was rough and it was a strain to talk, so that not a word was said for some time. The donkeys slipped and slid as they slogged on. Saengwon had to stop many times on the climb to get his breath back and to rest his legs. These days, each time he struggled up a hill he was reminded of his age. He envied Dong-i and other young men like him. Sweat poured down his back.

On the other side of the hill was the stream. The wooden foot-bridge, washed down in the rainy season, lay in the water with its end broken loose from their side of the bank. They had no choice but to ford the stream.

Taking off his thin shorts and tying them around his back, Saengwon jumped into the water looking absurd, half naked. The sweat had been pouring down his back, but now the coldness of the water at night stabbed him to the bone.

'So, who brought you up then?'

'Mother had no choice but to get another man as her husband and sell liquor. And my step-father turned out to be a regular villain. You wouldn't believe how much I was beaten, ever since I can remember. I didn't have a single day of peace. My mother herself got beaten and kicked when she tried to stop him beating me. She even had knives brandished in her face. You can just imagine what a state the house was in by then. So I ran away from home when I was seventeen, and I've been on the road ever since.'

'I thought earlier tonight that you must have had some reason for your behaviour at such a young age, and now I've heard your story, I can't help feeling for you.'

The water was deep and came up to his waist. The current was powerful, and the stones he groped for with his feet were mossy and slippery, and he felt as if he might slip and fall at any moment.

Cho Sondal and his ass had already neared the other bank, but Dong-i stayed behind to help Saengwon as he crossed, and these two fell back a long way.

'Was Jechun your mother's home county?'

'No, it's not. I've never heard the whole story, but I've heard that she came originally from Bongpyong.'

'Bongpyong! And do you by any chance know your father's surname?'

'How could I know that? I've never heard it in my life.'

'Yes, of course . . .'

As he was muttering to himself and blinking his cloudy eyes, Saengwon stepped carelessly and lost his balance. With a big splash he was thrown into the water over his head. The more he thrashed about in panic, the harder it was to get himself on his feet again. Dong-i came up shouting, and by the time he caught up with Saengwon he had already been carried a good distance downstream. He looked more wretched than a dog that's just crawled out of the water.

Dong-i was able to take him on his back without much difficulty. Although he was soaked through, it was no effort for a burly young man like Dong-i to carry the thin bony body.

'I'm sorry to have put you through all this trouble. I don't know what's come over me. I'm not myself today.'

'Oh, forget it. It's nothing.'

194

'And so, your mother, does she seem to look for your father at all?'

'She always said that she wanted to meet him once again.'

'Where is she now?'

'She's separated from my step-father now, and is at Jechun. I'm thinking of taking her to Bongpyong in the autumn. If I work my fingers to the bone, then we'll manage to survive, I suppose...'

'Of course, that's a very kind thought. So, in the autumn, eh?'

It was warm and comforting to press his bony body against the muscular back of Dong-i, and when they had finished crossing the stream, he felt sad to let go of him and wished he could be carried a little longer.

'What's up with you, Saengwon? You've been blundering into this and that all day,' Sondal said looking at him, and finally couldn't help bursting into laughter.

'It's because of the donkey. I lost my feet thinking about the donkey. Haven't you heard? Although my animal looks so run down now, he's fathered some foals, you know, from that mare at the Kangnung inn in the township. Those cute little things with the pointed ears playing about tinkling their bells... could there be anything more endearing than a young donkey? You know, I've often gone round the village on purpose just to see them.'

'It must have been some donkey to make a man fall into the water.'

Saengwon squeezed the water from his clothes and put them back on again. His teeth were chattering and his chest trembled. He was freezing cold, but for some reason he couldn't have felt lighter inside.

'Let's go on to the tavern and make a fire out in the yard and warm up. And don't forget to give some hot water to the donkeys. After the market at Daewha tomorrow, I'm off to Jechun.'

'Saengwon, do you mean you're going to Jechun as well?'

'Yes, it's been a long time. Are you coming with me Dong-i?'

When the donkeys started walking again, the whip was in Dong-i's left hand.

And Saengwon, who had been blind to the things happening in front of his eyes like some blind night goblin, couldn't help noticing that Dong-i, too, was left-handed. His steps were light, and the tinkling of the bells spread still clearer into the fields. The moon was riding steep in the sky.

THE FIRE

HYUN CHIN-KON

Translated by Kathryn Kisray

Though she was drowned in sleep, Suni, who was only fourteen and had been married just over a month, felt oppressed as if a huge rock was laid on her chest. If it were a rock, should she not at least feel its coolness? But what she felt on her chest, delicate like a dove's, was heavy like the stuffy and wet pre-monsoon air. It breathed heavily like a dog in the heat of mid-summer. And suddenly, Suni's waist and hip ached as if they were being chopped off, torn into shreds, and smashed into pieces. She could not stand the throbbing, burning pain. It was like an iron club thrust up her through the guts up to the throat and the sharp pain caused her mouth to open wide and her body to jolt.

If only she could wake up but with endless chores, carrying around water on her head, pounding crops in the mortar, water-milling, carrying meals out to the workers in the rice-paddies, her body, exhausted, was unable to get up in spite of all her effort. She was, of course, not unconscious. She thought, 'I must wake up, otherwise I'll die, no doubt I'll die.' Her eyes were tightly glued up. She could not chase away the sleep which was like thick muddy water. For a while her mouth kept on opening wide in agony, her body kept on jolting, and then like people who try to fight great pain, she even ground her teeth. After a while, which seemed ages, she was at last able

197

to open her eyes, as if released from the claws of a nightmare. She then saw her husband's face, which covered hers like the lid of an iron kettle. The dark area of his cauldron-like face was fused into the darkness, but from the blackness emerged the gleaming whites of his eyes and the lips – twisted and drivelling, revealing whenever they opened, the deeply yellowed teeth. This was clearly discernible in the dark. It was too frighteningly distinct. The huge face inflated more and more, his brown sun-tanned shoulder enlarged as well and soon seemed to her, like the bulk of a house. Suni shuddered and shivered with fear which she felt in her stomach, and also with the pain that wrung her guts. Alternately, she was pursued by the obdurate sleep and by the fear. Suddenly she opened her eyes to the horrifying reality.

At long last when she freed herself from the agony, the short June night had already started to dawn. The silhouette of this mass began to move and walked out of the room – a room hardly big enough to contain him. He must be going out to do his early morning stint in the fields. Only then Suni dared get up, letting out a long sigh of relief. The window was black as if it had been painted with Chinese ink. It turned slowly to grey and then the flickering yellow light sieved through the straw curtain. The shabby dressing table and its mirror reflecting light in one corner of the room, the fermenting soya-bean cake, all confirmed that this was the room of her 'arch enemy'. Above all, she was lying on a mattress. 'What happened?' She concentrated her thought. Last night, she had gone to sleep at some other place, and certainly not on this mattress. In order to escape this nightly torture for just once, as soon as she had finished the washing up she had sneaked out and hidden herself in the barn. With the two last remaining straw sacks as her companion, she spread one empty straw sack and hardly had time to stretch her legs when she fell asleep. How did she get back to this room again? That accursed enemy must have searched every corner with his lustful eyes and carried me without any difficulty and put me in this 'accursed room', and then must have done the accursed thing to me. These thoughts trailed off yet again as the sleepiness invaded her smashed body.

'Aren't you up yet? You've got to cook the mash for the cows,' came the frightful voice of her mother-in-law.

Even before these words were finished, Suni sprang up with jerk. While one hand was rubbing her sleepy eyes, the other gathered the clothes, which her husband had stripped off, and put them on. Did not the mother-in-law sleep till now? There was no difference between the matriarch and an army commander calling the attention of soldiers. Even in her sleep Suni was scared of her mother-in-law's shouting orders.

She hurried out to the wooden floor outside finding that it wasn't quite day yet. Through the thick mist, the lusterless pale moon was setting in the west, like a dead man's lightless eyeball.

She lit a fire under the mash she had prepared the previous night. Though it was summer, the early morning air was chilly, and the fire was delightful to look into. She enjoyed looking at the licking flames swallow the pine branches with which she fed the kitchen fire place. Suni's day started, her day rendered even more exhausting by the wretched night she had had.

When the cow mash was cooked, she had to fetch water to make breakfast. As she put the water jug on her head and stretched her arms to hold its ears, cool, damp air crept under her arms. She reached the stream, set down the jug, and stretched herself. The mountains and the hills still seemed to be wandering in dreamland, covered with white mist. The rain which had made all the farmers jump with joy a few days ago, had filled every single paddy. The paddies reflected the misty atmosphere, and were shimmering as if a blanket of mercury had been thrown over them. The replanted rice seedlings started to rub open their sleepy green eyes. In the midst of all this, the stream ran along, singing as if it were the only one awake while everything else was asleep. Its face was as clear as crystal, and was like an alert eye – wide awake and so aware. Suni dipped the gourd dipper into the water. The water rushed from all directions to that spot as if it wanted to heal the wound made by the dipper, but soon spread away in a larger and larger circle and merged with the rest, as if relieved that the wound was not at all serious. Suni drew more water with the dipper.

She brought back one jug of water, and went back to fetch another. This time she saw several minnows playing fearlessly on the surface. She has wanted to catch them before. She could not stand their teasing attitude. She held her breath and silently and carefully plunged both her hands to catch them, but they kept agilely slipping away. After having failed at several attempts, she burst into anger, fetching some stones and threw them blindly. There was quite a commotion, with water splashing everywhere – her face, her skirt – but those little devils managed to dodge away every time. Her irritation at not being able to catch any nearly drove her to tears. Again she tried to grab them, and at last an unlucky one got caught in her hands. As the water drained from her hands, the fish jumped in a desperate fight to save its life, and this amused her. Presently, the poor thing lay in her palm exhausted. She cruelly threw it down on to the ground. After a faint twist as if the drop hurt, the tiny fish's life came to an end: yet she was not sure and she touched it with her index finger. Then as she realized that the fish which was alive a minute ago was now a lifeless little piece of flesh, the fear of having taken a life seized her. From the very spot, she fancied its avenging spirit coming out. As she filled the jug in a hurry and started to walk away, she had the sensation that someone was pulling her hair.

She wasn't allowed even a moment to get her breath back. She had to mill the barley as soon as she had finished the breakfast. Her back was breaking as she pounded in the mortar. Dragged by the heavy weight of the mortar, she nearly fell head-first into it several times. She felt as if her arms were coming off, but she had to keep on working even if that meant generating superhuman effort.

Again it was lunch time. She must hurry over the meal and take it to the farmers planting seedlings in the field. She must carry the soup and the rice. The tray loaded with the soup and the rice on her head pressed upon her and pushed her neck in as if it were the neck of a turtle. She felt as if she was pressed down under the unbearable weight. She struggled forward step by step with the heavy load on her head.

Not a cloud could be seen in the clear sky, and the sun in the middle of the sky was shedding fiery light all over. In the broad and level rice-paddies, 'the sons of the Earth' were busy transplanting seedlings, as if they were playing with their mothers' breasts. The action of bending forwards and backwards lay bare, a deeply tanned back, and their faces were coated with mud as they tried to wipe off the sweat running off their faces. They did not want, however, a single moment to be wasted, trying to plant that one more, not letting escape a single sigh. On the contrary, they sang most freely and gaily as they laboured.

The soaked earth was drying its moisture under the sun. The weeds along the paddies resigned themselves to be stamped on by people walking indiscriminately over them, waiting for their feet to pass by, to lift back their faces to put on green smiles. There was joy of hardy and strong life, and the never ending effort to make life more fulfilling. It was a world full of the healthy life where the unhealthy had no place.

Suni was too frail to inhale this invigorating air in this ocean of bright and strong sunlight. She felt her eyes swivel and her head going dizzy. Her whole body was streaming with sweat and yet she felt a chill running down her spine. As she was just about to jump over a small puddle made by the rain, the sun reflected in it made her feel black in her eyes. All of a sudden, the minnow which she had killed earlier was pursuing her breathlessly, changing the form presently into a gigantic yellowtail and blocked her way. As she struggled to flee from it, she momentarily became aware of what was happening. Someone grabbed her hair and swirled her round. She heard thunder and dropped unconscious.

After a long while, she came round, but did not recover completely. Dumbfounded, and staring blankly, she vaguely recalled in succession that she was on her way to take the lunch tray to the labourers in the paddies, then the blinding sun in the wide plain, the minnow in gigantic form blocking her way. What had happened to the meal tray she was carrying? As she became aware of what had happened, she gave out a faint cry and sank. There she was again in the accursed room. Like a mad woman, she dashed out of it. Her eyes rolled with fear and horror as if possessed by an evil spirit.

Her mother-in-law, stirring wheat with a rake on the ground, cast a sharp look. Even if she were to forgive Suni for wasting the soup and the rice, she hated her for breaking the pieces of crockery among the precious few she had. But the old woman had to admit that she couldn't scold someone who had just recovered from fainting.

'Are you all right? Why don't you stay in your room and rest a little longer? Go back and lie down.' She seemed trying hard to sound kind and gentle. Suni, unsteadily but determined, came down to the yard.

'I'm telling you to go back to your room and rest!' She raised her voice a little.

'No, I feel all right.' She would rather die than go into that room again.

'Here you go disobeying me again!' And suddenly, as if she could not bear any more of her hatred, she rushed towards Suni holding the rake upside down and attacked her.

'You careless little bitch! How dare you creep out after breaking all the dishes, you shameless bitch. You smashed the two new bowls I had bought only on last market day.' Raving like this, she hit her with the handle of the rake wherever she could: head, back, legs . . . but she didn't feel any pain. On the contrary, she got a queer sense of pleasure as she felt her body smashed to pulp.

'Look at this stubborn bitch! Even this beating doesn't make her cry!' yelled the mother-in-law, and went on beating until she got tired, and throwing away the rake, she shouted. 'I can't stand the sight of you any more, get lost into the kitchen and cook the supper!'

Suni obeyed and prepared the rice for dinner.

And so, another day was setting. The kitchen was dark as if the night had already descended there. Dreadful night, hateful night was approaching her with its mouth wide open. The fear she felt at the advent of dusk assaulted her again. Each time she tried to escape it, and each time she had failed. Her small head was pulled apart in search of a way to save herself from the night. As she did not find a solution, she grew miserable, and pitied her fate. The fact that she was sent many hundred *li** away to be married, only to endure the unspeakable suffering, every night and every day, and above all to put up with the degrading beating she got from her mother-in-law today made her infinitely sad, and so much so that she could not

---

*li = a unit of measuring distance, 10 *li* is 4 km.

prevent her eyes from welling with tears. As she wiped the tears from her face, not only her fist but her forearm became wet with tears from the eyes. Right at that moment, someone shook her shoulder. It was her husband. She felt her liver shrivelling up in fear. He had finished the day's work and had come back. His frightening sunburnt face was wearing an unbecoming smile. She was like a chick caught in the grip of a hawk claw.

'Why are you crying? Don't cry please, please don't,' he whispered, trying to comfort her. He wiped her tears with his hand as big as the lid of iron pot, and then went out of the kitchen.

After seeing her husband, she could not endure it any more. The huge rock which pressed her body, the iron club which smashed her whole body . . . all of a sudden, the tears dried up, and she racked her brain for an escape from this loathsome night. No, it wasn't the fault of the night. It was because of that accursed room. If the room wasn't there, he would just wipe my tears and leave me alone. He would have nowhere to put me through that agony again. Wasn't there a way to make the room disappear?

The rice boiled over furiously. As she stood up to lift the heavy lid of the pot, she noticed the box of matches that was lying there. An idea flashed through her like lightning. She picked it up. Then casting a searching eye around her, she quickly hid it in her bosom.

'Why didn't I think of this before, it's so easy,' she thought to herself with a smile.

That night, without any apparent cause, a fire started from the room opposite the main one, and fanned by the strong wind, the whole roof was up in flames in no time. Suni watched the fire from beside the wall with the neighbour at the back. There was life in her face as she jumped to the right and skipped to the left with joy.

A LUCKY DAY

HYUN CHIN-KON

Translated by Chung Chong-wha

Demurely cloudy, it looked as if it might snow but, instead, it only rained drearily for a while. But for Kim Chomchi,* a rickshawman working around the little East Gate, it was the first lucky day he had had in a long while. Starting the day by taking the next-door mistress who wanted to go within the Gate – not that she really lived outside it – to the tram stop, he spent the day lingering about the station sending almost imploring glances at people getting off the tram until he ended up by taking a man dressed in a suit, probably a school-master, to Tong-Kwang School.

The first time he earned thirty *chon*,† the second time fifty *chon* – it was not a common occurrence in the morning rush. When ten *chon* pieces and three *chon* worth of nickel fell on his palm, Kim, who had not seen any money for almost ten luckless days, was almost tearful with joy. Besides, that eighty *chon* could not have come to him at a more opportune moment. He could not only wet his parched throat with a bowl or two of cheap liquor but could also buy his wife a bowl of *sullung-tang*‡.

---

*Chomchi: a title for a person at the lower class of society.
†*Chon*: a unit of currency, a one hundredth of one *won*, now obsolete.
‡*Sullung-tang*: a kind of beef soup with rice in it.

It was over a month since his wife started coughing. To the Kims, who went more days without eating than eating, there was, of course, no question of getting any medicine. It was not that he really could not afford it if he tried but Kim Chomchi stuck firmly to his belief that illness when made much of always returned with a vengeance. Also since she had never been to see a doctor, how could he knew what she had? But from the way she had lain there flat on her back neither being able to turn on one side or the other, let alone get up, she must have been seriously ill.

Her illness got to this serious stage about ten days ago when she got an indigestion from eating boiled millet. That time too, Kim had earned some money in a long while and brought her a bag of millet and a bushel of wood for ten *chon*. According to Kim, that confounded wretch had thrown the whole thing into a pot and boiled it. But being hungry and the fire slow to burn, the wretch had thrown the spoon aside and grabbed the still uncooked millet with her hands and stuffed it into her mouth until her cheeks bulged as if someone was after her. That evening, she started rolling on the floor, her eyes glaring, screaming that her heart burned and her stomach ached. Kim Chumchi had then fallen into a violent rage.

'You confounded bitch! Ill when there's not enough to eat, ill when there's too much! What do you want? Why don't you look at me straight?' Shouting thus he had slapped her hard across the face. Her glaring eyes gained concentration but dew drops formed on her lashes, and Kim had felt his own eyes grow hot with tears.

The ailing woman, however, still had not had enough of eating. For three days she had been plaguing her husband to buy her a bowl of *sullung-tang*.

'Confounded bitch, when you can't even swallow boiled millet, how are you going to swallow beef and rice soup?' Kim had yelled at her but he had not felt good about not being able to buy her a bowl.

Now he could buy her a bowl. He could also buy his two-year-old son, Gaetong, who had been crying from hunger, tugging at his ailing mother, some gruel. Clasping his eighty *chon* firmly in his hand, Kim Chumchie felt full in his heart.

His luck that day, however, did not run out there. It was when he was just coming out of the school gate, wiping his neck dripping with sweat and rain with a greasy towel. From behind came, 'Hey, rickshaw there.' Kim could guess at a glance that it was a student who stopped him. The student asked him brusquely, 'How much to the South Gate?' He was probably a boarder at the school on his way home for a winter vacation. He must have decided to leave today but was rather stuck with all his luggage in the rain. Then seeing Kim, he must have rushed out to call him; otherwise why should he have come after him his shoe-string still untied and getting his suit – though worn out – soaking wet in this rain?

'Do you mean the station?' asked Kim, hesitating for a moment. Was it because he didn't want to go that far in this rain without even a raincoat? Was he satisfied with his first, then his second earning? No, it was not that. It was because he was suddenly overcome with fear faced with such a string of luck. Also his wife's pleading as he was leaving the house in the morning troubled him. When the mistress next-door came to call him, his wife, with an imploring light in her unusually sunken eyes which seemed the only living thing on her emaciated face, had clung to him to stop him.

'Please don't go today. Stay at home, I am so ill...' Saying this in a faint and what sounded like a mere whisper, she had gasped for breath.

'Bloody bitch! I never heard anything like it. If I stay in, who's going to feed us?' As he was about to leave the house, not taking any notice of her words, the ailing woman waved her hand in the air as if to grab him. Soon afterwards, he heard her hoarse voice crying after him, 'Don't go out. Oh, then at least come back soon!'

The sight of his wife's almost tearful face, her unusually large eyes, and her hands which shook convulsively rose flickering before Kim Chumchie's eyes when he heard that she had said she was going to the station.

'How much to the station?' the student asked again. Then as if anxious, he gazed at the rickshawman's face and murmured to himself, 'There's a train for Inchon at eleven, then at two, I think.'

'One *won* and fifty *chon*.' Before he knew it, the word was out of his mouth. Though he called it himself, Kim Chumchie was amazed at the enormity of the sum. How long has it been since he had called such a sum! And his desire to earn such a sum drove away all his anxiety about his wife. She'll be all right for another day or two, he thought. Whatever happened, it was not possible to forego this stroke of fortune which was more than double the what he had earned earlier in the day.

'One and fifty is a bit too much,' said the student inclining his head a little.

'No, sir. It's more than fifteen *li** from here and in such a wet day, you should give a little extra.' The rickshawman's grinning face was overflowing with undisguised joy.

'All right then. But let's hurry.' The generous young customer hurried away in quick steps to dress and get his things ready.

Carrying the student on his rickshaw, Kim Chomchi's steps felt strangely light. Rather than running, he felt as if he was flying. The wheels too spun so fast that he felt that the rickshaw was sliding on ice like skates, though it was true that the frozen ground was slippery with ice.

But at last his legs grew heavier. It was because he was approaching his house. His heart felt oppressed by fresh anxieties.

'Please don't go today. I am so ill . . .' The words rang in his ears. The ailing woman's sunken eyes seemed to glare at him reproachfully. And at that moment, he thought he heard his son wailing. He thought he also heard the death-rattle.

'What's the matter? I am going to miss the train,' the customer's impatient voice barely reached his ears. Suddenly coming to himself again, Kim found himself standing awkwardly in the middle of the street his hands on the handle of the rickshaw.

'Yes, sir,' replying, Kim Chomchi started to run again. As the distance between him and his house grew, his steps again became light – as if he could drive worries and anxieties from his mind by moving his legs swiftly.

When that amazingly huge sum of one and fifty *won* came into his hand at the station, Kim, forgetting that he had trudged almost ten *li* in the rain as he himself had said a while ago, felt grateful as if he had been given it for nothing. He was

---

*li is a unit of distance; 10 *li* is about 4 km.

overjoyed as if he had become a millionaire overnight. To the young customer who was young enough to be his son, he bowed deeply several times saying, 'Good day to you, sir,' in an obsequious manner.

But the thought of going back in the rain pulling an empty rickshaw somehow daunted him. As sweat from his hard labour began to cool on him, chilliness began to spread from his famished belly and his dripping clothes; and he felt acutely what a wonderful and yet a painful thing this one and fifty *won* was. His steps as he was leaving the station were without any strength. He felt that his whole body was shrinking and that he would drop on the ground there and then and not be able to get up again.

'Going back with an empty rickshaw in this bloody rain! The bloody rain, it keeps on hitting my face,' he muttered to himself, getting angry as if rebelling against someone. At that moment, a new idea lighted up his mind: the thought that if he hung around here, he might be able to pick up another customer. Since this was such a lucky day, who knows whether such a stroke of luck would not fall on him again? And he soon came to a firm belief – a belief on which he was ready lay a bet – that another stroke of luck was waiting for him without fail. But because of the harassment of rickshawmen at the station, he could not wait in front of the station. So, as he had often done before, he parked his rickshaw on the pavement and on the tramway just a little away from the tram stop in front of the station and hovered about on the look-out for chances. A little later, a train came in and tens of people poured out of the station. Among them Kim, who was on the look-out for possible customers, spotted a woman with permed hair in high heel shoes and a cape, perhaps a retired *kisaeng*, a courtesan, or a high-school girl with fast habits. Slowly he approached her.

'My lady, take a rickshaw.'

The girl or whatever she was stood disdainfully for a while, her lips firmly pursed together and ignored him completely. Kim Chomchi, like a beggar, however, kept on importuning her, sending her imploring glances.

'My lady, tell me where you live. I will give you a better

price than rickshaw lads here,' said he with annoying persistence, about to handle her Japanese-style wicker trunk.

'Leave it alone! What a nuisance!' suddenly yelled the woman turning away from him. Taken aback, he retreated.

The tram arrived. Kim Chomchi glared reproachfully at those getting on the tram. But his intuition did not fail him. As the tram, now full, began to move away, there stood a man who had not managed to get on it. By the look of an enormous suitcase he carried with him, he must have been told to get off the crowded tram by the ticket man. Kim approached him.

'Take a rickshaw, sir.'

After haggling over the price for a while, he agreed to take him to Insa-dong for sixty *chon*. Curiously though, as his rickshaw got heavier, his body felt lighter, and as his rickshaw got lighter, his body heavier. But this time, he started to feel anxious. The sight of his house kept on rising before his eyes and now he didn't feel that he could afford to think about another stroke of fortune. Continually chiding his legs which felt like stubs of wood or something not his own, he could only rush along in a reckless pace. His steps were so hasty as to make the passers-by wonder why this drunkard of a rickshawman was rushing along the muddy road at such a pace. The sunless and rainy sky became dark and dusk seemed to be falling. Only when he reached Changkyong Palace did Kim stop to take a breath and slow his steps; and with each step as he approached his house, he strangely began to feel more relaxed. But that sense of ease was not coming from a real sense of relief; it was coming from his fear that the time was now come for him to face without any means of escape a great misfortune that was waiting for him around the corner. He floundered about to stretch this moment to stave off the misfortune for a little longer. He wanted to retain for as long as possible the happiness he felt in having earned such a miraculous sum of money. He cast his eyes about the place. It was as if he, now desperate, was pleading to someone to hold him back, to rescue him because it was no longer within his power to stop his legs from walking towards his misfortune.

At that moment, his friend Chisam emerged from a tavern in the street. His pink flabby face covered with black side-whiskers contrasted strangely with Kim Chomchi's sallow lean face marked by deep pits where a scrawny beard hung like pine needles stuck upside down.

'Hey, Kim Chomchi, you look as if you've been inside the Gate today and had a good day, eh? What about a bowl of something?' the fat man cried to the skinny man. His voice, unlike his appearance, was soft and suave. Kim Chomchi was overjoyed to run into this friend. He even felt grateful as if his friend had saved his life.

'You look as if you've already had a bowl or two. You had a good day too?' said he, his face relaxing into a smile.

'God, no. Is there any reason why a man should drink only when he's had a good day? But look here, old chap. You look like a drowning mouse. Come on in and dry up.'

The tavern was warm and cosy. Steam rose in great clouds every time a huge pot of loach soup was opened and on the grill was sizzling away beef, pork, liver, kidney, whiting and lentil pancakes. Sitting before the table laden with disorderly heaps of food, Kim Chomchi's empty stomach began to ache unbearably. If he had his way, he would have liked to swallow in one mouthful everything there and even then he would not have felt satisfied. But the hungry man first ordered a couple of lentil pancakes for they were rather filling and a bowl of loach soup. On tasting food, his famished stomach seemed to become even emptier and cried out for more and more food. In the twinkling of an eye, a bowl of loach soup with bean curds in it disappeared down his throat like water. With the third bowl of soup came two bowls of rice wine which had been heated warm. He drank this with Chisam and the liquor spread through his belly, empty till now, in no time and made his face flush with heat. Without pausing, he ordered another two bowls.

The hungry light began slowly to fade from Kim Chomchi's eyes. He ordered two pieces of rice cake on the grill to be chopped up and devoured them until his cheeks bulged. He then ordered two more bowls of wine.

'What do you mean two more? We've already had four bowls and that's forty *chon* already,' warned Chisam looking at Kim with puzzled eyes.

'Come, you stupid fool, what's forty *chon*? I made a fortune today. It was a really lucky day.'

'How much did you make?'

'Thirty *won*. I made thirty *won*. Where's the wine? Come on, it's all right. Swill it down. I made a fortune today, I tell you.'

'Gad, you're drunk. Now cut it out.'

'Fool, do I get sozzled on this? Come, have some more,' the drunken man cried pulling at Chisam's ear. Then he started picking a quarrel with a fourteen-year-old boy with a clean-shaven head who had come to serve him.

'You son-of-a-bitch, I told you to fill up.'

The monk-head merely giggled and glanced at Chisam as if asking what to do. The drunken man saw this and flew into a rage.

'Mother fucker, you don't believe that I have any money, eh?' He fumbled about his belt and produced a one *won* note and flung this before the boy. In the meantime a few pieces of silver fell on the floor clanging.

'Look, you've dropped some money. Why are you throwing money about the place?' his friend said picking them up.

Kim Chomchi fixed his gaze on the floor with his eyes wide open as if looking for his money even in his drunken state; then as if suddenly finding his behaviour disgusting, he suddenly jerked his head up and shouted angrily,

'Look, you bastards, do I have money or not? I'm going to break every bone in your body, bastards.' Then taking the coins from Chisam, he flung them against the wall.

'Bloody money ... son-of-a-bitch,' he cried. The coins fell back into a large brass washing basin clamouring loudly as if they were getting their just desserts.

Two more bowls of wine disappeared in no time. Kim Chomchi, sucking the wine from his beard and lips, sat back as if hugely pleased and stroked his beard.

'Fill up, fill up,' he shouted again. Gulping it down, he patted Chisam on the shoulder and suddenly laughed. His laughter was so loud that all the eyes in the tavern turned to him. The man laughed even louder.

'Look, Chisam. I'll tell you a funny story. I went to the station today with a customer.'

'Well?'

'It seemed a bit foolish to come back with an empty rickshaw, so I hung around the place for a bit waiting for customers. Well, there was this woman – a missus or maybe just a student, I don't know. It's so difficult to tell a lady from a whore these days. She was standing there in the rain wearing a cape. I approached her slowly and asked her whether she would like to take a rickshaw. I was just about to take her bag when she suddenly jerked my hand away and turned away screaming, "Leave me alone!" She sounded like a real nightingale, she did. Hah! Hah!'

Curiously enough Kim Chomchi imitated the sound of nightingale beautifully. Everyone burst into laughter.

'Little bitch, who wants to touch her anyway? "Leave me alone!" That was really unlady-like.'

Laughter got even louder, but before it died away, Kim Chomchi suddenly started sobbing.

Chisam looked at the drunken man, flabberghasted.

'What's the matter? Laughing one moment and crying the next?'

Kim Chomchi continued sobbing.

'My wife died,' he said.

'What? Your wife died? When?'

'Fool! What do you mean when? Today.'

'You madman, you're lying.'

'It's not a lie. She really died, really. . . . With my wife's dead body lying in the house, I am a bastard to get drunk, I am,' Kim sobbed even louder.

Chisam, as if suddenly finding that all the fun has gone out of the game, said, 'I don't know whether you are lying or not, but let's go and see.'

He took the weeping man's arm. But Kim Chomchi pushed it away and suddenly grinned, his eyes still full of tears.

'Who says she's dead?' he said triumphant. 'Why should she die? Why, she's as healthy as she can be, wasting a lot of good food. You've been tricked,' he laughed like a child clapping his hands.

'You're mad. I heard that your wife was ill,' said Chisam, telling Kim to go home as if he too felt some fear.

'She's not dead, not dead,' shouted Kim with conviction getting angry now, but in his cry could be heard his painful effort to disbelieve it himself. They came out of the tavern after drinking another two bowls of wine, managing thus to spend a whole *won*. The rain was still falling drearily.

Though drunk, Kim Chomchi arrived at his door-step, with

a bowl of *sullung-tang*. His house was, of course, a rented one and even that only amounted to a tiny room in the servant's quarter. For his rent, he paid one *won* a month and fetched water for the main house. If Kim had not been drunk that day, he would have noticed when he entered a fearful silence that reigned over the house. His legs would have gone weak at this silence which was like the stillness of the sea after a great storm had passed by. He could not hear the sound of coughing, nor did he hear the usual heavy breathing. Only a muffled sound of sucking, a child sucking his mother, broke this tomb-like silence – or rather than breaking it made the silence even more profound and ominous. Anyone with sensitive ears might also have guessed that since there was only the sound of sucking and no sound of swallowing, the child was only sucking an empty breast.

Perhaps Kim Chomchi too had already guessed this sinister silence. Otherwise, it was strange that he should come in shouting, 'God damn bitch, how dare you not look out when your husband's home,' – a thing he had never done before. But his shouting was, in fact, an empty bluster to chase away the fearful dread which was about to overwhelm him.

In a violent jerk, Kim Chomchi threw open the door. A sickening stench – a stench coming from the mixture of smells from the dust from under the reed mat, of human ordure from unwashed nappies, of dirty and greasy clothes and of the patient's sweat – came and hit Kim Chomchi's blunted nose.

Barely finding time to put the *sullung-tang* down on the floor, Kim Chomchi thundered at the patient.

'You bloody bitch! Lying there all day long. Get up, you bitch, when your husband's home.'

With this, he kicked the woman lying there. But what met his feet did not feel like human flesh; it felt like a tree stump. At that moment, the sound of sucking changed into wailing. His son, Gaetong, had let go of his mother's breast and started crying. But the child, though his face was all puckered up, was not really crying; he only looked as if he was crying and the wailing seemed to come not from his throat but from his belly. He must have cried and cried until his voice went and he was left without any more strength to cry.

Seeing that kicking had no effect, the husband rushed

towards where her head lay and grabbed her hair which was in a tangle like a bird's nest.

'Wretch, speak, I say speak. Have you suddenly turned dumb or something?' said he shaking her head. There was no reply.

'Look, she's not saying anything.'

'Are you dead, bitch, why don't you say something?' Again only silence answered him.

'She's not answering. She must be dead.'

Then Kim Chomchi saw her wide open eyes where the whites had completely covered the dark pupils.

'The eyes ... the eyes! Why don't you look at me instead of staring at the ceiling?' As he said this, his voice cracked. And tear drops as big as chicken droppings fell from the living man's eye and wetted the stony face of the dead woman. Suddenly Kim Chomchi started frantically to rub his face against the dead woman's face and murmured, 'I bought you some *sullung-tang*. Why can't you drink it, why? ... Oh, God! I thought it was a ... strangely lucky day. ...'

THE CRAG

KIM DONG-NI

Translated by Chung Chong-Wha

Geese came crying from the northern skies. Autumn was coming. There were no longer fireflies at night, and the Milky Way was slipping into the middle of the sky. To the homeless who might have to spend a night anywhere, the crying of the geese was not a welcome sound.

Under the railway bridge near the village a band of cripples, beggars and lepers were gathered. Some had their feet in rags, or had heaped sand over themselves where they sat; others wore sacking round their shoulders. To them the thought of the coming autumn was worrying.

'It's getting quite chilly at night these days,' said an old cripple.

'Chilly? It's so bloody cold my arms and legs shrivel,' retorted a man with a cankered arm.

Nearby someone was teaching begging songs:

> This singer in front of you
> Who was once the son of a minister and judge
> Who was once appointed to the governorship of
>   eight provinces
> Has now fallen so low
> And been sold for a penny . . .

The instructor raised his hand and stopped his pupils, saying, 'Gestures are important. Shake your bottom, shake your head. Stand crooked and drool when you sing. You have to get all these together.'

When the instructor finished, two ragged kids took up the song:

> Who's your master?
> You sing much better.
> Who's your master?
> You must have read the Shih Ching and the
>   Shu Dian;
> Your song is erudite.
> Have you read the Analect and Mencius?
> Your sentences are scholarly.

This time the head moving, the hand moving, and the bottom shaking all went well. Everyone burst out laughing.

A train rattled across the bridge above them. When it had gone, someone asked, 'Have you heard any news about your son, Auntie?'

The woman addressed as 'Auntie' just shook her head. She was one of the latest arrivals to the group. Silence came over them for a while and they were shrouded in dark despair.

'I hear the Japs are going to kill off all of us who have palsy,' said someone.

'We haven't done anything, they wouldn't kill us!' Auntie said.

'It's really getting cold,' remarked a young man who instantly reminded her of her son. She had had both a son and a husband until last year.

The son's name was Suri. Though nearly thirty, he had not been able to get himself a wife; and yet his friends envied him because he had saved up a hundred *won* or so. He used to say that when he had saved up around two hundred *won* he would get a wife and start family life. To this end, he never drank, and went without socks in winter. If his mother had not contracted leprosy, he would have been able to lead a normal family life.

He spent most of his money on his mother's medications, and when his savings were reduced to twenty *won* he squandered it in a night's gambling and drinking. Since then he was a changed man. He roamed the streets, half mad and violent, his eyes continually bloodshot, cursing and picking fights. He even tried to set his mother's hovel on fire. Then in early spring when the trees were just starting to bud, he suddenly left his family and disappeared from the village.

After Suri left, his father treated his mother more and more harshly. He came home dead drunk and beat her. For many days he didn't go out to beg food for her, but would say, 'Why don't you just lie down and die? If you died now I'd at least have the strength to bury your bones.' Every time he said this she cried. He wasn't the same man who had looked after her so well, when her leprosy had cost him his job as a servant. He had built her a hut behind the village, and fed her with food and scraps from the alehouse and the village where he did odd menial work. He fussed over her, saying tenderly, 'Eat as much as you can.'

It was early summer when the barley was about to ripen. There were rumours going round, saying that a wolf had been seen in a distant village and had carried off a child, and that a leper was hiding in a barley field. Dead drunk as usual, the old man came to see his wife in her hut one evening. He carried with him a handful of rice cake mixed with arsenic. The woman was scraping at the remains of a dried bean stew in her bowl. When she saw her husband through the open door, she put a grin on her wretched face, and brushed away the flies. The old man cleared his throat and felt the rice cake that he carried inside his shirt. With hazy drunken eyes he stared coldly at his wife and felt inside his shirt once again.

As she took the cake from her husband she twisted her face into a grin of gratitude. But when she realized the purplish streaks in the cake were arsenic, she looked angrily at him. A cuckoo called in the distance. She looked away from him at a corner of the floor. Tears gathered in her eyes and started to flow down her cadaverous face. The old man turned his head away and stood up, spitting. 'Why don't you drop dead!' he said, and spat once again to hide his guilt.

The next day the villagers heard that the leper cried for some time after her husband had left her, and that she finally ate the cake but did not die. She disappeared from the village, and it was said that she left in her hut a pile of red vomit from the poisoned cake.

The woman went round several villages, not just to beg, but because she hoped to find her son. A summer of begging and sleeping rough went by without any luck. The thought of meeting her beloved son before the autumn now seemed a futile dream. She even began to miss her old man: if he met her again he might build a hut for her to spend the winter in.

In the end she had to build a hut with her own hands. It was crudely constructed with wattle and daub on a hilly field near the railway bridge, but it was enough to keep off the frost. Building it took a few days of struggle. Sand got into her eyes, nose, mouth, and every crevice of her skin. Her bones ached and her skin was raw. She lay ill for two days. On the third day the owner of the field came to see her. He cursed her and said, 'If you don't pull this thing down by this evening, I'll set fire to it.' But she did not have the strength to build another hut, and there was no other suitable place as she did not wish to live far away from the railway bridge. So at the risk of being burnt alive she decided to stay.

The railway bridge crossed the main road that ran from the village to the market; and between the village and the bridge was a large rock. Some people called it the Crag of Good Fortune, because it was supposed to bring good luck. Some said it made wishes come true, and called it the Wishing Rock. And others, struck by its resemblance to a sleeping tiger, called it the Tiger Rock. All the year round women came to make wishes on the rock. They climbed to the top of the crag, each carrying a stone which was rubbed against the rock's surface all day. It was said that if the pebble stuck, your wish would come true. Some women sat on the crag for three days running, with enough food packed to last out the wishing-session. But not only women loved the crag: children from the village would come to play horses there, and the elderly people came to lean their backs against it and enjoy the view. The crag was dear to everyone in the village.

Suri's mother also liked the crag. It seemed to her that if she kept rubbing the rock she would meet her son. Often she had gone to the crag, avoiding the eyes of villagers, and rubbed

its unfeeling surface, calling out her son's name. After about
a fortnight of going to the crag, whether by chance or because
the rock had done its miracle, she met her son one day. The
market-place was bustling with pedlars. As she was about to
go into a food stall with a bowl in her hand, someone grabbed
her sleeve. Instantly she knew it was Suri. She raised her head
and saw her son's face. For a brief second her long white teeth
flashed in a smile.

Suri held his mother's hand and led her away slowly. At a
little distance from the market-place was the ruin of an old
fortress, with a path by it. The path was covered with autumn
grass and there was no one around. The two sat in the grass,
and wept.

'Mother!'

'Suri!'

Tears flooded into their eyes and flowed down their cheeks.

'Mother, how did you manage by yourself? How did you
struggle on alone?'

The mother just sobbed. Though her body was failing the
tears remained the same.

'Mother, how much did you miss me? How hard did you
look for me?'

Suri buried his head in his mother's lap and cried. A red-
tailed dragonfly alighted on the wild buckwheat among the
weeds growing on the path, and on the hill opposite a dappled
snake slithered through a stone crevice.

'Mother, I'll go and make some money. Don't die before I
come back.'

Suri caressed his mother's shoulders and arms. Tears constantly welled up in his eyes. They went back to the market
place. Suri took out three and a half *yang* and placed the coins
in his mother's hand, and before they parted at a rice cake
stall he promised to meet her again 'in three or four days'
time'. The sun was now slowly sinking. The market-place was
resounding to the cries of pedlars and shoppers. In the crowd
were a man bringing an ox to the market, a man carrying home
a pile of firewood on his back, a woman carrying something
in a wooden bowl on her head and a baby strapped to her
back, a boy riding a bicycle, a Japanese civil servant being
carried in a rickshaw ... they were all talking, laughing, fighting, eating ... Through the hubbub of the crowd Suri rambled

with an empty carrier on his back, looking at the ground and mumbling, 'Past the Crag of Good Fortune, under the railway bridge.' He also wanted to find news of his father while he was in the market, but no one could tell him exactly where he was. Some said that he was wandering the streets crippled by paralysis, and others said he had asthma and worked as an errand boy for a pothouse.

After the woman had met her son, her longing for him became even stronger. Acutely aware of his absence, she went looking for him round the market-place. The promised day passed by, then a fortnight . . . a month went by and still there was no sign of him. Now she had only the rock to turn to. It seemed to her that as long as that remained rooted in the ground, there was hope, and she would meet her son again and even perhaps cure her disease. 'I should keep on rubbing the crag whether it rains or snows.' Far into the night when all were asleep she would drag her aching, heavy body to the rock and rub herself on its surface.

But this time the rock did not work its miracle. She wondered if it refused her because she went there only in the dark. So she decided to go to the crag during the daytime when there were no people looking; but it wasn't easy to avoid the villagers.

One day she was spotted by them while she was praying on the rock. In an instant a rope whipped around her and she fell from the rock. She was dragged to the bridge, her whole body broken and spattered with blood; she lost consciousness. When she came round and opened her eyes, she saw the village servant drawing water and washing the crag.

From that day on, whenever she went past the rock, the woman would stop and gaze steadily at it. Every time she came near it she felt her feet stick to the ground and become immobile. To her it was endlessly dear and yet hateful. It seemed that her fate depended on the rock.

One evening she was coming back from the market-place after a whole day's search for her son. The hills, streams and the village were all wrapped in the glow of sunset. As usual, she was passing through the village with her begging bowl full of a mixture of food: rice, cake, toffee, soft persimmon, buckwheat curd, dates, bean curd, noodle, bean sprout, gilthead fish, pollock and other odds and ends. Her head was bowed down and she was dragging her feet heavily. She often stopped and peered into the bowl, muttering over to herself, 'Why didn't I go in and ask them?' She meant the conversation she had heard while she was getting buckwheat curd from a stall: an old man who sold persimmons was talking with another man.

'Still a long time before Suri comes out?'

'He's got six months. So he's got a long time to go.'

At that time she was busy with begging and couldn't afford to be distracted. Besides she would never have imagined that someone would be talking about her son. But now with the crag in sight she remembered what she had heard. She was sure that they had been talking about her son.

'Silly of me, they were talking about Suri.'

The more she thought about it the more certain she became. Their talk of 'Suri' rang again in her ears. She wanted to turn around and go back to the market-place, but changed her mind when she looked into her bowl. She walked towards the rock. Every part of her body began to ache. Her feet were as heavy as stone and she felt she might collapse on the spot. She was feverish and dizzy.

When she reached the crag the sun had already gone down and darkness was spreading its big wings at the far ends of the fields. As usual she stopped in front of the rock and looked at it for a while. When she turned her head towards her hut, there was no hut, only a sea of roaring fire. She couldn't believe her eyes, but the fire was there all right. She felt she was turning to stone. Even when she closed her eyes, there was the sea of flames. Fire, fire, it was fire everywhere whether she opened her eyes or closed them. Like a piece of wood she fell against the crag. She groped around for it with her already benumbed hands. Embracing it, she contentedly rubbed her dark, cadaverous face on it. A stream of cold tears flowed down onto the crag.

The next day the villagers gathered round the rock. They spat on the ground.

'Yuk! Why the hell did the filthy thing choose this place to die?'

'A leper died on our crag of good fortune!'

'What a waste of the crag!'
The tears on the woman's face had dried and begun to shine.

THE AFTERNOON OF MELLOW PERSIMMONS

SOHN SO-HI

*Translated by Angela Chung**

It had rained in the morning yesterday, but this morning the sky was clear and the air was fresh. Perhaps it was because the seasonal tide of the White Frost had come; the autumn was approaching.

Bobai started sweeping the stone steps that led to the temple of Chilsungdang. For exactly one hundred and one days Bobai had swept this path. One hundred and one days had been continued without interruption, and she swept it with her utmost sincerity.

'Na-moo-kwan-se-um-bo-sal, Merciful Goddess, have pity on me!'

When Bobai had finished sweeping, she put the broom back where it was. While she was washing her hands by the well in the back garden of the temple, she kept murmuring: 'Merciful Goddess, have pity on me!' She stood up and walked towards her room; her steps were quick, and her face was covered with a sweet smile. As she passed by the hall of worship she heard somebody calling the mercy of Buddha. The voice was coarse and loud, and yet, it seemed to Bobai, the owner of the voice was almost crying. She peeped into the hall, wondering

*Translator edited the original story in collaboration with the author, to make the English version read better.

whether it was the woman next door to her. Her guess was right.

Curiosity gripped her, and Bobai wondered why she was crying in her prayer. Her curiosity increased as she walked to her room. Once in her room, she started to paint her face. For three months and ten days she had neglected her toilette. She had wholly devoted herself to worship for a hundred days, and this was the hundred and first day at this temple. She laboured in making up her face as best as she could, hoping that her hundred-day prayer would bring a fruitful result. When she had finished making up her face, she found herself beautiful. Her skin was white and smooth, her eyes sparkling, her cheeks rosy pink as before, her protruded forehead glistening, her nose graceful, and her mouth elegant. A wave of satisfaction swelled over her and she couldn't resist a smile. Feeling happy, she took out a purse, in which a pair of small nail scissors and a thimble were kept. She put on her best clothes. She looked more beautiful. She exchanged a smile with herself in the mirror. Once in the good old days she had been devoutly loved by her husband, Ahn Doyong, for her beauty. He even now insisted that he loved only her. Perhaps it might be true.

'Excuse me, next-door mother, may we have breakfast together this morning? I don't feel like having it by myself,' said the woman who had been crying in the hall of worship. She smashed Bobai's happy daydream. Bobai was taken aback. Bobai felt terribly painful whenever this woman addressed her as 'next-door mother'. It was worse this morning. She wanted to refuse the invitation, but finding no adequate excuse she agreed reluctantly.

A few minutes later Bobai sat down with the woman over breakfast. She looked at Bobai several times with her swollen eyes, fascinated, and asked.

'You are going home today, aren't you?'

Bobai answered gently. 'Yes, I am. It is my hundred and first day here.'

'Oh, I see. You have finished your prayers then. So you must go back home now. That's why you look so beautiful today. I always thought you very beautiful. Even a sculptor couldn't carve a woman so beautiful as you.'

The woman paid Bobai various compliments, and she

answered with a sad smile, 'Beautiful? Not at all. It's no good any more.'

The woman shook her head and said, 'No, that's not true. Your beauty is in full bloom now.' Having said this, she swallowed a big spoonful of rice, and continued again. 'You are beautiful. Yes, you are a beauty,' she repeated in excitement. With a sigh Bobai finished her breakfast and put down her spoon. She said, 'Does it matter if one is beautiful? It doesn't. I am an abandoned woman.'

The woman expressed her surprise; she opened her swollen eyes in amazement. 'Abandoned? Good gracious! You can't be a rejected wife! You can't be a rejected one! It is unimaginable. No husband abandons a wife as beautiful as you. Perhaps you had a love quarrel and you are temporarily separated from your husband but not for good.' The woman watched Bobai carefully. She seemed very curious. Bobai smiled.

It was true that no husband rejected a beautiful wife. In Bobai's case, however, she had invited this trouble. To make her husband happy she had invited this abandonment. Doyong, her husband, was not an extremely wealthy man, but he was comparatively well off. So people called him a rich man.

Bobai had been married for fifteen years. Bobai was thirty-four years old and her husband just forty. They had loved each other and they had had everything they wanted except one thing, a child. For this Bobai had always felt responsible and guilty, and had very often suggested to him to take a concubine who would give him a child. But each time she mentioned this idea, the husband gave her a ready-made answer in a tender voice.

'Don't be silly! Let's not talk about it any more. We promised to forget about it. We shall live happily as we are now, and when we get old we'll pack everything and go to a temple to finish the rest of our lives.'

Sometimes he was angry at her hint. Then some time ago suddenly he started showing his strong desire for a child, even regretting not having one earlier, which made her very sad. But she couldn't blame him.

'It is true. I am deserted. Moreover, I am nearly forty. I am no longer young. But my husband didn't forsake me for my ugliness. I pushed him to desert me.'

'You pushed him to desert you? I can't understand that,' said the woman who had just devoured a bowl of rice and a glass of water. She lit her pipe. The woman seemed to have assumed that either Bobai had deserted her husband or she had cuckolded him.

Bobai regretted that she had talked about her private life, but it was too late to withhold. The swollen eyes of the next-door woman seemed to press Bobai to talk about her personal life more in detail. Bobai began to narrate in a calm voice as if she had given up everything. Some time ago Bobai had arranged for her husband to have a mistress, who became pregnant immediately. The woman gave birth to a baby boy in due course, and he was now six months old. As the boy grew, her husband changed; he was becoming indifferent to her. She didn't mind it at first because she believed in her husband's unshakable love. But as time passed, she felt hurt, which piled up to an unbearable extent. So she left her home and came to the present temple. Her husband came to see her every Sunday, each time insisting on taking her back. But she refused to go home with the excuse that she had to pray for one hundred days. However, since the temperature fell and the air was getting cool, she longed for her home. The next-door woman nodded her head several times to show that she had fully understood the situation. She continued to smoke her pipe for a while, and said:

'I thought only those ugly and old women suffer. But sometimes beautiful women also suffer. Yet your husband does not love another woman. If he turned away from you, it's not because he doesn't love you but because he wants children. Of course, it would be really ideal to have children where there is money and love. But you can't have everything. If you hear my story you'll realize how lucky you are. My husband is almost sixty, yet he keeps a mistress. He was very much devoted to me when he was young, but on the threshold of becoming sixty he went out for another woman. I was so disgusted that I left him and hid myself here. I won't go back, no matter how many thousand times he comes here to take me home, until he swears that this will never happen in the future.'

She found it hard to hide her laughter, but she had to refrain. She knew well that it was impossible to laugh at others when they were at the height of sincerity. Yet Bobai found it hard to hide a smile when she heard her calling her just 'you' instead of 'next-door mother'.

'So you said that this is your hundred and first day?'

'Yes.'

'Then you are going home before me.'

'It seems so. I am going home as soon as my husband comes to fetch me. If I don't go, it is I who will suffer. Won't you leave the temple with me? The temperature is going down everyday.'

The woman didn't answer. She just stared at Bobai.

In the garden where the sunshine was bright a whirlwind arose and drove fallen leaves. The fragrant air from the tens of thousands of cosmos flowers which stood on the hill outside the temple gate pierced Bobai's heart and stirred her. She shut her mouth tight as if to hide her excited heart, and glared at the woman. It gave her pain to look at the grey hair which reminded her of weird pine tree leaves and the thick vein on her dry, old skin which reminded her of an old, dying trunk.

'Is it Sunday today?' the woman asked.

'Yes, it is.'

'Will your husband come?'

'Yes, I think so.'

'You will be glad, I am sure. You stayed here long enough. I miss my home, though I've stayed here only six days. But I am determined to remain here until my naughty husband repents for what he has done to me.'

The woman seemed to get heated at the thought of her wayward husband. She repeated over and over again that she would give him a good lesson by remaining in the temple. Bobai asked her how many children she had. She said that she had two married sons and one married daughter and her youngest daughter was still at school. Bobai, again, asked if she was well off, to which she said 'yes', but she added that everything was chaotic at home without her.

Bobai left the woman telling her that she would like to see the temple once again before she went home. The whole area of the temple was very clean, though it was rather small, and Bobai attributed this to the fact that it was run by a priestess. Everything was tidy and in order. For one thing, the broom

227

for the main hall of worship and the broom for the floor were different.

Bobai came under a persimmon tree which stood by the stone steps leading to the temple of Chilsung-dang. She was suddenly seized by the temptation to count persimmons on the tree. It suddenly struck her that if there were more than a hundred persimmons, she would become pregnant in answer to her hundred day prayer, and if not, she would be forever barren. But she didn't have the courage to do that. She decided that the idea was flippant and silly.

While she was wandering around the cosmos flower bed outside the main gate, keeping an eye on the direction from which her husband would come, she saw the other woman coming towards her. She seemed to have painted herself. Her hair was shining – she must have put on hair cream. Her face looked whitish. All this made her look not bad at all. It was the first time she had seen the woman in full make-up. She smiled and said, 'You too are ready to go home, aren't you?'

She retorted hastily, 'No, I didn't make-up to go home. I just did it. I have to remain here and teach my husband a lesson. I had to squeeze out every drop of my courage to leave home. I can't go home so easily as this. Otherwise my neighbours would laugh at me.'

The woman seemed self-conscious about her make-up. Feeling uneasy, she wiped off lipstick from her lips once or twice using her handkerchief. She also looked nervous, and she was anxiously watching the direction from which any outsider would appear. It was the same with Bobai. Secretly, she hoped that the hilly path that reached the town was wider.

'I am sure you feel today that you are a newly married bride; you have been separated from your husband too long, while you are still in love with each other. He will be running out of breath on his way to meet you.'

'Do you think so? I don't know. I think your husband will be running on his way here.'

The conversation dragged on in polite tones, but each of them hoped that her husband would be the first to come to the temple. Bobai wanted to show to the woman the evidence of his love and devotion, and the woman hoped the same thing.

The sky was blue and high, with small whitish clouds. Autumn had come. The wind blew from down below the hills, and stirred the cosmos; the waves of flowers rose and died away. Bobai picked a red cosmos. The woman also picked a bunch of flowers; she smelt them and then said, 'They smell like a young woman's body: sweet and fleshy.' The woman laughed, amused at her own remarks, but Bobai couldn't join her. She just said, 'Why don't you put them in the vase?'

The woman toyed with the flowers, and smelt them once again, this time very deeply.

'I'll ask my husband to smell these, telling him that they reminded me of a young woman's flesh.'

The woman had a malicious smile on her face, and then she disappeared into the temple. Bobai instinctively knew that she went to her room to arrange the flowers in the vase. Bobai too left the flower bed and followed the woman. It was just ten o'clock, and it would be at least another two hours before her husband came. Bobai saw the woman watering the flowers she had brought in as she was passing by the woman's room.

There was nothing else Bobai could do. She had to wait. She came into her room, dusted the floor, and rearranged her belongings.

The clock struck eleven. There was no sign of her husband coming from the town. Not a single worshipper visited the temple. Bobai thought that eleven o'clock was too early for a visitor. She lay down on the floor, resting her head on her things that had been packed many times that morning. She tried to sleep, but it was no good. So she came out of her room once again and wandered around the temple. When it was ten to twelve, she saw a party of people climbing up the hill in the direction of the temple. The next-door woman also came out and watched the party, which, however, didn't stop at the temple but passed by. Soon the two women saw another party coming up towards the temple. The next-door woman fixed her eyes on the approaching party, shading her eyes with her hand from the sunshine. Bobai became impatient and then suddenly felt tired. She went again inside the temple. Once again the woman followed her. The women met the party in the garden, they had come for a day's excursion.

Bobai came out to the stone steps outside the temple when it was half past twelve. There was nobody to be seen on the road. Last Sunday her husband was very early. She suddenly had a thought that he might have had an accident on the way, and she trembled with fear.

'What's happened to them?' shouted the next-door woman, when Bobai was on the point of getting up. 'They seem to have made a vow never to come to this temple.'

'I am sure they will soon be here with us.' Bobai pretended that her mind was not stirred.

The two women came in once again, and sat down in the long corridor outside their rooms. The wind blew gently, touching Bobai's ears. The woman lit her pipe.

When the clock struck one, a middle-aged man came into the garden of the temple, carrying a baby with his two hands, who was soon followed by a young woman with a coloured parasol. The young woman carried a baby's blanket in one hand. Soon a young girl with a red parasol followed them, carrying a big luncheon basket in one hand. They were Bobai's visitors. She stood up from the corridor outside her room and welcomed them with a smile. The next-door woman cast a curious eye on the new party. The whole party saw Bobai and hurried towards her. Her husband smiled at her, but the young girl shut her mouth tight. When they met, Bobai took the baby from her husband, and said, 'He has grown quite a bit.'

The man retorted. 'Are you all right? I thought it would be nice to have lunch together. It took some time to get things ready for lunch. Have you waited long?'

'No, I haven't waited long. I was just worried whether you had had any accident.'

'Accident? No. I can't afford an accident. I'm not a child. By the way, I brought some beef and eggs. Do you want *pulgogi** and fried eggs? Since it has become cold, it's better to have a hot meal.' He took off his jacket and wiped his neck with his handkerchief.

'Shall I go in and ask them to cook these things for us?' said the young woman, the mother of the baby.

'Yes, do,' answered the man.

The young woman disappeared to order the dishes to be cooked. Bobai noticed a new amber ring on the finger of the

---

**pulgogi:* A Korean dish of beef richly seasoned in sweetened soya sauce and cooked usually on a charcoal fire.

young woman while she was tightening her long skirt. The new ring seemed to Bobai as if it was something she shouldn't have seen. She turned her eyes away, and said to the baby, 'You are now a big boy. You can play by yourself.' She touched the baby's cheeks with hers.

'Of course, he can play by himself. Now, Your Excellency, you must introduce yourself to your other mother.' The husband toyed with the baby happily and made him bow down before Bobai. He then turned to the young girl and said, 'Now, you have to introduce yourself. This young lady is the younger sister of the baby's mother. She came from Seoul a few days ago, where she studied.'

'Oh, I see. Welcome! The baby should be delighted to have an aunt like you.' Bobai said, while she was handing the baby to the father. 'What happened to your schooling, then?' Bobai turned to the young girl.

'I'm promised to get a place in a high school here.'

'That's good. I am glad to hear that.'

In the mean time the young woman returned from the kitchen and took the baby from her husband. When he handed her the baby, the husband took out a box, from which he took out an amber ring, but Bobai put it aside without showing much interest. The husband insisted that she should try it on, and she did. The ring fitted well. Bobai showed it to her husband, and then took it off. She put it back in the box and said she would wear it when she went home. The husband took out another box – a bigger one, this time, and said.

'I brought some persimmons. Won't you take one? All of us had some at home and left these for you.'

'You brought too much for me,' Bobai said, looking at the lid of the box. 'Would you pass me the lid and box?'

'Why?' The husband asked, while he was handing them.

'I'll dedicate them to the goddess. I can have them when I go home.'

'Certainly. You will have plenty of them at home.'

Bobai took the lid and box from her husband, and came out of the room. She saw the next-door woman outside her room with her things. The woman said to Bobai, 'I have decided to go home after all. My husband doesn't seem to be coming today. I may have to come back here again, but I am determined to teach him a lesson. He must have lost his head. Do please have a nice time and nice lunch here. You are lucky. I envy you. Your husband still loves you very much. No, no. Don't be sorry for me. I'll be all right.'

The woman hurried to the priestess of the temple to say goodbye. Bobai proceeded down the stone path slowly toward the temple of Chilsung-dang. She found her whole body trembling. When she reached the place, she found the door locked. She pulled the lock down hard; the door was opened. Once inside the hall, she shut the door firmly and then locked it from inside. She took out the wooden dishes and set them before the Buddha. She then put the persimmons on the wooden dishes. She lit candles and let incense burn. With her hands together she stood there for a long time without moving. Tears gathered in her eyes and fell on the floor.

Time passed. Bobai suddenly heard somebody knocking on the door.

'Brother-in-law asks you to come back quickly.' It was the young girl. Bobai lifted her head and glared at the Buddha. She then knelt down, took out a small pair of nail scissors from her purse, and watched them without thinking.

'Lunch is ready. Come out quickly, please.' The girl yelled outside. Suddenly Bobai took hold of her hair and started cutting with the scissors. When she finished cutting her hair, she put it in the box she had brought. She put the lid back on the box, while she tried hard to subdue her sobbing.

'The *pulgogi* is burning. Won't you come out quick?'

Bobai opened the door carefully and left the box on the floor outside the temple. She said in a quiet voice, 'Will you take this box to your brother-in-law? Ask him to open this by himself, and tell him that I won't ever come out from here in my life. Tell him that he'd better forget about me.' Bobai shut the door quietly.

THE TALE OF KIM TAKBO

YI MUN-GU

Translated by Shin Hyun-song

God almighty, just take a look at those weird flames dancing around in the dark!

If she muttered something about the will-o-the-wisp like this, she knew that all she'd get would be a tongue-lashing and looks of contempt from the others, and she didn't really fancy opening the day's account that way.

... What's wrong with you Yokmaldaek,* do you *have* to open your mouth? Are you worried that we won't have *enough* bad luck without you jabbering 'ghost' and 'goblin'? ... †

She just hoped she wouldn't spoil everything by opening that big mouth of hers.

She got a grip on herself again and prodded herself along. But in her haste she twisted her left ankle, and the flimsy rubber shoe came off her foot. Without thinking, she paused and was slipping her foot back into the shoe when the red-hot bowl of the long pipe in Tongshik's dad's mouth bumped into

---

*'Yokmaldaek' is not a name, but a form of address. 'Yokmal' is a place name, presumably her home village, and 'daek' is a suffix indicating that she is a married woman. 'Yokmaldaek' means, literally, 'the married woman whose home town is Yokmal'.

†In Korean, 'will-o'-the-wisp' and 'goblin' are often used to mean the same thing. This is because the will-o'-the-wisp (*ignis fatuus*) is called 'goblin fire' in Korean.

her and scorched her back, which was scarcely covered by the
shredded piece of rag she called her shirt.

'Ouch!!'

As she jumped aside and looked around, she couldn't help
smiling in relief. It was strange but she felt refreshed – as if
by crying out she had somehow chased away the bad luck that
was looming over her. It was a relief, like having a two-inch
thorn pulled out of her foot.

Now her cry had broken the ice, the tightly sealed lips of
the other, frozen solid from the moment they set out at cock
crow, began to thaw.

'Look over there! The goblin's really having a party this
morning!' said Malsun's mum, as if to let the others know that
their chatterbox was still alive and kicking.

'Hmmm, the market's going to be ruined again . . .' It was
Ojaeng-i's uncle, who normally paid back every remark he
heard with two more of his own for interest.

'I don't like it. It's bad luck to have the Jack-o'-lantern
playing about so wildly.' That trembly voice no doubt belonged
to Yungab's grandma, known for her habit of shaking her head
all the time, as if nothing in the world ever satisfied her.

The wet season had moved into its second spell, and it had
come to the point where people would shudder at the very
mention of the word 'rain'. So it was indeed a welcome change
to see the thick cover of cloud lift a little, and the people of
Galmori village weren't the sort to miss a prime opportunity
like that. It really was a long time since they'd last had a peep
through the clouds, and it was this change in the weather that
had led them to set out before dawn this morning to collect
salt from the saltern at Sobaeng-i.

The shriek that Yokmaldaek spat out a moment before
seemed to herald the formal opening of the day's business, or
at least the others must have thought so; because not long
after what had seemed an unfortunate accident, they all
became quite chatty and open.

'This is it, exactly half way,' Tongshik's dad announced as he
crossed the irrigation ditch dug by the watering co-operative.

That meant they still had four kilometres to go. They knew
from years of experience that the distance from Galmori vil-

lage to Sobaeng-i salt fields was exactly eight kilometres, not a step more, not a step less.

The southeast wind was blowing. It was cool and refreshing. Soon they'd be able to see the mud plains of Sobaeng-i and hear the undulation of the waves and the sound of ships setting out to sea . . . somehow like the sound of the dripping fog itself.

They could see Mount Songju in the distance, where the sun returned to the sky every morning after its nightly rest on the other side of the globe, regular as clockwork. The stars had disappeared from the sky above the horizon's protruding lip, but still it wasn't quite time for the sun to rear up its brilliant head.

And yet, in spite of the half-light, they forged nimbly ahead along the tortuous banks of the rice paddies, which were as irregular as the path left by an earthworm sliding along on its belly. After all, they did have ten years of experience behind them. These peasants, these wretched peasants, made their living by collecting salt at the saltern and then selling it in the local township, subsisting on the meagre difference they were able to pocket.

Tock . . . tock . . .

The sound of the hollow wooden clappers of the Buddhist monks could be heard pulsating from the Paeju Rock, far away on Mount Wangdae. These people, too poor to own a watch, told the time by the sound of the clappers.

Yokmaldaek herself stirred awake at their sound every day at dawn. She drew a couple of pails of water from the well, and put a battered pot on the fire . . . and being too poor to afford rice, threw in a handful of barley. As she fanned the fire with one hand, burning damp sawdust, the hem of her *chima* would begin to soil from wiping her smoke-filled eyes and nose. Scooping out the sticky mess, too watery to be considered 'cooked', and too viscous to be called gruel, she sat herself across the kitchen stove, poured in cold water to make soup, and shovelled it down noisily.

With her stomach full, she would get her things ready for the day's trek – the round wicker basket and the dirty cotton sack to carry the salt on her head, the small pickle dish she used for a measure, a few sheets of newspaper and millboard ... these sorry pieces of junk were all she needed for her trade.

The peasants assembled under the Giant Pine before setting off. It might be expected that when trades people gather, they would exchange early morning greetings with one another. But although such be true elsewhere, this particular group's 'greeting' was the absence of it, and silence had become the recognized and accepted form of acknowledgment; in fact the only one.

And so they all held back from saying anything, thus perpetuating the rather nasty piece of folklore that the first person to utter a sound would lose all his luck to the others.

In the mud plains around Granny Rock, the goblins were particularly boisterous and seemed as if they were trying to tease the wayfarers on their way. Some goblins would come together making a floweret, then separate, turning into spinning columns of fire, or perform tricks like jumping on top of one another and jumping down again. Sometimes they would even play hide and seek, all disappearing at once, then slowly reappear one by one.

The group from Galmori moved down from the paddy banks and over the dyke into the mud plains, through which their short-cut lay. From here, Granny Rock wasn't far ... on Granny Rock they would be able to stretch their legs a little, as they always did. Indeed, it had become their custom to loosen their belts and rest on top of the rock. As they approached the rock, dancing flames seemed to run away from them; whatever the reason there was certainly a decrease in their number.

'I don't know what I'll do if the price of salt's gone up ...' Yokmaldaek worried.

'I know, it's awful, isn't it? And they won't have any of it roasted, not in this weather anyway.'

'Even if they did, it'd still be as heavy as lead with the moisture.'

This was more than true. In the wet season, it was all too easy to get pushed into the red if you were a salt pedlar.

They looked up at the sky, united at their hope that the sun might shine on them, at least for today.

'Must have been last summer ... well, you see, there was

this high-school kid, down from Seoul on a holiday . . . Tong-shik's dad started telling his story. 'You see, I went down to Daechon beach selling salt, and set up my A-frame on the sand and took the cloth off the salt, and guess what? This bloke comes up and asks me if the salt won't melt in the sun! So I told him it not only melts but it goes bad and rots as well, and . . .'

'You know, the same thing happened to me once. I was working away in the fields when this young kid walks up to me, points at the pile of rice plants, and asks if that "tree" was a rice "tree"! So I told him it was, and the next thing I know he asks me to sell him one stem so he could plant it in his flower pot and take it back to Seoul!'

Ojaeng-i's uncle had hardly stopped talking when Tongshik's dad started up again.

'You have to be careful crossing streams, you know, if you slip on one of those mossy stones . . .'

After seeming to give some relevant advice for a change, he delved deep into his story bag and began unwinding the old yarn about the time he once caught a pair of goblins single-handed.

. . . Long ago, before all these hard times, when Squire Yun's house was still in its heyday and rich enough to own several large fishing boats, he went out one day before dawn to inspect his stone walls on the beach. These walls were a sort of primitive fish-trap, a structure arranged in a U-shape, so that at high tide fish would unknowingly swim inside the U shape of the wall; when the tide went out, any fish too big to swim through the gaps in the wall would be stranded.

That particular period was the end-of-month fishing season, so that he happened to be carrying his harpoon and pike in a woven straw bag. When he got there, goblins were playing about, and ran away as he approached. But a pair of them were so busy having it off that they were totally unaware of what was happening around them, so he sneaked closer and piked both of them with one almighty thrust. When the two of them, as tall as totem poles and with horns on their heads, came at him together, he had to admit he was a little scared. But he brought them down with one swift kick of his left leg, and impaled them to the ground with his harpoon. Well, there they were, hopelessly struggling on the sand. He dragged them over to his wall and tied them up. But when he returned after daybreak, all that was left was a rotting old broom. And judging from the fact that a goblin had left it there (by the way, the broom was absolutely covered in dead oyster shells) he reckoned it must have been the goblin's mistress or his concubine . . .

'They say there are all sorts of goblins and monsters going around,' said Ojaeng-i's uncle.

'Well when I told Squire Yun about it, he said the things must have been water goblins.'

By the time Tongshik's dad had come to the end of his story, they had already reached Granny Rock, and as for the goblins, there were none to be seen.

'They've run away. They must have seen us coming.' They were busy looking round, and no one noticed Mount Songju rise up against the sky.

Sitting on top of the rock, the party unpacked the little bit of food they had each brought, and started to eat. After a brisk four kilometres cross-country, the few bites of food they'd gulped before setting out had gone down long ago, so they were all quite hungry by the time they reached the rock.

'What the hell's the matter with that woman, does she think she'll get anywhere by giving all her food to her old man while she starves herself to death?' Malsun's mum pushed a piece of gummy wheat bread in front of Yokmaldaek and eyed her disapprovingly. For years, Yokmaldaek had continued to come along with an empty basket, and watch the others eat as if her eyeballs would drop out.

'Go on, take it.'

She put the bread into her mouth with show of reluctance, as if she had been persuaded by her friend. She took only a tiny morsel, but the sound of her chewing was the noisiest and most vigorous of them all.

'Tut tut . . . poor wretched thing. What's the use of fattening your husband like some farm animal if you're starving yourself . . .' Yonkab's grandma also got into the act, tearing off a piece of burnt barley cake studded with beans, and put it in front of Yokmaldaek.

'Oh, you know, you really don't have to . . . I mean, eating between meals. I ate a lot before leaving.'

Even as she said this, she snatched the hard lump from the old woman's hand and started chewing noisily.

For ten years, the routine had been the same. Yokmaldaek would sit around drooling, watching the others eat. Then she'd be given a few scraps, and she would eat it in her own cheeky and annoying way. It had become almost a ritual. The funny part was that she accepted food from the others without batting an eye.

'Ooh, my back.'

Finishing off both her scraps, Yokmaldaek put her hands to her back and gave a long moan of pain. But nobody took any notice.

'I'm not pulling your leg, it really hurts. There, look.' She peeled her skirt down from her hip and tried to show them the black and blue marks on it, but it was still dark and nothing could really be seen.

'He did it to me yesterday.' She went on to explain how her husband had thrown the wooden head-rest at her. But still no one turned their head.

'And what about my thighs ... bloody hell, how can I walk with this, look!' This time she pulled up the leg of her drawers. 'He kicked me with that sledgehammer of a leg, and phew, I don't know when he's going to come to his senses.'

'Oh you've really got nothing to moan about. I ask you, why do you still feed him three times a day and give him money to drink like a whale? You deserve everything you get!' Hairy Mister Shin's new daughter-in-law burst out, pouting her lips, as if she couldn't stand any more of Yokmaldaek's two-faced carrying-on.

During this fuss, the darkness had lifted completely and the sun started to raise its head.

'I wonder what the market's going to be like today ... my dreams weren't too peaceful last night.'

'Yes I think the market duty collector's going to be a pain in the neck again today. Do you remember he threatened to get all the back duty that's piled up, this time? Well, I don't know ...'

'I'd rather throw my salt all over the ground than get taxed by that bastard.'

'Don't be stupid.'

Tongshik's dad and Ojaeng-i's uncle straightened their hats and stood up. The women also got ready, tying their towels around their heads.

'Better get up now ...'

'Yes, let's!'

There is a story that once long ago an old woman was on her way to see her grandchildren, carrying five pretty little jackstones in her apron to give to her favourite grand-daughter. As she was crossing this mud plain, the sea rushed in and drowned her. But not everything perished. One of the jack-stones swelled up and became a huge boulder, and Granny Rock was this jackstone-turned-boulder.

The sun was shedding its warm rays on the rock. Soon the sunlight itself would no doubt come for a rest atop the rock.

At the foot of the cemetery on the hill behind Galmori village, next to the coffin chamber, stood a shabby hut on the verge of collapse. The peak of the roof had caved in, leaving a myriad of dips and bumps, from which reeds and purslane grew thickly.

From pits in the ground where the fence had been ages ago, tall mugweed was thriving, lifting its head. In the yard and in the fields outside, dense grass was flourishing. So much so that a tigress rearing her cubs wouldn't have been noticed in the thick vegetation.

The doorless kitchen and the chimney, already fallen to pieces, gave the house a deserted look. No one would have guessed that somebody *did* live in this hole. The only clue was the swarm of flies buzzing around a cluster of wild rose bushes in one corner of the yard. Behind the bushes was a deep ditch serving as a toilet.

The sun somehow found its way even to this God-forsaken place. The whistle of the first morning train came over from the ridge. There was something stirring in the main room. With a thud, the frail wooden-framed door opened and a hairy mess, more like a bear than a man, came crawling out.

Mr Kim Samshik, or as he was better known, Kim Takbo,* the tippler, had at last awoken!

---

*'Takbo' is a common Korean nickname, meaning someone who likes 'Takju' (or *makoli*) very much. From this origin it has passed into general usage, meaning a person who drinks a lot.

'Is the sun so high already . . .' he mumbled as he crawled over the threshold.

Takbo looked out onto the mud plains, shielding his eyes from the sun. There was no one to be seen. He turned his eyes to Granny Rock. Granny Rock seemed very small . . . small enough indeed to be a jackstone. He guessed that his wife would be resting on the rock, on her way back from the salt fields.

The sound of the train was getting nearer. It sounded as if it was coming round the bend on the hill. Whenever he heard the sound of a train, he was taken back in his memory to the time when his wife ran away from him and fled to Seoul to work as a maid, and how he eventually brought her back.

Giving a mighty yawn, he raked his belly with his fingers and had a slash, right in the middle of the yard. The hempen shirt and the band around his ankles – his knee-breeches – clung to his skin, they were so damp.

Where the chimney had collapsed long ago, rain came in and soaked through the mattress and saturated his clothes. It was quite useless to burn fuel because it would only scorch the fire-mouth and do little else.

Takbo went into the kitchen. The charred stove was only just supporting a battered pot above it. He lifted the blackened lid; a rancid, vinegary smell stabbed his nostrils. Two flies, as if put off by the smell, circled the pot once and flew onto his chin, and eventually flew off behind his ear. The dingy pot of cooked barley was still warm.

'Silly cow! She should have made some soup if she knew I was drinking yesterday . . .'

He put the bowl of barley down on the stove and picked up his chopsticks. But there was nowhere for them to go.

'Bitch! How can I eat the barley on its own . . .'

Mumbling to himself, he came out of the kitchen in search of something that could go with belly-filler. Ojaeng-i's pepper field was not far: just across the little stream that flowed on the other side of the yard. This stream, which went past his chimney, was dug to drain rainwater from the vast expanse of the public cemetery.

Picking nine or ten heads of heavy, ripe green pepper, he came back to the kitchen. A puddle of water had formed on the kitchen floor, and clear water was trickling past the threshold and onto the bare earth floor of the next room. It was probably water that had accumulated behind the chimney. This little trickle dribbled on, day and night, week after week, and flowed into the thick jungle of grass in the garden.

Sitting on the stove, Takbo shovelled in a couple of spoonfuls of barley and chewed a pepper, which he was occasionally dipping into a pot of fermented bean sauce, before he discovered two maggots crawling out of the pot.

'Stupid cow! You can't do anything right, can you!'

Rushing into the other room again, he started to look for something, looking in every corner of the room. He was going to check under the clothes in the crate on the other side of the room but decided not to, after considering the chances of finding anything there. He moved along the walls of the room, groping into every crack or hole, but nothing came out. Takbo stopped his search for a moment and fell into deep thought. He remembered his wife's habit of never hiding anything in the same place twice, after it had been dug up once. He left the room: it had to be in the kitchen somewhere.

On the kitchen floor, a frog was busy licking up the maggots from the sauce pot. He stood there awkwardly as he racked his brains trying to work out where she had hidden it. But it wasn't easy, especially if you had a wife like Yokmaldaek, who was renowned for her cunning and shrewdness.

But at length he was able to pull out a hundred *won* note from the sack of sawdust. At once his face lit up with joy.

'Ha! Were you saving up for your own little trip to Heaven?'

He patted some water on his face and changed his clothes.

It is said that market day is the peasant's birthday party, and true to this saying, tradesmen and pedlars filled the road leading into the market. They all seemed like friends in Takbo's eyes. Now his busy hours would finally begin.

Takbo and his wife were not merely inhabitants of the village, but pretty notorious local celebrities as well. They were both around fifty, but they didn't have any children. As for 'property' and 'savings', they didn't know the meaning of those words. They just lived each day as it came.

Their life was so wild that no one ever came to offer them comfort, and no one invited them to share in times of festivities. Wherever they went, they were uninvited, unwelcome guests, and were the object of much nudging and gossip.

A whale of a drinker ... literally 'Takbo'. This nickname was an appropriate one when you think that even after pouring down gallons and gallons of wine, he never had any trouble with his bladder, but would wake up as good as ever.

But whenever he had had too much to drink, his favourite pastime was beating the hell out of his wife.

'You! Do you call yourself a woman? Why can't you whelp a little blighter that looks like you, the way the other women do? In the old days they would have kicked you out of the house for committing one of the Seven Crimes!' And once he started beating her there was no stopping him.

'Huh, you can talk! What about yourself, are you so sure the seed you're sowing is healthy?' She wasn't stupid enough to take all the blame. In fact, it was difficult to know whose fault it was. Takbo had had his share when he was young but he had not produced any children. As for Yokmaldaek who was Takbo's third wife, she had not been able to bear a child before their marriage, so that in a sense she had not 'proved herself' either.

Although they had lived together for twenty years as intimate strangers, they had nowhere else to let out their personal grievances, and no one to confide in. They would turn and face each other in mortal combat at the slightest provocation.

But for all of that, their lives were not completely devoid of affection. After being beaten to a pulp, Yokmaldaek would mourn and howl so sorrowfully that Takbo himself would break into tears. At this unbecoming sight her wailing would get even sadder.

'I'm sorry, please stop crying now.'

In the end Takbo would hold her by the hand and pull her up. After giving her nose a good blow, Yokmaldaek would smile at him. Soon they'd be smiling and chatting with each other as if nothing had happened.

On these nights after their battles, Takbo opened a book under the flickering light of the oil lamp, and read to her. When he came across a difficult passage he added some improvisations and guesses and glided smoothly over the lines. It was said that he had entered primary school at twenty but had quit after only a year. The fluency that Yokmaldaek had in retelling 'The Fallen Flowers and Flowing River', 'Love at Sandy Beach', 'The Tale of Ok Dan Chun', and other love stories of the sort, was largely due to the fact that Takbo had read them to her time and time again, year after year.

At night, after her day's work, Yokmaldaek often dozed off while having her supper, and it was no surprise that she grew leaner by the day. Partly this was because of the hardships she experienced; but more importantly it was due to her anxiety at not being able to have a child. She was also distressed to see her ageing husband lament day and night at the passing of time, and worry about the dismal future that lay ahead of them. It was a wonder she managed to limit her feeling to 'distress' and nothing worse.

The roof, which had not been thatched since . . . God knows when, leaked whenever it rained. The walls had crumbled down in places so that stars could be seen at night from inside the room, but not a thing had been repaired. The least Takbo might have done was to cover the holes with some mud, but he couldn't be bothered even with that.

As Yokmaldaek shrivelled up day by day under the crushing weight of the salt, the opposite was true of Takbo. To him, any house with a gathering, whether for a celebration of some kind or for commemorative mourning for departed ancestors, was *his* house. And if there was anything that wasn't lacking in those houses, it was food and drink! Thus as his wife withered away, he grew fatter as the months wore on.

More than any other problem that Takbo presented to the villagers, his habit of bursting into tears and asking for 'Malsun's mum' when he was drunk was particularly annoying and embarrassing. It made them all feel awkward and uncomfortable, but for a certain Yom Kilsong it was downright painful. He and Takbo were both living in the same village and were both growing old; but with this the similarities stopped, and there was a particularly important difference. Yom Kilsong was none other than Malsun's father.

How Takbo came to be in such a situation is a long story. Many years ago, when Yom was employed as a servant for Squire Yun, Takbo and the woman who was now the mother of Malsun were husband and wife. Even in those days, Takbo was notorious for his drinking, and it was more than understandable that he couldn't make a success of his job as a farmhand. Indeed Takbo himself didn't think much of his employers, but unfortunately for him the antipathy was mutual. His notoriety had spread to such an extent that he could not get a job, even in his own village. And without a job the future looked bleak, especially concerning his unpaid drinking bills.

But to top the lot, a rumour began to float about that his wife was seen going into the hemp field with Yom. Far from being ruffled by the news, however, Takbo adopted a very businesslike attitude, and people said it was Takbo who contacted Yom first and put his case to him.

'Look, they say that a rumour is only a rumour, and I'll go as far as to say that I won't get angry even if the rumour about you and my wife sharing the same pillow is true. But you've got to think about my feelings. Suppose you were in my position . . .'

'What do you mean?'

It wasn't because Yom didn't know what Takbo was talking about that he asked this question.

'You know what kind of a rumour is going around, and so I suppose you know I'm in a bit of a fix. I can't really let things take their course, but on the other hand . . . Come on, don't just sit there blinking your eyes. Tell me the truth!'

'All right, I've got your message. Give me a chance to think about the best solution. I can't promise you much, but I'm not an ungrateful person.'

'Thank you, I hope things will turn out for the best. Anyway, you won't make me too sad, will you?'

The deal was concluded the next day. It was said that Yom went to Takbo's house in the middle of the night. As soon as he came into the house, Takbo's wife, whom Takbo thought was still asleep, jumped out of the quilt and put on a new pair of socks which she took out from under the sewing box.

'Who is it? Is it you, Yom Kilsong?'

When she opened the door nervously there was Yom, looking very smart in his overcoat.

Takbo just closed his eyes. Rather, he closed his mind. It was said that when he opened his eyes again, the oil lamp was out. Relighting the lamp – *voilà!* – he found Yom and his wife were nowhere to be seen, but on the mattress lay a five won note.

245

Even these days when Yokmaldaek referred to that incident he would lose his temper and say, 'Five *won* in those days was a lot of money, and if I wanted to raise that kind of money again I'd have to sell three or four like you put together.'

When Takbo returned to the village after less than a year's absence, his former wife had already given birth to her first son, and after that she bore six daughters in succession, and in consecutive years. Malsun was the youngest of the six.

As she gave birth to one child after another, Takbo's drinking got worse and worse. So in effect, as Yom got richer in daughters, Takbo became more of a boozer.

Yokmaldaek at the time was a lonely woman who'd been deserted by her former husband for her alleged barrenness, and was growing old and searching for some support. Takbo was doing the same. It was perhaps inevitable that these two, sharing the same lonely fate, came to live together. It was a good thing in many ways.

Although once, unable to stand Takbo's drinking, she ran away to Seoul, but she couldn't help returning to him later at Namdaemun Police Station. Perhaps she was won over by his sincerity, but whatever the reason, she had not regretted coming back with him.

'Love and affection are nothing special . . . you get to love someone by sharing your life together. It's nothing special, really . . .'

That was what Takbo would always say to her.

When Takbo left the house and reached the inn on the newly built main road, he saw the wife of Kang the tax collector walking past him. It wasn't her that drew his attention, but the basket she was carrying on her head because he saw the necks of a couple of bottles of . . . something! sticking out of the basket. She was on her way to the rice paddies.

'So, the day's first drink is here!'

Takbo turned and followed her with consummate skill.

Day labourers were scattered across Kang's fields. If the rain had not been so heavy recently, no doubt Kang would have had to hire even more hands to irrigate the land, by means no more modern than bucketing water in by hand.

The work seemed to be progressing slowly and the workers were ready for something to eat. When they've had this rest,

Takbo thought, it will be around ten o'clock. After splashing about for an hour or two it'll be lunchtime, and when they've finished commenting on the food and had an afternoon's nap, it'll be about three or four, and after another short spell, it'll be the afternoon break when they'll be having another snack. After a puff or two on a cigarette the sun will be slowly sinking into the west. On top of that they'll get a free packet of cigarettes as a bonus. It was small wonder that Chunsob, who had left for Seoul in search of something better, had come back before a month had elapsed, back to the well-worn, familiar handle of his hoe.

So Takbo was able to scrounge a bowl of rice and a glass of *makoli*.

'Talk about the good life! Takbo, your life is the best of the lot.'

'Yes, nothing could be better than that,' the workmen said, sounding really envious.

Scrounging a cigarette this time, Takbo sat under the shade of a tree with the others. He made some comments on the moves in a game of chess, and then got up and headed towards the market, joining a party of pedlars heading in the same direction. It was only a twenty minute walk from where he was.

At the cattle market, which was situated near the entrance to the main market, Takbo happened to bump into Kim Chasun. Kim Chasun had also lived in Galmori before the end of the war in '45. At that time he was quite penniless, but Takbo had heard that after moving to Wa-ryong Gorge in Hyngkyo County he had somehow come into some money, and was now able to lead a fairly comfortable life.

'How's the farming? How are your wife and children?'

'Fine, fine . . .'

For him, the very idea that he was acquainted with someone like Takbo was embarrassment enough. He was also afraid that Takbo might dirty his brand new ramie overcoat. Takbo himself wasn't so stupid not to know that.

'It's been a long time. Let's go somewhere and have a chat over a snack. How about it?'

Takbo held on to Chasun's coat, and didn't look like letting go. Chasun's face turned a little darker.

'I'm rather busy at the moment...' Chasun said, trying to shake Takbo off.

'What do you mean "busy", we're all busy in one way or another. I'm so busy I haven't the time to look at my prick after I've had a piss these days!'

Takbo pushed Chasun's back, and they entered the inn. He ordered dog-meat soup and rice whisky.

'Did you come to buy an ox?'

'No, I came to see the mayor, but he wasn't in, and they said I should wait.'

'Have as much as you like, come on. I've got plenty of money. If that's not enough, then you can fill the gap and pay the rest.'

Takbo wrapped a garlic in some dog skin and gobbled it down. He was sweating heavily.

After eating everything on the table, Takbo took out the dirty hundred *won* note speckled with sawdust.

'That's funny, there should be some more somewhere... I'm sure of it...' and pretended to search his pockets.

Chasun watched this farce and produced the four hundred *won* left to be paid.

'We've stuffed one twentieth of an acre of land down our throats.'

Today, business was quite good for Yokmaldaek. Scarcely an hour after she'd opened her stall, she had already sold one *mal* and seven *doi*.*

The markets were always busy in summer, right from the very beginning. And due to the good supply of crops after the rain, it was as lively as any market just before a public holiday. At the rate business was going, Yokmaldaek would be able to leave before closing time; and this meant that with luck she could avoid being taxed by the market duty collector, and take home every penny she had earned that day. If the salt didn't sell quickly enough, she would soon have to give it away at a bargain price.

But not everything went according to plan. It was a bad

---

*The *mal* and *doi* are measures of volume; 10 *doi* make 1 *mal* which is 18 litres.

omen to have had the will-o'-the-wisp jumping around so early in the morning, and true enough, the sky began to cloud.

On either side of her stood Yonkab's grandma, Ojaeng-i's aunt, Tongshik's sister and Malsun's mum. And from the way they were all able to nibble on some starchy bread for lunch, their business wasn't doing too badly either.

It was past midday, and she felt hungry. She had to have something to eat. Suddenly she remembered that there were some over-ripe melons selling for next to nothing.

'Malsun's mum, could you look after my things? I think I have to go to the toilet . . . I've been trying to hold off, but . . .'

'Sure, go and relieve yourself,' Malsun's mum answered without turning her head.

Yokmaldaek hurried toward the crop stalls, which sent a thick, sweet aroma floating across to her. At this time of the year, the melons came cheaper the bigger and heavier they were.

Threading her way past the merchants, she found herself at last in front of the vegetable stand. She had a good look all around to see if anyone she knew was watching her. Seeing that nobody was near, she squatted in front of the stack of melons, and from a separate pile of rejected ones, she picked up the biggest and gave it a shake. From the watery sound it made, it was obviously over-ripe, or rather it had been 'baked' in the humid heat of the rainy season.

'Well I suppose it's better than eating green, unripe ones. It'll be softer and sweeter . . .'

She asked how much they were, and was told three *won* each. She bought two for five *won*, and fearing she might be seen, started eating one without even peeling the skin. She soon felt full.

'Blimey, these days you can't even go to the toilet without waiting ages. I mean, there were so many people!'

She returned to her usual position behind the salt basket. It was only then that she really wanted to go to the toilet.

'You know, I think we should all go and have a rotten melon, seeing we're all so bored . . .'

As Malsun's mum said these words, the others looked up to see the melon seeds clinging to Yokmaldaek's upper lip.

At a distance, Takbo appeared from under the drapery stall's
tent. He stood there inconspicuously, and studied Yokmaldaek
with his beady eyes. His face was flushed with drink.

He was planning to get up to his old tricks – he would go
up to the stall and shake the salt basket about, pretending he
was drunk – then Yokmaldaek would have to give him some
money.... He was waiting for a suitable moment to put his
plan into action.

Takbo, with his big, broad forehead, the pillar of a back
which could carry thirty *mal* with strength to spare, and his
big, bulky body... from any angle he looked a dignified old
man. However, with his wife he was no more mature than a
three-year-old infant crying for his mother's milk.

After waiting a bit, he started towards the salt stands, thinking the best time had come for his assault.

Two middle aged women holding parasols were being served
by Yokmaldaek. Takbo had it all worked out. He would first
embarrass Yokmaldaek by going up to the stall saying, 'Come
on old woman, press the salt down hard when you're measuring it!' and pick up the measuring scoop himself. If anyone
took a picture of Yokmaldaek's face then he'd be able to sell
it at quite a high price.

But he had hardly started towards the stand when a disturbance flared up. Takbo stopped in his tracks.

'Oh, no!...'

'Oh, sir, please...'

Amidst these shouts, the people from Galmori could be seen
rushing about with their salt baskets in their hands.

'Let go of my arm! I warned you last time, didn't I?'

The man in the old suit raising his voice was none other
than the market duty collector.

It was customary for the county office to collect a fee for
clearing the market afterwards. Usually it was about ten *won*
altogether, and it varied according to how much space a stall
occupied.

If the day's trading was not good the salt sellers from Galmori would stand firm in their refusal to pay up; but even if
business had not been too bad, it was their nature not to oblige
the tax collector. It so happened that their tax had been piling
up over several market days, as they tried to put off paying it
for as long as possible; so that now it was equivalent to the

price of more than a *mal* of salt. And last market day he had warned them that he would take the tax in salt if he wasn't paid in money. So here it was. The official must have asked for the money, and apparently one of the Galmori people had again resorted to the old excuse that they would pay on the next market day 'without fail'. It must have been this that had made the duty collector so angry.

The official, with the help of an office boy from the county office, was making his attack, starting with the stalls at either end of the row. It was Tongshik's sister and Yonkab's grandma who were the first to have their baskets seized. Tongshik's sister, making a show of maidenly innocence, and hairy Mr Shin's new daughter-in-law, still not quite aware of the realities of a pedlar's life, ran away, half frightened to death, leaving their baskets behind.

'Oh, sir, please, I beg of you!'

Ojaeng-i's aunt fell on top of her basket, pleading and weeping. Malsun's mum was being held and kicked by the duty collector, as she tried desperately to save her tin bowl of salt.

'Look here, do you think I like doing this sort of thing? You can't imagine how many times you've annoyed me with your lies and broken promises!'

He kicked the basket until it was knocked out of all shape, beyond all recognition.

'This is the last time you're going to fool around with me. This time I'll teach you a lesson.!'

There was some justice in what the duty collector said.

'Oh, please, I have four children to feed, please. . . .' Ojaeng-i's aunt wept.

Had the men been here, the pedlars would not have had to go through this degradation, but Ojaeng-i's uncle and Tonshik's dad had gone back home after helping to carry the salt to the market.

'All right, you bastard, I'll do it for you!'

Yonkab's grandma, after trying everything from begging to blackmail, and failing at both, now let go of her basket and went for the office boy, trying to grab him by the collar.

The boy, not really in a position to abuse the old hag, nor to push her away forcibly, went red all over and then suddenly snatched the salt basket and tried to run off with it.

'Oh no you don't!'

The ha*g* shook her head and reached under the counter for a jug of dirty dish water, which she poured over her sack of salt.

'That's too much, there was no need for that ... What's wrong with that woman ...'

There were comments from the thick wall of spectators that had formed around the scene.

Meanwhile, Yokmaldaek was able to get away in the confusion with her salt basket intact. It went well up to that point, but where could she go from there? She had no time to think. The first place that crossed her mind was the shop opposite. She rushed into the shop's living quarters behind the counter, but a fierce dog was guarding the entrance, ready to tear anyone apart. The toilet behind the main door caught her eye.

Unfortunately the duty collector had seen her entering the shop and followed her. He also was nearly bitten by the dog, and stopped abruptly. Then he saw the toilet. There was nowhere else she could have gone. But first he gave a knock.

Knock knock ...

Knock knock ... came the reply.

Yokmaldaek put her heavy basket down on the floor.

'It's occupied. You can't come in right now,' she said and locked the door.

'I know you're in there. Come out now, come on.'

The duty collector was hardly able to keep from laughing as he spoke. He continued to tug at the door handle.

Yokmaldaek, not daring to let out a cough, or even a moan, was beginning to regret having opened her big mouth.

'No, I'm not your salt pedlar. I'm having a crap at the moment, really I am ...'

'What, are you trying to make a fool of me!'

As he forced the door open with an almighty heave, Yokmaldaek came tumbling out still holding on to the door handle.

Takbo, having seen enough, slowly turned around and headed towards the stalls selling odd bits and pieces.

It wasn't because he didn't want to help his wife that he turned away; it was because he knew he wouldn't have been able to do anything despite his size, and thought the best thing to do was to save face and forget he saw it happen.

Takbo spat out his phlegmy spittle and stood thinking. The

alcohol was rising to his head, but far from feeling good, all he felt was irritation . . . Now, where can I go to sweeten my mood . . . Okay, there's that travelling medicine man's show I saw earlier today . . .

Takbo searched around for the medicine seller. He noticed a loud-speaker tied to an electricity pole, next to the public lavatory. A young woman with her hair in two plaits was singing 'Speak to Me, Mount Yudal'. The audience seemed to be made up of the usual mixed bunch who came to market. They had never seen a proper show in their lives, and there was no applause, in spite of the size of the audience.

The repertoire moved on through songs like Lee Mija's 'The Camellia Girl', but still there wasn't much response from the crowd. Perhaps it was because of the weather. The farmers, already depressed to the limit by the wet season, could see the sky beginning to darken again, struggling under the thick quilt of black clouds.

The day was steaming hot without a breath of wind to cool it. Takbo began to miss the sharp and tangy taste of a glass of rice whisky.

He left the show and wandered around the market a few times, but couldn't find anyone he knew. The only place he could get a drink on credit was the inn at Galmori.

'Okay, off to Galmori then . . .'

So for the first time in his life he left the market place before sunset.

Takbo woke up from his sleep. Rather he woke up from the effect of alcohol. All he could see in front of him was total darkness. He couldn't tell where the line of the earth ended and where the sky began. It was just one huge blurred mess.

He didn't have the slightest idea where he was. A dog was barking in the distance. His neck burned. His limbs ached as if someone were pounding them to a pulp. It was cold. His stomach felt sore. Perhaps he was hungry. Slowly, his eyes got a little brighter. He stumbled to his feet and looked around. At last he realized that he was in a heap of straw next to the compost pit in Yom Kilsong's yard. He felt faint. A fear came over him that he may have made a scene again, asking for Malsun's mum. Oh, no . . . he thought to himself.

He was rubbing his mosquito-bitten limbs, and trying to get

hold of himself, when he heard a racket going on at a distance. The sound was getting nearer. He saw a lamp slowly moving towards him.

'Calm down, father. Let's go back into the house. You're quite drunk now, and you need some rest . . .'

'No, I must have it out with him once and for all!'

It was Yom Kilsong and his son.

'You can do that tomorrow when it's light and you're sober.'

Yom's son, Il-yong, was trying to restrain his father by hanging on to him and holding him down. Il-yong was said to be on leave from his military service. Takbo felt something gush up inside; he felt sorry for himself. He had no children who would do for him what Il-yong was doing for Yom. There was no one to help him off the dirt right now. He envied Yom.

'Let go of me, boy, I'm not drunk. This time I'm going to teach that Takbo a lesson. I'll squeeze it out of him why he always cries for 'Malsun's mum' whenever he's drowned himself in drink. The bastard! Let go, I say, let go.'

Takbo felt the sky crumbling on top of him. He couldn't remember a thing that had happened, but since he found himself lying there, there was no doubt whatsoever that he'd made a scene again.

'That rascal Takbo, he's still lying there on the straw pile, isn't he?' said Yom as he rolled up his sleeves.

'No, father, he's long gone.' Il-yong was doing his best to cool his father down.

Takbo got up quietly and sneaked out past the pig sty behind the compost heap. He followed the edge of the hemp fields and headed home in the darkness. A rumble of thunder went rolling past him towards Mount Songju.

He reached his house but there was no one to welcome him except the humming of the mosquitoes.

'Where is that bitch, hasn't she come back yet?' Takbo mumbled and sat down in the entrance to the room.

'Why are you so late? Where have you been?'

Yokmaldaek stuck her face out of the kitchen. A flash of lightning made her jump as she did so. She went on.

'The rain's too heavy, and it looks like a flood.'

Before Takbo arrived she had been about to bury the day's takings in the sack of sawdust. She had discovered that the hundred *won* note was missing and she was lamenting her miserable existence when she heard Takbo coming in. It was only after she had hurriedly put the money in the tin of chilli powder and snapped the lid tight that she dared put her head out.

'What are you doing there without a light?' he asked.

'Do you really think we have any oil left for the lamp?'

'Well then go and buy some, or borrow a lampful from somewhere.'

'If we'd paid back what we borrowed last time we might be able to borrow some now!'

'You're the one who's supposed to be earning the money, what do you do with it all?'

'I buried it in the sack of sawdust, why do you ask?'

'Oh, shut up, I don't want to speak to you.'

'Oh, my rotten luck! I lose my salt and my basket, and when I come back to this hole I call my home I find there's a thief under the roof . . . and it's my fate to call this thief my husband. Oh, why do I have such bloody awful luck!'

'Shut your trap before I tear your arsehole out!'

Takbo sprang up and swung his fist at Yokmaldaek, but missed her completely.

'Have you made supper yet? Why aren't you asking me to have something to eat?'

'How can I make supper after what I've been through. I've bought something instead.'

Yokmaldaek came out of the kitchen, holding a paper bag.

'Aren't they dumplings from the Chinese restaurant?'

'No, buns.'

'Stupid cow, how do you expect me to swallow those cotton balls on their own without anything to go with them, like some soup or something?'

Takbo crawled into the room. He took off his shirt and chased away the mosquitoes, swinging the shirt around. He dropped to the ground and started snoring. Yokmaldaek put the buns back in the kitchen and followed Takbo inside.

There was an acrid smell of sweat in the room. She lay down with all her clothes on because of the mosquitoes. Using the sack of barley as a pillow, she rested her head and stretched out her legs.

The sound of thunder rolled through the air as if it would split the sky, but Yokmaldaek could only hear the humming mosquitoes around her. It was said that when the will-o'-the-wisp was active near the stream, rain would follow. True to this lore, it started to pour down in the middle of the night.

The room was letting in water, and puddles were starting to form on the floor. The water rushing down from the cemetery was bringing earth and sand with it. And the little trickle that used to flow past Takbo's chimney had now swollen a hundred, a thousand fold, and had begun to overflow.

'Ahhh!!'

Takbo opened his eyes as something struck him very hard. The force was so great that he felt he'd been hit by lightning. The roof had collapsed, and as it came down it struck him on the back of the head.

'Hey, hey, wake up!'

He tried to escape by twisting his trunk, but the main crossbeam of the roof had fallen and he couldn't budge an inch. Luckily for him he had not taken the full force of the collapse. If the beam had fallen on him directly, no doubt his back would have been broken. But the beam's fall had been checked by the wooden chest and the pile of quilts. And even though this piece of wood was called the 'cross beam', it was barely the thickness of his arm.

'Come on, wake up, you salt-selling bitch!'

'When I shook you, you were a corpse!'

Yokmaldaek was lying nearer the chest so she had a little more freedom of movement than Takbo. Before anything else, Takbo was glad that his wife was unharmed.

'What the hell's happening?'

'The whole lot's come down!'

With a crash the floor had collapsed and gave way under the added weight. Takbo went down with it. Now he could move more freely. But there was not a moment to lose. The water level had started to rise rapidly.

Pressing against the ground with his arms and legs, Takbo pushed up with his back. The old roof had been so much weakened by years of wear, that one man's force could move it a little. Supporting the weight with his burly limbs, as strong as the branches of an oak, he pushed the beam up with a thrust of his backside. Then a rafter lying across his head snapped. It was a piece of rotten wood as thick as a child's arm.

'Quickly, get under me!'

'If you'd done something to it before . . .'

Yokmaldaek only just managed to crawl under him. Takbo started to push against the wall. It was made of layers of dried sod, and under Takbo's pressure it looked as if it would give way at any minute. If it didn't crumble inwards they would be able to escape to the outside.

'Ouch!!'

Takbo shrank back as he gave a sharp cry of pain. He had felt something moving on his back, and soon found out what it was: a rat. The rat had bitten him on the buttock, which had been shaking and heaving in an undignified manner.

'Are you hurt?'

'It's that damn rat. Huh, it serves him right to drown. That's his punishment for gnawing through the walls and the beams. Good riddance!'

'Oh be quiet. That's what the rat should say to *you*. If you had seen to the house before, this sort of thing would never have happened. Think how much the rat must have hated you to bite you with its last breath . . .'

At last the wall gave way, collapsing outwards. With this the roof, or rather what was left of the roof, fell down flat. But Takbo was strong. After all, he had done nothing but eat and sleep, and it wasn't too difficult for him to push away the flimsy cover that passed for a roof.

By the time they got out to th world outside it was quite light. The little streamlet had turned into a raging torrent, and the water level had risen to Takbo's navel, and was jostling against the land.

Takbo and Yokmaldaek climbed the hill behind the house. Sitting on the slope, they watched their house being engulfed in reddish brown water. They saw a large cooking pot floating on the surface, tied to a mugwort reed. Yokmaldaek got up.

'Well, we'll have to rescue the pots and pans at least . . .'

'Don't be silly. We're lucky even to be alive. And when have we *ever* saved anything for the house?'

Takbo was clutching the place where the rat had bitten him and massaging himself. But even in this sort of crisis, he was unruffled. There were two cuts on his back, bleeding from where the rafters had struck him.

'Oh, that, that is . . .'

Yokmaldaek discovered the chilli powder tin entangled in some shrubbery next to the toilet. She remembered that every penny she had was inside the tin.

'We have to save that tin!'

'Bitch, what the hell are you going to do with it? Hang it around your neck and beg on the streets, I suppose.'

'Without that tin we'll be even poorer.'

Takbo pulled her down, and made her sit.

'You can't go in there barefoot. It's full of broken bits of china, and apart from that you might fall into the toilet.'

'I don't care. We have to have it.'

'Why are you so keen to get that tin? I mean, you let the pots and pans go . . .'

But Yokmaldaek didn't tell him about the money.

The rain kept pouring down, and the water was rising by the minute.

'We'll have to go into someone's house and rest a bit. Otherwise we'll get ill or something.'

'Where on earth can we go? Especially looking like this . . .?'

Yokmaldaek looked at herself. Her appearance was untidy to say the least. In fact she looked awful. It was only then that Takbo guessed what must have been in the tin.

'Oh yes, and what was in that tin, anyway?'

'Leave it. It wasn't much anyway . . .'

'What do you mean, "leave it"? Do you know how much the price of chilli has risen recently because of the bad harvest?'

'Just leave it, you might fall into the toilet.'

'If I do, I'll have a bath.'

Takbo staggered down to the water. The wild muddy torrent, like a monster from the underworld, was pushing the large cooking pot into the stream.

'It's all because of booze! Oh, the demon drink! Why do you drink so much? I mean, you must be the only person in the world who's washed away his house in wine and whisky. Do you drink because you like the stuff, or is it just a habit?'

Yokmaldaek took the opportunity to see if Takbo had learnt anything from the calamity.

'I don't drink because I like the stuff, I drink because I like money . . .'

Takbo cracked this remark as he reached out for the tin.

'Ah, my wretched life . . . just take the whole tin and get

something to drink at the inn. I'll go to Malsun's to get a mouthful to eat.'

Yokmaldaek squeezed the water from her drawers. Takbo opened the tin.

Part 3

'WINTER, 1964, SEOUL' AND OTHER STORIES

ECHOES

O YONG-SU

Translated by W. E. Skillend

The days can be as much as an hour shorter in the valley than on the plains, but it is a broad level valley, with the huge Mount Chiri behind it to the southwest, and the River Tokchon flowing to the northeast. Across the river, the county town of Sanchong is perhaps five miles away. Once or twice a year a priest from the Taewon Temple goes through it, with a rucksack on his back. There is a smaller valley going off it to the southeast, where one might see a shack covered with eulalia and pine branches. This is where Yang Tong-uk and his wife live.

They found this place the spring after the mopping up of communist guerillas on Mount Chiri had been completed, set up camp here, and began to clear the ground.

They had been refugees in Pusan. Struggle as they might, they had not been able to make a living. They had no skills. There was nothing they would not have turned their hands to, but there was no work, nothing they could do.

They knew quite well that they only needed medicine to keep their child alive, but they had none to give it, and had had to let it die. When their shanty on Youngson Pass was pulled down as well, they gave up and drifted away.

They lived for several months in Chinju. Tong-uk tried working as a carpenter's or plasterer's mate. It was only for a

263

few days a month, and even then work was short. He did not even get his share of work, never mind any wages.

His wife set out as a pedlar, with a tin bowl on her head. She sought out mainly the country villages, but since she could not reduce her prices below cost, she made no sales.

There was nothing to be done to keep themselves alive.

They went to Sanchong.

Here there was less than nothing to be done.

'We are fish out of water, dear. Let's give it up and go right into the hills and work a bit of land.'

So they sold everything that they could raise money on. They bought two bags of wheat flour and thirty pounds of seed potatoes, and purchased a bundle of cabbage leaves. They packed up hoes, a saw and sickle, and other such tools; several bowls of soy bean paste, two gourdsful of salt, and besides all this a bottle of paraffin and an oil lamp. Leaving Sanchong, they set off for the hills.

After a mile or two they were in the hills. Tong-uk's pace slowed. Out there in the world everyone was going on living, everyone was alive, yet they were unable to live there, were being driven off like this to an uninhabited valley, he thought. The sadness that welled up and choked him was a sort of defeatism. It made him feel all the more sorry for his wife who was following behind him, and yet at the same time he was dependent on her.

'What shall we do? The valleys are all much the same, aren't they, everywhere?' Tong-uk said, as he stared around the valley.

'They may be all the same, but go on. Let's see if we can get as far as the end of this track.'

The sun stood nearly halfway across the sky already. The pale glint of a river could be seen around a bend. They walked listlessly, just gazing at the distant spot where the river was. They skirted round a cliff a little way, and there was the river flowing at their feet. The water was low, and they crossed it. They followed the track, which sometimes seemed to be there and sometimes not, went round the foot of the hill, crossed over several ridges, and then entered the valley. The further in they went, the broader it got. By the side of the path they saw fragments of earthenware.

'Does it look as if it used to be a village?'

'It does look like it.'

These fragments of earthenware made their hearts beat faster, as welcome to them as discovering an ancestor's grave. As the valley widened there were many fields that had been cultivated the year before and were tangles of weeds now.

Tong-uk and his wife, as if by agreement, put down their loads by the side of a fair-sized rock in this branch valley.

Tong-uk took out the saw that very day, and began to cut up some wood to build a hut. They passed that night sitting back to back, with blankets around them, and a good fire to frighten off any wild animals.

In four days they had fastened together what might be called a hut, and dug over the fields. They burnt off some of the fields that had almost gone back to nature, and started digging the burnt patches. Tong-uk took up the hoe while the stars were still shining, and put it down only when it was dark. His wife pulled out the roots of the weeds and made furrows.

By near the end of March, they had planted about a sixteenth of an acre with potato. Since they did not have enough seed potatoes, they broke them into pieces, planting each eye separately. Mrs Yang's fingers were scratched and torn, and the blistered palms of Tong-uk's hands hardened into callouses.

As April set in, the wild vegetables sprouted everywhere. At a stage when they were counting every cabbage leaf, nothing could have been more useful than wild vegetables.

As soon as they had had some rain, the potato shoots came up too. With them came a carpet of weeds which covered the ground completely, all from seeds that had fallen in the previous autumn. The weed shoots were too small for Tong-uk's wife to get hold of, and she picked them out with her fingertips, like nits, but she did not mind the tedium of it. Only when the sun had set and Tong-uk had put down his hoe and told his wife to get up, because her hands must have been sore with all the weeding, did she stop work.

As she did so, she would always look back over the furrows in the field that she had been weeding and scratching at all day and say, 'If we could spread a layer of manure from an ox on it...'

It was true that what they lacked was manure.

Tong-uk went up along the brook as far as the next valley back. He took off his coat and washed his hands and feet. He wrung out the towel tucked in at his waist and, sitting down on a nice round rock beside the brook, rubbed his face as he gazed up at the hills. This had become a sort of habit with him morning and evening, from the time they had come here.

Tong-uk liked hills. Perhaps it was because he had grown up in a mountain valley. The deeper he was in the hills, the better; the more trees there were, the better. And not pines particularly: the thicker the trees were, the better he liked it. He liked the spring for being spring and the summer for being summer. He liked the autumn more, and did not even dislike the winter.

If he was gazing at hills like this, he felt safer and more secure. He was pleased and happy at having come to the valley, just as if he had returned to his childhood home. He congratulated himself on having come to the valley.

There are times, now and again, when the hills boom. It could be every day, or it could be a few times a month. The deeper you are in the hills, the more they do it. It is a faint, yet clear and heavy song, as if coming from the ends of the earth. Every time the mountains sang, Tong-uk felt awed at what seemed to be the livingness of the hills. He heard the echo of the cry of a buck deer from another valley somewhere. Twilight fell.

He went down to the shack. At the shack the twig fire was blazing for supper. After filling themselves up with a gruel made of flour mixed with wild vegetables, they relaxed into absolute exhaustion. They went to bed early to save paraffin too.

'When I've finished weeding the potato patch, I must dig up and lay in a really good stock of fern shoots and wild roots – pick and dry the wild vegetables before they're too old.'

'The first clearing'll be finished in a day or two.'

'The potatoes are sprouting all right, aren't they?'

'Not bad. They could do with a layer of manure.'

'D'you think we'll get a couple of bagsful?'

'We'd better leave them.'

'I wish the new potatoes'd be ready soon.'

Tong-uk was silent.

'Darling!'

He had fallen asleep already, but his wife had too much to think about. What would they grow along the side of the field, where should they plant spring lettuces . . . but time was getting on and they had no seeds . . . she must not forget maize and pumpkin seeds, she reminded herself as she fell asleep.

Hardly wasting a moment after finishing weeding, she raced to dig up some of the roots like *todok*, and went off to market with them on her head. Tong-uk saw her off as far as the other bank of the River Tokchon.

'Should I come to meet you?'

'Why? I'll soon be back.'

'Sell them for any price you can get and come back before the sun goes down.'

'Of course.'

As she rounded a cliff, the path was almost lost among bushes. From time to time a squirrel cut across in front of her, but in several miles she did not see a single person.

The crown of her head was numb, her neck pushed down into her chest. She had to lean on a rock and put her bundle down. She opened her blouse and wiped away the sweat. She had a sudden thought: what if she should meet someone in such a valley? And if it were a man, would he simply step aside to let her pass? Her head throbbed at the thought. She hastily dragged the bundle up onto her head and stumbled out of the valley.

The market had just started at Sanchong. She put her bundle down by the bus stop at the market and straightaway two old ladies, who were waiting for the bus, saw her *todok*. They were delighted, and asked her whether she was selling them. When she said she was, they asked her how much she wanted for the lot. She asked them to give what they thought, and they asked whether four hundred *hwan* would do. She accepted, and the ladies packed the roots up in two bundles, sharing them between them. The stouter one, who seemed to be a couple of years older, added another hundred *hwan*.

'They're wild *todok*, aren't they? My goodness, this must have taken a lot of work, digging out every root.'

They were probably grandmothers from some big city in Kyongsang Province, out visiting a temple or something like that. Tong-uk's wife took the money and folded it away in a cloth, but did not walk away quickly, perhaps because she felt as if they were two grannies from her own neighbourhood, like old and close friends of hers. The two old ladies got on the bus, and as it edged its way round, Tong-uk's wife said, 'Thank you. Thank you,' although they would be unlikely to hear her, and awkwardly bowed her head at each word. If she still lived in the valley in Kangwon Province, up near Hamgyong Province in North Korea, her mother would be just about their age, she thought. Her eyelids burned.

The sun was nearly halfway across the sky. She made for a seed shop. She bought a hundred *hwan* worth of turnip and cabbage seed, and ten *hwan* each worth of onion, leek, red pepper, pumpkin and gourd seed. Then she bought a bag of maize, and as she was about to leave she suddenly thought of buying twenty *hwan* worth of tobacco seed. After all, her husband enjoyed tobacco even more than wine.

She took a look up at the sun and counted her remaining money. There was still three hundred *hwan* left. She was thinking of what they were without as she came to a dried fish shop. It was not much of a dried fish shop, but it did have a few things like pollock, bream and mackerel. She threw caution to the winds and bought a mackerel covered with salt. Now she must go, she thought, pulling her skirt string tight, and looking at the sun once more. But she still had some money left. She could take it with her, but it would be no use in the hills. They still had some paraffin for the light, and some salt left too. What were they short of? She was still thinking as she left the market. Some rough-made noodles being sold by the roadside caught her eye. Her mouth suddenly watered, and she felt an unbearable hunger. She asked the price first, and then had a bowlful. As she paid the fifty *hwan*, she asked, 'If I bring some wild vegetables, will you give me some soy bean paste for them?'

'That depends on what sort of soy bean paste. Where do you live, my dear?'

'In the valley on the way to the Taewon Temple.'

'Is it all right there now?'

'Yes, indeed.'

'Before the war, we used to live in a valley about seven or eight miles from here. The war made us abandon all our fields and come here.'

Mrs Yang said nothing. The lady drew in her breath: 'If our lad came back, we'd have to go there ourselves.'

'But we had nowhere to live, except the valley.'

'My dear, you bring me fern and aralia shoots, and I'll give you as much paste as you can eat for them.'

'Thank you. All right, I'll come next market day.'

Having eaten noodles by herself, she felt guilty about her husband, and spent all the money she had left on tobacco before she raced away. She felt really pleased. She was delighted just to think of giving her husband an unexpected gift of tobacco. She wanted to see his face too when she boiled him a piece of mackerel. On her way to market, the load had been so heavy that she had not been able to turn her head, but now she gazed round the valley at the cliffs and the rest as she hurried along. In every little valley, at every cliff, there were masses of azaleas blooming. Between almost black-green pine trees the new shoots of the bushes were as soft as a coating on rice cakes and prettier than maples in the autumn. A pheasant, out in the daytime probably guarding his territory somewhere, beat his wings and cried.

In the hills, the sun was already shaded. She crossed the river, turned a spur, went over a ridge, and as she entered the valley she saw the shack. She wondered whether to shout 'Hello!' she was so glad to see it, but decided against it. She could see her husband's back, about as far away as the shack. He was hoeing.

'Have a bit of a rest.'

At the voice Tong-uk jumped and looked around.

'Oh, you're back! I was just wondering whether to come and meet you,' he said, as he went up to her.

'Why? Did you think I'd take the wrong path?'

'I wondered whether you might have been carried off by a wood-cutter.'

'It'd be terrible to be carried off, but there'd have to be someone to do it. But look at . . .'

'What's this?'

'You look!'

'Mm, it's tobacco!'

Tong-uk sniffed the tobacco, and rolled some up rather thickly in newspaper.

'And did you get all the seeds?'

'I got just all the most urgent things.'

'You should've bought a rake before tobacco. Did you?'

269

'I didn't think of that! I'll buy one next market day.'

Tong-uk put a cigarette in his mouth and took up his hoe again, with a glance at the lingering rays of the sun.

'Here!'

'What? Something else?'

'Open it!'

'Tobacco seeds! What's this – is this all you've got?'

'There's more than enough there for an eighth of an acre, they said. That's the way with tobacco seeds.'

Tong-uk was charmed enough by this wife of his to want to pinch her cheek.

On the supper table that night there was a piece of mackerel. Tong-uk's nostrils dilated.

'Where did this fish come from?'

'I had some money left, so I bought it.'

Tong-uk ladled up a couple of spoonsful of thick gruel, and picked off a morsel of mackerel and chewed it.

'This is going to ruin my palate, but . . .'

'What d'you mean? That we shouldn't even brighten up our lives by buying some salt fish?'

'Oh, I suppose you're right, but taste's a very misleading thing.'

'You can say misleading or anything you like, but you'll just have to put up with it.'

Tong-uk had already emptied one bowl and taken a second. He indicated the fish dish with his eyes, and said, 'Why aren't you having any? Shouldn't we share it?'

'Oh, not that little piece! I had a bowl of noodles today.'

'Well done! But when you say noodles, do you mean they were buckwheat noodles with winter pickles?'

'What would you say to wheat noodles with minced pheasant?'

'Yes, but we ought to have a bit of buckwheat.'

'In the autumn, let's plant some wheat!'

'Manure's the problem. We really should keep a pig for the manure.'

'I'd like to manage somehow to get and keep a pair of chickens.'

'They'd be difficult because of lynxes and weasels and things, chickens.'

'What's that? Are there a lot of them, lynxes and weasels?'

'I'd say so, out in the hills like this.'

'Do they come out in the day?'

'They probably do.'

However, in his heart, Tong-uk wanted to keep chickens no less than his wife. To keep out lynxes and weasels you have to keep a dog, and in their situation now, when they could not even spare themselves a taste of food, they could not dream of a dog.

'Still, let's try keeping just one pair.'

'We've no time for chickens. I should be using every minute to cut up wood so that we can at least have a house up before it turns cold.'

'You make a house sound easy, but how much would we have to pay to get one made?'

'If someone just put up the pillars for us ... I believe that a long time ago there used to be an old man living in a hut at the top of the hill who used to make wooden bowls and things. They say he goes to the temple sometimes. Perhaps I ought to go and look for him.'

'When we get our crop of new potatoes, take him a couple of gourdsful.'

'The potatoes seem to be growing.'

'If only we got three or four sacksful.'

'My, there's nothing like wishing. . . . The paraffin's running out. Let's go to bed.'

The next day, Mrs Yang chose a sunny side of the field, where the soil was warm, and planted the seeds. She was happy going up and down the hill. She carefully broke off fern shoots, dug up roots of *todok* and *toraji*, and carried them home. At night she split the fern shoots. It was true that *todok*, chopped up in soy sauce, were a seasonal dish, but fern shoots and *toraji* roots could be dried and, if kept carefully, could be sold or used the whole year round. For, according to the custom of this part of the world, at times of ceremonies, whatever else they could not do, people never left out vegetables like fern shoots and *toraji* roots.

She had to pick and dry a good supply of wild vegetables before their flower stalks appeared. In the hills, it was essential for a balanced diet to have some dried wild vegetables instead of cabbage leaves.

The next market day she did not forget to break off some

aralia shoots to exchange for soy bean paste. However, the aralia in the sunny spots were now too old, and she had to scrabble around for them in the shady spots.

Tong-uk stayed by himself, and worked away to dig over several more patches before the weeds grew thick, never putting down his hoe. Even the long days of April and May were too short for them, they were so busy.

Day by day the hills grew more luxuriant. As soon as the azaleas began to die off, the wild vegetables were past their best. Tong-uk's wife had wrapped up, in bundles of a fistful each, *toraji* roots and fern shoots that she had dried under the paraffin lamp. Tong-uk rolled a cigarette with tobacco eked out with wild aster.

'We may be late, but by a fortnight after midsummer we should have some millet seeds in too.'

'I must buy some buckwheat and bean seeds.'

'When's midsummer?'

'Oh my, when I went to market the day before yesterday, the barley was yellow already, and they were just transplanting the rice.'

'How about the strawberries?'

'Not quite yet.'

'D'you think it'll rain?'

'It must. It's been so dry lately.'

A week after midsummer they had planted most of a quarter of an acre with millet and a couple of furrows with buckwheat. It was a little early, but in the hills, while the season comes late, autumn comes early. Meanwhile the flowers died on the potatoes and eventually the leaves turned yellow.

It was time to dig them up.

'Shall we dig the potatoes up tomorrow?'

His wife did not reply.

'Why should we leave them in any longer?'

'We'll leave them because I don't like to dig them up,' his wife smiled.

Certainly they had dug this field when they had to warm their hands in their breath in a hill wind which was still sharp. And when they had planted the potatoes, they had been so short of seed that they had divided the seed potatoes each into three or four pieces about the size of pheasant's eggs. So they were more than a little worried that they would not even sprout. They dug in those hollows where no shoots had appeared. There were a few rotted seed potatoes. They weeded such hollows and piled soil over them, sad, and hating the look of them all, like holes where teeth had fallen out. After the shoots came up, they could not be at ease in their minds unless they looked over the ridges in the field once or twice a day, morning and evening. From about early July, the earth swelled up, as if showing the movement of moles, and through the cracks in the earth red potatoes could be seen growing. They wanted to tear at them with their fingers, dig up some of the fatter ones and eat them. However, they would quickly cover them up with earth, as if someone might spot them. Far from digging them up too early, they took such care of them that their fingertips were sore. If they were left one more day, they would be that much bigger, they thought.

Tong-uk understood thoroughly his wife's feeling that potatoes grown with such affectionate care should not be carelessly dug up, but, with a laugh, he said to her, 'We've done the farming; don't you like the idea of harvesting?'

His wife laughed with him: 'So long as the weather is fine, let's dig them up tomorrow.'

The weather in the hills was capricious. A clear blue sky can cloud over completely in a moment, and clouds can be dispelled completely without warning in a moment from across the hills.

The next day Tong-uk dug over the ridges with his hoe, and his wife, following behind him, picked up the potatoes. Although it was poor soil and the potatoes looked scruffy, they were a good size and solid, and half of them still remained to be dug. In the pleasure of digging up the potatoes, Tong-uk and his wife forgot their hunger. They went along one furrow each, and then back down it, as the sun approached the head of the hill.

'It's not worth trying to dig them all up today,' he said, straightening his back.

At that moment they were surprised to hear from behind them the sound of a wooden clapper. They both heard it together. They flashed a look at each other, and then they looked round. On the edge of the field there was a priest, hands together, with a rucksack on his back.

'D'you think he's the priest from the Taewon Temple?'

'It looks like it.'

Tong-uk was the first to approach the priest, who looked over fifty, handsomely aged.

'I thought I'd call in on my way past to say a prayer.... Praised be the Goddess of Mercy.'

Tong-uk and his wife were so hungry for human company that they were exceedingly pleased and grateful to see the priest.

'We're glad you've come, because I was intending to call on you one day when the work eased off a little.'

They asked him to go to their shack and rest a while before going on.

'You are very kind,' said the priest, who kept his hands clasped all the time.

Tong-uk, who had gone in front, looked back at his wife: 'Wash some of those potatoes quickly and cook them.'

However his wife was already carrying a scoopful away. Tong-uk set a straw-filled cushion beside the shack and offered the priest a seat.

'Early in the spring I was going past – on my way to a minor temple in Sanchong – and saw you from a long way off. I wondered whether the people who used to live here had come back.'

'How many families used to live here before?'

'Four did. In the war all their houses were burnt and the people scattered all over the place. Whether they're alive or dead ...' he sucked in his breath '... Praise to the Goodness of Mercy.'

'They'll come back gradually. But, your reverence, I've heard that there is in this valley an old man who makes things of wood. Perhaps ...'

'There is. Why do you ask?'

'I'll tell you exactly why. When we've got our harvest in, and before it gets cold, we must build a house. You can see how we're fixed now.'

'Of course, of course.'

'We've got to have a house, to keep out the rain and wind at least.'

'I'll bear it in mind and ask. The old man does come down to the temple sometimes. If there are any simple repairs to be done to it, he comes and does them.'

'I'd be grateful if you'd do that for me.'

At that point the potatoes appeared.

'It's not a feast, but help yourself.'

'I'm sorry to be such a nuisance.'

'You happened along just as we collected the harvest of our first farming, so . . .'

'I'm sorry to be such a nuisance.'

They were not perfect, split open all ways, with bits of potato stuck to the skin, perhaps because they had only just been dug up, but they were creamy and tasty.

'They taste really good.'

'You must have a good appetite.'

The potatoes filled the wooden scoop, but he ate nearly all of them, and had a cup of water. Then he stood up, gazing at the last few rays of the sun on the ridge of the hill.

'I don't know how far you have to go, but the day is almost gone, so . . .'

'It's about six miles, but I'm used to the way, so please don't be concerned.'

'From about the middle of November would be fine, so please be sure . . . the old man . . .'

'Don't you trust me? Please don't worry.'

The priest clasped his hands again, bowed from the waist and set off back. The two of them followed him as far as the end of their field.

'Any time you are passing, your reverence, please call in on us.'

'I'm sorry to be such a nuisance.'

He did not hurry. He disappeared slowly into the valley along a path at the foot of the hill.

'Shall we dig one more furrow?'

'Let's do it tomorrow – the sun's gone altogether.'

Tong-uk and his wife became even busier. He had to take good care of the tobacco patch, and cut grass and compost it. He had to cut wood for their house and leave it to dry. His wife's job was to take care of the vegetable patch and to sort out the smallest potatoes, even though they did not have so many of them, to store as seed potatoes. She had to transplant the young peppers, and pick strawberries once or twice before they died. While they were doing this, the maize, which they had planted as a fence because their shack was very exposed, was already sending out side-shoots from its base, and had grown to half waist height. The pumpkins which they had put up on top of the ditch were sending out creepers and blooming with dazzlingly yellow flowers.

At about harvest moon time, the red of the maples began to appear on the peaks of the hills.

There was still about a month to harvesting time, so Tong-uk and his wife took the opportunity to begin carrying down the wood for their house; all this time they had been cutting down timber.

One day, after they had dragged the pieces for the pillars down to the bottom of the valley, Mrs Yang said that she was going to look for some bunches of wild grapes. She went over a ridge into the next valley. Her husband, after carrying a few more rafters, sat down on a tree stump and waited for her to come back.

It was nearly mid-day and she still had not returned. He shouted in the direction of the next valley: 'Time to come down!' But there was no answer, only the echo coming back to him. He cupped his hands round his mouth and shouted once more: 'Where are you? Come on down!'

As he turned his head to listen he caught his wife's clear voice: 'Come here!' in the echo of his own voice. He shouted again across the hillside. 'Where?'

'Here.'

Following the voice, he saw his wife through the trees examining the ground and digging at it with her fingernails.

'What's this? Have you dropped something? Or don't you know how grapes grow?'

But his wife just kept examining the ground without looking round or answering him.

'Where you come from do grapes sprout in the earth?'

Only then did his wife turn round to him. She had a sweet smile on her face as she waved some pine mushrooms in front of his eyes.

'Ah, you've found some mushrooms!'

Then he became conscious of the spreading smell of pine mushrooms. He looked round his feet and got down.

'Are there any more?'

'It looks like a whole patch of pine mushrooms. Don't trample all over it.'

'Should we leave them for now and come after it's rained?'

'Yes, let's.'

'And grapes?'

'There aren't any at all.'

'Shall we go down?'

'Yes, let's go.'

As she said so, she sniffed the appetizing smell of the mushrooms. She noticed that their hats had not yet opened and she giggled. Tong-uk looked over at her.

'What?'

'This!'

She showed him a mushroom and giggled even more. Tong-uk was affected by her giggle.

'Naughty!'

His wife's eyes softened. The warm rays of the sun soaking them through the trees, the patch of soft dried grass, were distinctly better than their gloomy shack.

It was better because the hills are tolerant and do not find fault.

It can happen that way.

During the summer they used to go to the stream at the back every day to wash off the sweat. They would strip off in the shack and go up just holding something across the front of their bodies. One time Tong-uk gave his wife a push in the back.

'You've put on weight lately!' he said, giving her backside a slap. She turned with a giggle and sat down, sending a great splash of water up at his stomach. Tong-uk stood his ground, as if daring her to look at him. She kept on splashing water at him.

'What a terrifying sight!'

As she turned away from him again, Tong-uk said, 'I was only saying hello to you.'

'A funny sort of hello ... cheeky ...'

That day Tong-uk, completely naked, carried his completely naked wife down on his back.

'What about you carrying me?' he asked.

'Don't be silly!'

Two days later the rain came. Tong-uk's wife picked a whole basketful of pine mushrooms, and the next day took them to Sanchong. Tong-uk trimmed the bark off the wood for their house all day. His wife came back with three chicks and a puppy in her arms.

Tong-uk was really extremely pleased, but only said: 'Aren't nails more urgent if we want to build a house?'

'All right, then. I'll go again.'

Tong-uk lifted up the puppy in his arms. 'Can you always find mushrooms somewhere?'

'It's only the first crop yet. I'll gather a few more.'

'After it rains again?'

'I'll go and see tomorrow.'

'Did the mushrooms sell quickly?'

His wife pulled the chicks out of the basket.

'The passengers on the bus were in a tearing hurry to get off and buy them! Look! D'you think they're a local breed?'

'Is this one a male?'

'It looks like it by his comb.'

'But how are we going to keep them?'

'We can start by breaking off some sticks to make a coop for them.'

Still, Tong-uk liked the puppy better than the chicks. In the hills there are times when a dog's more necessary than several people. The deeper you are in the hills like this, the more reassuring it is to have a dog barking morning and evening. Even after supper, when he was in bed, he would hold the puppy and stroke it.

'Did you buy the puppy too?'

'I'll tell you how I got it. It's a puppy from a dog belonging to the lady who gave me the bean paste, remember?'

'So, did she just tell you you could have it?'

'She said I had to take her a basket of maize or something next time.'

'Is it a female?'

'She said it was better to have a male in the hills.'

The next day Tong-uk broke off some sticks and made a chicken coop.

'The coop's finished. Shall we put them in it?'

'Ah, the poor little things!'

'But what can we feed them on?'

All they had to eat was a few bowls of wheat flour and the potatoes.

'Should we pull some ears of millet for them?'

'Let's just let them out in the day-time. They can find something to peck at for themselves.'

'Are you sure there won't be any weasels?'

'Hardly in the day-time.'

'What would we do if they disappeared into the hills?'

'Let's keep them cooped and give them feed and water for a day or two, first.'

Mrs Yang had put out an enamel bowl of water and gone to pick some millet. She came running back.

'There's someone coming over there!'

Tong-uk had had his eyes glued to the chicks in the coop, and he straightened up in surprise. Across the millet patch, where his wife was pointing, he could see clearly that someone was coming. It was an old man. He was wearing what looked like an army jacket, and he had slung over his shoulder a net which obviously contained tools.

'Can it be the old carpenter from up the hill?'

'It looks like it.'

'Is he coming here?'

'He must be.'

Tong-uk tramped out to meet him and spoke to him first, when he was a few yards away.

'Are you from the hut up the hill?'

'Yes. The priest from the Taewon Temple . . .'

Tong-uk welcomed him with great joy.

'It's good of you to take so much trouble,' he said, as he helped the old man off with his tool bag. He was perhaps over sixty, judging by his drawn face, and a quiet man of few words, but still obviously in good health. Tong-uk nodded to his wife to get the old man some lunch.

'My name is Yang Tong-uk.'

'Pleased to meet you. I'm Pak.'

'I didn't expect you to come so soon.'

'When I went to the temple a month ago, I heard about you from the priest. I was so pleased to hear that someone was living in this valley again, so I didn't waste any time in coming.'

'Thank you. But we haven't got our harvest in yet, though we'd like to give you something to eat.'

'What do you two have?'

'Nothing much, I'm afraid.'

'No, tell me really what you have.'

'Vegetable gruel with potatoes . . .'

'That's fine. I'll just have what you two have. By the way, have you cut some wood for your house?'

'Yes, and we've dried it off and brought it down, but . . .'

'Let's have a look.'

Mr Pak stood up first, and looked at the wood that they had brought down the valley at the back.

'Let me just run my adze over the logs and set them up.'

'Ah, all right. All we need is to keep out the wind and rain with some thick plastering.'

'The wood will do fine for that.'

'But since I haven't collected any eulalia yet to cover the roof . . .'

'There's plenty of it, so let's get the pillars up and you can collect it at your leisure.'

They had potatoes for lunch, and for supper they shelled some new beans and boiled them up in a flour and vegetable gruel. A dish and a half satisfied Mr Pak, and he relieved himself with a belch.

'I came to the hills, and have been living here for nearly twenty years, because I disliked people and couldn't trust people. However, I was wrong. If people live with people, they get a true sense of values.'

Tong-uk took out some of the first tobacco he had picked and dried and offered it to the old man.

'Help yourself.'

'Where did this tobacco . . .'

'We planted a bit, but the soil was poor, so that's why it's like that.'

'Before, just round here alone, there used to be several hundred families living, squeezed into every odd corner, but in that damn war, many of them died, and . . . eh, it's a wicked world.'

'And were you in the hills all . . .'

'No. I used to go to the temple.'

'How are things now?'

'Empty hills, not a soul!'

'If it's twenty years since you came here, you must have been young then. What made you . . .'

Mr Pak stopped smoking, and for a while was sunk in thought.

He had lived near Chongsong, North Kyongsang Province, and had been a carpenter-plasterer. He had got married at forty, but had had no children. One spring he had been given a building job at a village fifteen to twenty miles away, worked there for a month and saved a good bit of money. The day he returned home, he had bought some material and some shoes for his young wife. There was transport half the way, but he had had to walk the rest. Since he had set out late, he had not reached home till late at night. It was a moonlit night. The village was sleeping as if dead. In front of the house, he wondered whether to give a cough to announce his arrival, but decided against it. Thinking to give his wife a surprise, he went up to the stoop. There was a strange pair of shoes left outside the door. His heart sank and his legs shook. But why . . . he hung the shoes on his hands and looked at them in the light of the moon. They were not shoes that he had worn. He put his eye to a hole in the door. Inside, the room was dimly lit by the light of the moon filtering in through the window. It was utter disorder. He looked more carefully, wiping his eyes and blinking several times. It was clear that it was that fellow Yun Pang-gu that he had had along with him when there was a rush job. His wife was asleep, stretched across him, with her head on his arm and one leg up over his stomach. He stepped down to the ground. He turned back. Taking a bundle of straw, he piled it up in front of the door. On top of that he placed the material and the shoes, and set a match to it. As soon as the flames caught, he tore away from the house, with only his bag of tools on his shoulder. By the time he had got as far as the back road out of the village, the flames had already spread to the eaves. He screamed madly: 'Fire! Fire!' a couple of times, and then turned his back on the village. It was a month after that when he came to Mount Chiri, via Hadong.

As if waking up from a sleep, Mr Pak lit his cigarette again. 'It's not much of a story, but, ah . . . all that . . .'

Mrs Yang had boiled some maize and gave it to them. The next day, early in the morning, Tong-uk started to pick one row of millet. It was still a bit early, but there was Mr Pak to feed.

From that day, the sound of Mr Pak's adze smoothing the pillar timbers echoed round the valley all day. So, six days later the foundation stones were laid and the pillars erected next to the shack. The rafters were tied on with arrowroot, and four days later the roof was covered with eulalia. They covered the roof as thickly as possible. When they had the roof covered, the work seemed to be more than half finished.

They tied lespedeza and arrowroot along the walls, and put on the first coat of plaster. While the walls were drying they decided to lay the stones for the underfloor heating. As he was going around looking for stones for this, Mr Pak said, 'Judging by the look of it, there used to be a mill here.'

'Was it a treadmill?'

'No.'

Next day Mr Pak found the mortar stone where the mill used to be. This made Mrs Yang the happiest of them all, because she had been just about to press Mr Pak to dig out a mortar for her when the work on the house was finished. While the walls and the second coat of plaster were drying out, they decided to saw up the wood to make the doors. Mr Pak said that they had only to dry out the wood for the doors, and in the meantime they would begin putting a fence around. When Tong-uk asked what they wanted with a fence, Mr Pak said that having a house without a fence was like wearing a hat but no coat. It would not be a proper house. The more shabby and isolated a house was, the more it needed a fence, he insisted.

After they had put the fence round, as Mr Pak said, they were happier than ever with the marvellous cosiness of it. The more they thought about it, the more they thought that they had done well to have a fence around. Mr Pak said that they should have a gate, even if only a token one, and he put up a gate as well.

As soon as the floor was nearly dry, they moved their eulalia-filled mattresses to sleep on, since, as Mr Pak said, the shack was cramped. That night, Tong-uk's wife snuggled up to his arm-pit, as she had not been able to do for a long time.

'The house is almost finished. What are we going to do about paying Mr Pak?'

'I don't know. It looks as if he'll be staying on here.'

'Would that be the best thing to do?'

'Huh, that's the way it is. Let's leave it.'

Three days later they put up three doors, a door to the kitchen and a shelf in each room too. When the work was about finished, Mr Pak took a walk several times round the house, putting on the final touches, until night fell. After they had had supper Mr Pak rolled a cigarette and said to Mrs Yang: 'It's late in the season, but you should try the mushroom field.'

The word he used for the 'mushroom' brought a light to Mrs Yang's eyes, because the sort of mushroom he mentioned had been a Mount Chiri local product from time immemorial.

'Where is it?' she asked. 'I'll go tomorrow!'

Mr Pak told them that the people who used to live here before had picked a sackful each of these mushrooms every year and sold them for spending money. Mrs Yang went to bed consumed with a desire to go to the mushroom field the next day without fail. In the morning she rushed out early carrying a basket. Mr Pak was tidying up his tools.

'Goodbye! I'm going today.'

Mrs Yang was too surprised to say anything. She went back to the shack.

'Tong-uk, the old man says he's going!'

'What?'

'Oh dear, he's getting his tools ready to go.'

'Going? Where?' He came out, round-eyed, and went straight over to Mr Pak.

'I'll be off now. You've been very kind to me.'

'Hey, if you go, where . . .'

'I must go into the hills.'

Tong-uk and his wife were dumbfounded. Tong-uk gulped and grasped the old man's sleeve.

'Not going like that after building the house? We were expecting that you'd just stay on with us.'

'When I came, I'd just cut some wood. I must go and get some washing paddles and things shaped up before the New Year.'

Mrs Yang rubbed her hands together. 'Can't you do it here?'

'I've left the sawn wood there,' he said, as he slung his tool bag over his shoulder.

Tong-uk took hold of it: 'How can you . . . and to tell the truth, your wages . . .'

'What are you talking about, wages? You've kept me, that's enough. I'll be off. Goodbye!'

However Tong-uk held onto his bag more tightly, and his wife stood in Mr Pak's way: 'Even if you go, undo your bag!'

'Yes, and stay just one more day before you go.'

'He's right. In a month or more you haven't had a single day's rest.'

'She's right. Just today . . .'

Mr Pak was forced to put down his bag and accept the situation gracefully. Mrs Yang briskly set about mixing and grinding some potatoes that she had sliced and dried with a gourdful of buckwheat.

Mr Pak, feeling that he could not just be idle, made some bowls for oil lamps and an ashtray out of the odd bits of board, and repaired some of the defects he found in the hen coop.

Mrs Yang had made a dough of buckwheat flour and gestured to her husband to come up. She asked him to kill a chicken.

The autumn days, though they seem leisurely, are short. For lunch and supper they had good satisfying meals of chicken broth with buckwheat noodles.

'I suppose you'll have to go,' said Tong-uk, offering Mr Pak a roll of his nicely dried home-grown tobacco, 'but come and see us soon.'

'Let's see how it goes.'

'We're all by ourselves, and you . . .'

'I had the same thought, but . . .'

'When we have got our harvest, it would be easy to feed three, and since we've got two rooms . . .'

'If I come, please don't turn me away!'

'What a thing to say!'

'Anyway, I am grateful that you have come to live in this valley.'

It was not clear to whom he was grateful. The next morning he started to leave early, because, he said, he would call in at the temple on his way and see the priest. Tong-uk took a jacket lined with artificial fur out of a bundle and held it out to Mr Pak.

'In case you feel the cold in the spring wind up the hill . . .'

But Mr Pak refused, jumping up and down to show that he simply could not accept.

'Please,' said Mrs Yang, 'I was going to make you a suit of padded clothes, but do accept this.'

Mr Pak gazed into the distance for a moment and then gave in and took the coat. As he did so, he turned his head aside, sniffed loudly, and with that went out of the gate.

'When you've finished your work, come and see us.'

'Please give our regards to the priest when you meet him!'

They saw Mr Pak nod as he went off around the bend the way the priest from the Taewon Temple had always gone. That day Tong-uk's wife went in search of the mushroom field, but the mushrooms Mr Pak had told them about were already finished.

Suddenly the maples burst into a blaze of colour, though the lacquer trees had seemed to be racing them. Every morning a heavy frost lay thick, and the distant ridges grew barer day by day. They had to hurry with their harvest.

They reaped the millet first. Then they shook the buckwheat, pulled up the pepper plants, and picked the pumpkins. All they had to do was sow the barley, and there would not be much more autumn work.

Mrs Yang went off to market in Sanchong with about a peck of peppers on her head, plucked while they were still green, and then dried. She bought barley and wheat seed, and things like old bags and newspapers, and paper for covering the doors and windows. Without manure, she could only plant half the barley seed. She had planted one row of garlic in ash which she had frugally kept, and she put down the pickles in brine for the winter.

Now there was really nothing urgent for them to do.

They began papering the walls. First they pasted newspaper onto the walls and undid cement bags and pasted them on the floors. When they had pasted paper on the doors too, the room looked much more cosy. They got out the oil lamps which Mr Pak had made for them before he went, and lit them. The cosiness of the light in the room pleased them.

'Our honeymoon room?' said Tong-uk.

His wife wiped the room over with a cloth.

'Now we've papered the walls, it will be our honeymoon room.'

'Yes, just like the room where newly-weds first meet.'

That night Mrs Yang spent a surprisingly long time noisily

busy in the kitchen. The autumn nights were almost too long. They slept stretched out in comfort in the warm room, until they had really had too much rest, and still the day did not dawn. The bright moon shone through the door.

'It is pickling time,' said Mrs Yang, 'so the price of peppers should be good.'

'Should we grow a lot of peppers next year?'

'Yes, and garlic too.'

'And next year we must keep a baby pig somehow, for the sake of the manure.'

'How much would one cost?'

'I don't know. What would we do for money?'

'The hens are broody.'

'They're bound to hatch some chicks in the spring.'

For a while they stopped talking.

'Is it light?'

'Not yet. By the way, darling, why doesn't Puksuri bark ever?'

'He's a fool!'

'Do you think even a dog behaves better when he comes to the hills?'

'When he sees something, he'll bark. He's got to have something to bark at!'

It was true that though Puksuri had grown into a full-sized dog, he hardly barked at all, except once or twice at the moon as it came up. Perhaps it was true that even a dog became more tolerant-minded in the hills.

'I meant to give him some acorns.'

'We've got enough food. What do you want giving him acorns?'

'If we've got enough food, there's all the more need to be careful with it.'

'Huh, we've got about five bushels of millet, two sacks of potatoes, soy beans and red beans, buckwheat – one way and another at least another half bushel, haven't we? And several basketsful of pumpkins on top of all that!'

'If you mash acorns properly, you get a good dough and a good jelly.'

Day broke. There was nothing particular to get up early for. They would wriggle around with their backs on the warm floor, and then just open the door of the chicken coop, or something like that. After a late breakfast, when the sun was well up, Tong-uk might carry his hoe out and dig a furrow, or bring in some dead branches. His wife might set Puksuri in front of her and bring him some acorns. The chestnuts and acorns she collected in three days filled a sack.

The winter nights were stubbornly long. Tong-uk and his wife went over all their plans for farming again. Tong-uk rolled and made cigarette after cigarette, and his wife wrapped up into bundles fern shoots and *toraji* roots to take to the New Year market.

'When you think of how we're making a living, isn't it natural?'

'When I think back to when we were refugees, it's really like a dream.'

'D'you remember how we used to crawl under the wire every night to get a few tins thrown out of that damn back door?'

'Yes, the way we used to use them for selling drinks at the quayside. Call that being human . . . tit and bum for tit-bits . . . ugh . . .'

'I wish he were still alive.'

Mrs Yang made no comment.

'Where was that hill behind Taesin-dong, where he was taken and buried?'

'He was supposed to have been properly buried, but he was just taken and thrown away.'

'But why was there no suspicion afterwards?'

'What's suspicion?'

'Sign of pregnancy, I mean.'

'It was a good thing there wasn't, because if there'd been a child to look after in that situation . . . Look at Myong-suk's mum!'

'Yes, I wonder how she's living.'

'Living? If she's surviving, she's living.'

'Do you remember how she quarrelled with you over a squid?'

'It's difficult to remember how valuable a good squid was at that time.'

'I wish she'd come to live here with us.'

'Indeed!'

The next night Tong-uk was making traps, because he'd seen

pheasants landing in the barley field. His wife was sorting out dried fern shoots.

'D'you think we'll catch a pheasant tomorrow and have it to eat with some noodles?'

'Have you heard that there's a blind pheasant somewhere?'

At that moment Puksuri suddenly barked. Their eyes met in a spasm of fear.

'What is it?'

'I don't know.'

Tong-uk shuffled across the floor sitting down, half opened the door, and looked out. The moon was as bright as day. He could see clearly two people walking towards the far end of the fields.

'Somebody's coming.'

His hand trembled as it grasped the door handle and his voice quivered too.

Even though they missed human company, yet they were also fearful of people. What they were thinking was that the people swiftly appearing up there might be partisans – they were still being picked out like lice – who had been in hiding somewhere.

Tong-uk pushed his wife into the next room and stepped out onto the stoop. He had no idea what he was doing. As soon as he came out, Puksuri got more excited and ran out of the gate, barking.

'Oy, Puksuri! Puksuri! It's me!'

'Ah, Mr Pak!'

Tong-uk ran out towards the gate. His wife chased after him. They each took hold of one of Mr Pak's hands, overwhelmed with relief and pleasure.

'Why have you come so late?'

'Huh, that's the way it happened.'

'Go on in!' said Tong-uk, and, looking back at the man who had come with Mr Pak, 'You too!'

When they got into the yard, Mr Pak asked whether the shack was still empty. 'Why the shack?'

'I wondered whether we might have a fire there.'

'Why? The other room's huge, so why d'you say that?'

'Let's go into it later.'

So saying, he went round to the shack, taking the man with him. Tong-uk got an armful of twigs and lit a fire, while his wife hastened to prepare some food. Mr Pak and the man undid and sorted out their tool box and bundle, and laid out mattresses in the shack.

The meal was ready.

They sat facing each other over the bowls of mixed grain, which were steaming with an appetizing fragrance. They ate like hungry sows, blowing on the dishes. Their noses ran continuously, and they wiped them with the backs of their hands. They munched hungrily at turnip stems soaked in brine.

The man looked a few years older than Tong-uk, perhaps a bit more than forty. He looked weatherbeaten and worn, perhaps because of the tufty beard on his dry face. He never said a word.

'Oh that was such an excellent meal I don't know how to thank you,' Mr Pak said.

So saying, he pushed the table away. Tong-uk offered him a cigarette.

'Is it icy up on top of the hill by now?'

'The wind's so strong . . .'

'Then you're going to stay with us now?'

Instead of replying, Mr Pak took a handful of tobacco for the other man.

'You'd better get off to bed early.'

The man stood up and went out without a word. Tong-uk stood up. 'I wonder whether the fire's going.'

'I'll see,' said Mr Pak, 'Sit down. There's something I've . . .' He puffed at his cigarette and looked from Tong-uk to his wife.

'I've a favour to ask you.'

'What d'you mean, favour?'

'I don't know. I could set up a workshop, make things of wood, and earn my living, but – how are you doing for food now?'

'What sort of miserable talk is that? We have a good crop of millet, potatoes, and so on, several bags. There's no need at all for you to worry about food.'

His wife added: 'We've gathered in a dozen peck of soy beans, red beans and maize, and a couple of dozen pumpkins. And there's a sack of acorns left, and . . .'

'That's right,' Tong-uk agreed. 'If you want to know how things are, it's missing human company that . . .'

'That's so. If you think of people, it's a matter of people living together. Before the war, there used to be people living in every valley. There used to be villages in every valley, and several houses in each. It was reassuring. You never felt lonely. At the very worst you could get by if you saw a fire burning a long way off, or heard a dog barking. Since the war there's not been a person to see. I feel so isolated and lonely that . . .'

'We know. We came to this valley because we didn't know where our next meal was coming from. It's been a plain and simple life here, though we don't starve. But it's true, what we miss now is not food, but people.'

'That's why I rushed to put up the house, I was so terribly glad that you had come.'

'Come and live with us now. Be one of our family.'

An appetizing smell wafted in from the kitchen.

'It's only by living in loneliness in the hills that one realizes how precious and important people are. I mean, ugly or beautiful, they're all living people.'

Mrs Yang brought in some boiled potatoes.

'By the way, that man . . . just now you saw . . .?'

'Who is he?'

'I used to know him at home in Chongsong. I used to employ him if I had a rush job. He did something wrong and couldn't stay there, and went off to a coal mine, I think in Samchok. So, when the war broke out, he couldn't get home. He was dragged off by the red army and later driven up here. He was nearly killed a dozen times, and often half gave up the ghost. One way or another he was sure to die, I thought, so I hid him. At one time I hid him in a temple. So, he was the very last red left here in the hills. What should I do with him? Where could I send him? I'd die rather than tell him to leave me. I'm sure he wouldn't live a minute if he left me. So what am I to do with him?'

Tong-uk and his wife swallowed, and could not take their eyes off Mr Pak's lips. He gulped down some more of the potato which he had been chewing.

'So, what am I to do with him? Here I am, stuck with him. When I rushed back up before, in fact it was because of him. When I got there, he was nodding off beside a bonfire of rubbish, but you should have seen the happy way he came running out as soon as he saw me. What am I that he should trust me, wait for me like that, run out to meet me so happily? When I think of this, I feel so sorry for him. He's just helplessly . . .'

Tong-uk asked his wife to bring some more potatoes to the shack, but Mr Pak refused firmly, saying that it was time he was going to bed.

'The peaks are already covered with snow. When I'm locked up in the snow with him, I can't prepare enough food, and the winter days are so terribly lonely that I've brought him here.'

'You've got to come down. You certainly did well to come down.'

'So, what do you think? He's all right to get on with. He does whatever you to tell him to. He can help me with my work, and do farming for you.'

'There's no question. Whether he likes it or not, we'll hold on to him.'

'Thank you.'

Mrs Yang said quickly, 'It's we who should say thank you to you.'

'All right,' said Mr Pak, 'I'll start building a workshop tomorrow.'

'No, you can sleep here. Look how much room we've got.'

'As if we could do that!'

'D'you think we could just sleep in comfort ourselves and . . .'

Mr Pak opened the door and went out. After he had returned to the shack, Mrs Yang said, 'While he's building his workshop, make sure that he adds another room. Mr Pak's got to have somewhere to sleep, and the shack's so . . .'

'Yes, you're right.'

The next day Mr Pak started work with his adze, and Tong-uk and the man carried the wood. He said that his family name was Yun and his personal name Pang-gu, and that he was also known as Yun Saengwon.* Four days later the shed was up, and ten days later it had its extra room, with its second coat of plaster on and its doors hung.

Mr Pak, with an eye on the New Year market, rushed to

---

*'Saengwon' was a title given to a man of letters in the Yi dynasty of Korea, although in popular usage it subsequently took on the general meaning of 'Mr'. The term is very rarely found in Korea today.

cut washing paddles, cattle food dippers and rice serving spoons. Yun Saengwon was beside him, sawing or drying the wood, or he would use his spare moments to go into the wooded valley to cut wood for axe handles or flail spokes. Tong-uk, as the fancy took him, would dig in the fields or, if he preferred, give a hand in the shed.

'Pang-gu, the day after tomorrow's market day in Sanchong. Will you take a load?'

'I won't go to market.'

'Who'd catch you if you went to market?'

Yun did not reply.

'All right, then, will you carry it part of the way?'

'Of course I will.'

When market day came round, Yun put on his back a dozen dippers and two dozen rice serving spoons, and Mrs Yang put on her head a bundle of fern shoots and *toraji* roots. Mr Pak set out early with them to Sanchong market. Yun carried his load about four miles, and then panted and puffed his way back. That day Tong-uk and he dug in the fields all day. At digging Tong-uk was incomparable, so good and strong.

Mr Pak and Mrs Yang returned only when the sun was almost down. They were loaded with purchases: some clothes – dyed army uniforms – for Pang-gu, two pairs of socks, newspapers, salt, paraffin, lamps, empty oil drums, and besides all this a pair of dried mackerel, nails, wire and the like.

They buried the empty drums between Tong-uk's house and the workshop and made a cess pit. They had long planned to have a cess pit because they were so short of manure. The wire was for Pang-gu to use for making traps.

On the last day of the New Year market, Mr Pak and Mrs Yang went there. Mr Pak sold all the things he had left over from the previous market day, and Mrs Yang took some fern shoots and *toraji* roots to sell as vegetables for sacrificial dishes. That day Mrs Yang bought oil and lard. This was for making savoury muffins and pumpkin pancakes for the New Year feast, she said. It was a long time since the aroma of frying had wafted round this valley. It made it seem less like a valley in the hills.

On New Year's Eve the night was bright everywhere with the burning of midnight oil. Tong-uk went to the shed with two handfuls of tobacco in his hand. Mr Pak was carving a pipe

from some tree root, and Yun Saengwon was making a noose
of wire to catch a boar.

'Where are the boars?' asked Mr Pak, rolling some tobacco.
'The wild animals have all died out with the war, so . . .'

But Yun had a broad smile on his face: 'I've seen their
tracks.'

'Where?'

'In the wooded valley.'

'Big ones?'

'Yearlings, I should think.'

'Just see them being caught by you!'

But Yun just kept smiling gently.

'Talking of pigs,' said Tong-uk, 'we ought to keep one for
the manure.'

'You're right,' said Mr Pak. 'We could certainly keep pigs.
How much would a three-month-old one cost?'

'I don't know. The price of pigs lately might be . . .'

'Berkshires are dear,' said Yun, 'but you don't have to give
much for the local breed.'

'Let's find out,' Mr Pak suggested to Tong-uk.

'It's a stupid idea. What would we feed it on?'

But Mr Pak took him to task. 'You only have to give it
acorns, damn it. I should think . . .'

'All right, I'll buy the pig – will you keep it?'

'I'll have a go. You just buy it!'

At this point Tong-uk's wife brought in a small 'dog's legs'
table with some pancakes and a little brown jug on it.

'What's this?' asked Tong-uk, looking at the jug.

'What d'you think? Wine, of course!'

'Wine!' All three of them were astonished.

'That day we went to market, I bought a lump of yeast. It's
New Year, after all, and then I thought of you being here, Mr
Pak, so . . .'

'Huh, I don't know what this . . .'

'It's millet wine. What's it taste like?'

As Tong-uk poured some wine into a cup, Mr Pak put his
hand across to stop him.

'Not yet. Tonight everyone is observing the ceremonies.
Although we can't do so at our ancestors' graves, we depend
for our lives on the hills, don't we? Let's go and make an

offering to the spirit at the foot of Baby Ginseng Rock, behind here. What d'you think?' He looked across at Tong-uk.

'You're right, we should do that!'

'Let's then! How's the time? We've got to go before the cocks crow.'

'Cock-crow? It's still . . .'

'Right, then, madam,' Mr Pak said to Mrs Yang, 'Please prepare this table again.' As she took the table out, he added: 'And let us have a wash, etcetera, before we go.'

With that they stood up. The three of them broke the thin ice on the brook at the back and washed their hands. Mr Pak and Yun Saengwon changed their socks.

Yun took the table and Tong-uk took a straw mat rolled up. Mr Pak went first, carrying a torch, and the three men went up to the foot of Baby Ginseng Rock. The night sky was pitch black, and there was only the smoke from the pine pitch lit by a flickering flame. No one said a word.

After they had spread the mat and set down the table, Mr Pak poured some wine. He first sprinkled some on the earth and then lifted up the cup, stepped back two paces, and gestured to Tong-uk to stand at his left and Yun at his right. He bowed once, and then again, the second time kneeling and remaining bowed low.

'Spirit of the Mountain, we are people whose lives are at your mercy. Look well upon our afflictions, yet be not angry with us. Give us our life here, for your mercy is infinite. Preserve our crops next year from calamity, and bring back to live here those who used to live in this valley, we beseech you, Spirit of the Mountain!'

At the end of his prayer he scattered the remaining wine on the earth, and tore up one pancake and scattered the pieces. Then they returned. On their way down Mr Pak told them that in the old days there had been a ginseng root here, at the foot of the rock, in the shape of a baby, which had turned into an immortal spirit and descended to Sanchong market. This was where the name Baby Ginseng Rock came from.

In the room next to the workshop there was a table, as before. Mr Pak took a cup of wine first, and next Yun. As Yun lifted the cup, he said, 'I've been teetotal. What will happen to me?'

'We've worked so hard in the fields,' rejoined Mr Pak, 'that you're hardly likely even to half fill your belly with wine.'

Tong-uk agreed enthusiastically as he took his turn. He drank a cupful, Mr Pak had two, and Yun three, and the jug was empty. A cock crowed twice, and Tong-uk went back. He felt somehow that Mr Pak was a good solid fellow, and that he had done well to perform the sacrifice.

They took a day or two off, but then Yun set out with a hoe, saying that he felt restless all over if he had to be idle. There was also the reason that they had to put a layer of manure down before the ground was covered with snow, and they had to add water to the manure where it did not fill any hollows and ladle it out over the barley field. Mr Pak too said that he was bored with being idle, and went up the hill to cut wood.

The first month of the New Year passed with one thing and another. One night early in March, after supper, they were smoking as usual.

'The azaleas are out already,' said Mr Pak.

Tong-uk's wife took him up: 'In no time the vegetables will be coming up well.'

'Vegetables are early on the lower hills. Here, deep in the hills . . .'

'All right,' said Tong-uk, 'shall we plant the potatoes?'

'Have you got enough seed potatoes?' asked Mr Pak.

Tong-uk's wife replied, 'I picked out only little ones, and it came to a bushel.'

'When are we going to buy the pig?' Yun blurted out.

Mr Pak looked as if a thought had only just occurred to him: 'Before New Year, someone asked me to sell him two troughs. If I sell two troughs, will we be able to buy a pair of pigs?'

'If not,' Yun replied straightaway, 'we can get rid of all our axe handles and flail ribs.'

'When the vegetables come up, I'll be able to make up the difference with them.'

Two days later Tong-uk and Yun began to plough their newly dug field. They attached an arrowroot rope to a spade and Tong-uk pulled while Yun guided the spade. They planted about an eighth of an acre. It took four days work, night and day. After finishing the potato planting, Tong-uk and Yun went with Mr Pak to get some wood to make the troughs from the hill. They had been doing this for a few days when the 'flower wind' began to blow, and the sap began to rise on the hills day by day.

The hens were looking for places to brood. Tong-uk and his wife were setting them to brood on the sunny side of the yard.

'Tong-uk, we still need to add another room.'

'Another room? What for?'

'What about Yun Saengwon?'

Tong-uk was watching closely what his wife had to say.

At last he realized what she was getting at, and a smile spread over his face as he said, 'D'you mean to get Myong-suk's mum here too? Would she come?'

'She'd be bound to. She's thirty-six, with a child. Where d'you think she'd live?'

'It'd be lovely if that happened.'

'I know that Yun is three years older than you, forty-one. Forty-one is the prime of life. How could he live out his life here unmarried?'

What she did not add was that Yun had been looking at her more strangely as the days went by.

'Let's try that!'

'If only we have the fare, I'll go before the wild vegetables are ready.'

'All right. Shall I see to getting another room put on?'

'We've got the room next to ours for the time being, so there'll be plenty of time after she comes.'

A few days later Tong-uk and his wife discussed the matter with Mr Pak. He seemed to be delighted with the idea of having what would virtually be a daughter-in-law: 'That would make me really happy,' he said.

One day about a fortnight after this, Yun carted two troughs to just past Twin Rocks, and Tong-uk's wife went to market in Sanchong with Mr Pak, carrying a bundle of axe handles on her head. Tong-uk and Yun were waiting in the workshop room for news of the marketing.

Tong-uk was worried about whether they would have got rid of the troughs and axe handles easily, and if his wife had left for Pusan. However, Yun waited patiently for the pig.

'If you plant chestnut trees, you pick chestnuts in three years . . .'

'Only chestnuts? We should plant some persimmon trees too.'

'If we had beehives, we'd attract bees.'

'Where are the bees?'

'There are lots. They like it here in a hill valley.'

'For honey, you've got to go where I come from. Everyone knows Kangwon Province honey.'

'The honey here's called "clear white". In the old days it used to be supplied to the court.'

The sun was just about setting when Mr Pak came back by himself. Tong-uk guessed that everything had gone well, and felt relieved. Yun, on the other hand, had his eternally gloomy expression as he looked for the pig.

'Did she go?' Tong-uk asked.

'She did,' Mr Pak replied promptly, with a smile.

Yun could not wait: 'The pig?'

'The pig? There wasn't a suitable one, so we decided that Mr Yang's wife should buy a good one.'

He exchanged glances with Tong-uk and laughed.

'Will she buy a pair of pigs?'

When Yun butted in again like this, Mr Pak turned on him: 'You don't know anything but pigs. She dislikes you so much that she'll just buy one sow,' and he guffawed again.

Tong-uk saw the joke, and Yun smiled contentedly: 'I'll take Puksuri round the snares,' he said, as he opened the door and went out.

After a while the hills sang with the sound of Puksuri's barking in some valley. The echoes faded away from valley to valley, like ripples from a stone thrown into water.

A BETRAYAL

OH SANG-WON

Translated by Kim Chong-un

It was an evening in the late autumn of 1946. The joy of liberation, now torn asunder in chaotic conflicts, was already a year old. The bulletin board in front of every newspaper office drew enormous crowds. The centre of attention was a large handbill written in black ink with many flashy red underlines. The crowd of people, hastily reading the news item, turned pale instantly and exchanged doubt-ridden and uneasy looks with one another. News Extra! News Extra! Small handbills carrying the news printed in extra large type were racing along the streets at an incredible speed.

It was a small drinking place in one of the back alleys of Seoul. The outer wall of the house was permanently wet with urine and the pungent smell filled the whole alley; it was the doing of senseless drunkards who filed out of the place every night. But the place was nearly empty now; perhaps it was too early. Only two, over-thirtyish men sat at a table, tipping their glasses and talking quietly. They seemed to be talking about politics, for the names of some prominent political figures could be overheard from time to time. The only other customer in the place was a young man of twenty-five or six who sat drinking alone at a corner table. The way he listened to the conversation of the others between gulps of his drink somehow

298

gave the impression of listlessness. A shadow of uneasiness flashed in his eyes from time to time.

'A nationwide drive to abolish the 38th Parallel must be launched,' said the stout, tall one of the conversing two, wiping his wet lips with the back of his hand.

'We shouldn't be . . . I mean what they say shouldn't always be taken at face value. It is obvious that, despite what they profess, some of them, at heart, wish to maintain the status of the 38th Parallel, at least for the time being anyway. This is a tendency which is especially prevalent among the leftwingers. They want to earn enough time to gain a base of power,' observed the other, in a soft, weak voice which was not in keeping with his strong, round face just as his unexpectedly small, narrow eyes were unbecoming to his facial outline.

'They can be *removed* one by one as the occasion arises. That's no problem,' said the first.

At this the narrow-eyed one frowned visibly. 'Terrorism isn't the whole of politics. It's only a single indispensable ingredient at best, and only an expedient at that.'

At that moment, the young man drinking alone at the corner-table looked up and gave a sharp glance at the two men. For some reason, the young man's face darkened.

Just then, the errand boy of the place rushed in breathlessly with a small square piece of paper in his hand. 'Listen! Did you hear the news? The whole town is topsy-turvy,' he cried.

The proprietor, an old man, hesitantly took the piece of paper. The two men drinking together looked up at the proprietor. The old man, with the aid of eye-glasses, began to read the paper, but he broke off with a deep sigh. The man with narrow eyes, who had been watching the old man read, then took the paper from the old man and read. The stout, tall one also joined in reading. The instant they had finished reading they crumpled up the paper in disgust.

'Another great man has fallen!'

They said nothing for a while, but seemed tense and alert.

'Who could have shot him?'

'Someone from the opposing camp, who else? Sure it must be them,' said the stout one.

After a while the narrow-eyed one reflected: 'But we cannot jump to the conclusion that it was the doing of the opposite side. Assassinations are not always carried out by political enemies alone. It could well be the doing of the closest ally. They have the advantage – I mean they could kill a person and still look most grieved over the death. It's only the public that gets deceived. That's how politics works . . .' As he was talking, his face flushed darkly.

At this point the young man drinking alone looked up again, glancing briefly at the two men. When their eyes met, the stout man got up and walked over to the young man's table. Smoothing out the crumpled paper, he put it on the table for the young man to read, asking: 'Do you want to read this?' The young man finished up his drink, without so much as glancing at the piece of paper he had been offered, calmly made his payment, and left the place with his face averted from the others.

It was a dimly lit office room cluttered with desks and chairs. From the way the noise of the street was muffled, one could judge that the place was a secluded one, far from the main streets.

'Let's toast, he'll be here soon,' one of the two men in the room said. Glasses with clear liquid touched with pleasant clinks.

'He's the damnedest professional I ever saw. I was nearly beside myself with worry that he might mess it up, but just as I had finished lighting my cigarette I heard the two shots. I had seen him loitering in front of the tobacco shop even when I was pulling the cigarette out of the pack. He's as quick as lightning, that's all . . . But I wonder what's keeping him this late?' The man who said this had a triangular face with slit eyes which gave an impression of malice rather than of sharpness. He gave a quick glance at his wristwatch.

Just then a man in a felt hat opened the door and entered the room. Pushing up the rim of his hat slightly, he nodded to the two men and threw a bundle of newspapers towards them.

'Read these papers, everything seems to have come off well,' said the newcomer, this time nodding to himself. The other two hastily ran their eyes over the newspapers.

'The assassin is a jobless young man.' 'No progress made in the investigation into finding the masterminds because the culprit is still unconscious.' There was a picture of a young man fallen unconscious with his face all smashed up. As the man with the triangular face quickly read the headlines and captions, a queer smile crossed his lips. 'We did it again!' he said.

'You'd better read the next newspaper,' said the man in the felt hat, with a wink, wrinkling up his forehead. But the queer smile did not disappear from the triangular face. His companion opened the next newspaper. 'The arrested suspect may not be the true culprit.' 'Who then is the true criminal?' There was a picture of a girl sobbing into her handkerchief who was identified as the sister of the arrested suspect. There was also another picture showing the mother of the suspect, who had fainted at the news of her son's arrest.

'What does it say?'

'According to the sister, the suspect had gone into town to borrow money, needed to care for their long-ailing mother. "My brother could never have done such a thing. I swear to God that he is not the criminal . . ." It was then reported that the girl had been unable to continue answering the reporter's queries . . .'

The queer smile still lingered on the lips of the triangular face even while he listened to the report of the paper. He then said: 'In any event, the case is closed. That's important, and we needn't concern ourselves with anything else. Hey, have a drink, Kim.'

The man in the felt hat picked up a glass, and the triangular-faced man poured him a drink. Then glancing at his companion who was still eyeing the newspaper, the triangular-faced man snatched the papers up, then folded them neatly. Pushing them into the friend's pocket, he said: 'It may have a bad effect to let our boy read this when he comes in. Take it home and read it there if you want.' Then he turned to the man in the felt hat and addressed him: 'Kim!' Kim finished his drink first, and putting the empty glass down on the table, looked up at the triangular-faced man.

'You have talked to Mr Chung, haven't you? Is everything ready?'

The man in the feltt hat nodded.

'The girl is ready, too? A pretty one?'

The man in the felt hat grinned broadly as a way of saying yes. Seeing that, the man with the triangular face also grinned.

But this grin was immediately replaced by an unnamable shadow. 'Don't you think our boy has been acting a bit queer lately?' he asked.

The lanky, nervous man, pulled the folded newspaper out of his pocket and remarked ruefully: 'Seemed a bit downcast since his mother's death, yes.'

The man with the triangular face spat on the floor in disgust. 'Could it be that he has begun to have doubts about our cause?' he asked, but he broke off in haste and turned towards the door, for it was slid open at that very moment from the outside. A gust of cold wind raced through the room.

'Welcome! What kept you so long? Congratulations, anyway,' said the man with the triangular face to the new arrival, lifting the glass towards him.

But the man who had just stepped in, stood by the door for a moment eyeing the others, and then slowly approached the table. He picked up the bottle and drank from it without paying any attention to the others. He was the same young man who had been drinking alone in the back-alley bar awhile before. Though his face was beginning to turn red from drinking, his eyes seemed shadowed with some dark clouds. His wet, red lips contrasted sharply with the shadowy eyes.

'You've already had a few somewhere else? We've been waiting all this time so that we can celebrate together . . .' said the man with the triangular face in a tone of mock-rancour, offering an empty glass to the young man.

But the young man showed no sign of accepting the glass. Instead, he glanced at it, and then at the triangular-faced man.

'Have another drink, and then let's go to where the girl is. That'll make you feel much better. Everything is ready for you including the girl, and it's not polite to keep a lady waiting too long, you know,' said the man with the triangular face. With the habitual queer smile still on his face, he spoke in a domineering tone which suggested that he had complete control over the other's feelings as well. He went on: 'I know how nervous one becomes after the violent moment, and then how it is followed by a dark, shadowy feeling. This always happens after killing a man, and when that happens a girl is the best cure. One can unload the residual passion into the flesh off the girl. After that you can sleep in peace, and all will be restored to normal.' Saying this, the man with the triangular face watched the eyes of the young man. The young man's face grew even darker.

'Have another drink and go to the girl. Her soft flesh is waiting for you, all right?' pursued the man with the triangular face.

The young man looked sharply into the eyes of the other. 'Send the girl away,' he said.

A derisive smile curved the lips of the triangular-faced man. 'Where do you want to go, then?'

'Home.'

'Home?' The inquisitive eyes and the dark, troubled eyes met in silence. 'Cut it out. What home?'

Again the dark shadow seemed to pass over the eyes of the young man. 'My home . . .' he half mumbled to himself, looking up again at the other's face. The man with the triangular face blinked his small eyes, and suppressed a sigh.

They exchanged no more words after that. The young man poured out a drink, gulped it down, and left the room. The man with the triangular face watched the closed door for a while in a leaden silence, and then, grabbing the bottle, he began to drink directly from it. A trickle of drink flowed down from his chin and neck. He paused for an instant to catch his breath and resumed drinking. When the bottle was finally empty, he threw it into the corner of the room spitefully as if to vent his anger.

In the dark, cold sky the stars twinkled like so many beads set on ice. Every time a gust of wind swept through the branches of the streetside trees, dead leaves snowed on to the pavement near his feet. The young man was leaning against a tree watching the sky. So far he had been unable to drive away his heavy-heartedness. He drew a crumpled piece of newspaper out of his trouser pocket. For an instant, the picture of the old woman in the newspaper, with the caption saying 'The suspect's mother who fainted at the news of her son's arrest' was superimposed in his mind's eyes on his own mother's image. An imaginary voice telling him: 'All this for the sake of our fatherland' rang in his head. The voice continued: 'We have all sworn to offer our lives to the fatherland. We are well aware how you must feel, but some things must be sacrificed for the sake of nobler causes in life.'

It had all started about two months before. The underground society to which he belonged had concluded about that time that they must assassinate a certain political figure. He had been chosen to be the gunman. But on the very night which was chosen for the assassination his own mother happened to be dying from a long illness.

That night, it was exactly half an hour before the pre-arranged time when the car-horn sounded curtly outside his house. The second hand of his luminous watch was circling the dial with precision. Another short sound of the horn was heard. He confronted the darkness in silence. 'Postponing it is out of the question. Just think what kind of time and effort we've been putting into this so far ... Besides, if we fail today, all our plans will come to nothing. It means we will have to start everything from scratch. All this when success is nearly in our grasp. Don't worry about your mother. We'll take care of her. Haven't we sworn to offer everything for the fatherland?' All this was said in a low but anxious tone. He closed the lattice-door behind him quietly. The sound of his mother's groan followed him outside.

Following the liberation of 1945 the country was flooded with hastily banded political parties, and in the midst of ideological disorder created by the chaotic conflicts an aroused political consciousness drove the youth of the country into the ranks of clashing political forces. Everyone professed to be on the side of the fatherland. The young man was working for a small firm after graduating from high school when he too was persuaded to join this underground society by the man with the triangular face, former student of the same high school. The ignominious and fallen history of the fatherland had been and was steered by unpatriotic traitors, and it was the aim of this underground society to single them out and *remove* them before they could do serious harm. Those that must be removed would be removed in the name and honour of the fatherland. He learned how to handle a gun. A well coordi-nated person, he soon became nearly perfect in his marksman-ship. He felt the upsurge of pride and excitement whenever the clay-bottles burst and fell one by one in target-practice. Then there were the nightly debates and discussions. The com-mander of the American Occupation Forces knew little of the situation in Korea. Who then was the man manipulating things for his own benefit by supplying distorted information to this commander? A name often came up in the course of their discussions. Careful plans were made and remade. The young man's home became a more and more distant affair to him everyday. And while all this was happening, his mother's illness was getting worse. On the evening before the day he was to assassinate the man, he went back home to see his mother for the first time in several days.

His bed-ridden mother opened her eyes at the sound of the lattice-door being slid open. The low-ceilinged room was dark and stuffy. He knelt quietly before his mother. Her eyes, questioningly searching her son in silence, reflected the dimly-lit kerosene lamp. They looked more like dying embers.

'Mother . . .'

The old woman seemed to nod faintly as if she had recognized her son.

'Mother, has the doctor been here?'

But the old woman gave no sign that she had heard him. Thinking she hadn't, he repeated the question once again, this time leaning closer to her ear. He then studied her expression. Her wrinkled lips fluttered faintly. Her hand seemed to grope for something. Sliding one of his hands into hers he said, 'What do you want, Mother?'

She said nothing; she merely gripped his hand meekly. Then she guided his hand onto her cheek. Slowly she moved his hand over to her lips and pressed tightly as if the mere sight and touch of his hand was not enough. He felt a lump rise in his throat. He recalled the short conversation he had with her when he had last left home several days earlier. 'When will you be back?' 'I won't be able to come back today. I've asked the lady next door to come in often to look after you. I gave her some money, too, so don't worry. The doctor will come to see you again in the evening.' 'Good . . .' Then after staring aimlessly at the ceiling for a long time, his mother mumbled, half to herself: 'The son is everything to the mother. More so as she gets old. . . . But I guess the reverse is not always true. The son has more important business to attend to . . .' His heart choked when he heard her say that, for he had to leave her in spite of himself.

And now recalling the scene, he imagined he could see his

mother fondling his hand and pressing it against her lips. The limp movement of his mother's hand had ceased after a while. He had turned his eyes from her bony, weak fingers to her eyes. Her dim eyes, looking up at him, seemed like lustreless glass beads in the dust. For an instant, he reflected darkly that she might not be seeing him at all, but merely feeling his presence.

The following day he stayed at home, not going to the rendezvous place. It was near noon. A car had rattled outside his house and screeched to a stop. 'What's the matter, Min?' agitatedly called out a fellow-member of the Society. Min (that was the name of the young man) motioned his friend to be quiet and led him outside. When he had finished explaining the situation, the friend seemed visibly upset. 'All right, let me take charge here in your place, but you must go to the rendez-vous place right away. Everyone is waiting for you,' he said.

'I'll go to the spot directly instead of joining the others at the rendezvous place, you go and tell them.'

At this his friend's face darkened again. 'Why?' he asked. He seemed worried that Min might be undergoing a change of heart at the last minute, and he gave a keen searching glance at Min's face.

'I only want to . . .'

'Only want to what?'

'I only want to stay with my mother as long as I can,' he said in a low tone.

'But . . .'

'I know. I'm supposed to sacrifice everything for the cause . . .'

He did not leave his mother's bedside. The doctor made two or three visits in the course of the afternoon. When the sun dropped over the high, elevated wall next door, his little house was instantly immersed in grey shadows. As the darkness of night swarmed in through the windows of the sick-room, the mother seemed to slip into a coma. The doctor, with a black bag that contrasted too sharply with his gown, sat silently and gravely by the old woman feeling her ever-weakening pulse.

A car-horn clamoured noisily outside. But he did not budge. The shadow of death was hovering around his mother's eyelids. Another curt, insistent blast of the horn broke the silence outside. He had to go, leaving his dying mother in the hands of his friend.

Later that night his mother passed away. His mind could now picture the face of his dying mother calling his name. He would never forget the description of the last moments which his friend later related to him. Placing hand on the shoulder of the sobbing bereft son, the friend said: 'I am sorry, but don't grieve so much. Your mother seemed to be contented as she passed away. She kept calling your name towards the end, so I played your role. When she groped for something, I gripped her hand, and placing my hand onto her lips she pressed them against it for a long time. Then she passed away. Though you weren't there, she passed away believing you were. Of course it wasn't you, but that did not make any difference to her. I think that should lessen the burden on your conscience. Now stop . . .'

Now in the cold night under the twinkling stars, he was recalling all this in his mind. Feeling again for the crumpled newspaper in his pocket, he looked down on the ground at the burning cigarette butt. He pictured himself as a man trying to loosen himself from the web of the memory of those heart-breaking scenes. 'Mother!' he cried to himself. The picture of the old woman in the newspaper who fainted at the news of her son's arrest was again superimposed with his own mother's face. It flashed before his eyes again. At that moment, almost unconsciously, he drew the newspaper out of his pocket. Sighting a street-lamp nearby, he walked towards it. Under the light he opened the newspaper to the local news section. Rapidly running through the report, he noted one item of interest.

'Taxi!' he called out. Once in the taxi, he said calmly to the inquiring driver: 'To Han River Boulevard.' As the taxi made a U-turn and was gaining speed, he again sank into the heavy-hearted thoughts.

A scepticism had slowly crept into his heart since his mother's death. He had begun to see that his actions, while serving one cause, were defeating another at the same time.

The political situation of the country was sinking ever more deeply into a quagmire of confusion and disorder – a breach and jealousy among the political leaders, open denunciations

and physical violence in the meetings, proliferating conspirac-
ies and rebellions of a complex nature entangling themselves
to no end.

It was now a rainy evening, a month or so after his mother's
death. Min stepped into the office, and immediately noted
the tense atmosphere reigning over the room. The eyes of the
triangular-faced man were almost venomous, and his habitual
queer smile lingered around his lips.

A man appeared through the narrow door leading down to
the cellar, wiping his hands with a piece of rag. His fingers
were bloodstained.

'Any change?' asked the man with the triangular face. The
man who just stepped in merely returned a grin.

Min cautiously climbed down the narrow steps to the cellar,
bowing his head down low. A small iron-grilled rectangular
window opened on the ground level, and in the dim light
coming through that window Min could see a young man lying
prostrate on the floor, as if dead. After a hesitant moment
Min walked over to the young man. Noting the footsteps, the
young man raised his head in a rebellious gesture. The young
man's lips quivered, and from between his lips a line of blood
trickled down. His eyes glared with curse and resistance. Min
stared down at him in silence. Under his left ear, strands of
hair were matted in blood, and his neck was all bloodstained.

'You want to *interrogate* me, too? Why don't you guys simply
kill me and do away with it all?' panted the young man. When
he said that, more blood trickled down from his mouth. Min
watched the young man in silence for a while, and then showed
his empty hands to the young man.

'What do you want, then?'

Min merely held his breath for an instant. To Min it was
unbearable to see this bleeding young man who would soon
die without having the chance to see the light of the world
again. He turned and started to walk back towards the stairs.
A foot on the first step, he stopped. When their eyes met, the
man on the floor mumbled something, his mouth still bleeding.
'You, you too, think I'm a turncoat?' said the man, sitting up.

Min made no sign to this question. The troubled, penetrating
eyes of the man on the floor were darkly clouded once again.

'True, I often met and conversed with men of the opposing parties,' the man on the floor said, 'but the only purpose of that was to know "myself" more clearly. It was a way of redefining myself. But you guys now accuse me of squealing the secret of our party, damn it!' His eyes flew into a mixture of curse and rage. He went on, biting his bleeding lips: 'The political platform of our society sounded first-rate, and that was why I joined it. Maybe I'm not the only one; perhaps all other young men have joined it for the same reason. And this only proves how naive we all were politically. No political training or experience to speak of. The most favoured word on our lips was "fatherland", but in reality we had no clear idea of what it was. Just a blind and raw passion, and it is this that the politicians took advantage of. I didn't realize this in the beginning. But soon I got confused, for I learned that the platform of every other political party was equally impeccable. Do you know what I talked mostly about with the men of the opposing parties?' Here the man gave a series of big political names, and went on: 'Well, all of them were so-called patriots in the past. But we don't know who among them will be the true patriots in the years ahead. Can you single them out? The ones whom we can follow, at the cost of life if necessary? These politicians, it's true they fought against the Japanese colonialism, but they are now trying to take advantage of that political asset and each one is doing his best to grab the power by enlisting as many members as possible into his own party. But we young people did not enter politics for the same reason. Perhaps we were naive, but at the same time we were pure in our passion to rebuild the fatherland regained after a long subjugation. But the greed of the political leaders knows no end. Just take a look at the disorderly mushrooming of political parties and their behaviour. We got caught in it and are being manipulated by them. Our pure passion for the fatherland is soiled by their greed. Take a look at the bloody clashes among youth organizations. What better proof . . .? Think of the cunning and complex forces working behind these clashes.' He spat a lump of blood on the floor and went on: 'You fellows cleverly lured me out here this morning, but when I wanted to go home giving up everything, politics included, you wouldn't let me do so. My only reason was that I no longer wanted to waste my passion on this dirty game. I wanted, and had the right, to talk to any young man of my own generation, that's all, but in your eyes it's a betrayal!' The young man stopped, and suddenly coughed up an amazing amount of blood. Then, with a burning curse in his glaring eyes and pallid face, he toppled onto the ground and lay motionless. Min had to avert his eyes from the ghastly scene.

The fierceness of political strife became even more stormy and violent. Behind all the political schisms and collusions, there always were betrayals. Soon in his organization people began to talk of the necessity of 'removing' a political leader by the name of X. Their reasoning was that, though X outwardly professed to be on their side, he was secretly bargaining with Y, a leader in the opposing camp. When the simmering of such talks came to boiling point, the organization decided to remove him and a plan was set. But this time Min was spared because the leaders of the organization decided to give him a rest after his recent undertaking. Instead, another young man was chosen as the sniper. But the assassination failed because the inexperienced gunner bungled it at the critical moment.

A new plan was drawn, and this time Min was marked out as the gunman. 'You'll do it again, won't you? I mean you can do it easily just as you did the last time,' said the man with the triangular face to him.

Min gave a hesitant look.

'What's the matter?'

'I'm not convinced of the necessity.'

Eyes of suspicion and outrage immediately shot at him. But he tried to look self-composed, and soon his friend's eyes softened.

'You are still thinking of your mother, I see. But you mustn't forget that for us our cause is first and foremost.'

'That's enough!' Min broke in, 'You simply ask me to shoot, and I'll do it. But no preaching, please.'

But to carry out the plan was extremely difficult. For one thing, the time was to be at four in the afternoon in broad daylight. The shooting part was easy, but the problem was the get-away. The only advantage was that the place was to be a spot with few or no passers-by. So a careful and ingenious plan was developed. Min, along with another man, were to loiter for about twenty minutes before the time, in front of the tobacco shop, across from the house from which X was to come forth. Min was to turn his back to the house while his friend kept the entrance of the house under surveillance. He was to cross the street after giving a sign to Min if he spotted X. Then Min was to follow him across the street and shoot X, taking cover behind the friend. While Min was to get away through a back-alley, several of his colleagues, waiting in the neighbourhood, would run after Min pretending they were chasing the culprit. If by a lucky chance the spurious chase party should run across a young man on their way, they were to grab him and beat him up as if they had caught the criminal. They were to make sure that the man was beaten to unconsciousness in order to delay the police investigation. If in the unlucky event there were no likely passers-by, they would have to act improvisingly so that Min could get away while they themselves made out to assist the chase.

This plan had been carried out, and it had worked. Fortunately, a young man passed by the spot at that critical moment, and he was captured as the gunman. The newspapers reported accordingly. Following the get-away, Min hid in the house of one of his colleagues and changed his clothes. A while later, to drive away the depressed feeling, he visited a small drinking place in a back-alley and drank alone. After leaving the place, he had bought a newspaper.

The taxi screeched to a stop. So deeply was Min immersed in thought at that moment he did not notice the taxi had stopped. 'This is Han River Boulevard!' the driver had to remind him.

He got out of the taxi, and stood blankly by the streetside for a long time as if he were lost. Then he reconfirmed an address in the newspaper, and asked for directions at a small store. But locating an address in this area was not an easy job. Nearly an hour had passed before he finally found the rambling shack by the railway. The sliding doors pasted poorly in old newspapers opened. The girl who answered was certainly the sister of the arrested suspect whose picture the newspapers had reported.

'Are you from the police?' the girl said, fear-stricken.

He did not say anything. He merely dropped his head.

'My brother . . .' she began, but a sob choked off what she

was going to say. 'My brother is not a criminal. He's not that sort of person. Won't you let him go, please?'

'I'm sorry, but I'm not from the police,' said Min.

'Then, what're you here for? I see, you must be a newspaper man,' she cried, and tears flowed down her cheeks. 'Please write that my brother isn't the culprit. You'll know in time that he is not. Just one single line is enough. My poor mother. My brother was out to borrow money to buy medicine for our sick mother. She'll die soon, and I can't stand the idea of her dying while her son is still accused of a false and unjust charge.' She sobbed. But when she looked up, she was astonished to also find tears in the eyes of this stranger.

Min averted his eyes, trying not to show his tears to the girl. 'Has the doctor been to see your mother?' he said.

The girl merely stared at Min, not being able to grasp the turn of events. Min placed a bundle of banknotes in her hand, and she stood there dumbfounded. He turned, not knowing what more to say.

'I, I should at least know who . . .' the girl muttered.

Min turned to the girl for a second. 'Your brother will come home soon. Don't worry about him, just look after your mother, all right?' And with a little nod he turned and left. The girl began to cry again.

The following day Min was sitting in the organization office with his colleagues. The atmosphere was tense.

'So?' said the man with the triangular face.

'Let's get one thing straight here,' said Min, looking calmly into the eyes of the other. 'I'm not here for a cross-examination.'

The habitual queer smile played about the lips of the man with the triangular face. 'I see you've worked yourself up pretty much. But you are not such a fool to bungle up everything at the last moment.'

But Min went on as if he had not heard what the other had said: 'Listen, my position is simply this: now I want to love as many simple, ordinary people as possible. I now prefer the life of simple people to any grandiose accomplishment we dream up.'

'You don't yet understand what history is.'

'I don't need your kind of history, the kind that demands sacrifices.'

'Do you then deny our cause, too?'

'I now prefer the kind of life in which there is no need to talk about causes.'

'Does this mean a betrayal?'

'Think what you please. Anyway, I'm going.'

'Going where?'

'Home.'

'Home?' A contemptuous sneer ran darkly across the man's triangular face. 'Are you thinking about surrendering yourself to the police?'

'I'm not that naive,' said Min, standing up.

But the other pulled out a gun at the same time. A tense excitement filled the air. But Min turned, unperturbed, and started to walk towards the door. Just when he was passing through the door, a shot exploded. Min froze; he felt his head was shattered in pieces, leaving a white, paper-like blank in its place. A moment later, however, he felt that the shattered pieces seemed to fit themselves back again as the sound of the shot echoed and re-echoed in the faraway places. He passed through the door as if nothing had happened.

Other colleagues stared after Min, and then at the blank hole on the floor made by the shot. 'I didn't think this kind of threat-shot would stop him,' observed the man with the triangular face, half to himself.

Min walked down the street slowly in measured steps. In his mind's eye, faces of the girl, her dying mother, and his own dead mother were all jumbled together and superimposed. He now really felt like going home for the first time in a long, long while.

TWO RESERVISTS

KIM DONG-NI

Translated by Chung Chong-wha

Towards the end of March, 1951, on the main road between Kimhae and Pusan two young men walked slowly and painfully towards Pusan. They were in rags, soiled in dirt, oil, and urine, and stinking; and their tattered clothes were torn to pieces noticeably on the parts of the shoulders and hip. Looking like two beggars they had the appearance of sick, starved dogs. Their two eyes were sunken as if they were just from the tomb, and their cheeks were deeply hollow. Their nostrils were large and dark, and they were like the dens of badgers.

The taller of the two, a man with broad, bony shoulders, wore a pair of black sneakers patched together with white thread. They afforded no protection for his feet. The other, an inch-and-half or two shorter, had put on a pair of boots which were more or less his size but torn open at the sides and in the soles. His face was swollen. He seemed to have an eye trouble, for his eyes were wet and held a sticky fluid in their corners. He carried a small bag.

When they arrived at Sasang, the day was nearly gone and evening was setting in.

'We should kill our hunger,' said the taller of the two to the man with the swollen face, who silently followed into a small inn.

'What should we eat?' the taller – whose name was Ui-kwon – said to the smaller whose name was Sang-bok.

Sang-bok looked round the inn but did not answer, with his neck stretched. He seemed to be looking for the cheapest and the most filling food. Of course it was not possible to find the two in one. So he remained silent.

'Can we have some hashed rice?' Ui-kwon asked.

'We don't have hashed rice. We only have soup and rice.'

'How much is that?' Sang-bok asked this time.

'Seven hundred *won*, a bowl.'

Sang-bok was startled at the price, but he didn't show it.

During the three months of isolation at the Second Reserve Training Camp they had rarely been out in the world. They could not imagine that prices had gone up so much. Sang-bok was busy with mental calculations; seven hundred *won* for one bowl of soup rice and they had about five thousand *won* each. To be exact Ui-kwon has four thousand *won*, because he had bought a packet of 'Peacock' cigarettes, not a real one, at Kimhae, paying six hundred *won* out of his five thousand *won*.

'We have no choice. Let's have it.'

Ui-kwon ordered two bowls of soup and rice. Sang-bok was not easy, but he couldn't help it. When Ui-kwon had one or two spoons of soup and rice, he said, 'Let's have a glass of rice wine each.'

In fact, Sang-bok also wanted a glass of rice wine before eating his soup and rice. But he kept quiet, because he was reluctant to spend even a single penny from his slender resources. Two glasses of rice wine were soon in front of them.

'Drink up!'

Ui-kwon emptied his glass in one gulp and Sang-bok did likewise.

'Kyongsang Province brews good rice wine!' said Ui-kwon. Sang-bok remained silent.

'How about having one more glass each?' Ui-kwon said again.

'Well ... but ... the money ...' Sang-bok said vaguely, wiping out the liquid that lay thick on his eyes. Ui-kwon paid no attention to Sang-bok.

'Give us half a bottle of rice wine and something to go with it. What have you got? That cuttlefish will do.'

There was no hint of hesitation in Ui-kwon's ordering. He

seemed to be determined to eat whatever he could get hold of, regardless of his pocket situation.

'You must eat while you can. When you are dead, the money in your pocket is no good. You have to eat and survive.'

'Well ... but ... the money ...'

Sang-bok's answer was unfinished and vague as before. He only seemed to mean that he would like more to drink and that he was merely worried about money.

'Don't worry so much! You can't live if you don't eat. Once you are dead money is no use to you. You have been in training for three months, so you should have changed by now. You shouldn't be that narrow-minded!'

The more Ui-kwon drank the more he boasted. Still Sang-bok kept saying 'Well ... but ... the money ...' but Sang-bok never refused the wine Ui-kwon offered him.

Ui-kwon paid for the food and rice wine from his pocket which came to four thousand *won* altogether. Sang-bok, whose face was flushed with the drink, just watched Ui-kwon, dumbfounded.

Once out of the inn, they started walking towards Pusan again. Both were silent; both were thinking. Sang-bok was thinking that Ui-kwon had changed too much. Ui-kwon was thinking that Sang-bok had changed too much. Both had been discharged from the reserve corps at Kimhae that morning, and were on their way home.

Reservists, when they are discharged, return to their home. However, the reservists from the provinces of Kyonggi, Kangwon, Hwanghae, and Chungchong didn't expect to find their home there. The house might be where they had left it but it was certain that their families had moved. They said that the people of those areas had all moved down to the south. Ui-kwon and Sang-bok were both from Anyang, only twelve kilometres south of Seoul, but they had heard that their people had moved south, which was only natural. Yet they did not know where their families were. They thought that they had probably come down to Pusan. But Pusan is a big city with a population of over a million. It would be extremely difficult to find their families there.

It was commonly believed that all refugees had gathered in

Pusan, and since that city was not so far away from Kimhae they decided to try there. On that point they agreed.

But their agreement ended when it came to the matter of dealing with the rice and money they had received from the camp on their discharge. Ui-kwon insisted that they should give the small amount of rice (two *dois* each) to Mr Lee, without whom they might have died of starvation and hunger and thus to whom they were greatly indebted. But Sang-bok had a different opinion. He admitted that they were deeply obliged to Mr Lee, but he strongly objected to giving away rice to their benefactor. Sang-bok said that they would face starvation as soon as they disposed of the rice, and he proposed that they offer half of their rice to Mr. Lee. After all, he said, there was not very much difference between one *doi* and two *dois* if it was only a sign of their gratitude. Ui-kwon had finally brought their argument to an end by saying, 'All right, you give just one *doi* and I'll give two *dois*. That will make three *dois* altogether.'

'What you have done for us will be remembered till we die. And we won't forget you, Mr Lee. We hope we'll soon be able to pay you back for your generosity and kindness. Today we have brought a small amount of rice just to show how grateful we are. Please accept it.' Ui-kwon spoke eloquently.

The difference in opinion between the two was no greater than the difference between one *doi* and two *dois*, and both were right in their own way. But this small difference got on each other's nerves very much. After three isolated months in the training camp they tended to worry about small things. In Sang-bok's eyes Ui-kwon had suddenly become a tough and prodigal man with no care at all for the future, and to Ui-kwon Sang-bok had suddenly become a miser and a coward.

A prodigal and a miser; then mutual disbelief and suspicion had increased after the incident at the inn. To Sang-bok Ui-kwon had undoubtedly become a scoundrel and to Ui-kwon Sang-bok had become a miser and fool. It was true that their minds were developing along diametrically opposed lines. Sang-bok certainly had become a coward. He had decided to cling desperately to any outside help, however small it may be. He said that, although there was no reason to refuse help from an individual, they should go to the authorities or the government to appeal for their understanding and sympathy.

To which Ui-kwon objected. To him the idea of appealing to others for help, understanding, and sympathy was disgusting. There were always plenty of food to eat, clothes to wear, and places to sleep that were to be gained if one had the initiative. Why should one degrade oneself to the position of a beggar. He not only found it difficult to understand Sang-bok's frame of mind but also hated and despised Sang-bok intensely. It was the same with Sang-bok. Not only did he think the scamp-like, rough and prodigal behaviour of Ui-kwon wrong, but he also wanted to avoid the sight of Ui-kwon's face. This situation made both of them silent while they walked towards Pusan. In the bottom of their hearts both were full of disbelief, suspicion, and hatred of the other.

Both of them came from Anyang. Ui-kwon had a small bicycle shop in the town and Sang-bok had worked on his uncle's vineyard about six kilometres outside the town. They thought that they had met once or twice before in their native town. Their friendship, however, had developed while they were undergoing training, partly because their serial numbers were only a few digits apart, partly because they were from the same town, and partly because they happened to be in the same squad whenever on duty. Besides, Sang-bok had once saved Ui-kwon's life. In the training camp Ui-kwon was, like all others, terribly undernourished. He caught a bad cold which later developed into pneumonia. There was almost no hope for him. But Sang-bok didn't give in; he did all he could and knocked at every door in the town to beg for food and medicine for the dying patient. Ui-kwon in the end miraculously came round.

The next morning the two came to the city of Pusan. Sang-bok was to search for their families in Pumil-dong district, and then go on from one district to another. Ui-kwon was to earn some money. They were to separate during the day but meet in the evening.

That evening they met each other at Pumil-dong tram stop. They told each other that their whole day's struggle had been fruitless. Sang-bok seemed to have missed his lunch and dinner. His shoulders were sagging and he kept wiping out tear drops from his eyes. Ui-kwon, on the other hand, seemed to have met someone he knew and had been offered something to drink and eat, because his face was a little flushed and his shoulders did not sag. There was a smell of death about Sang-bok, but there wasn't any in Ui-kwon.

'Let's have something to eat,' said Ui-kwon curtly.

Sang-bok said nothing, his eyes looking into the other's face.

'You have money, don't you?' Ui-kwon shouted to the other.

Sang-bok looked into the other's face, as if he could believe nothing.

'Don't you want to eat?' Ui-kwon shouted again.

'But ... until I see my family ... this money won't ...'

When Sang-bok said, Ui-kwon spat, making a loud sound. The saliva almost touched Sang-bok's face and passed close by his ear.

Without further exchange of words, they went to a district office. The district office usually shared the same building with the young men's defence guard, and this young men's defence guard had a shelter for destitute people for a night in the office.

That night, a young man in the defence guard came to them and told them that they could get rice, money, clothes and medicine either from the Ministry of Social Welfare or from the Ministry of Health. He said that either of these ministries looked after reservists wonderfully well. This seemed to have roused Sang-bok's curiosity. He said, 'Did the newspaper say that?'

The young man said it did.

'Where is the Ministry of Social Welfare?' Sang-bok asked again.

Suddenly his face took on colour and became alive. His long-awaited dream and hope that the government would save them seemed to have come true. So he said once again, 'You said that everything will be all right if we go to the Ministry of Social Welfare?'

Ui-kwon was displeased at Sang-bok's animated conversation with the young man. With his face frowned he stood up and went to the window. He opened it and spat once again. When he came back to his place after he had closed the window, he found it difficult to control the desire to spit into Sang-bok's face.

The next morning when Sang-bok awoke Ui-kwon was not beside him. Suddenly a premonition flashed into his mind. He felt in his inner pocket. The five thousand *won* was gone. He had a feeling that somebody had hit him on the head with a heavy iron bar. His head reeled. 'Ah . . . ah . . . ah . . . ah . . .' he cried.

He once again touched his inner pocket, but the five thousand *won* was not there.

He remained lying down all day long. In the depths of his heart he waited for Ui-kwon to come back. Throughout the day he shut his eyes, as if he was asleep, and repeatedly groaned.

The day after he had left Sang-bok in the district office having taken five thousand *won*, Ui-kwon was approaching the roundabout in front of the city hall from the bridge that connected Yongdo Island and the city. It was about midday. Ui-kwon saw a crowd gathered in front of the city hall.

'A man is dead!'

'A beggar has collapsed!'

People shouted to one another. Somebody then said in the crowd, 'No. That's not a beggar. He is a reservist from the training camp! I supposed he's been just discharged!'

Immediately Ui-kwon dashed into the crowd.

'Ah! Sang-bok!'

The name crossed his mind in a flash. He felt something in his throat.

'It's just mere faint, mere faint. A reservist going home . . . Such an incident happens so many times a day,' a man said.

'We should take him to the Ministry of Social Welfare, the Ministry of Social Welfare!'

A man in a green suit and another in a grey overcoat and a dark hat argued over the collapsed body of Sang-bok. They were shaking Sang-bok's head and arms whilst they were arguing. A man in yellow overalls with a crew-cut approached the body and heaved it over his back.

'To the Ministry of Health!' the man in a grey overcoat shouted.

It was at that moment that Ui-kwon, who had been watching the scene absent-mindedly, ran after the man in yellow overalls and snatched Sang-bok from him. He put his friend on his back.

'Clear out!' Ui-kwon shouted and looked askance at the

crowd: the green suit who insisted on taking Sang-bok to the Ministry of Social Welfare, the man in the grey overcoat who insisted on taking Sang-bok to the Ministry of Health, the man with the crew-cut wearing yellow overalls, men, women, the old, the young.

He disappeared into a back alley which led neither to the Ministry of Social Welfare nor to the Ministry of Health.

RETREAT

HWANG SUN-WON

Translated by Chung Chong-wha

It had been the same for two days; nothing was visible except hills and valleys. There were no moving creatures. Even the air was still.

Captain Chu's shoulders sagged despite the support of two comrades who were carrying him. He had been shot in the thigh and had applied a temporary styptic treatment to the wound with a bandage. Fortunately, neither the artery nor the nerve system was damaged. He had managed to escape capture by the enemy, but suddenly this morning an unbearable pain started, as if something had gone wrong.

Nothing was definite in their southward movement; they had merely walked in that direction. Captain Chu knew well how the sense of distance affected a wounded soldier on the retreat. During the battle a soldier has been shot in the stomach, but he had come back to the camp with his dirty uniform stuffed into the bleeding hole. It had taken him half an hour to get back; as soon as he had reached camp he fainted. The soldier had managed to get back only because he knew how far he had to go.

However for Captain Chu there was no destination. Yet he didn't dare tell either Lieutenant Hyun or Private Kim to leave him behind: to remain alone without help in a place like this meant a sure death. So Captain Chu let the private carry him on his back. The private was only seventeen, but having come from a farming family he was sturdy enough to carry a wounded officer on his back for a considerable distance.

When it was Lieutenant Hyun's turn to carry the captain, he glanced at the waist of the wounded officer where his pistol was hanging. Already they had all thrown away their rifles, knapsacks, helmets and jackets. The only weapon they had was the pistol. Captain Chu knew why the lieutenant looked at his gun; he could easily guess what he was thinking. Since the captain couldn't walk on his own he was nothing more than a useless burden to the two men. But they couldn't abandon him; for one thing he was their commanding officer. Perhaps they were waiting for the captain to use the pistol on himself.

Captain Chu, however, ignored the lieutenant's look. To make himself lighter, he took off his trousers and boots before he let the lieutenant take his turn. The lieutenant was not so heavily built as the private, but he was stronger than the captain and managed his job quite well.

For two days they had had nothing to eat except arrowroot and other wild plants. When they were lucky enough to stumble across a spring, it was their chance to take a long drink. The early summer sun was scorching. Sweat ran down the face of the man who carried the officer on his back, and the salty streams worked into his eyes and mouth. Yet he couldn't use his hands to wipe his face; all he could do was blink the sweat out of his eyes, or blow out and shake his head when it got into his mouth.

The further they advanced the more often they had to take turns at carrying. Strangely, Captain Chu gained the greatest sense of being alive from the rubbing of his wet shirt between his own chest and the sweaty back of the man who carried him.

With the captain on his back once again, Lieutenant Hyun struggled under his burden, sweat pouring down his face. A scene from his previous night's dream repeated itself over and over in his mind's eye.

In the middle of a vast yellow sky the sun was burning fiercely; the sun was also yellow as if it had been infected with jaundice. The earth stretched endlessly until it touched the sky. He was standing alone, sweating, and his naked legs were covered halfway up his shin with yellow dust. He was worried about his legs, as there was something very precious there. On the day before he was called up for service in the army, his girlfriend had teased him about hair on his legs being too long. She said jokingly that the longest hair belonged to her and he should look after it carefully. And now that longest hair was being covered with yellow dust.

But Lieutenant Hyun was also worried about something else. He saw an ant-hill in the dust right in front of him. Although he was not ordered to guard it, he felt compelled to do so. A stream of ants was coming continuously from the ant-hill, ants as yellow as the earth itself; and outside the hole was an exceptionally large yellow ant, killing each small ant as it emerged from the ant-hill by biting it on the neck. Soon a heap of dead ants had accumulated. Yet the strange thing was that the heap of dead ants didn't remain merely a pile of dead carcasses, but soon disintegrated and became part of the yellow earth itself. He was beginning to wonder if the endless yellow earth was made entirely of dead ants. He stood still watching the ant-hill under the yellow sky and the jaundiced sun.

Lieutenant Hyun felt oppressed by the weight of Captain Chu on his back. There was just one way to get rid of that weight; if the Captain could only give up the wish to go on living, everything would be alright. Otherwise the three of them would perish together.

Lieutenant Hyun was thirsty. Five days ago he had received a letter from his sweetheart, part of which read, 'My lips will never wither; the happy memories you have given me will water them always.' Once long ago, after a long passionate kiss he had whispered into her ear, 'Your lips are a many-petalled, multi-folded flower. The more I open it, the more there is to open.' In the letter there was something unusual, something different from her previous letters; for the first time she began calling him 'darling', instead of the semi-formal 'you', which meant their relationship was now sealed. As he read the letter and looked at his hairy legs, he had felt the warm smiling eyes of his beloved were watching him.

Even now, carrying Captain Chu on his back, he tried to quench his burning thirst with happy memories of his sweetheart's lips. Thinking of the smiling eyes, he felt guided by her, his sweat-soaked eyes shining brightly.

It was Private Kim's turn to carry Captain Chu. They came to a steep hill, from which they had either to go down into the valley and then climb up the opposite hill, or to wind around the slopes. Lieutenant Hyun insisted on going down the valley, which was shorter in distance but harder. Private Kim didn't agree, objecting that they might get lost in the bottom of the valley where they had to pass through a thick wood. Cutting into their indecision, Captain Chu suggested, 'Lieutenant Hyun, shall we follow Private Kim?'

Lieutenant Hyun looked at Captain Chu's pistol once again. He remembered his dream. High in a vast yellow sky the jaundiced sun was blazing, and the yellow earth stretched as far as the rim of the sky. He stood still, sweating, at the centre of this bleak landscape, and watched the ant-hill. From it a colony of yellow ants emerged, only to be bitten to death by the giant ant, as regularly and mechanically as the movement of the ants from their hole. The killed ants immediately turned into yellow earth. The more ants were killed, the higher the earth piled up to cover his hairy legs. He grew impatient and anxious, and yet there was nothing for him to do but to stand motionless. This time he noticed another hole which he had not seen before; it was a hole he himself had dug to let the ants escape. But the ants kept coming out of the same hole as before, to be bitten to death. Lieutenant Hyun was soaked with sweat, although he was not carrying the captain on his back.

At sunset the three of them caught a snake and shared it for dinner. When they finished it, Lieutenant Hyun moved off as if he wanted to relieve himself. They waited for him; and when he did not come back Captain Chu said to Private Kim, 'You might as well go now.' But the private did not understand what the captain meant.

'Lieutenant Hyun has left us, he was tired of waiting.'

'Waiting for what, sir?'

'Waiting for me to kill myself.'

For a long time there was no sign of Lieutenant Hyun.

Captain Chu, avoiding Private Kim's eyes, said again, 'You'd better go now.'

Private Kim, after a moment's hesitation, looked at the sun setting behind the western hills and, without a word, offered his back to the captain.

Since he had to carry the wounded man entirely by himself, the going was a great deal harder. They had to rest more often. When it was quite dark, the two of them stopped the day's march and lay down on the ground. They missed the army biscuits which they had thrown away along with their knapsacks. In the dark they thought of Lieutenant Hyun and wondered how far he managed to go. Private Kim thought him cold-blooded and cruel; but Captain Chu was hoping that the lieutenant would bring a rescue party. He remained awake after the private had fallen asleep. His wound no longer hurt, but he was obsessed with the idea that if he went to sleep he would never wake again.

He suddenly remembered a woman with whom he had gone to bed in Pusan, where he had leave about three months ago as a reward for his role in recapturing a strategic hill. After love making the woman had told him a story. She had been in Seoul working in a bar during the January 4th retreat. One day she had helped a girl escape through the back door because three foreign soldiers were pursuing her. Consequently she had been forced to take the girl's place. She fainted while they raped her and came round only at dawn the next morning. She couldn't remember what the girl looked like. Then the day she slept with Chu, many months after the incident, she had met the girl by accident on the street. The girl recognized her and greeted her very warmly, and she was touched by the girl's offer to do anything she could to help her. When the woman had finished her story, Captain Chu had asked her, rather sarcastically, whether she would do the same thing again just to be thanked for it. She had replied, lighting a cigarette in the dark, that things of that sort couldn't be repeated just because one wished to do so. When she had let the girl slip out, she had done it without knowing what the consequences would be. She added, 'There are times when you do things which you later think would be impossible. It was the same then. I just helped her without much thought, and had to take

326

what came afterwards. If it happens again I might do the same thing, or I might not. It all depends.'

In the dark Captain Chu thought of her and of what she had said. Suddenly he realized that he had done the same thing she had. Battle after battle, always under unexpected circumstances, he had always done unexpected things. When he had asked her sarcastically that night whether she would do the same thing again, he had in fact hoped secretly that she would. Now on a dark hill he seriously thought he had no right to expect the woman to go through all that again. And the same with himself; no one had the right to ask him to keep repeating the terrible experiences of war. He wanted to get up and shout out that no one had the right to expect him to put up with what he had suffered. But there was no one to hear; only the thick wall of darkness. After a while he fell asleep.

Next morning the two of them began moving; they had to stop more often than the day before. Private Kim took off his trousers and boots; he knew that it would be difficult to walk barefoot in the hills, but the boots were unbearably heavy. Soon his feet began to bleed, as he could rarely find a soft path in the rocky hills.

Nothing was visible except hills and valleys, and nothing was audible in the profound silence of the wild except the private's panting. There was no sign of a rescue party, nor could they hear their army's cannons in the distance. Yet Captain Chu was constantly alert, determined not to miss a single sound. Once he pointed in a certain direction and told the private to move towards it, and they found a stream running through rocks.

That day they did not advance more than four kilometres. They managed to catch a few frogs and ate them raw. Private Kim was exhausted, with buckling knees and stooped back. The more his back bent, the less hope for life the captain felt.

Towards evening, while they were climbing a hill, a crow suddenly flew up from the other side. From the top they could see that the way down was a steep cliff, and they had to turn back. Private Kim looked aimlessly down and saw two or three crows land on something. It was a man's body. He knew at once it was Lieutenant Hyun. He wore the same clothes that he had on the night before: shirt, army trousers and boots. Crows were pecking at his face. When they noticed two people at the top of the hill, they started; but seemed to change their minds, cawed aggressively and went on pecking. Already the eyes had gone and the sockets were dark hollows.

The two men moved back and dropped to the ground when they could no longer see the crows. The last wave of energy seemed to be ebbing away from both of them. Private Kim got up again and staggered to the edge of the cliff. He began to stone the birds, which flew away from the corpse but kept returning to it immediately, fluttering and croaking wildly. The private, tired of throwing stones, came back and stretched out on the ground. He saw the captain shut his eyes and keep quite still. The private thought it strange to feel the approach of death in such a peaceful silence, while in the mist of fierce battles he had been completely unaware of death. Perhaps tomorrow the crows would be pecking at their eyes too. He hoped he would die first and become food for the crows, instead of having to see the birds land on the captain's face. Suddenly he felt like crying, but he was too weak even for that.

Private Kim was woken from a deep sleep by Captain Chu's voice. It was starry night.

'Listen to that!' said the captain again weakly. 'That's the sound of cannons.'

Private Kim felt suddenly wide awake and raised his head to listen. He could hear the faint roaring of cannons from far off.

'Which side is it, sir?'

'Ours. That's a 150 mm cannon.'

Private Kim thought the captain was right. Before he had time to ask him how far away it was the captain said, 'Unfortunately, it's a bit too far for us, not less than sixteen kilometres.'

Sixteen kilometres was out of reach. The private lay down again. The captain felt that he was slowly dying. He felt his mind become lucid, and could clearly see death coming closer every minute. He was finally confronting an idea he had long tried to suppress, to kill himself with his pistol. Had he finished himself with it sooner, much trouble might have been avoided.

For a start the lieutenant wouldn't have run off and fallen down the cliff trying to travel in the dark. Yet it was still not too late to get rid of himself. When he was dead the private would have a better chance of rejoining his regiment. He shouted to the private, 'The cannons are firing somewhere to the southeast. Keep to the left of the cliff.' He pulled the pistol from his waist and raised it to his head.

At that moment he heard another sound in the midst of the dull roaring made by the distant artillery. At first he wasn't sure what it was and said to the private, 'What's that noise?' The private raised his head from the ground and listened. After a while he said, 'What noise, sir?'

'I can't hear it now.' At once he heard the sound again as if carried by the wind. 'That's it, coming from over there.' Still the private couldn't hear anything at all.

'It's like a dog barking,' said the captain.

At the mention of a dog, the private sat up and crawled in the direction the captain pointed. If it was a dog barking, there must be a family living somewhere in the valley.

'It's on the other side of that hill,' the captain called.

Still the private could hear nothing. He crawled back to where he had been lying.

Captain Chu wanted to give something to the private, and at the same time he wanted to give himself something, too. The private murmured to himself, but loud enough to be heard by the captain, 'Perhaps there will be more crows tomorrow. This is the last night that I'll have my eyes.'

Suddenly the private heard a pistol shot. Astonished, he turned to the captain, who was pointing his pistol at him, shouting in a weak but clear voice, 'Carry me on your back now!'

Without knowing what was going on, he got up and turned his back to the officer, who ordered, 'Now, move!'

Private Kim felt the muzzle of the pistol pressing behind his right ear. When they reached the other side of the hill, the captain ordered him to stop for a moment in a dark wood. He listened attentively and said, 'To the left!' After a while he said, 'Stop here,' and then, 'Move forward!'

While the private struggled to the left, then the right, and forward at the captain's command, he heard nothing. He thought the captain was dying and delirious. If he was dying, why did he order Kim to accompany him on his journey of death? He felt waves of anger surge up which he had not felt before. However, he had no choice but to stumble on as he felt the pistol touching his right ear. It was as if only the force of the pistol pushed him forwards step by step.

When they reached the foot of the hill the captain ordered, 'To the right!' and again a few minutes later, 'Straight on!'

Finally the private too heard a sound, and the barking of a dog became clearer and clearer as he moved on. But he still couldn't tell how far it was. He felt something burning in his throat, and each staggering step seemed to fall into a bottomless pit. He wanted to sit down every moment, and yet he couldn't stop while the pistol compelled him.

He saw nothing in the dark. He wasn't sure whether he was on his feet or not. He walked on and on. Then suddenly the barrel of the pistol was withdrawn and the dead weight of the captain fell from his back to the ground, just as he thought he saw, though dimly, the dark shadows of a thatched house, a man in front of it and a dog barking.

WINTER, 1964, SEOUL

KIM SUNG-OK

Translated by Chung Chong-wha

Anyone who was in Seoul during the winter of 1964 would know well the street stalls which appeared after dark and sold fried beancurd or fish-cakes on small sticks, roast sparrows and three kinds of drink. As soon as you lifted the shabby curtain fluttering in the cold wind which already swept the frozen streets, you faced a carbide bottle's elongated flame, waving in the passing wind, and a middle-aged man in a dyed army jumper, serving drinks and something to eat with them. In one of these mobile stalls three of us met that night, by chance. By three of us I mean a postgraduate student with very strong glasses; another man, thirty-five years old, of obscure background, which, though obscure, still betrayed his poverty; and myself.

A conversation of a kind took place between the postgraduate student and me, and in the course of quite unremarkable introductions I learnt that his surname was Ahn, his age twenty-four, that he was specializing in a subject which I, ignorant and without college education, had never heard of before, and that he was the eldest son of a rich family. In return I suppose I told him something about myself; I was twenty-four years old, born in the country, and after high school had applied to the Military Academy unsuccessfully, and then I enlisted in the army where I at one point had

331

gonorrhoea, and now I was working in the City Council's local draft office.

After this we had nothing else to say to each other. For a while we drank quietly. As I picked up an over-cooked, charred sparrow, an idea occurred to me. So I thanked the dead sparrow in my heart, and said: 'Do you love flies, Mr Ahn?'

'No, not yet,' he said. 'Why, do you love flies, Mr Kim?'

'Yes,' I answered. 'Because they can fly. No, not for that reason alone. Rather because they can fly and at the same time they can be caught in my hand. Have you ever caught in your hand anything else that can fly?'

'Wait a minute.' He looked at me vaguely through his glasses. He hesitated for a while and then said, 'No, except for flies ...'

It had been unusually warm during the day and everything had melted, making the road muddy. But with nightfall the temperature had gone down and the wet earth begun to freeze beneath our feet. My black shoes made of real leather were not enough to protect my feet from the cold air coming from the freezing earth. A street pub like this is good enough for a few minutes and a glass or two on your way home from work, if you feel like it. But it is not a place to stay for a considerable time and engage in conversation with the man next to you. As I came to realize this I heard the bespectacled fellow ask a brilliant question. I said to myself, 'Ah, there's a chap,' and asked my freezing feet to wait a bit longer.

'Do you like the things that wriggle, Mr Kim?' he asked me.

'Of course I do,' I answered, feeling exalted. Sad memories make us quietly exalted and happy memories make us boisterously so. I said, 'After I failed at the Military Academy, I shared a room in Miari with a fellow who had failed at university. I had never been to Seoul before. I was rather depressed after my dream of becoming an officer had been shattered. I suppose I lost all my hopes for good then. As you may know, the bigger your dream, the greater you despair. During that period I enjoyed getting into a crowded bus in the morning rush hour. As soon as we finished our breakfast my roommate and I dashed to the bus stop on the top of Miari Hill. Honestly, we were panting like mad dogs. Do you know what the greatest attraction and the greatest novelty of the big city are for a country fellow like me? The greatest attraction is the numerous lights in the windows of tall buildings; no, it's the people moving here and there under these lights. And the greatest novelty is a pretty girl standing right next to you in the bus. Sometimes you can rub, flesh to flesh, your arm or thigh against hers. Because of this I once spent a whole day on buses, changing from one to another. That night I was so tired that I vomited.'

'Wait a minute, please. What are you driving at?'

'Well, I was going to say that I love things that wriggle. Listen to me. Like two pickpockets, my roommate and I got on a very crowded morning bus and stood in front of an attractive young girl who had already taken a seat. Surreptitiously I had a look at the lower part of the girl's belly while I hung onto a strap, leaning my head against it because I had become a little dizzy after a run from home to the bus. Though I didn't notice right away, I could see her belly moving up and down quietly when my eyes cleared in a few minutes.'

'Moving up and down? Was it due to her breathing?'

'Yes, of course. You never see the abdomen of a corpse move. Well, anyway, I felt strangely peaceful and clear in my mind as I watched the lower part of a young woman's abdomen moving quietly in the crowded bus. I like that movement enormously.'

'Well, it's a pretty obscene story, I must say,' said Ahn in a very strange voice. I was angry with him. In fact I had prepared the story for a radio panel discussion; if I was ever invited to a panel and was asked the question, 'What is the freshest thing in the world?' I would certainly argue that the freshest thing in the world is that movement, in contrast to other members of the panel who would say that it is a lettuce, a May morning, or an angel's forehead.

'No, oh, no! It's not an obscene story at all,' I protested strongly. 'That's a true story.'

'What is the connection between being true and not being obscene?'

'I don't know. I don't know anything about the connection as such.'

'Well, it is just moving up and down, not wriggling. So, Mr Kim, you don't like something that wriggles, I assume?'

We lapsed into silence again, so I just rubbed my glass with my fingers. I thought to myself, 'Son-of-a-bitch, all right, so it's not wriggling then.'

'I have come to the conclusion that your movement up and down is a kind of wriggling,' Ahn said suddenly.

'It is!' I shouted happily. 'It's certainly wriggling. I love a woman's belly most. What kind of wriggling do you like most, Mr Ahn?'

'There isn't any special kind of wriggling. Wriggling is wriggling. A thing just wriggles. For instance ... a demonstration.'

'Demonstration? Well, a demonstration ...'

'Seoul is a huge assembly of all kinds of human desires, you see?'

'I'm afraid I don't see,' I answered as clearly as I could.

Our conversation stopped once again. This time the silence lasted longer. I lifted my glass to my mouth. When I emptied it, I saw him do the same, with his eyes shut. Feeling somewhat sad, I thought it was time to leave. I said to myself, 'Well, that's the way it is; it's just as I've always thought.' I was hesitating whether I should say, 'See you next time', or 'I have had a very good evening', when Ahn took my hand suddenly but gently. He said, 'Do you think we were telling lies to each other?'

'No,' I answered, feeling a little bit annoyed. 'I don't know whether you told lies, Mr Ahn, but what I told you tonight is the truth.'

'Well, I have a feeling that we told lies to each other.' His flushed eyes blinked once or twice behind his glasses. 'Whenever I make friends with anyone of my age I am tempted to talk about wriggling. This is why I start talking, but the conversation does not last more than five minutes.'

I thought I could understand what he was talking about, though only in a vague way.

'Let us talk about something else,' Ahn said.

I wanted to bully this man who liked to talk about serious subjects. I also wanted to enjoy the drunken man's privilege of hearing his own voice. So I said, 'The eighth street lamp from the east in front of the Pyungwha Market was not lit ...' As I saw Ahn look puzzled, I continued more excitedly: 'And the fifth floor of Whashin Department Store had only three lighted windows.'

But this time I was taken aback, for I saw a glow in his face. He said very rapidly: 'There were forty-nine people waiting for buses at the Sudaemoon bus stop, among them were seventeen women, five children, twenty-one young men, and six old men.'

'When was that?'

'A quarter past seven, this very evening.'

'Ah!' I said desperately, but the next moment I regained my confidence, and feeling very happy said, 'There were two chocolate papers in the first dustbin in the side alley by Dan-sung Cinema.'

'When was that?'

'At nine o'clock on the evening of the fourteenth.'

'The walnut tree by the front gate of the Red Cross Hospital had one broken branch.'

'In an inn without a sign in Ulchiro Third Street there were five girls whose names were Mija, and they called themselves the First Mija, the Second Mija, the Third Mija, the Fourth Mija, and the Last Mija, in the order of their arrival at the place.'

'Others would know that, because you cannot be the only one who has been there, Mr Kim.'

'Oh, yes, you are right. I didn't think of that. I slept with the First Mija one night. The next morning the girl bought me a pair of pants from a woman who sold goods on daily credit. She keeps her money in an empty rice-beer bottle, and there are a hundred and ten *won* in it.'

'Well, that makes sense. The fact belongs to you and nobody else, Mr Kim.'

The tone of our conversation became more and more polite. When we started our stories at the same moment, one of us gave way to the other.

'I . . .' it was his turn. 'I saw a tram heading for Seoul Railway Station from Sudaemoon, and its trolley sparked exactly five times. This happened at twenty-five past seven tonight.'

'You were around Sudaemoon tonight, Mr Ahn, I suppose?'

'Yes, that's right.'

'I was around Chongno Second Street, tonight. Underneath the door handle of the lavatory in the Youngbo Building is a nail mark two centimetres long.'

He laughed heartily. 'It is your nail mark, isn't it?'

I felt ashamed, but I had to admit it, by nodding. 'How do you know?' I asked.

'I do the same sometimes,' he said. 'But a thing like that is not a happy memory. We should just observe and discover facts and keep them secret. If you don't, you have an unpleasant taste in your mouth later.'

'I've done that sort of thing a lot, but I rather en...' I meant to say that I enjoyed it, but a sensation of shame for what I had done overwhelmed me, and I didn't come out with the next words. I acquiesced, by nodding. All of a sudden I was seized with a strange feeling. If what he said half an hour before was true, this bespectacled man next to me should be the son of a rich man and highly educated. Then why does he behave in this manner? I wondered.

'Mr Ahn, is it true that you come from a rich family and are a postgraduate student?'

'Well, you may call a man rich when he has property worth thirty million *won*. Of course it is my father's. And as for your doubt whether I am really a postgraduate student, I can show you my student ID card,' he said. He searched his pocket and took out his wallet.

'No need to show your student ID card. To tell you the truth, I had some doubts about you, Mr Ahn; it just occurred to me as being rather strange that a man like you should sit down with me in this cheap place on a cold night and talk about things, about secret thoughts, to a fellow like me.'

'Well, that is, that is...' he stammered in a rather heated voice. 'Well, damn it. I have a question to ask you, Mr Kim; why do you come out in this cold weather and walk around in the streets?'

'It's not from force of habit. A pauper like me can come out onto the streets only when he has a bit of money in his pocket.'

'But why do you come out to the dark streets?'

'It's better than watching the walls of my room.'

'Don't you feel somehow rich when you are wandering in the streets?'

'What is rich?'

'Something. Perhaps it is life. I think I understand why you ask a question like that. Well, my answer is this. Night falls, I come out of my house, and I am free from everything. Perhaps I am not free, as a matter of fact, but at least I feel so. Don't you feel the same, Mr Kim?'

'I don't know.'

'I am not among things then, but outside them, and I can watch them in perspective. Don't you agree?'

'Well . . .'

'Do not think that it is difficult to understand. I mean this. When night falls everything shows its real, naked self, while in the day-time it shows us only its surface. Do you think that is meaningless? I mean, to enjoy observing the naked core of things at night.'

'Meaning? What sort of meaning? I never count the number of bricks in the buildings in Chongno Second Street, because that has any meaning. I just . . .'

'Exactly. It is meaningless. There may be some meaning in it, but what it is I don't know yet. You don't seem to know either, Mr Kim. Well, then, let's go out and find out what it means. Of course, we shouldn't create any artificial meaning.'

'I am a bit puzzled. Is that your answer, Mr Ahn? I am a little puzzled really. This word "meaning" suddenly comes and worries me.'

'Oh, well. I am sorry then. Perhaps my answer is this. I come out onto the streets at night because I feel full inside.' He lowered his voice this time. 'Mr Kim, you and I were taking different ways and arrived at the same point. Even if this point is the wrong spot, it is not our fault.' Then he raised his voice and said cheerfully, 'Well, we shouldn't stay here any longer. Let's go to a warmer and more proper place to drink, before we say good-bye. I will go round the town and then go to a hotel. I always go to a hotel whenever I come out onto the streets like this. The hotel is the climax of my night out.'

To pay the bill, both of us put our hands into our pockets at the same time. It was then that a man said something to us. He was the man who had taken a seat next to us with a glass of rice beer, warming his hands over the anthracite fire; he gave the impression that he was there to warm his body and not to drink. He was in a clean coat, and his hair, on which reflected light moved whenever the carbide flame danced in the wind, was neatly oiled and combed. He looked about thirty-five or so, and he carried a vague air of poverty about him; perhaps it was his shabby jaw and reddened eyes. The man addressed one of us, it might have been me or Ahn, in a weak voice 'Excuse me, can I join you? I have some money with me.'

He didn't seem to insist on joining us, but it was clear that he wished to go out with us. Ahn and I exchanged glances for a second, and then I said, 'If you have money for drinks . . .'

'You are welcome to join us.'

Ahn finished my sentence.

'Thank you,' said the man, still in a weak voice, and followed us.

Ahn's face had an expression which showed that things were moving in directions other than he had intended, and I also had a premonition that things might not go well. I had met strangers drinking several times and found that I enjoyed being with them; all it took was a facade of boisterous enjoyment; they were there full of vigour and adventurous spirits. But I had never met anyone with a dying voice. We walked slowly, looking round like men who had suddenly forgotten where they were going. A pretty girl on a medicine advertisement-board, hung on an electricity pole, was looking at us with a sad smile, and she seemed to say, 'It's cold, but what can I do?' On the top of a tall building one neon sign was blinking incessantly, advertising *soju*,* and next to it was another, advertising some medicine, which flickered as if it had forgotten to go off and then stayed on for a few seconds. On the streets, which were completely frozen by then, beggars crouched rock-like, and people passed by them hurriedly. The wind blew and drove a sheet of paper in our direction from the other side of the street. The paper fell at my feet. I picked it up and found it was an advertisement for a beer hall; the paper read, 'Beautiful hostesses at your service, prices specially reduced.'

'What time is it, please?' asked the weak-voiced man.

'Ten to nine,' said Ahn after a short silence.

'Have you had supper? I haven't had any yet. Would you like to have it on me?' This time he looked from Ahn to me in turn.

'We've had supper,' Ahn and I answered at the same time.

'Why don't you have yours?' I suggested.

'No, I won't bother,' the weak-voiced man replied.

'Go on. We will come with you,' Ahn said.

'Thank you. Then . . .'

We went to a nearby Chinese restaurant. When we were

---

*soju is one of the most popular drinks in Korea, distilled from rice.

settled in our room, the man entreated us to change our minds and order something for ourselves. We declined his offer. He asked once again.

'Can I order something very expensive, then?' I only said this as a way of turning down his kindness.

'Yes, by all means,' the man said eagerly, in a strong voice for the first time. 'I've decided to spend all of my money.'

I felt a little bit uneasy with him, not knowing what he was up to, but all the same I asked him to order me roast chicken and a drink. So he told the waiter to bring what I had asked for as well as his own meal. Ahn looked at me, bewildered. But I was more interested in some ecstatic cries coming from a woman in the next room.

'Please, do order something,' the man asked Ahn.

'No, not for me, thanks,' Ahn declined, surprised.

All of us listened silently to the panting sounds in the next room. A long way off the trams seemed to be squeaking, the traffic sounded like a river in flood and in the restaurant the bell rang occasionally. In the room we were wrapped in an awkward silence.

'I have something to tell you,' the kind man began. 'I should be grateful if you would listen to my story. Some time this afternoon my wife died. She had been in Severance Hospital.' The man looked at us with a face which was no longer sad. 'Really?' 'I am very sorry,' Ahn and I offered him our condolences.

'My wife and I lived happily. Because she couldn't have any children we were closer and happier. We were not rich, but whenever we had some money we went everywhere together and had a good time. During the strawberry season we went to Suwon, and during the grape season we went to Anyang. In summer we went to the Daichon Beach, and in autumn we went to Kyungju. In the evening we went out to the cinema or theatre.'

'What was the trouble then?' Ahn put it cautiously.

'Acute meningitis, that's what the doctor told me. She had had acute appendicitis and acute pneumonia in the past, but she survived them. But this one finally killed her . . . she was finished.'

The man dropped his head and murmured something inaudible. Ahn touched me on the knee with his finger and sent a silent signal with his eyes that we should leave him alone. I agreed, but we couldn't leave, as he suddenly lifted up his head and continued his story again.

'My wife and I were married two years ago. We met by chance. I heard from her that her home was somewhere near Taegu but she didn't go to see her parents. So I didn't know how to get in touch with them. I couldn't help it.' He dropped his head again and started murmuring inaudibly.

'What couldn't you help?' I asked.

He seemed not to have heard me. After a few minutes' silence he looked up at me, almost imploringly, and said, 'I sold my wife's body to the hospital. I couldn't help it. I am a mere door-to-door book salesman. I couldn't help it. They paid me four thousand *won*. Until shortly before I met you both, I hung around outside Severance Hospital. I wanted to locate the morgue where they were keeping my wife's body, but I couldn't find it. I just sat down by the wall and watched the whitish smoke coming from the chimney. What would happen to her? Could it be true that students in their anatomy class would cut her head open with a saw and dissect her stomach with a knife?'

We had to remain silent. The waiter brought a dish of yellow turnip pickles and leeks.

'I am sorry that I have told you a very unpleasant story. But I couldn't help telling it to somebody. Now I would like to ask your advice. What shall I do with this money? I would like to spend it all tonight.'

'Do, by all means,' Ahn answered without hesitation.

'Could you stay with me until I spend this money then?' the man asked, but we couldn't decide immediately. 'Please stay with me,' he implored. We agreed.

'Let's spend it in a splendid way.' He smiled. It was the first smile he had shown us since he had joined us that night. But his voice was still weak.

When we came out of the Chinese restaurant, the three of us were quite drunk. One thousand *won* we'd spent there. The man was crying with one eye and laughing with the other. Ahn told me that he was now tired of scheming to get away from the man. I kept shouting to myself, 'Everybody made mistakes in accentuation, in accentuation.' The streets were as cold and deserted as those of colonial towns one sees on the cinema

screen. The neon sign for *soju* blinked as busily as before, and
the neon sign for the medicine advertisement went on and off
as lazily as before. The girl on the electricity pole smiled at
me and said, 'Well, well.'

'Now where to?' the man said.

'Where to?' Ahn said.

'Where to?' I said after them.

There was nowhere to go. There was a foreign goods shop
with the show-window facing the street, right next to the
Chinese restaurant we had just come out of. The man pointed
at it and dragged us into the shop.

'Choose neckties. It's a present from my wife,' the man
shouted.

We picked striped ties and the man spent six hundred *won*.
We came out of the shop.

'Where to?' the man asked.

There was still nowhere to go. There was a man selling
oranges in front of the shop.

'My wife liked oranges.' The man dashed to the orange cart
and spent three hundred *won*. We peeled off the skins with
our teeth and hung around the Chinese restaurant.

'Taxi!' the man shouted.

A taxi stopped before us. As soon as we got into the vehicle,
he said loudly, 'To Severance Hospital!'

'No! It is useless,' Ahn stopped him.

'No?' he mumbled. 'Then where to?'

Nobody answered.

'Where do you want me to go?' the driver asked us in an
irritated voice. 'Will you get out, if you've got no place to go
to?'

We got out of the taxi. We were still not more than twenty
paces away from the Chinese restaurant.

From down the street the other way came a loud siren, the
sound coming nearer. Two fire-engines passed us noisily at full
speed.

'Taxi!' the man shouted.

A taxi stopped in front of us. We got in and he told the
driver, 'Follow that fire-engine!'

I was peeling my third orange.

'Are we going to watch the fire?' Ahn asked the man. 'No
we haven't time for that. It's half-past ten already. We should

341

spend our time in a more exciting way than watching the fire. How much have you got now?'

The man searched his pockets and took out all he had. He then handed the money over to Ahn. Ahn and I counted the money. There was one thousand, nine hundred *won*, as well as a few coppers and a few ten-*won* notes.

'That's enough,' Ahn said, and returned the money to the man. 'Fortunately there are girls who know all about female charm.'

'Are you talking about my wife?' the man asked in a sad voice. 'The charm of my wife was that she smiled so much and so often.'

'No. I was only suggesting that we go to the brothel district of Chongno Third Street,' Ahn said.

The man smiled contemptuously and looked at Ahn. Then he turned his head away. Meanwhile we arrived at the place where the fire had broken out. We paid thirty *won* for the taxi. We soon learned that the fire had originally started in a paint shop and now it had spread to the first floor, which was used as a ladies' hairdressing school.

Flames were belching from the windows. The whistle of policemen, the sirens of fire-engines, the crackling of the fire, and the hiss the jets of water made against the walls were the only sounds I heard. Strangely enough there was no human voice; people were like still-life, reddened by the fire, as if they had been caught doing something shameful. Each of us crouched down, sitting on the tins of paint which were at our feet, and watched the fire. I secretly hoped that the fire would last for a long time. I saw the flames catching the signboard of the hairdressing school. Soon the flame began at the last letter of the signboard.

'Mr Kim, let us talk about ourselves,' Ahn said. 'Fire means nothing. If it means anything, it means that we are watching tomorrow morning's newspaper story in advance. That fire belongs neither to you nor to me, nor to this gentleman. Fire belongs to all of us. Yet fire does not break every night, and therefore I am not interested in it. What do you think, Mr Kim?'

'I agree,' I said inattentively. I was only interested in the flame catching the second last letter of the signboard.

'No, no. I was wrong. Fire does not belong to all of us. Fire

belongs only to fire. We mean nothing to fire. And that is why
I am not interested in fire. What do you think, Mr Kim?'

'I agree.'

A jet of water landed on the burning second last letter of
the signboard, and grey smoke rose where the water extinguished the flames.

'It's my wife,' the weak man suddenly shouted, standing full
of energy, with his eyes wide open and pointing at the blazing
flames with his finger. 'My wife is shaking her head violently.
She says her brain is going to crack, with unbearable pain. Oh,
darling . . .'

'If she complains of unbearable pain, it is a symptom of
meningitis. But that is not your wife, it is the flames that are
shaking in the wind. Sit down. Your wife can never be in those
flames,' Ahn said, dragging the man down to the tin again. He
then whispered to me, 'This man makes you laugh, doesn't
he?'

I saw the second last letter catching fire again. Streams of
water were again directed at it. But the water missed the spot,
dancing in the air. Meanwhile the flames swiftly licked the
third last letter. I secretly hoped that the fire would soon catch
up with the very first letter and that nobody else in the crowd
would notice the process of fire spreading up the signboard,
except me. Soon I was seized by an idea that the flames were
alive. So I cancelled my previous wish. I noticed something
white flying into the burning building from our direction.
The white pigeon dropped into the fire.

'Something flew into the fire, didn't it?' I asked Ahn, turning
round.

'Yes, something flew in there,' Ahn replied and turned to
the man. 'Did you see that?'

The man said nothing. A policeman caught the man by the
hand and asked, 'What did you throw into the fire just now?'

'Nothing.'

'What?' the policeman shouted, with a threatening gesture.
'I saw you throw something. What was it?'

'Money, sir.'

'Money?'

'I threw money and a stone in a handkerchief, sir.'

'Is it true?' the policeman asked us.

'Yes, that was money. This gentleman believes in a superstition that his business will prosper if he throws money into a fire. Well, you may think that he's a bit mad, but he is an honest businessman,' Ahn explained.

'How much was it?'

'One copper,' Ahn replied.

When the policeman was gone, Ahn asked the man, 'Was it really money that you threw away?'

'Yes, it was.'

'All you had?'

'Yes.'

For a long time we listened to the crackling flames without talking. Ahn broke the silence after a while and said to the man, 'Well, you've spent it all now ... Our promise is over and we must say good-bye to you.'

'Good-bye, then,' I said to the man.

Ahn and I turned away from the man and started walking. He came running after us and caught us by our hands.

'I'm afraid to be left alone,' he said trembling.

'It will soon be curfew time. I must hurry to a hotel,' said Ahn.

'I'm going home,' said I.

'Can't we go together? Please, stay with me just for tonight. Please, will you come with me for a moment?' said the man, waving my arm, which he was still holding, as if it were a fan. He was probably doing the same to Ahn's arm.

'Where do you want us to go?' I asked the man.

'I want to see somebody near here to get money, and then we can all go to a hotel together.'

'To a hotel?' I asked, counting the money in my pocket with my fingers.

'I will pay the bill. Don't worry about money, but let's go together anyway,' Ahn said to the man and me.

'No, no! I don't want to give you any further trouble. Just please follow me for a few minutes.'

'Are you going to borrow money?'

'No, no. Somebody owes me some money.'

'Does he live near here?'

'Yes, if this is Namyong-dong.'

'It certainly looks like Namyong-dong,' I said.

Ahn and I followed the man and we moved away from the fire.

'It's too late to go and claim your money,' Ahn said to the man.

'But I've got to have my money back.'

We entered a dark back alley. After turning several corners, the man stopped in front of a gate under a street lamp. Ahn and I stopped about ten steps away from the man. He rang the bell. Soon the gate was opened and he started talking to someone inside.

'I want to talk to the master of the house.'

'He is asleep.'

'Then the mistress . . .'

'She is asleep too.'

'I must see one of them.'

'Wait a minute, then.'

The gate was shut. Ahn rushed up to the man and took hold of him by his arm. 'Let's go.'

'No, it's quite all right. They must pay me.'

Ahn walked back to his previous position. The gate was opened once again.

'I'm sorry to bother you so late at night,' the man bowed his head to the open gate.

'Who are you?' It was a woman's voice, befuddled with sleep.

'I'm very sorry that I've come rather late. As a matter of fact . . .'

'Who are you? You look drunk . . .'

'I've come to get the money for the books you had on hire purchase,' the man said in a high-pitched voice, almost crying. 'I've come to get the money for the books you had on hire purchase.' The man leant his hands against the doorpost and burst into tears, burying his face on his outstretched arm. 'Money for the books you had on hire purchase, on hire purchase,' he kept sobbing.

'Come tomorrow in the day-time.' The gate banged in his face.

The man cried for a long while, calling 'Darling!' from time to time. We waited until he had stopped, keeping the same ten steps away, and when, after a while, he came to us, staggering, we walked back through the dark alley, with our heads down. A cold wind swept along the deserted street.

'It's very cold,' the man said in a worried voice.

'It is cold. Let's hurry to a hotel,' said Ahn.

'Shall we take a room each?' Ahn asked us when we were in the hotel. 'That would be a good idea, wouldn't it?'

'Better be in one room, all of us together,' I said, anxious about the man.

The man said nothing and stood absent-mindedly, as if he were at our mercy and did not know where he was. We all felt awkward as soon as we got into the hotel, the awkward feeling one has after coming out of a theatre and not knowing what to do next. Now we were inside the hotel, the streets seemed much better. We had to go into separate rooms, next door to one another.

'What about going into the same room?' I said again.

'I am very tired now,' Ahn said, 'Let's take a room each.'

'I hate to be left alone,' the man grumbled.

'It will be much more comfortable to sleep alone,' Ahn said.

We parted in the passage, and took three separate rooms adjoining one another, as the porter indicated.

'Let's play cards,' I said before we parted.

'I'm terribly tired. If you want to, please go ahead by all means, but leave me out.' Ahn vanished into his room.

'I'm tired too. Good night,' I said to the man and went to my room. I drank a glass of water which the porter had brought and went to bed. I slept very soundly, without a dream.

The next morning Ahn woke me up very early. 'The man, he's dead,' Ahn whispered into my ear.

'What?' My sleepiness vanished instantly.

'I have just been to his room and found him dead.'

'Well, as I thought . . .' I said. 'Do they know about it?'

'Nobody yet. It may be better to slip away now.'

'Suicide, isn't it?'

'Of course, yes.'

I hurriedly put on my clothes. An ant crawled towards my feet. Feeling he was going to bite my foot, I moved out of the room quickly.

Outside, in the early morning, hail was falling on the street. We walked as fast as we could away from the hotel.

'I knew he was going to die,' Ahn said.

'I didn't know.' I spoke the truth.

'I knew.' He had the collar of his coat up. 'But I couldn't do anything for him.'

'No, you couldn't. I didn't dream of it,' I said.

'If you had known, what would you have done?' he asked me.

'Hell, what could I have done? What did he want us to do for him?'

'Exactly. In fact, I thought that he might not die if I left him alone. That was the best and only help I could think of for him.'

'I didn't dream that he was going to kill himself. Hell! He was carrying poison with him then?'

Ahn stopped in front of a bare tree which was covered with snow. I did likewise. He looked at me and asked me in a wondering voice, 'Mr Kim, we are certainly twenty-four years old, aren't we?'

'At least I am.'

'I am too.' He shook his head once. 'I am afraid.'

'Of what?' I asked.

'Something, that is . . .' he said as if he were heaving a sigh. 'We seem to have grown old, too old, don't you think?'

'We are only twenty-four,' I said.

'Well, anyway . . .' he extended his hand towards me.

'Well, let's say good-bye here. Have a good time.' I held his hand.

We parted. I dashed to the other side of the street where a bus had just pulled in. In the bus I looked out through the window and I saw Ahn deep in thought with the snow falling on him through the bare branches of the tree.

A JOURNEY TO MUJIN

KIM SUNG-OK

Translated by Moon Hi-kyung

When the bus curved round the mountain, I saw a sign-post, 'Mujin 10Km.' Looking the same as ever, it stood out among tall weeds on the roadside. I listened to the conversation that started up again between the two people who sat behind me.

'Only ten kilometres to go.'

'Yes, we'll be there in about half an hour.'

They sounded like agricultural inspectors, but perhaps I was wrong. At any rate, they were wearing short-sleeved colourfully patterned shirts and polyester trousers, and were making remarks about the passing farms, hills and villages in a jargon which only those with professional knowledge could have used. Since I changed bus at Kwangju, I had been listening to their low-toned and polite conversation in a state of half-sleep. There were many vacant seats on the bus. According to the inspectors, it was because nobody had time to travel, it being a busy season on the farm.

'There aren't many things that Mujin is noted for, are there?'

'No, there aren't many. It's odd that it should be so populous, though.'

'It's near the port, so I suppose it could develop as another harbour.'

'You'll see when you get there that it's not really suitable for a port. The sea is shallow and you have to sail out several hundred *li* before you reach the real sea where you can see the horizon.'

'It must be a farming district.'

'Well, it hasn't got too many open fields either.'

'Then how does a population of fifty or sixty thousand manage to survive there?'

'That's why there's such an expression as "struggling along somehow." '

They laughed in a somewhat dignified manner.

'Still, a place ought to have at least one special local product,' said one of them shortly.

But it is not true that Mujin has no special product. I know what it is. It is mist. When you go out in the morning, the mist would completely encircle Mujin like an enemy troop that had advanced silently through the night. Hidden by the mist, the hills would look as if they had been banished to some distant land. The mist was like the breath exhaled by the ghost of a woman who, restless with some unavenged grievance, nightly haunted the place. Before the sun rose and the wind changed, it was not within human power to dispel the mist. Though it could not be touched, its presence was palpable and it encircled and isolated the inhabitants. The mist, the mist of Mujin, the mist that you met in the morning in Mujin, the mist that made men wait anxiously for the sun to rise and the wind to change – that mist was the most distinctive speciality of Mujin.

The bus began to jolt less. I could feel whether the jolting got better or worse through my chin. Since I was sitting completely relaxed, my chin jogged up and down with each bump as the bus went over the pebbly country road. I knew perfectly well that it was more exhausting to slouch and let my chin jog up and down in this manner than to sit up stiffly, but a summer breeze that crept through the open window and mercilessly tickled my bare skin lured me into a state of drowsiness, making it impossible for me to sit up. It seemed to me that the breeze had turned into countless little particles, each bursting with as much sedative as it could hold. Pure sunlight, a still and innocent coolness that had yet to be touched by sweaty skin, a saltiness in the air pointing to the presence of the sea beyond the mountain, which embracing the road, seemed to be making a lunge towards the moving bus – the

349

breeze contained all these, mixed and melted together in a strange alloy. The innocent brightness of the sun, the coolness of the air which gave elasticity to the skin and the saltiness of the wind from the sea – if I could mix these three and make a sleeping pill out of them, it would be the most effective of all the sedatives displayed in the drugstore window. And I would become managing director of the most successful pharmaceutical company in the world, simply because falling into a sweet sleep is a pleasant thing which everyone, without exception, wishes for.

When this thought occurred to me, a bitter smile came to my lips. At the same time, I felt more acutely that we were approaching Mujin. Whenever I went to Mujin, such fantastic ideas always came to my mind and everything became topsy-turvey. In Mujin, fantastic ideas that never occurred to me anywhere else came to me without any shame or hesitation. Without any conscious effort on my part, these thoughts, formed elsewhere by themselves, seemed just to push themselves into my head.

'You're looking unwell. Why don't you spend a few days in Mujin. You can say that you are visiting your mother's grave. Father and I will get everything ready for the general shareholders' meeting. Go get some fresh air. You haven't had any for a long time. When you return, you will be managing director,' my wife had said to me a few nights ago, tentatively fingering the sleeve of my pyjamas. I had responded to her earnest suggestion by muttering something under my breath, like a child forcibly sent on an errand. It was like a reflex reaction conditioned by my past experiences in Mujin, which had always left me feeling rather lost.

Since I had become older, I had paid only a few visits to Mujin. I seemed to visit it only when I needed to escape from Seoul due to some failure or when I needed to make a fresh start of some sort. It was not by accident that I sought Mujin on such occasions. Nor did it mean that fresh courage and new plans came to me more easily in Mujin than in other places. On the contrary, Mujin always gave me the sensation of being sunk in stagnation. Sallow-faced, I would lounge about in dirty clothes in a back room. The memories I had of Mujin were generally about things like losing my temper with the old couple who used to look after me, or masturbating to chase away insomnia and empty thoughts, inhaling cigarettes strong enough to make my tonsils swell, and waiting impatiently for the postman. But these, of course, were not the only memories of Mujin. When my ears suddenly get tuned to the external world in the streets of Seoul, making me reel under the shock of a merciless onslaught of noise, or when I drive up the narrow street before my house in Shindang-dong, suddenly there would rise before me the image of a country town with a brimming river, whose grassy banks stretched out more than fifteen *li* towards the sea, a town with small woods and many bridges, with narrow streets and mud walls, a school-ground surrounded by tall poplar trees and local offices with front yards covered with black pebbles from the seashore where people would put out bamboo mats at night. Such a town would come to my mind and the town was always Mujin. I also thought of Mujin when I felt a sudden longing for some quiet. But in those moments Mujin was merely a cosy spot that I had painted in my head and it was always empty of people. Most of the memories I have of Mujin were of my dark youthful days.

But it would be untrue to say that the memories of my days in Mujin followed me about like shadows. On the contrary, now that those dark years have passed, I can say I have almost forgotten Mujin. Even as I was getting on the train last night, the dark memories of Mujin had not come to me in any vividness, perhaps because I had been too busy leaving instructions to my wife and to some people from the office who had come to see me off. But this morning, a mad woman whom I saw in Kwangju as I was leaving the station suddenly pulled those dark memories out from the shadows and threw them before me. The woman wore with some elegance a Korean-styled skirt and a blouse and on her arm was a handbag which looked as if it had been carefully chosen to suit the season. I thought her rather pretty but she was heavily made up. Because of her ceaselessly roving eyes and the way she was teased by a group of half-yawning shoeshines who had gathered around her, I knew that she was crazy.

'She went mad because she studied too hard.'

'No. Her lover left her.'

'She can speak English. Shall we ask her to . . .'

The boys exchanged words loudly. A slightly older looking boy with a face covered in spots fingered the front of her blouse; every time he touched her, the woman, her face always expressionless, just screamed. Her screaming suddenly brought to my mind a line I had written in my diary in the backroom in Mujin.

It was when my mother was still alive. Because of the outbreak of war, classes at college had been suspended and having missed the last train, I had to walk several thousand *li* from, Seoul to Mujin, my feet covered in blisters. Once in Mujin, my mother made me keep to a dark back room so that I could evade the recruitment of volunteers and later conscription. While my classmates from Mujin Middle School were leaving the town square in army trucks for the front, cotton bands tied around their heads and singing, 'If the Fatherland survives, though I die,' I sat in my dark room, listening as they went past the house. Even when the news came that the battle-front had moved north and that classes had resumed at college, I still hid in the back room in Mujin. It was all because of my widowed mother. When everyone else was going to war, I lay hidden in the back room, masturbating. Whenever there came any news that a neighbour's son had died in action, my mother rejoiced over my safety, and if a letter arrived from a friend at the front, she tore it up. She did this because she knew that I preferred the battle-front to my back room. The diary I wrote in those days, though all burnt now, was full of self-contempt and effort to bear the ignominy of the situation.

'Mother, if I were to go mad now, it would be because of the following reasons. So please take them into consideration when trying to find a cure.' The woman I saw in the morning had conjured up before me the memories of the days when I wrote such words in my diary. Through her I sensed the nearness of Mujin and the dusty sign-post that stuck out from among the weeds, which we had just passed, made the nearness real for me.

The bus was entering the town of Mujin. In the blazing sun of late June, all the roofs – of tile, tin and thatch – shone like silver. The sound of hammering from the smithy rushed towards the bus, then retreated. The smell of manure seeped in from somewhere and as we passed the hospital, the smell of disinfectant floated in. From a loudspeaker in a shop came flooding out a sleazy pop song. The streets were empty and people crouched in the shade under the roofs. Toddlers, naked and unsteady, stumbled about in the shades. Only the dazzling sun filled the town square in which a pair of dogs, their tongues hanging out, were copulating in silence.

The People I Met at Night

Just before dinner, I went over to the street where all the newspaper agencies were located. My aunt did not subscribe to any paper, but a newspaper had become for me, as for everyone else living in the city, an essential part of my life, marking the beginning and end of every day. I entered an agency and left my aunt's address and a map showing the way to her house. But as I was leaving, I heard voices murmuring behind my back. Some people in the agency must have recognized me.

'Really? He looks arrogant.'

'He's a real success.'

'A long time ago ... consumption.'

Amid such whispering, I secretly longed for some acknowledgement but none came. That was the difference between Seoul and Mujin. Without knowing it, the people at the agency will probably be drawn more and more into a whirl of their own whispering; losing themselves in it and oblivious of the emptiness that they will face when thrown out of it, they will go on whispering and whispering.

The wind was blowing from the sea. The streets were more crowded than they were a few hours ago when I got off the bus. Children were returning from school. As if they found their bags burdensome, they whirled them about in the air, or slung them over their shoulders or even carried them tightly in their arms, all the time blowing saliva bubbles with the tips of their tongues. Schoolmasters and local officials also went by with drooping shoulders, their empty lunch bags rattling. Then suddenly it flashed across my mind that it was all a game – going to school, teaching children, going to work and returning home. Everything seemed just an absurd game. And I thought it comical that people should cling to such things, making endless efforts all to no end.

While I was having dinner at my aunt's, I received a call. The visitor was someone by the name of Park, my junior by several years at Mujin Middle School. He seemed to have conceived a certain respect for me, for I had been a real bookworm in those days. Park, too, had been crazy about literature. He said his favourite author was an American author, Scott Fitzgerald, but unlike Fitzgerald's heroes, he was well mannered, serious and poor.

'I heard from a friend at the newspaper agency that you're down. What brings you here?' He was genuinely delighted to see me.

'Is there any reason why I shouldn't come down?' I said, but my own words irritated me.

'No, it's just that you haven't been down for a long time. It's your first visit since I left the army, which means that it's . . .'

'Already four years.'

I came down to Mujin four years ago when I had lost my job as an accountant at a pharmaceutical company, which was being merged with a larger firm. No, that was not the only reason why I had come down to Mujin. If only Hee, who had been living with me then, had stayed with me, there would have been no journey to Mujin.

'You're married now, I hear,' Park remarked.

'Yes. And you?'

'No, not yet. They say that you married well.'

'Do they really? Why aren't you married yet? How old are you?'

'Twenty-nine.'

'Twenty-nine. Well, nine is supposed to be an unlucky number. But still, you should try to do something about getting married.'

'We'll see,' said Park, scratching his head like a boy.

Four years ago I was twenty-nine and at about the time when Hee left me, my wife's first husband died.

'I suppose there's nothing wrong?' asked Park, who knew something of my former visits to Mujin.

'No, I'll probably get a promotion, so I took a few days' holiday.'

'Well, that's nice. People here say that you are the most successful person from Mujin since the Liberation.'

I smiled at this remark.

'Yes, you and Cho, your classmate.'

'Do you mean the chap who used to hang around with me?'

'Yes, he passed the Civil Service Examination last year and is now the head of the local tax office.'

'Really?'

'You didn't know?'

'I've lost touch with him. He used to be a tax officer here some time ago, wasn't he?'

'That's right.'

'That's a welcome bit of news. Perhaps I'll go and look him up this evening.'

My friend Cho was short and rather dark. He had often told me that he had an inferiority complex when he stood beside me, for I am tall and pale. 'Once upon a time, there lived a boy who was told that he had inauspicious palm lines. Digging lucky lines into his palms with his nails, the boy worked hard. He succeeded and lived happily ever after.' Cho had been a boy who was easily impressed by such a tale.

'What do you do these days?' I asked Park.

He blushed and hesitated and, as if he was ashamed, muttered that he was teaching at the old school.

'That ought to be nice. You have plenty of time to read. I don't even have time to read a magazine these days. What do you teach?'

As if encouraged by my words, Park replied in a brighter voice, 'I teach Korean.'

'That's good. From the school's point of view, they're lucky to have found a teacher like you.'

'Not really. With all these people from education colleges, it's difficult to get a job with only a teaching certificate.'

'Is that so?'

Without replying Park only gave a rather bitter smile.

After dinner, we had a drink or two and set out in the direction of Cho's house. The streets were dark. As we crossed the bridge, I saw dim reflections of the trees in the water. I remembered that I had once cursed those dark crouching trees. They had stood there as if they would leap on me if I were to let out a scream. I had even thought how nice it would be if there were no trees in the world.

'Things haven't changed much here,' I said.

'Perhaps,' muttered Park.

In Cho's sitting room were four other guests. I saw that Cho, who was shaking my hand heartily, almost painfully I should say, had become smoother-faced and less dark.

'Come and sit down. I'm sorry it's such a mess here. Must get myself a wife.'

The room, however, was not sordid.

'Why aren't you married yet?' I asked him.

'Well, it just turned out that way. While I was struggling with law books, you know. Sit down.'

I was introduced to other guests. Three of them were men from the tax office. The last was a woman and she exchanged a word or two with Park.

'Come on, no secrets here, Miss Hah. Let me introduce you to my old classmate Yun Hee-hung. He is manager of a big pharmaceutical company in Seoul. This is Hah Insook, the music teacher at the old school. Miss Hah graduated from a music school in Seoul last year.'

'So you and Park both teach at the same school,' I said, pointing to Park and then at Miss Hah.

'That's right,' she replied, breaking into a smile.

Park bowed his head.

'Are you originally from Mujin, too?'

'No, I'm just down for the school, so I'm on my own here.'

She had a face which was not without character. It was oval-shaped, her eyes were large and her complexion was rather sallow. On the whole, she gave an impression of being rather delicate, an impression which, however, was dispelled by her high-bridged nose and full lips. Her high-pitched and firm voice enhanced the impression created by her nose and lips.

'What did you major in?'

'Vocal music.'

'But she plays the piano beautifully too,' Park, who was standing by her, added in a cautious voice.

Cho joined in. 'She's a wonderful singer. Her voice is really something.'

'Ah! Are you a soprano?'

'Yes, I sang "On a Clear Day" from *Madame Butterfly* in the graduate concert,' she said in a voice which had a nostalgic note.

Silk cushions were on the floor and scattered on top of them were playing cards. They were the same cards as those of the old days when I used to get up almost at noon, and a cigarette almost burning into my lips and bleary-eyed with tears from the smoke, I would cast the luckless day's fortune. The same cards as those of the gambling table at which I had flung myself, the cards that had made my whole body feel numb except for my burning head and trembling fingers.

'You have some cards here, some cards,' I muttered, picking one up and throwing it down and repeating this.

'Shall we play for money?' asked one of the men from the tax office.

But I didn't feel like playing.

'Another time, perhaps.'

The people from the tax office grinned. Cho left the room and returned soon. A little later drinks were brought in.

'How long will you be staying?'

'About a week.'

'What do you mean by getting married without inviting me to your wedding? Not that I could have gone as I was stuck in the tax office counting numbers all day long.'

'I know I was rather remiss. But you must send me an invitation when you get married.'

'Don't worry. You'll get one within the year.'

We drank some beer which was none too foamy.

'A pharmaceutical company is where they make drugs, isn't it?'

'Sure.'

'Well, you won't ever have to worry about getting sick there.'

As if this were a tremendously funny joke, everyone roared with laughter, slapping their thighs.

'You must be a popular teacher, Park. You never come and see me, when I'm only five minutes away.'

357

'I've been meaning to but . . .'

'Miss Hah keeps me informed, though. Miss Hah, have a glass of beer. Beer isn't really alcohol. Come, why are you so shy this evening? She's not really like this normally, you know.'

'Thank you. Please leave it there. I'll help myself.'

'You've had beer before, haven't you?'

'When I was at college. I once locked myself in with some friends and drank *soju*.'

'I didn't know that you were a closet drinker, Miss Hah.'

'Oh, no. I didn't drink it because I wanted to. I just wanted to see what it tasted like.'

'How did you like it?'

'I really don't know. The moment I put the glass down, I fell asleep.'

They all laughed. Park looked as if he were forcing himself to join in.

'As I always said, that's what's so nice about Miss Hah. She always tells a story in the most amusing way.'

'I'm not trying to make it amusing. I always used to talk like this when I was at college.'

'Ah, now here is precisely what's not so nice about her. Can't you leave out the bit "when I was at college"? I haven't been to college and it makes people like me jealous.'

'I'm sorry.'

'Then will you give us a song in the way of apology?'

'Yes, a song, a song.'

'That's right.'

'Let's have a song.'

Everyone clapped. She hesitated.

'We have a special guest from Seoul tonight. What you sang the other night was lovely,' Cho urged her.

'All right, then.'

She began to sing; her face was almost expressionless and only her lips moved a little. The tax office people began to beat their fingers on the table in tune with her song. She was singing 'The Tears of Mokpo'. I wondered to myself how much affinity there was between 'On a Clear Day' and 'The Tears of Mokpo'. And what could cause a popular song to flow from a throat trained to sing arias. In the way she sang the song, there was none of the shrillness that the song had when it was sung by a prostitute. Nor did it have the hoarseness and mawkish sentimentality common in such songs. As she sang it, it was no longer a popular song, but it was still less an aria from *Madame Butterfly*. It was a completely new song. It had a kind of pitifulness different from the one usually found in such songs; it had a pitifulness which was even more brutal and a shrillness which was even more high pitched than that of 'On a Clear Day'. The song was permeated with a cold smile of a wild-haired mad woman and even more with the smell of Mujin, the smell of a rotting corpse.

When her song ended, I forced myself to give a rather foolish smile and clapped. I became aware – was it through intuition? – that Park was longing to leave. My eyes met his and he got up from the seat, as if he had been waiting for me. Someone begged him to sit down again but he declined with a feeble smile.

'I'm sorry I have to leave before you. I'll see you again tomorrow,' he said to me. Cho accompanied him to the door and I saw him to the street. Though the night was still young, the street was deserted. From somewhere distant came the sound of a dog barking, and some rats, which had been nibbling at things in the street, darted away, startled by our shadows.

'Look, the mist is falling,' Park said, and even as he was saying it, from the far end of the street, dark silhouettes of distant houses with lights shining here and there began to fade away.

'You're in love with Miss Hah, aren't you?'

Park smiled rather feebly again.

'Is there something going on between Cho and her?' I asked him.

'I don't know. I think Cho is thinking of her as a possible marriage partner.'

'If you like her, you should be more assertive. Good luck.'

'I'm not sure,' Park stammered like a boy. 'It's a shame to see her singing a pop song to those Philistines, that's all. That's why I left,' said Park in a low voice, as if he were repressing his anger.

'Well, there is a place for everything, for classical songs and for pop songs. I don't think you need to think of it as being a shame.' I consoled him with a lie. He left and I returned to the company of Philistines. In Mujin, everyone has the same habit of regarding others as 'Philistines'. I too have the same tendency of thinking that everything that other people do is merely a game which is no different from pure idleness.

When we got up from our seats, the night was far advanced. Cho pressed me to stay the night but I thought of the discomfort I would suffer in the morning and insisted on leaving. The tax office people went their different ways, leaving the school-mistress and myself to walk together. We were crossing the bridge. In the shadowy landscape, the stream stretched out in silver, its distant end disappearing into the mist.

'It's a really beautiful place at night,' she said.

'Really? That's something.'

'I can guess why you said it was something.'

'What have you guessed?' I asked.

'You said it because in reality this is a dull place. Am I right?'

'Almost.'

We came to the end of the bridge. There we had to part. She had to take the road that ran along the stream while I continued down the same road.

'Is this your way? Then . . .' I broke off.

'Will you take me a little farther? The street is so quiet and I feel a bit frightened,' she asked in a slightly trembling voice.

We started to walk again, side by side. I felt as if we had suddenly become very close. From the end of the bridge, from the moment she asked me to escort her in a voice that really did seem to tremble with fear, I felt that she had leapt into my life – like all my friends, like the friends whom I can no longer drop, the friends whom I sometimes wounded but who had more often wounded me.

'When I first met you, how shall I put it? Was it that you had an air of Seoul about you? I felt I had met you before. Isn't that strange?' she said suddenly.

'A pop song,' I said.

'Yes?'

'Why do you sing that kind of song? I thought music students usually avoided them?'

'It's because they ask me to sing only pop songs,' she replied and then laughed gently, as if embarrassed.

'If I were to point out to you that you don't have to be with

360

them if you really didn't want to sing those songs, would I be
meddling in your affairs?'

'No. I don't intend to go any more. They're really a worthless
bunch.'

'Then why did you go before?'

'Because I was bored,' she replied, depressed.

Boredom – yes, that was the most accurate word.

'Park said he was leaving because it was a shame to see you
sing such a song.'

I looked at her searchingly in the dark.

'Mr Park is too stuffy.'

She laughed aloud, as if delighted.

'He's a good person,' I said.

'Yes, too good.'

'Did it ever occur to you that he may be in love with you,
Miss Hah?'

'Oh, please don't call me Miss Hah. Considering your age,
you might even be an older brother.'

'What shall I call you then?'

'Just call me by my first name, Insook.'

'Insook, Insook!' I murmured in a low voice. 'Yes, that
sounds better. But why are you evading my question?'

'What question?' she asked, smiling.

We were walking along the rice paddy. It was a summer
night. I was listening to the croaking of frogs from the rice
paddies far and near, a sound which was similar to that of
thousands of shells being rubbed together. Suddenly I felt as
if the sound were changing into countless stars twinkling within
my senses. There had occurred within me a strange sensation
of a sound changing into a visual image. Why had my feelings
been in such a turmoil at that moment? It was not as if I
heard frogs croaking when I saw bright stars almost showering
down from the sky. Staring up at the stars, I had seen clearly
before me, as if my eye-sight were becoming more acute, the
tantalizing distance between myself and a star and between
that star and another star. Bewitched by the sight of that
inaccessible path, I had stood dumb and still, my heart bursting
within me. Why had it been so difficult to endure it? Why had
it been such an anguish to endure the sight of those innumerable stars twinkling in the sky?

'What're you thinking about?' the woman asked me.

'Frogs croaking,' I replied and looked up at the sky.

Veiled by the settling mist, the stars were fading.

'Oh, yes. The frogs. I hadn't noticed. I thought the frogs croaked only after midnight in Mujin.'

'After midnight?'

'Yes. After midnight the landlord turns his radio off and I can hear the frogs then.'

'Why do you stay up so late?'

'Sometimes I just can't go to sleep.'

Just can't go to sleep! That was probably true.

'Is your wife pretty?' she asked suddenly.

'Yes, she's pretty,' I replied, smiling.

'You're happy, aren't you? You're rich, you have a pretty wife and adorable children.'

'I have no children, so I guess I am a bit less happy.'

'Why don't you have any children? How long have you been married for?'

'Just over three years.'

'Why do you travel alone when you're not on business?'

Why was she asking me such questions? I laughed quietly.

She said to me in a livelier tone, 'From now on I am going to treat you like my older brother. Will you take me to Seoul?'

'Do you want to go to Seoul?'

'Very much.'

'Don't you like it here?'

'No. I think I'm going crazy here, even at this very moment. In Seoul I have many friends. God, I am dying to go to Seoul.'

She clutched my arm but immediately let it go. I suddenly felt very excited. I frowned and frowned again. The excitement died down.

'But now, wherever you go, it won't be as in your college days. And since you are a woman, wherever you go you'll feel that you are going crazy, unless you get married and have a family.'

'I thought of that too, but at the moment I feel as if I would go crazy even if I did have a family. Even if there were someone I really cared about, I still wouldn't want to live here. I would beg him to leave.'

'But in my experience living in Seoul is not the best thing. There are responsibilities, only responsibilities.'

362

'But here there are neither responsibilities nor irresponsibilities. Anyway I want to go to Seoul. Will you take me?'

'I'll think about it.'

'You'll promise, won't you?'

I merely smiled. We reached her house.

'What're you doing tomorrow?' she asked me.

'I'll probably visit my mother's grave in the morning. I have no plans after that. I may go down to the sea. There's a house I used to lodge in. I might go and look it up.'

'Why don't you do that in the afternoon?'

'Why?'

'Because I want to come too. Tomorrow is half-day.'

'Let's do that then.'

We fixed the time and place to meet and parted. Feeling strangely depressed, I walked slowly through the dark streets back to my aunt's house.

When I lay down, the siren blew to announce the curfew. It came suddenly and loudly and blew long. Everything and every sound became absorbed into it and there was nothing left in the world. Only the siren remained. I felt as if the siren too would go on just long enough so as not to be felt any more. At that moment it suddenly lost its strength, and faded away in a long moan. Thoughts revived within me. I thought of the conversation I just had with the woman. Though it felt as if we had talked of many things, only few words remained ringing in my ears. Eventually these words too would move from the ears to the head and from the head to the heart and I wondered how many would remain then. They may even all disappear. Let me think slowly. She said she wanted to go to Seoul. She said it in a frustrated tone. I felt a sudden desire to clasp her in my arms and ... No! This desire would be the only thing remaining in my heart. But once I leave Mujin, even this would be erased from my heart. I could not sleep. It was partly because of the afternoon nap. I smoked a cigarette in the dark, staring hard at the white dresses hanging on the wall, which were staring back at me like cheerless ghosts. I shook the cigarette ash somewhere above my head, a place where it could be easily swept clean in the morning. From somewhere came the sound of 'frogs that only croaked after midnight'. The clock struck one, two, then three and four. A little later the siren lifted the curfew. Between the clock and the siren, one of them was not on time. The siren came suddenly and loudly and blew long. Everything and every sound became absorbed into it and there was nothing left in the world. Only the siren remained. I felt as if the siren too would go on just long enough not to be felt any more. Somewhere husbands and wives were probably copulating. No, not husbands and wives but whores and their customers. I didn't know why I suddenly had such a ridiculous thought. A moment later I was fast asleep.

A Long Embankment Stretching to the Sea

It was raining lightly in the morning. Before breakfast I took an umbrella and visited my mother's graveyard, which was close by the town. I rolled my trousers up to my knees and knelt in the rain to kowtow before the grave. The rain turned me into an exceptionally dutiful son. I pulled out some long weeds on the grave with one hand and thought of my father-in-law, who, with his boisterous laughter, would be calling on various important people to get me promoted to the position of managing director. This made me want to leap into the grave.

On the way back, I decided to take the road along the grassy embankment, although it was a detour. The wind blew the rain into a haze and the landscape danced. I closed the umbrella. As I was walking along, I saw standing about on the grass below the slope of the embankment a throng of children from distant farms, who were probably on their way to school. Among the crowd were also a few adults, and a policeman in a raincoat was crouching on the slope smoking a cigarette, his eyes fixed on a distant spot. Clicking her tongue, an old woman managed to make her way out of the crowd. I went down the embankment and asked the policeman as I went past him, 'What happened?'

'Someone's committed suicide,' he answered in a voice completely devoid of interest.

'Who was it?'

'A whore from the town. Every summer one or two of them kill themselves.'

'Oh!'

'This one was a tough one. I thought she would survive but maybe she too was human.'

I went down to the river bank and joined the crowd. The dead woman was facing the river, so I couldn't see her face but I could see her permed hair and plump white limbs. She was wearing a thin red sweater and a white skirt. It must have been rather cold early in the morning. Or maybe she had a liking for that outfit. Her head was resting on rubber shoes with flowery patterns and lying on the ground in the rain and a few feet away from her limp lifeless hand was a white handkerchief, which, as it did not blow about in the wind, seemed to be wrapped around something. To get a glimpse of her face, the children stood in the stream facing my way. Their blue school uniforms were reflected upside down on the water and were like blue flags surrounding the corpse. Strangely, I felt rising within me a great surge of physical desire for the dead woman. I hurriedly left the scene.

'I don't know which drug she took but there may be something that we could still do,' I said to the policeman.

'Women of that kind usually take cyanide. They don't create scenes with a handful of sleeping pills. That's something to be thankful for, at any rate.'

I recalled that I had played with the idea of making a new kind of sleeping pill on the bus. The innocent brightness of the sun, the coolness of the air which gave elasticity to the skin and the saltiness in the wind from the sea – if only it were possible to make a sleeping pill with these three elements! But perhaps such pills already existed. It suddenly occurred to me that perhaps the reason why I could not go to sleep the night before, tossing and turning in bed, was because I was keeping some kind of vigil over the last hours of the dead woman. The siren must have sounded and then she must have taken the pills and I had fallen asleep. All of a sudden, I felt that she was part of me, a part which gave me pain but which nevertheless had to be cherished. Shaking the rain off my umbrella, I returned to my aunt's house.

A note from Cho, the head of the local tax office, was waiting for me. 'If you have nothing to do, please drop by,' it said. I made my way to Cho's office after breakfast. It was no longer raining but the sky was still overcast. I thought I could discern what was on Cho's mind. He wanted to impress me with the sight of him sitting in his office. No, maybe I am being unfair. I decided to think otherwise. Was he content with his job? Probably. Cho was someone who was completely at home in Mujin. Again, I decided to think otherwise. Knowing someone well – not pretending to know someone well is a great misfortune from that person's point of view. The reason that we can criticize people or at least pass judgement on them is because we happen to know them.

Cho was fanning himself in his chair with his jacket off, his trousers rolled up to his knees. He looked shabby and when he made gestures that showed that he was proud to be sitting in a revolving chair covered with a piece of white cloth, I felt very sorry for him.

'Aren't you busy?' I asked.

'There's nothing for me to do. If you are in a position of responsibility, you only have to say a few words about assuming all the responsibility.'

But Cho, in fact, was not as idle as he made himself out to be. Several people came in asking for his signature on documents and more documents piled up in the box containing business yet to be dealt with.

'We are a little busy today because it's the end of the month and a Saturday,' he said.

His face showed pride in his being so busy. Busy, so busy as not to have time even to be proud of it – that was what my life in Seoul was like. Perhaps this showed that people down here had little finesse about living. They could not even be busy without clumsiness. I felt that clumsiness in one's job, even if it was burglarizing, was pitiful and irritating. The ability to deal with things smoothly and efficiently is reassuring to say the least.

'You know Miss Hah from last night? Is she a possible candidate for marriage?' I asked him.

'Is that all you think I'm worth?' he asked.

'Why, what's wrong with her?'

'Look here, my clever boy. When you're so well off with a rich and influential widow, do you expect me to be content with some skinny music teacher from God knows where?' As if enjoying himself hugely, he laughed loudly.

'You are well off, so what does it matter if she is a beggar?'

'I know, but that's not how it is in this world. Since I have no connections, my wife's family should have some,' he explained. From the way he talked we were no less than fellow conspirators.

'It's a funny world we live in. When I passed the Civil Service Examination, I was suddenly beseiged by match-makers. They only brought miserable matches, though. Some women think that just being women is good enough for them to get husbands. It's a piece of impertinence.'

'Is Miss Hah one of those women?'

'She's a typical example. The way she chases after me is a real nuisance.'

'She looked quite intelligent to me.'

'Oh, she's intelligent all right. But I looked into her family background and it's rather shabby. If she were to die here tomorrow, there's nobody who could come down to see to things.'

I felt a desire to see her again soon. I felt that at that very moment she was dying somewhere and I longed to see her soon.

'Park, who doesn't know these things, is in love with her,' Cho said, grinning.

'Park?' I pretended to be surprised.

'He writes her love letters and she shows them to me. It amounts to Park writing love letters to me.'

My desire to see her vanished completely. But it revived in a moment.

'I took her to a Buddhist temple last spring. I was hoping to get somewhere with her but she was very clever and said she wouldn't give an inch before marriage.'

'So?'

'I was rather put out, that's all.'

I thanked her.

When it was time for our meeting, I went down to the embankment which was a few minutes' walk from the town. A yellow parasol could be seen in the distance. It was her. We walked side by side under the sky overcast with clouds.

'I asked Mr Park lots of questions about you today,' she began.

'Did you?'

'What do you think was the most important question?'

I could not guess at all. She giggled to herself and said, 'I found out your blood type.'

I was silent.

'Yes, your blood type. I have strange faith in blood types. If a person's character is ruled by his blood type – like in biology books – then there would only be so many different kinds of persons, wouldn't there?'

'That's not faith. It's wishful thinking.'

'What kind of blood type is that?'

'It's a type called foolishness.'

In the warm stuffy air, we laughed with an effort. I glanced at her profile. She had stopped laughing and was gazing straight before her with her big eyes, her lips firmly set. At the tip of her nose was a drop of sweat. She was following me like a child. I took her hand. She seemed taken aback. A moment later I tried again. She didn't seem surprised this time. Between the palms of our hands a faint breeze filtered through.

'What will you do in Seoul when you get there?' I asked.

'My nice older brother will look after me, won't he?' she looked up at me smiling.

'There are plenty of eligible men. But wouldn't it be better for you to go home?'

'I would rather stay here than go home.'

'Then why not stay?'

'Then you don't want to take me?'

Her face crumpled up and she threw my hand away. In fact, I didn't know what I was thinking. I was past the age of being ruled by mere emotion and compassion. Though I didn't marry a 'rich and influential widow', as Cho termed it a while ago, out of calculation, I had come to accept it as a good thing in the end. I felt a different kind of love for my wife from that I felt for the woman who had left me. Yet, in spite of this, walking along the embankment that stretched toward the sea under the cloudy sky, I took her hand again. I explained to her about the house we were going to.

One year I had taken a room in that house to clean out my polluted lungs. It was after my mother's death. Frequent in the letters I sent during that year I spent by the sea was the word 'lonely'. Though it is now a rather common word, a dead word which no longer provokes any feeling in anyone, in those days it was the only word that held any meaning for me. The tedious hours I spent walking up and down the sandy beach in the morning; the sense of emptiness that overcame me when I woke from an afternoon nap and wiped cold sweat off my wet brows; the anguish with which I waited to hear the piteous wail of the sea, my hand pressing down the heart which was beating loudly from having woken up from a nightmare – these things had clung to my life like oyster shells and I had summed up my life with a single word 'lonely', a word which, looking back on it now, seemed empty of meaning. What would a person who lived in a city where the sea cannot even be imagined have felt when he read the word 'lonely' in a letter handed to him by an expressionless postman? Had I received such a letter in the city, would I have responded with a sufficient amount of sympathy to all the feelings that had been packed into this single word? Was sympathy even needed? To be more honest, I think I had vaguely felt these doubts and questions even as I was moving towards my desk to write such letters and the answer to the questions had always been, I think, 'No.' Yet I still wrote those letters with the word 'lonely' and sent everyone postcards with crude pictures of the blue sea.

'What sort of person do you think wrote the very first letter in the world?' I asked.

'Oh, letters! There's nothing more wonderful in the world than getting letters. I wonder who it was? It must have been a lonely person like you.'

Her hand moved in mine. I felt that those words were uttered by her hand.

'Also like you.'

'Yes.'

We looked at each other and smiled.

We arrived at the house. Time seemed to have bypassed the house and the people in it, leaving no imprints. The landlord treated me as in the old days and I became my old self. I gave them the presents I brought with me and the old couple gave me my old room.

In the room I took away her impatience, as if I were snatching a knife away from a man who was rushing towards you with it. Like snatching a knife away from a man desperate

369

enough to stab someone if no one took it away from him, I took away her impatience. She was not a virgin. We opened the window and lay there for a long while, silently gazing at the rough sea.

'I want to go to Seoul. That's my only wish,' she said, breaking the silence. I was drawing meaningless figures on her cheeks with my fingers.

'Do you think there are truly good people in this world?' I asked, relighting the cigarette which had gone out in the wind from the sea.

'Are you reproaching me? Unless you want to believe in their goodness, I don't think you will find any.'

I thought we could only be Buddhists.

'Are you a good person?'

'As long as you trust me.'

I thought again that we had to be Buddhists. She nestled closer to me.

'Let's go down to the sea. I'll sing for you,' she said.

But we did not move.

'Let's go down to the sea. It's too hot here.'

We got up and went out. We walked across the sandy beach and sat on a rock from which no houses were visible. The waves came, carefully hiding in their arms the foam which they splashed out before our feet. She called me. I turned my head.

'Have you ever hated yourself?' she asked in a voice whose gaiety sounded forced.

I searched through my memories and nodded.

'Yes, it was when my roommate told me that I snored. I really didn't feel like living any more then.'

I said this to make her laugh. But she did not laugh. She merely nodded her head quietly. After a long pause she said, 'I don't really want to go to Seoul.'

I asked her to give me her hand. Holding it firmly, I said, 'Let's not tell each other lies.'

'It's not a lie,' she said smiling. 'I'll sing "On a Clear Day" for you.'

'But it's cloudy today,' I said, thinking of the parting which the aria sang of. Let's not part from each other on a cloudy day; let's put out our hands and if anyone should come and take them, let's draw him closer to us. I wanted to tell her that I loved her. But the awkwardness of the word 'love' chased away my desire to utter it.

We returned to the town when darkness had fallen. Before entering the town, we kissed on the embankment.

'I'm going to have a wonderful fling while you're here, so I warn you,' she said to me as we parted.

'But since I am stronger than you, you'll end up being dragged up to Seoul,' I said.

When I returned to my aunt's house, I learned that Park had come and gone. He had left a couple of volumes of something with a note saying 'Just in case you get bored'. My aunt told me that he had said that he would return later in the evening. Pleading fatigue, I told her that I didn't feel like seeing anyone that evening. She said she would pretend that I had not yet returned from the sea. I didn't want to be bothered by anything. No, by nothing at all. I asked my aunt to get me some *soju* and drank myself to sleep. I woke up suddenly early in the morning. My heart was pounding away in fear for no particular reason.

'Insook,' I murmured. Then I fell back asleep.

'You Are Now Leaving Mujin'

My aunt shook me awake. The morning was advanced. She handed me a telegram: 'No need to attend the conference on 27th. Please return immediately. Young.' The 27th was the day after tomorrow and Young was my wife. I rested my aching head on the pillow. I was breathing heavily. I tried to breathe more evenly. My wife's telegram made me clearly recall all my actions and thoughts since my arrival in Mujin. Everything was due to my preconceptions. That was what the telegram asserted. I shook my head in denial. Everything was because of the freedom that a traveller feels, the telegram asserted. Again I shook my head in denial. Everything would be erased from my memory in good time, the telegram insisted. But I shook my head saying that the scars would remain. We argued for a long time. In the end the telegram and I reached a compromise. Let's affirm, just for this once, for this once only and for the last time, this Mujin, the mist, maddening loneli-

ness, pop songs, a whore's suicide, betrayal, irresponsibility –
for once and for the last time let's affirm these things, just for
this once. After that I will pledge to live within the bonds of
my responsibilities. Oh, Telegram! Let's make this compromise.
I will pledge myself to adhere to it. So we promised.

But turning my back on Telegram and avoiding its eyes, I
wrote this letter:

'I am suddenly called to Seoul. I wanted to come and tell
you myself but talking always takes one in an unexpected
direction. So I am writing to you instead. I will be brief. I love
you. Why? Because you are myself, because you are the image
of my former self, which I love though perhaps only faintly.
As I have done my best to turn my former self into what I
am today, so I will spare no effort to draw you into sunshine.
Trust me. As soon as I get everything ready in Seoul, I will
contact you. Please leave Mujin then and join me in Seoul. I
think we could be happy together.'

I wrote this and read it through. I read it again. Then I tore
it up.

Sitting on a jolting bus, I saw somewhere along the road a
white sign-post. On it was written in clear black letters 'You
are now leaving Mujin. Good-bye'.

I was overcome by an acute sense of shame.

THE HEIR

SUH KI-WON

Translated by Kathryn Kisray

The boy did not hear the rain. As she turned the page of the book, Sukhi's hair tinted the air with the smell of dry straw. Outside, the heavy rain of the wet season was pouring down.

'Cousin, Cousin Sukwun, why do you think the man left his home?' Sukhi asked, the man being the hero of the novel that he was reading to her. He had finished the first chapter of that book.

'Let's stop here for today,' he shut the book.

She twisted her waist in protest and insisted that he read more. He opened the book again and looked into the printed words. He blushed feeling embarrassed. He secretly wished that she would leave him alone. He thought it was a big mistake to have remained with her in the same room for so long.

He heard faintly his grandfather's voice drowned in the noise of the rain.

'Hush, I think Grandfather is calling me.'

He lifted his head and turned his ear to the guest room. Sukhi was staring into his face, and didn't seem to care the least about her grandfather. This time, he heard more clearly his grandfather calling.

'Yes, sir,' he answered in a deep, mature voice, and trying to put on a composed face to meet senior persons, he left the

373

room. Younger cousins Sukbac and Sukkon had not been around since morning. Their generation names all began with 'Suk' and with his indistinct pronunciation owing to his paralysis, when the grandfather called, they would often reply two at a time.

'Greet this gentleman,' said the grandfather in the room clouded with tobacco smoke, before he could even close the door.

He saluted the man in the coif, just like the one his grandfather was wearing. He blushed every time he had to make the deep formal bow. He had never succeeded in getting used to it. He had to put both his hands one on top of the other in front of him, as he knelt down and lowered his head onto his hands. Every time, he invariably felt degraded.

'What a fine looking fellow! Sit down there.' The guest spoke softly, stroking his thin long beard, which looked like a dried maize tassel.

'Carbon copy of his father, isn't he? Do you remember his father?' asked the grandfather.

'Yes, of course.' replied the guest, tut-tutting his tongue as if he was sorry about the boy's father.

The boy remained with his head down, one knee drawn to his chest, while the grandfather and his guest talked about the boy's father. He stole a glance at his grandfather, and could sense his distress as he tried to satisfy the guest's curiosity about his father. He seemed to look back upon his son with pity – the son who had died in a far-off place, but at the same time, he seemed somehow angry with him.

'You may go now,' the grandfather ordered.

In the middle of the yard, a muddy pool was formed by the rain which was not likely to stop soon. He stood at the door and watched the opposite room where Sukhi must still be waiting for him. The boy had a white forehead with long black brows. He frowned as if he had something sour in his mouth, and his face showed obvious shyness.

The boy went to the store room at the end of the yard, walking along the eaves to avoid the rain. A hot damp rotten smell emanated from the straw compost. Under the bare roof, the darkish wooden frames were visible through the clay. Every time a rat ran across, an acid smell of earth pervaded the air.

He looked up at the small window, way up near the roof.

The parchment of the window was torn, and through it, spread an opaque light like in the early morning of a rainy day.

One half of the shed had been screened off and was being used as a tool shed where spades, picks and hoes, and all sorts of farming tools were left around in a disorderly manner. On the worn clay walls, buckets, grain-sorting trays and other things of the sort were hung. The room had no ventilation and smelt damp.

He picked up a hoe, and made the gesture of ploughing a couple of times. Every time he saw a hoe, he felt a tickling smile come to his face. The curved line of the hoe seemed to have some magic in making him laugh. He wandered around the barn. He stared for a while at the iron padlock on the door leading to the adjacent room. Unexpectedly, the padlock was not really locked. His heart began to beat. This was the room which had attracted all his curiosity ever since his arrival here. It was a mixed curiosity of fear and mystery. He thought it would be proper to obtain permission from his grandfather or his uncle before he went into the room. He hesitated for a moment, then he unlocked the padlock and stepped inside pushing the door.

'I am the eldest grandson in the family, and as such, I'm going to inspect what I am to inherit . . . there's no harm in that . . .'

The word 'eldest grandson' never did sound real, however hard he said it to himself.

This room was even darker than the barn. There was a small window, about the size of a tray, but as it led to the main door which was closed, it let in only a faint bluish glimmer.

He remembered then that there were five or six charcoal-coloured cardboard boxes on the shelf in the corner. As he moved lightly, each step made the old floor boards bend and creak. Books tied with string were stacked up dangerously high. He of course was more attracted by the cardboard boxes than the books. The sound of the rain did not reach his ears. The very next day after his arrival here, his grandfather had taken him alone to his room to show him round. The grandfather had taken out from one of the boxes, a roll of paper.

'This red paper is the Red medallion and it is awarded to one by the King if one passes the Higher Civil Service Examination.'

The boy asked what the Higher Civil Service Examination was.

'If you want to become a very high official, you had to take the Civil Service Examinations.'

'Did you pass the examination?' asked the boy.

'I could not pass.'

'Why not?'

'When I was young, the Japanese were already here, and the Civil Service Examination had been abolished.' He explained, seeming a little embarrassed.

Since then, he had heard from his aunt that his grandfather, when he was young, had enjoyed drinking too much, and had never worked hard. The aunt, as if she was revealing to him a great secret, related what the grandmother used to say when she was still alive, that the reason he couldn't pass the Civil Service Examination was not because of the Japanese, but his own lack of will to study for it. This amused him, especially when he thought about the layabouts among his own friends.

The grandfather used to say, 'You are the ninth generation of the family among which five Red Medallions have been awarded.' It was then that the boy had fun in recalling his grandfather's absolute aversion to study.

He picked out the chest that his grandfather had opened and handled it carefully. In the box were many rolls of paper, all alike, and it seemed that there was nothing else. He plunged his hand deep in the box between the rolls but there were still more of them, all strained from being handled often. He unrolled the long red paper which his grandfather had called the Red Medallion. It looked like floor paper dyed red. The boy, who was in the second year of middle school, frequently enjoyed reading grown-ups' books. He looked carefully at the red paper, and recognized among the badly faded brush strokes, his ancestor's name. The three characters were familiar to him. He rolled the paper back as it was, and put it in the box, closing the lid.

Then he lowered to the floor a leather case that was hung on the wall. It looked like a rough wooden box. It was unmistakably made of leather but it was as heavy as an iron box. The grandfather had told him that it was a gunpowder box. It had a broken padlock, just like the one that one puts on a rice chest, only a little smaller and unmended. In one corner, its key was hanging out but there was no need to use it.

The boy's eyes were caught by what seemed to be a pencil case among the personal ornaments and pile of junk. He picked up a pair of round jade rings with holes in the middle. The jade rings were attached by the holes with a string and its colour was milky.

The boy had no way of knowing what its use was. The hole would be too small even for Sukhi's little finger. Perhaps it was an ornament women wore on their upper garments.

He struck the two pieces of jade lightly one against the other. It gave a very clear sound as it vibrated. He listened to it again and again. He threaded the two pieces back together and put them in his pocket. He felt his legs shaking. Everything in this room was mine I was told.... The white hands of the boy which were placing back the powder box lid trembled. He had no intention of touching other boxes. He tiptoed out of the room. The rain had become lighter and had almost stopped.

At breakfast and supper, the boy sat at the grandfather's table with Sukbae. His tongue which had been accustomed to the sweet dishes of the city, found the country food bitter and salty. He disliked even more the flesh of Sukbae who sat right close to him. Sukbae, his cousin, was two years his junior, and was epileptic. He hated the fact that his cousin looked so much like himself. When he looked at Sukbae's face, he felt as if he was being insulted. He had only learnt about his cousin's epileptic fits a week after his arrival. It was at an evening meal that he had his first fit.

His stomach turned at the smell of stinking prawn sauce mixed in the braised tender courgettes. From the dark brown earthen soy sauce bowl came a stinking smell. The idea that he had to live on this kind of food for days and days to come (he did not know how long), brought him an infinitely sad loneliness.

Suddenly, Sukbae fell on his back throwing his spoon on the floor. His eyes squinted and only the whites of his eyes showed. From his mouth, pulled to one side like a hare-lip, bubbled out a foam of saliva. The boy could not stand the sight and left the table. The grandfather put his spoon down on the table, turned to his side, and let out a long sigh. His eyes were blood-shot, difficult to tell whether he was angry or he was suppressing the tears that welled in his eyes.

The boy cast a piteous look at Sukhi who was just then pushing in the bowl of rice water to the room. She could not cope with his look. Immediately, she became tearful and ran away, turning her head. The uncle moaned continuously, and then he spat harshly, 'Take away the table!'

'Why are you upset all of a sudden? Even though he is not normal, he is still your son, isn't he?'

The grandfather scolded in a tone that showed a slight reproach. The uncle's forehead now showed a thick vein in the centre.

'Sukwun, don't be afraid, he breaks my heart like this from time to time.'

It was his aunt who explained in tears. The boy felt like dashing out of the room, but he thought he somehow had to remain with the family and watch until Sukbae's fit passed. Sukbae's twisted arms and legs presently stretched long and his breathing calmed down but he still could not open his eyes. His body was supple like a snake's. The cold liquid seems to have run through his body, while his limb was stretched limp.

The boy took a sip of water, and went outside. The long midsummer day was setting in the western sky, and the red sinking sun coloured the clouds.

At the edge of the front yard, clear water ran down along the ditch. It was said that in that spring, surrounded by moss-covered stones, lived a huge dark carp.

His grandfather had told him that when his great grandfather had come back from a long exile, and had to go south, he had chosen this spot near the spring to settle down. Between the spring and the gate there were five ghinko trees which separated the patch to the cottage and the outside courtyard.

'I wish my brother was dead.' Sukhi's preposterous voice was heard from behind him. The boy could not understand straightaway whom she meant by 'brother', but he was not surprised to realize a little later who she meant; even if she had not meant Sukbae, but him, he could have accepted what she had said without being embarrassed. The boy stared at Sukhi, while she was approaching him. He tried to look at her

in the face calmly, but, in actual fact, he was almost breathless.
She looked maturer than he, but she chattered smilingly.

'Cousin Sukwun, I want to hear more about Seoul.'

The boy smiled back in reply without a word. Sukhi sat on
a stone around the spring and stretched her rough red legs.

'I am the second tallest in my class.' She shrank her neck
and giggled.

The boy wanted to know more about his cousin's epilepsy,
but he sensed that she feared such a question.

'You'll be going to middle school in town next year, won't
you?'

'Grandfather said that he won't let me go,' Sukhi retorted.

'I don't believe it,' mumbled the boy.

'You don't know,' said the girl, rolling her eyes as she inhaled
deeply, but she was unable to speak up.

Without a breath of wind, the twilight approached. From somewhere far, an old man coughed. The sound was so much like
his father's – his coughing in those early mornings – that he
pricked his ears. But it was his grandfather. He was looking in
all directions as if he was searching for something in the thick-
ening darkness.

From the kitchen, the smell of something frying in sesame
oil struck his nostrils. He could see white steam blow up hard
in the faint lamp light which was shining through the kitchen
door. The grandfather advised the boy to get some sleep until
he was called again. Sukbae and Sukkon seemed to like commemoration day a lot. They had been peeping in the kitchen,
and were told off by their mother. It was the boy's first experience of a commemoration. He remembered his mother used
to remind his father of the day and ask him to send some
money for the purchase of some fruit. And every time, his
father strongly disagreed and kept his lips tightly sealed and
refused to discuss it.

'There's not a single month without a commemoration for
one or the other ancestors, so how can I cope with them all?'
Those words spat out by his father were starting to make sense
to him now.

Preparing the ceremony table, the expression his uncle had
on his face seemed as irritated and gloomy as his father's who

hated being reminded of the day. He could also guess that it was disturbing his uncle in the same way.

He tried to calm down his heart which was beating hard without any reason, and looked at the slightly inclined flame on the wooden lamp stand. He spread out the mattress and lay down, but was not sleepy. In the large parquet room, where the special table was set, the two candles at the ends were burning. The candlesticks made of brass were smeared with a greenish rust. The grease-proof paper that covered the table stank like fish that had gone bad. The grandfather pulled out from the wall cupboard, a bundle of clothes made of unbleached ramie fibre. He chose from the bundle a ceremonial gown and put it on. It covered his thin body raising a light cloud of dust. He knelt before the ceremonial table and lit the incense in the burner. From the burner, which age had turned into a dull black, rose a thin line of bluish smoke. The whole fish on a flat round plate was giving off an unpleasant smell.

'Broiled meat must be on the left hand side, like this. Is this the first time you are setting up the ceremonial table?'

He rolled up his right sleeve and stretched his withered hand and changed the dishes around.

'This is your great grandfather five generations removed.'

The boy had heard it for the third time that evening. The two grown-ups in their gowns began to make their deep formal bows and the youngsters imitated them just behind. The boy nearly burst into laughter as he brought both his hands to his forehead after the deep bow. Curiously, the wiggly body of Sukbae had a very becoming movement as he made the deep bow. For the next boy, he lifted his hands together up to his chest, and then dropped then foolishly, and Sukbae, lifting his arms above his head – arms that looked longer than his height – started the bow. The grandfather cleared his throat and started to read the remembrance address. His voice was thin and it trembled sadly. As soon as the address was finished, the wail started led by the grandfather, whose wail was the only distinct and sad one. The uncle mumbled in a low voice.

The boy closed his eyes and his mouth. To him, it was not boring; he felt tension which was unbearable. He half opened his eyes and sneakily lifted his head. Small insects gathered around the candle light. Every time the smoky flame flickered, it cast a ghostly shadow over the table. The far side where the tablet was placed, looked much darker, and it felt that from inside the tablet, some stranger was staring at everyone present.

He remembered how his father had become a total stranger when he breathed his last breath, and had raised a cold wind. The boy had shaken off his father's strong grip and fought to avoid being caught again. The boy could not touch his father and cry. It was only when he had left the room that tears had sprung up.

He shut his eyes again. The wail was going on ever more sorrowfully. The boy's shoulder was moving up and down in his effort to suppress the weeping.

As soon as the ceremony ended, the boy dashed out to the spring. Stars were twinkling in the sky between the clouds. Bluish star beams glittered on the slowly circling surface of the spring. The boy washed his hands in the cool water. He washed and washed until the smell of the ceremony had evaporated completely.

'Sukwun!' called the grandfather's voice.

In the main hall, there were three tables and all the family were seated face to face.

'Food of fortune, it's called, you must eat the food which served the ceremony,' said Grandfather, pointing to a seat in front of him with his chin. The rice bowl with two holes in its centre where a pair of rusty chopsticks were planted, now stood under the grandfather's beard.

The boy sipped the rice wine which his grandfather had handed to him, and winced. Everybody had put the rice in the beef soup, and were eating it noisily. The grandfather appeared to be displeased because the boy was not eating. With the pretext that he had a stomach ache, he left the table and went to the other room. He could hear his grandfather. 'It's incredible how he resembles his father.'

The grandfather went to town in the morning in his new ramie overcoat which Sukwun's aunt had finished making late last night. The boy brought down his leather case from the cupboard after having made sure that all his cousins were out to play, and investigated its contents. The first time he was searching the inside of the case, the children gathered around him as though it was a mysterious spectacle not to be missed. The boy wanted to keep his belongings in a private place. There were four or five novels, a few school books, a glass paper weight in which a red goldfish was swimming, a telescope made of cardboard, and the wallet his father had given him the day before he died ... they were the boy's precious possessions. He held up the jade rings he had taken the other day in the storage room. The milky jade still made the same clear beautiful sound when he struck the two pieces together. He fancied that he could hear it even more clearly because the weather was fine.

That very moment, without warning, a dark shadow suddenly walked into the room. It was Sukbae.

'What are you doing, cousin?'

'I'm sorting out my things.' The boy replied hiding quickly what he was holding in his hands.

'Cousin, are you going anywhere?' Sukbae asked him sitting down very close to him.

'No,' the boy replied.

Sukbae turned his eyes towards the case, and suddenly he plunged his hand in it and fished out something and said, 'Cousin, will you draw my portrait?' It was a box of pastels with half the colours missing. Sukbae's eyes almost closed completely as he smiled.

'All right, I will.'

The boy not only wanted to show off his gift at drawing but he was particularly pleased and relieved that Sukbae had not noticed anything suspicious in his behaviour.

He put a sheet of paper on the case and made Sukbae turn around and face the door. He picked up the yellow to start with, and had a good look at Sukbae. The model was sitting quite dignified with his lower lip protruding. The boy's eyes were caught by the eyes of Sukbae and remained thus for a good while. He was lost as to how he should draw another boy who looked so much like himself. If one were to look at Sukbae's eyes, ears, mouth, and nose separately, he did not resemble the boy at all, but the face altogether gave him the impression that he was not looking at another being, but at himself. Impatient, Sukbae said, 'Why aren't you drawing me?' lowering his eyes. The boy silently started to move his hand over the paper in strokes. Sukbae's complexion was slightly darker than his own. It was dark, plumpish and oily. His skin looked shiny and slippery. Sukbae licked his lips from time to time with his red tongue.

The boy suddenly wished that Sukbae would start another fit right there and then. His heart was mingled in fear and curiosity. The boy deliberately moved his hands in slow motions.

'There! It's finished.' The boy put on an unsure smile as he handed the portrait to Sukbae.

'It's more like yourself.' Sukbae protested in a sulky voice.

'No, it's like you,' the boy retorted.

'Then write my name on the drawing, will you?'

The boy wrote Sukbae's name in thick black ink.

The grandfather had discovered the disappearance of the jade rings. The boy was sitting on the side corridor facing the back yard. There was the fragrance of balsam flowers in the air, and over the mud brick wall under the ash grey sky, the sharp tip of the Moon Mountain was stabbing the sky.

In the front yard, the grandfather was heard scolding someone. The boy could understand what was being said with just the intonation.

'You ignorant lot, did you think it was some sort of toy?' It was the grandfather's angry voice.

'Please stop it now. I'll get it back for you when he comes home.' The uncle was pleading with the grandfather to stop nagging.

'Do you realize that it's because you are so uneducated? You should have at least taught the kids the way a dignified noble family should behave. It's altogether inconceivable . . .'

From the beginning, the grandfather never bothered whether his grandchildren were present or not when it came to him to rebuke his adult son. The boy's heart sank deeply. There was no doubt that Sukbae was going to be blamed for the crime.

'He has sold every single thing worth anything. . . . Now he loses his temper on a small nothing.' It was his uncle complaining to himself after the grandfather had retired to his room. The boy could feel his whole body tremble like gentle waves. He just could not go out of the room to face the rest of the family. When he imagined the scene which would take place when Sukbae returned, he wanted to go straight to his grandfather and confess his guilt; that seemed much easier, but he could not make the move.

'Do you at least know what it is?' The grandfather was speaking in a voice full of mockery as he came back again to them.

'Did you not say it was jade *Kwanja**?' the uncle spoke.

'Jade *Kwanja*, do you think they're all the same? It's real jade fastener of the highest quality used only by government ministers.'

To these words, the uncle had no reply. The grandfather was shaming his son, as if he was a perfect stranger. The boy did not know what jade rings were for. He only realized that it was a very precious thing to his grandfather even though it was not worth much money.

The boy shuffled out in rubber shoes that were too big for his feet. He counted in his mind the money left in the wallet which his father had given him. There was enough for five or six months' boarding. The house which had a sunny east facing study was sold by his uncle after his father's death. He, however, never forgot the thick volume in his wallet whose four corners were well worn.

'Cousin, let's go out to catch some killifish,' Sukhi said, holding an armful of fresh greens that she had just picked from the vegetable bed.

'It looks like rain again soon,' said the boy.

Sukhi crouched up comfortably at the well and started to wash the tender young turnip greens.

'Pretty, isn't it?' Sukhi opened her wet hand and showed her little finger wiggling with the nail dyed red in the juice from balsam flowers. Then she smiled shyly shrinking her neck and blushing slightly. The boy laughed loudly like a man, pulling back his head. The sight of Sukhi in her blue skirt and the white dress made him forget for a moment that she was his younger cousin.

'Sukhi, what is the jade ring for?'

'Have you noticed the thing on grandfather's jacket, the thing which looks like a black button, well, that's what's called *Kwanja*, I believe,' Sukhi whispered, blinking her eyes.

'But that isn't jade, is it?'

Kanja – a fastener for hat strings.

This time, she just twisted her lips and bent her neck in reply.

'Cousin, don't you hate my brother?' It looked that Sukhi was also thinking that Sukbae was the one who had stolen the jade rings.

'Why?' He pretended he didn't understand the question.

'Some time ago, grandfather told us that there was no one like him in our family,' Sukhi stopped for a moment and looked at him.

The boy shut up. What he had just heard hurt him.

'My brother had his head cauterized when he was small with mugwort leaves,' Sukhi said with pity in her voice. He picked himself up, and kicking a stone, he strolled towards the brook.

In the evening, it started to rain. The thunder struck and the rain grew heavier and all of a sudden, the whole house was in turmoil. The grandfather, all rain sodden, was rushing around the house.

'Where's the kids', father gone? What a calamity!'

The grandfather, shaking off the water from his beard, asked the same question repeatedly.

The boy began to feel uneasy as he started to realize that something had gone very wrong. He closed his eyes. He could see in his imagination, his cousin Sukbae being thrown against the rocks, and swept away by the reddish muddy current. The whites of his eyes were showing in their hollows, his bubbly saliva was being washed off by the dirty water.

... Grandfather, grandfather, it wasn't me ... not a single groan came from the mouth which had gulped too much water.

The boy's knees were shaking violently. His uncle, who had just returned holding a torn grease-proof paper umbrella was seen going out again with Sukkon.

'I'd like to go with you,' proposed the boy.

'You have nothing to worry about,' said the Uncle watching the boy out of the corner of his eye.

'All the same, I'd like to go ...' the boy said resolutely.

'I tell you, you'll be of no use at all!' This time, the uncle snapped at him losing his temper with his insistence.

The grandfather kept moaning noisily for a while, then repeated, 'Take some men from the village with you.' The uncle replied that he would, in an irritated voice.

In the room, the smell of mildew had become thicker. A centipede crawled slowly into the room. The sound of the falling rain did not reach the boy's ears. He felt that he should be in the guest room with his grandfather and wait for news, but he did not have the courage to do so. He lit the wick of the lamp. He touched his forehead. His hands must have been burning, for in spite of the chill running down his spine, his head was ice-cold. In the end, he could stand no more, he spread his bedding and lay down. He heard the sound of the jade rings, clear as crystal, mingling in the noise of the rain. Suddenly, he surprised himself wishing with all his heart that the wiggly serpent-like body of Sukbae would never reappear. Even after his departure from this house ... never show up again in front of the grandfather.

When he woke up, he found Sukhi sitting by his head with the lamp shining from behind her. The little girl's silhouette looked more like that of a mature woman. He felt a cold hand on his head. He did not shake his head. The cold hand warmed up little by little and became a little sticky and wet.

'What news of Sukbae?' asked the boy turning to her.

'Only Sukkon has returned. Father went to the Moon Mountain with the people from the village,' Sukhi answered.

The boy was silent.

'It has happened before. The following morning he came back but he couldn't remember where he'd been,' the girl said. The uncle came home after midnight, completely exhausted.

'It's the punishment for my offence ...' His aunt wailed banging the floor wearily.

The boy could not sleep a wink that night. The next day, the weather did not improve, and it rained on and off. Early in the morning, neighbours came to inform the family that Suh Moon Bridge had been flooded and washed away.

It was difficult to tell whether the uncle was laughing or crying as his face crumpled up. He sat on the parquet floor and ordered a tray of drinks, and asked in all those gathered in front of the gate and offered them.

'Have you searched the Snake Gorge?'

'Do you know where that is?'

'It rained so hard last night.'

'It's been five years since the bridge was washed out last ...'

'It would be wise to report it to the local police, I think.'

The uncle stood up suddenly without a word, and pulling up his trousers, led the way. Everyone stood up wiping their mouths with the back of their hands and followed. One could tell from the way he walked out that he held no hope whatsoever.

'It's my fault... I'm being punished...' From the main room, the wailing of his aunt leaked out. His aunt had been suffering from a bout of heartache since yesterday, and had stopped eating altogether. She would go on with her cry – one could even say chant – even on the verge of losing her breath. The aunt seemed absolutely incurable as long as Sukbae did not return safe and sound. Perhaps it was her fate to weep thus... and it almost seemed as if she was not letting go of the illness in her own will, but stubbornly holding on to it.

The boy could not help feeling that the disappearance of Sukbae was something that was unbreakably tied to him. Had he never come here in the first place, there would have been no change at all in the daily life of this family, with its dry acrid smell of earth and the fungi... He felt like putting all the blame on to himself.

There was no one in the yard. It was covered with dark shadows, and only a misty chilly air filled the space. The rain which now turned into thick cords, fell hard on the stone resounding noisily. The boy held the jade rings tightly in his hand and went to the storage room. He was trembling with excitement and fear, like a burglar who had set out to steal a bar of gold.

The old floor board of the storage room moaned under the slight weight of his body. He could not help but stand still like a stick. On the powder box there was a brand new padlock instead of the old and rusty one. The shiny silvery colour of the padlock sneered at the boy's surprised eyes. Knowing in every detail the secrets of the boy, being aware of the irresistible temptation to open the box again, the padlock was waiting with a malicious smile which it now openly showed in the dull store room. The boy felt faint and leaned against the earthen wall.

Deep in the valley somewhere, among the rocks where the flood water had drained away, stuck the body of Sukbae. He used to run fast and agile in the roasting sun like an alert snake, but now he'd become a sodden trunk. His shiny oily skin had turned into a muddy yellowish colour. The uncle carried the body on his A-frame; he came down the mountain path, staggering under the weight.

The boy thought he had to run away as far as he could from this house before Sukbae's body was brought in. Like a murderer who could not face his victim, he had to hide himself.

The boy returned to his room and immediately started searching his case. He got the leather wallet his father had given him.

'Cousin, are you going anywhere?'

The boy nearly jumped with surprise, but he couldn't turn and face her.

'Don't go, please don't . . .' Sukhi begged him in tears.

He turned and stared in her eyes, the eyes that were looking right through him.

The boy impatiently shook his head and just twisted his lips. His throat was so tight that he could not even breathe normally. Sukhi let her face fall and began to sob. The smell of dry straw emanated from her tousled hair. The boy left her in the room and went out. A heavy shower was starting. All that he possessed was an umbrella, the wallet with the worn out edges, and a pair of jade rings. He did not release the cold touch of the jade stones in his pocket. He walked slowly under the downpour towards the main road. . . . Everything in here is yours . . . Grandfather's blunt voice sounded in his ears.

As he reached the main road, he began to run.

LAUGHTER

CHOI IN-HUN

Translated by Lee Sang-ok

There was still a bit of time left before the appointed time,
but she went straight to the corner and turned into the lane.

When the familiar signboard, 'Bar Havana', came into her
view, she felt strange, as if she had come across an old, dead
acquaintance.

The bar seemed to be a distant place. Today the lane which
she had passed through so many times seemed to be a strange
space filled with obstructions to the passers-by.

Even after she opened the door and walked into the hall
her funny feeling didn't disappear – it grew worse: there were
piles of chairs along the walls, the legs of the topmost chairs
were pointing towards the ceiling, the piles were covered two-
fold with screens, and the vacant floor which used to have a
well-oiled glossy black surface now looked mealy and dreary.
She recognized first all the empty floor, and then the piles of
chairs behind the screens with their upside-down legs sticking
out. It was not the same place where she drank and laughed
until a month ago. It was not the place where, in expectation
of gratuities, she would leave her face and tipsy body to the
discretion of the fun-seeking customers. It looked like an
entirely different place, a place that she had never been to.
Her heart felt a strange pain, a feeling similar to that she
would have felt if she had come face to face with the haggard

389

trunks of thorny cacti in the arid desert like she had once seen in a motion picture.

Feeling sorry about her own stealing steps, she went to the counter at one end of the hall. On the counter she placed her handbag with a thump and said, 'Anybody here?'

Under the cupboard there was a door that opened into the kitchen, and near it stood a noodle bowl. The wet bowl told her that the noodles had just been finished by somebody who should be around somewhere in the kitchen. But nobody responded. Again she asked whether anybody was in. She was holding her handbag with one hand, and with the other she knocked hard on the vertical wall of the counter on which she was leaning.

She heard someone inside the kitchen. She was about to ask again when the door opened and an unbelievably familiar face appeared. It was Sunja's chubby face.

'Wow, you are here!'

Sunja strained her neck to look up and smiled at the visitor. Then she disappeared from behind the door. Presently she reappeared and came out to the counter.

'So you are still here!'

'Yes.'

Sweeping back hair from her forehead, Sunja smiled again. She was a kitchen maid when the bar was closed, but she had been imitating the manners and make-up of the bargirls so eagerly that she was becoming quite a lady herself. The visitor recollected how she would give away her leftover manicure liquid and lipsticks to the maid.

'Was the Madam here today?'

'No.'

'When was she here last?'

'Well – she came here about four or five days ago. She said she would open the bar again in the near future.'

'Did she?'

She thought that if what Sunja said was true the Madam would certainly keep her word. There was no doubt that the Madam would wish to re-employ her and that the first thing she would do to keep her in the bar would be to pay back the overdue wages. She sat down on a chair, the only one left on the floor, and asked Sunja, who was still standing behind the counter, 'Did she say she would come today?'

'No.'

'That's all right. I'll wait here. I need the money to carry out my plan,' she thought to herself. The plan seemed to be something she was destined to carry out at any cost.

Sunja felt a little uneasy because the visitor seemed to have fallen deep into thought and apparently had no more questions. Picking up the empty noodle bowl, Sunja asked her to wait until she returned. Even after Sunja went out, the visitor was still sitting on the chair propping up her jaw with a hand.

The hall was quite dark because the front door was double-glazed with opaque glass and the long upright windows were covered with heavy curtains. When viewed from the dark spot where she sat, the outside looked like the pupil of a certain sun-glassed male eye, an illusion effected by the sunlight seeping through the curtains. Suddenly a clean, pale image of sun-glassed eyes appeared to her, but the anger lurking in her mind erased it quickly and relentlessly. When she felt her face blushing, she became angry with herself. She opened her handbag, picked out a manicure file, and began to trim her fingernails.

As usual, she could recover her composure by trimming her fingernails. She habitually resorted to that pastime whenever she was disgusted by the noise around her, when she hated to listen to others or wished to evade their eyes. The habit of filing her fingernails when she was happy or unhappy was so well known that her fellow bar-girls used to tell her state of mind from the way she trimmed her nails. She tried to detect the smallest flaws on the already well-trimmed fingernails and corrected them meticulously. Since the hall was dark, the filing took more time and needed more care. Applying the file carefully against the shining nails, she kept on trimming.

Both sides of the lane were lined with bars. At a little after one in the afternoon it was so quiet that she could hardly hear any noise from outside. From time to time she would lift her head to look up at the front door and the piles of chairs in the corner. She appeared as if she wanted to make sure that the door and the piles of chairs were kept in their right places while she was trimming her fingernails. She didn't look like a person waiting for the appearance of somebody at the door. Like the second hand of a clock her eyes would move from the door to the piles of chairs and then slide back to the nails.

Her fellow bar-girls were awed by her habit. At the sight of her nail-trimming, novices became aware of the superiority of an experienced bar-girl, her competitors felt disgust, and the Madam sensed the weighty position assumed by the Number One girl of the hall. When this Number One deviated into some amorous affair which was quite unworthy of her position, the Madam tried to admonish her but not necessarily for the sake of saving her own business. The Madam's voice was trembling because she thought she was telling the bar-girl something very near to truth about life. Listening to the words of warning, she would slowly produce a file from the bag.

Sunja didn't return for a long time. The Madam didn't appear at the appointed time, either. According to Sunja, the Madam was to show up sooner or later. 'If the Madam doesn't come, what shall I do?' At this thought the forlorn sight of the hall overwhelmed her. 'If she doesn't come?' All she could imagine was a life as forlorn as the sight of the hall. At that time as well as before she was enjoying the rotten feeling of security of a person clinging on to the last step surrounded with coloured lights, but what about now? The darkness of a cave. The mountain of the thorny cacti jerking up toward the sky. There her mind was floundering along to gain some ground from the last step. She was thinking about these things, never stopping the movement of the file.

It was not until a full hour after the appointed time that the Madam showed up. What Sunja had said was true. The Madam said the bar would reopen soon. She also said she would have the hall redone and spend as much money as was needed for making the place look new. What the Madam said failed to reassure her, however, for she thought that the Madam might be telling a lie to put off the payment of the overdue wages. But soon it proved to be an unnecessary worry, for the Madam produced a cheque from her handbag while the girl was wondering what to make of the Madam's extravagant project.

The Madam said to the still unbelieving girl, 'You must have been busy these days. You are different from other girls anyway. You wouldn't have been hard up for lack of this money. By the way, have you caught that damned man of yours?'

The Madam talked as if it were immoral to pay the promised money to the girl. Apparently she was trying to soothe the girl for fear that she might be embarrassed by such quick payment. She was so sure that the girl would return to the bar.

Asked whether she had caught her man, the girl became as angry as a cat whose sore wound was touched by an unscrupulous hand. Without saying a word she folded the cheque and put it into her handbag, thinking 'Now I can afford to die.' All of a sudden she suspected that she might have been wishing that the money wouldn't be paid. This suspicion made her even angrier.

The train to P. Spa leaves Seoul Station at four in the afternoon. She took it on the following day. It was a weekday, and there were many vacant seats in the second-class coach. A few seconds before the departure of the train a stout, middle-aged man took the seat facing her. The man got on her nerves because she wished to be alone, but she thought it improper to move to other seats right away. She looked out of the window at the colours of May. To her the rushing scenery looked no different from the dreary scene of the bar she had seen on the previous day.

There was no doubt about it. Everything was up to her. She had made up her mind to die, and now she was hurrying towards the place where she was going to lay her dying body. She hated to die in her boarding house. It was abhorrent to her to think of those tenants who would be looking into her room making a great fuss over her suicide. It was also as horrible as death itself to imagine that she would have to look up to the ceiling until the pills made her fall asleep. She had disposed of all her personal effects and made enough money to pay what she owed to the landlady and to the owner of the nearby store. She still kept intact the money she had received from the Madam. She chose P. Spa because she was pretty familiar with the resort, which was not too far from Seoul. Now that everything had been settled, she had only to proceed to her death, which was as tightly planned as the timetable of a railway station. In the meantime, everything was quite unreal to her, and the feeling of unreality vexed her very much. She felt as if her own fate were controlled by somebody in such a way that her last wish in this world wouldn't be realized no matter how hard she might struggle to achieve it. She was annoyed not a little by the thought that her death wish, apparently a personal matter of her own, was to be interrupted by other people and that she would have to fight the interference to get to her goal.

To her great regret she found her annoyance being aggravated by an outside interference there and then in the train. It came from the passenger sitting in front of her. The man with a pale forehead was staring at her through his cigarette smoke. The stare which she felt on her skin seemed to say, 'Well, I know what sort of a girl you are!' She found herself immobile. No sooner had she sensed her own immobility than she felt a heavy feeling of fatigue. She opened her handbag with as nimble a manipulation of her hands as possible. The file was nowhere to be seen. Then she began to feel a heavy and voluminous feeling that she hadn't felt for a long time. It was a feeling of despondency which seemed to open its mouth to show an abysmal depth, but soon it was closed.

She felt relieved when the train vendor appeared before her as if to keep an appointment. She bought an apple and borrowed a knife. She began to peel the apple with a slow movement of her hands.

'Are you going far?'

The fat man spoke at long last. She felt like pushing the knife-point towards the direction where the question came from, but she could easily tell that the man was grinning. She was peeling the apple as if she were carefully removing the thin skin of a tomato. The deliberate movement of her hands showed how hard she was trying to suppress the desire to make a lunge at him with the knife. She wondered whether any sign of her fatal plan had appeared on her face. That didn't really matter at all anyway. For she hated the man for the saucy stare which seemed to say, 'I know you are a girl of easy virtue.' When she felt like killing this fat man, it wasn't a false feeling. 'If I take this man along with me, will he interfere with my suicide? Of course I could put some sleeping pills into his glass and proceed myself to the place where I want to kill myself. Why not do that? Isn't it as easy a thing as could be!' To her the premeditated murder didn't look merciless any more than her own intended suicide looked real. All right. Let me kill him . . . ah!'

'Ah!'

The man's astounded voice struck her ears before she uttered the painful exclamation herself. When she pressed her slit thumb hard, the apple dropped from her hand. Blood seeped out between the thumb and the pressing finger.

She stood up as if she had been waiting for the arrival of the moment. She took down her trunk from the rack and moved to a seat at an end of the carriage. Feeling the throbbing pain in her thumb which she had wrapped up with a handkerchief and was pressing hard, she leaned against the back of the seat with her head resting upon it. Looking out of the window she felt comfortable for the first time since she got on the train. The outside scenery constantly rushing away from her view looked like a desert stained in green. It made her sad to think of the unfeeling heart of the man, who was apparently regarding a woman harbouring a desert-like feeling, as an object of his desire.

The sun was about to set when she arrived at P. Spa. She liked the room assigned to her at the hotel. She had no appetite for supper, so since she had nothing to do in the room she came out to wander along the streets.

Here and there she could see the street stalls. People were passing by them. To her all the passers-by looked like tourists. She was sure that no one had a forlorn feeling like hers. All of them looked cheerful, but she had no reason to envy them. Now that she had reached her chosen place, her heart was emptier than ever before. It felt like a desert without cacti. Cacti without thorns. That is why the whole thing grew more unreal with her intended suicide of the following day.

There was a church in a lane. The street-side windows were lit. She stopped to look through one. There were two rows of benches along the walls and a vacant aisle in the middle. The gilded body of Jesus on the cross above the pulpit told her that it was a Catholic church. The empty nave didn't look strange at all, and she was obsessed with the feeling of its familiarity. At last she came to recognize that what she was actually seeing through her mind's eye was the vacant hall of the bar she had visited the day before. The nave was hardly more spacious than the hall. She looked up to Jesus. The two gilded arms that looked limp were raised and the head was bowed to the chest. In front of the cross there was a plaster statue of the Blessed Mother with her Blessed Baby. Mary looked like a widowed mother with a baby born after its father's death. In this small house where the Mother and her

Baby, different from any other mothers and babies in the world, had their home, she was actually seeing a family that had its own troubles and problems.

Suddenly a fantastic feeling obsessed her that the gilded arms of Jesus were going to drop and eventually crash onto the pulpit. She stood there watching them with one hand constantly sweeping back the hair from her forehead. She looked as if she were waiting for the crash to happen. Soon another fantastic vision dawned upon her mind. 'If the man on the cross should wave his hand and call me to him, I might as well give up death. Of course it's not because I'm afraid of dying. It's because such a miracle would be as valuable as my own death.' She wished that such a miracle would happen and that her own death would stop being unreal and hang on to her ankles like a heavy solid stone. She was sitting on one scale with her determination, the fatal decision placed on the other scale. However, the determination, like a soap bubble, was so light that it could hardly counterpoise the physical weight of her body. That's why she was so fretful and restless. She wished that Jesus with his gilded arm would press down on the other scale. She was looking up to Jesus almost like a worshipper in prayer. But Jesus would never lift up his head. Mary wouldn't move, either. Nevertheless, she stood waiting a long time. Nothing happened. She was ashamed of herself. She turned her back to the church.

The next day was nice and clear. She took her time dressing up. She came out of the hotel around noon. Located at the foot of a hill, the hotel overlooked the town. The place where she decided to kill herself was somewhere on the hill. She had chosen the spot right after she made up her mind to commit suicide. She had already been to the spa three times. Each time she came to enjoy the hot spring she would spend a lot of time at that spot in the hill. The moment she decided to carry out suicide, her mind drifted to the spot like a sleepy person walking to his bed. The hill was exhaling; the warm air mingled with the freshening and intoxicating smell of the grass.

Climbing up to the spot she panted for breath, but her short breath was not necessarily due to the steepness of the hill path. As she came nearer to the spot, she realized that the determination placed on the other scale was gaining as much weight as the truthful feeling on her side of the balance. It was really a cozy place, the kind of nook a hiker would come across sooner or later. People like to bury their family members in such cozy places, but her chosen place was certainly much better than most burial sites. From afar she tried to spot the nook. Hidden behind the trees, however, the place was nowhere to be seen. Now the path led downwards. Walking carefully step by step, she cut across the slope. When the nook appeared from behind a curtain of leaves, she stopped short. Leaning forward she began to gaze at the spot behind the trees.

Somebody was there.

She walked forward a few more steps. But she couldn't go any farther. For it was virtually the end of the forest, and farther ahead she could see only a thinly wooden slope. Moreover, a small cliff obstructed her progress. She hid herself behind the trees and tried to command a better view of the nook. Since the place was surrounded by trees whose sprigs were waving in the breeze, she couldn't see the whole figure. It was a couple lying on the grass. They were facing each other, the woman resting her head on the man's arm. She crashed herself down to the ground. It was certainly more a dropping on the thick grass than an ordinary sitting down. As the weight on the other scale was slowly removed, the scale on which her mind was placed was hopelessly coming down. She didn't look toward the nook anymore.

She tried to remove one by one the burrs stuck on her skirt. She never lifted her head to the spot. She thought she heard over the winds, a short laugh from the woman, but still she didn't turn her head that way. When she had removed all the burrs, she wound blades of grass on her fingers and snapped them off their stalks. She got a whiff of warm air mingled with the smell of the broken grass and the rumpled top-soil. The smell made her as giddy as if she were falling from a high place. She felt nauseous. Then she lost her sense of time. When she arose she thought she had been there in that posture for a long time. The man and woman were still lying there. She thought she heard another short laugh by the woman. As if driven away by the laughter, she hurried back to the hotel.

All night her sleep was disturbed by nightmares. The couple on the green grass were laughing happily. On a more careful observation the woman proved to be herself. The woman said,

'I want to die this way with my head in your arms. How can one die a happier death?' The man said, 'Why do you want to die? The sky is so beautiful. Why don't you try to smell the grass? You'll have nothing like these after death.' The woman continued to talk to the man like a child: 'I want to die. Now. I want to be in your arms forever.' The man turned out to be Jesus. With one gilded arm under her head, Jesus grinned drearily, exposing his white teeth. The dreamer thought that Jesus's face looked like somebody she knew. Patting her on the head with his free gilded arm on which the sunlight glittered, Jesus said, 'You shall never die as long as I don't want your death.' The woman said, 'Why not? What do you mean by that?' 'It means you can die only in my arms.' 'I want to die in this manner.' 'No, you shall not.' Saying this, Jesus produced sun-glasses from his pocket and, still lying on the grass, put them on. The dreamer thought the clean, pale image of the sun-glassed eyes was reminiscent of somebody she knew. Why not? She began to rub her face on the gilded arm. Jesus said, 'It's a sure business. Do lend me some money.' At last the dreamer identified the 'somebody'. The next moment the woman slid off the gilded arm and dropped aside, and the dreamer woke up. It was only midnight.

The next day she went to the hill at the same time as the day before. Since the familiar path seemed much shorter, she walked as slowly as possible. She arrived at the spot where she could have a good view of the nook. She looked at it reluctantly, as if she were afraid of some terrifying scene. The couple was already there. She saw that the arm on which the woman's head was placed glittered like gold in the sunlight. The man was in a chrome yellow shirt. She could not recall whether he had been in the same shirt on the previous day. The woman seemed to turn around in his arms, and then the morose laughter followed.

She turned away from the scene and returned to the hotel. She took a chair out to the end of the porch and sat on it. With a fan in her hand, she began to think about the unforeseen situation. The whole thing was quite undreamed of, and it was difficult for her to make a decision on how to carry out her plan. It was very likely that the couple would come to the nook every day while they were staying at the spa. How long were they going to stay there? Nobody knew that. Of course she could wait until they left the spa. Even if one day she found the nook unoccupied, it wouldn't necessarily mean that the couple had left the spa or that they wouldn't come there anymore. Suppose they came to the place after she had taken the pills. Then her suicide would be foiled. Moreover other people might also come to the spot. Considering all these possibilities, the place was not safe at all.

Now there were only two ways to go. She could give up the idea of killing herself in that place – but that was unthinkable. Since she had made up her mind to commit suicide, she had been thinking of the nook as the only place for her death. She was obsessed more or less with the thought that either she should die in that place or she would never die at all. So this left only one way for her – to go to the place at night and take the sleeping pills. However, she had never thought of waiting for her death at night. She was afraid her suicide wouldn't be the same as originally planned. It was during the daytime that she had found the place for the first time, so she couldn't think about the nook without the clouds overhead, the whispers of the surrounding trees, and the bright open air. As she had never been there at night, she couldn't imagine what it would be like to make a nocturnal visit to the nook.

Even after she went to bed, she couldn't make a decision. Neither could she enjoy a sound sleep. No sooner had she fallen asleep than she dreamed about the couple in love at the nook and then she woke up. Like an insomniac she made all kinds of futile efforts to fall asleep. Noises from a room a few doors away stopped. She thought herself to be the only person in the hotel who still remained awake.

Like an innocent reader who dares to open a terrifying passage in a horror story, she reluctantly opened a door of her mind. She saw a grass field where she found herself lying in an amorous manner with 'the man' who had dark sun-glasses on his clean, pale face. The vision infuriated her. She felt as if she had come to recognize at last that the nook was the very place where she had had a most unforgettable affair with 'the man'. As the significance of her suicide plan became more evident, she became more enraged. She hated the couple for they seemed to destroy her plan by deliberately taking up the place in the forest.

She never thought that she had given away her heart to 'the

man'. The relationship between them was in no way struck up on a heart-to-heart basis. It was a relationship about which she used to feel sorry because she knew that she never gave away her genuine heart to him. When he asked to return his money that she had owed she gave it him back, not because she felt serious about their relationship, but because she wanted to alleviate her guilty feeling. She would have as willingly lent the money even to Mr Kang or Mr Han if only she had felt sorry about her false relationship with them.

When she had seen the couple in the nook for the first time, she thought she had seen a fantastic vision. She and 'the man' were lying there. It was a pleasant vision and was as valuable as her death. But soon the vision was destroyed and she fell into deep despondency. Then she was fully aware of the significance of the fall. Only she hated to think about it. Now everything was becoming evident. She had been in love. She must have given away her genuine heart to 'the man'. Otherwise, she wouldn't have lent him the money – the whole amount of money that she had earned through prostitution. Genuine heart.

She giggled at the thought. She giggled and giggled. She woke up feeling as if the laughter were ringing not from her own throat but from another woman hidden in a dark corner of the room. She had been giggling in her dream. Soon the dream disappeared from her mind; she only thought she had heard somebody else's laughter. She thought it was the short laugh of the woman that had been barely audible in the forest.

For the remaining hours of the night she tried hard to squeeze out what meaning she could from the dream. She also tried to put the dream on the other end of the scale which was coming up as the weight on the other scale was being removed. In the meantime she kept her mind on this side of the scale. She tried to think about the day when the woman, betrayed like herself, would visit the nook alone. Upon these thoughts her mind became incredibly composed. She felt reassured as if she had come to a conclusion after a night of sleepless effort. Soon she fell into a deep sleep which was not to be disturbed until late in the morning.

It was two hours later than the day before that she woke up. Her head was clear and she had no feeling of fatigue at all.

Soon it was lunch time. She ate a little and then climbed up the mountain. She said to herself, 'This is going to be my last visit. I won't come here any more.' The malignant wish for the ill-fated future of the couple had made her sleep well last night, and the wish, still alive, was reassuring to her. Today she was not fretful or restless while going up the path. She was sure she wouldn't be so disappointed as the day before to find the nook already occupied by the couple. What should she do then? It wouldn't really matter to her anyway. She was sure she would find them there. In her mind she put 'the man' and herself in the place of the man in the chrome-yellow shirt and his woman.

When she arrived at the top of the cliff, what struck her was a ring of ten or so persons looking down at the spot. Instantly she felt nauseous. The next moment she began to climb down the cliff carefully. She came near the people.

No one bothered to look at her. No one noticed her even after she had elbowed herself into the ring.

The spot where the couple used to lie was covered with a straw mat. The heads, arms, and legs of the couple were sticking out from under the mat. The woman's head was lying on one of the man's arms. She saw that the arm sticking out of the golden sleeve and shining in the sunlight of the high noon was putrefying into a blue-black colour.

Somebody beside her said, 'When do you think they died?'

'That bespectacled detective over there says they died a week ago.'

She was listening to the dialogue as if in a dream. It was at that moment that she heard the laughter coming up from the mat. It was the same short laughter of the young woman that she had heard on the previous day. Feeling giddy, she thought her legs were being drained of strength. She fell down on the grass.

She stayed at the spa a week longer and then got aboard a train bound for Seoul.

At a window seat she was carefully trimming her fingernails with a new file she had bought at a store. She looked out of the window from time to time.

As before the scenery looked like a desert stained in green, but now she had a vision of a certain specific scene in it. A couple is lying side by side in the shadow of a cactus. The man is a stranger to her. The woman's face hidden behind the cactus is not to be seen. Presently a short laugh by the woman comes from behind the thorns of the cactus. While she was listening to the laughter, her hand ceased to move the file. It was a very familiar and soul-searching voice. The morose voice ringing on her ear-drums. It was her own laughter.

THE REVELATION

SUNWU HWI

Translated by Chung Chong-wha

It is not quite clear whether I was sixteen or seventeen. Nor is it clear whether I became politically conscious because I had hated school work or hated school work because I had become politically conscious. It seems, to be honest, the former was more likely the case. Anyway I had decided to perform an act of terrorism, though it now seems very vague in what form I had meant to carry it out. What is clear to me is that I had felt an intuitive call to do something about a 'certain person' and I had actually wanted to fulfil this call in real life.

The 'certain person' is no other than Yi Kwangsu (better known by his pen-name Chun Won), whose work had left not a little influence on me during my sensitive years. I even admired him in my quiet way. However, his *To My Fellow Countrymen* (written in Japanese), in which he had tried to persuade Korean people to adopt a pro-Japanese attitude, made me, sensitive and young as I then was, furious with him. My admiration for him turned into hatred. I suppose that I was not alone, that the majority of people felt this way; in other words, my reaction against him was that of just one of thirty million people.

For a few days I planned various intrigues. The fact that I had been especially proud of Chun Won because we shared the same home town made me quite ashamed and pained. I

was then more subject to naive exhibitionism than was usual
with teenagers. I should have gone to Chun Won directly and
sworn at him or knifed him, but instead I went to see my form
master and told him what my 'convictions' were. There was
something more than the ordinary teacher-pupil relationship
between him and me, owing to the fact that there were only
three or four Korean teachers among a hundred in the whole
school where seventy per cent or more of the pupils were
Japanese.

After his supper the form master came to the living-room;
his Korean costume struck me forcibly and I became more
excited. When I finished my eloquent speech (perhaps I might
have stammered) about 'convictions', he seemed unmoved.
Frustrated, I was suspended in the void for a while. When the
wife of the form master brought a cup of tea, I blushed with
embarrassment at my excitement before her refined beauty
and her calm manners. Feeling confused and out of place I
gulped a mouthful of tea, and the hot liquid made tears come
to my eyes. Seeing the teacher still relaxed and cool, I even
hated him.

After a short silence the teacher asked me if I would like
to join him for hill-climbing on the coming Sunday.

'Hill-climbing, sir?' I could not help asking him.

'Yes, hill-climbing,' he said. 'To be free and lofty, nothing
can beat hill-climbing.' He inhaled his cigarette and then puffed
out pale smoke.

First I thought, 'Bah! This coward is beating about the bush.'
But the next moment an idea flashed through my mind and I
reflected, 'He is going to tell me something in confidence on
the hill.' So I accepted his invitation. Given the circumstances
I decided that he had communicated by telepathy more than
he had said in words.

On Sunday we went to Dobong Hills. The form master
started with his old-fashioned preaching, saying that I should
not neglect my school work; that if I thought lightly of it I was
mistaken; that whatever I wanted to be in future my school
work would be very important, that what Chun Won had said
– *'We survive only by learning; learning is power* – was an
unmistakable truth, and that if I did not work now I would
regret it sooner or later. Then he said: 'Chun Won himself was

to join us for the hill-climbing and I am very sorry that he couldn't make it today.'

This aroused my interest.

'Is he not very well?' I asked, slowing my pace. The teacher proposed to have a rest on the grass. He sat down.

'I think he is very poorly; his old complaint, tuberculosis, seems to have gone to the marrow of his bones now.' As if he knew that I was going to say, 'Then he should be lying quietly in bed. This is only a very poor excuse for his pro-Japanese campaign,' he said again, 'It is the tuberculosis that damaged his health not his poor health that is the cause of his campaign.'

'Then?'

'He truly believes that it is the only way to save the people.'

'But I can't believe that.'

'What I am quite sure is that he is not doing it under hard pressure from the Japanese police, as others do.'

'How can the pro-Japanese way be the salvation for our people?'

'A good question. I do not understand it very well myself. As one friend to another I tried to understand him, but I don't seem to have really grasped the meaning of his campaign. However, what is clear to me is that he is not doing it because he is afraid of gaol or torture. Nor is he doing it for worldly success. In other words his campaign springs from his conviction.'

'Would you call it a conviction when it is so obviously wrong?'

'Wait a minute. Don't be too critical.' He assumed a contented smile and raised his hand to stop me. 'This is only my guess; I think he has offered himself as a lamb to the sacrifice. To put it in other words, he volunteered himself for the position if someone had to be in it.'

'There is no such position as you talk of and there is no need to volunteer.'

'The question presupposes that the salvation of our people lies in the union of Japan and Korea. He has volunteered to be a villain at the cost of his personal reputation while others are hesitant to do so.'

'So there is no difference between him and Yi Wanyong, you think?'

At this the teacher laughed heartily and said, as if he was

talking to himself: 'You mean they are birds of a feather? I should not have said anything.'

There was an expression of regret on his face for a moment, and I thought that my accusation against Chun Won had gone too far. So I lowered my voice and said as if I too was talking to myself: 'He should have stayed quiet. If he changes his attitude as suddenly as this, where should his young followers go now, sir?' My voice was shaking a little bit in self-pity.

'Naturally you will have to stop following,' the teacher murmured. He seemed to be immersed in his own thoughts for a while, and then he changed his tone and said, 'Well, then, would you like to hear the story of a man who chose to be quiet?'

'The one who chose to be quiet, sir?'

'Yes, the one who shut his mouth like a shell in the deep sea.'

'Who is he?'

'Perhaps you know of a poet called Suh Rang who started writing poems of aesthetic nature at almost the same time as Chun Won started his literary career in Tokyo?'

'Ah, that Suh Rang!' I shouted in spite of myself.

The following is the rough transcription of what the class master told me about the man.

Suh Rang was born in Seoul, in the same year that Chun Won was born. Suh adopted Rang for his pen-name. Suh Rang and Chun Won were literary rivals, but they were friends because Suh wrote mainly poems and Chun Won novels. If both of them were engaged in the same field, either poetry or the novel, their rivalry might have sharpened the blade of enmity which in the end could have cut their friendship to bits. Chun Won regarded himself as inferior to Suh Rang in poetry, and Suh Rang seemed to have given up the ambition of writing a novel as well as Chun Won. However, Suh Rang often teased Chun Won, 'I would never wish to write such a thing as a novel. Even if I had to write in prose I would never write a novel as archaic as yours. Yet I grant you that your novels are not too bad.'

Chun Won replied to proud Suh, 'Of course you are right. An aesthete like you who luxuriates in words could never write a novel. Perhaps at best you might be able to write a *conte*. But with the density of your poetic phrasing, even in that you would be as clumsy as an inexperienced cook who makes tasteless meat soup.'

Chun Won, though he had been vain in his youth, had to concede something to Suh Rang. First, Suh Rang was handsome and well dressed, and anything he did was an expression of beauty. Chun Won sighed with envy because he had nothing on which he could beat Suh Rang except his eyes in which, as everyone agreed, the three Buddhas of Paradise dwelt. Secondly, there was Suh Rang's art of speech; Chun Won, in his local dialect of Pyung An Province, praised Suh Rang's standard Korean so highly as to call it music. The silk-soft language of the capital could easily take on a feminine tone, but Suh Rang was free from this fault. When Suh Rang talked, Chun Won, with his eyes shut, listened to him attentively as if he was appreciating music. Besides all this, there was something mysterious about the way Suh Rang acted. Whenever he went to a discussion or a meeting he was the central character and his speech exerted strong influence, and yet he made people feel that he was only a man behind the scenes. When Suh Rang and Chun Won did things together, it was always Chun Won who appeared in the foreground while Suh Rang remained in the background. Chun Won noticed this himself, thinking that Suh Rang's way was a sort of perfect art and that there was an inborn elegance in him. Finding himself in the foreground with Suh Rang, willing and content, a few steps behind, Chun Won came to the conviction that he was nothing but a country scholar, and that he could not be equal to Suh Rang.

Suh Rang enjoyed drinks and gay social evenings, and yet there was nothing lewd about him. Neither did he lose his head in his drinking. Once weak-headed Chun Won was persuaded to have a little too much to drink and he lost consciousness. He was taken to his lodgings by Suh Rang. When Suh Rang came to see him next day Chun Won said: 'I am ashamed of myself for passing out just with that amount of drink. You stay sober after so much and this is proof that you are a true gentleman.'

Suh Rang became rather grave and said: 'No, that's my trouble. No matter how heavily I drink, one corner of my head stays sober. I wish I could get completely tipsy and forget myself once in a while, but I can't. In that sense I envy you.'

What Suh Rang seemed to think unfortunate was that he watched himself coolly from one corner of his mind.

Suh Rang had another outstanding attribute; he was very sharp at analysing a situation and at coming to an accurate judgement of it. After the nationwide rising for independence from Japanese occupation on 1st March 1919, many of his Korean fellow students wanted to go back to Seoul from Japan, but Suh Rang stopped them. He argued that the liberation of the country from Japanese rule was impossible in view of the international balance of power at the time. When a hot-headed student shouted that the independence of a people 'was not given but taken', he answered, with a cold contempt on his comely face, 'Japan is a rising star at the moment and its international share price is soaring. Fighting bare-handed against the guns and swords of Japan who defeated the Ching Dynasty and Imperial Russia can only end one way.'

When Chun Won decided to exile himself in Shanghai, Suh Rang did not stop him but advised, 'If this is romanticism, all right; but you must not believe that it will get us independence.' When Chun Won came home from China, Suh Rang said, 'At last the fish is back in the water. Play with words as much as you can.' It was partly due to Suh's advice that Chun Won became the bestseller of his time after his return from Shanghai. It is not clear whether Suh Rang did not write any poems at all during this period or just did not publish his work. However, what is clear is that he went to public meetings along with Chun Won and earned enormous popularity with his audiences by his eloquence. He strongly influenced a limited number of people with his theories of aestheticism.

Suh Rang had a wife who was so beautiful and virtuous that Chun Won described her as symbolic of Korean women. It is also said that Chun Won used her as the model for the heroine of his novel, *Indifference*. Chun Won often wondered whether the reason why Suh Rang had refused to join him in exile in Shanghai was not because he believed that the independence of the country was not to be found in self-exile, but simply because he could not leave his beautiful wife. And indeed Suh's love for his wife as almost blind. Once Chun Won invited an American missionary to dinner along with the Suhs and the

American told him later, 'By meeting Mr Suh and his wife I have confirmed that Korean people are a beautiful people.' Chun Won did not take his remarks simply as a compliment for his dinner.

The friendship between Suh Rang and Chun Won did not change even after Chun Won had come out more and more publicly in support of the Japanese colonial policies which forced all Korean leaders to co-operate with the Japanese military police. Once Suh Rang went with Chun Won to give a public lecture on literature, which, while not yet openly a lecture of a political nature, was bound to be a sort of prelude to incite Koreans to co-operate with the Japanese. At the lecture in what was then the Citizens' Hall, but is now the House of Parliament, for an audience mainly of students, it was arranged for Suh to talk first and to be followed by Chun Won. There was nothing unusual in Suh Rang's behaviour on that day. The public applauded quietly when he appeared, handsome and graceful, on the stage. After he took a drink of water, his beautiful words, which Chun Won called music, began to flow as smoothly as a roll of silk. And then a strange thing happened.

Scarcely a minute had passed when the eloquent flow of his speech stopped all of a sudden. At first the audience did not think it strange. Some of them laughed when Suh Rang hurriedly drank the remaining water from the glass. However, Suh Rang did not continue his talk even then. The people in the front rows saw Suh Rang's face growing pale. Suh raised his hand and rubbed his lips several times. Then he dropped his hand and massaged his neck with the other hand. By this time the audience finally realized that something had happened to the speaker. Suh Rang covered his mouth with his two hands, and uttered animal-like sounds several times through his fingers. A number of people in the audience started getting up, so did the chairman on the stage. In the middle of this great disturbance, Suh Rang walked away from the stage quickly, with his two hands still on his mouth, and disappeared. The chairman who had followed Suh Rang came back to the shouting audience and in an excited voice asked the people to calm down. He said, 'Mr Suh Rang suddenly coughed blood from his mouth.'

Chun Won's behaviour in this utter chaos was very odd. He

remained calmly seated with his closed fists in his lap and his eyes shut. When the chairman hurriedly introduced him, Chun Won stood up quietly, proceeded to the platform and began speaking on his literary topic in an utterly composed way. Towards the end of his talk Chun Won, in the same calm tone, argued that the Japanese and Korean cultures had come from the same root. There was no visible reaction to this from the audience, but the majority of people in the theatre felt that something ominous was afoot.

That day marked the beginning of Chun Won's open advocacy of co-operation with Japan. There was a rumour that Suh Rang had not coughed blood but had been struck dumb. The first reaction to this rumour was a wave of public sympathy for the unfortunate man, but as Chun Won's pro-Japanese pronouncements became more frequent there followed another rumour that Suh Rang had feigned his dumbness. The story was that unusually sensitive as he was to developments in political situations, Suh Rang had pretended to be dumb rather than be forced to work for the Japanese war cause. This became a kind of analgesic to soothe the intellectuals, frustrated by Japanese colonial policies. When people heard that Suh Rang had left for the Diamond Mountains for treatment, they took it as his going into political hiding, referring to him as a modern Poi and Shuch'i.

'But, sir, there is another, more widely accepted story that he literally became dumb,' I suggested to the form master after I had heard this long story.

'Naturally there will be all sorts of stories about him in this rumour-infested society.'

'I have heard that there was a student who believed that Suh Rang had gone dumb deliberately and was so overwhelmed that he went all the way to the Diamond Mountains to get a glimpse of his hero. He wanted to have a written conversation with him if possible. However, not only did he get no response at all, but he found that the dumb man was like one bereft of his senses.'

'Could he have trusted him and confided that he was only acting dumb?'

'But his wife is said to have begged the student to leave her husband alone.'

'Well ...'

'They say that he has become deaf as well. Fearing that Suh
Rang might influence Koreans a great deal, if the rumour of
his pretence were true, Miwa, the Japanese detective, went to
see him. The detective fired his pistol right behind his ear,
without giving Suh Rang any warning, but he was entirely
unmoved.'

'I've heard the story that the detective's firing killed his dog
but Suh Rang remained unresponsive.'

'If he was feigning would he remain so unmoved?'

'You could also say that it is very odd he showed no reaction
at all.'

'Why then would the thorough Japanese military authorities
leave him alone?'

'That's simply because they put a different value on him. If
it had been Chun Won, they wouldn't have let it go just like
that. The Japanese military authorities, though they might have
been sensitive to the rumours, decided that a dumb Suh Rang
couldn't do any harm to anybody.'

'What does Chun Won think of this case?'

'He went to see his friend, who remained withdrawn into
his dumbness. He was very distressed.'

'Would he ever have thought that Suh Rang's feigning was
successful and that he was beaten, that Suh Rang had done it
again?'

'Well, if it were me, I would just exclaim, "That could
happen!" If I had myself done what Suh Rang did, I would
have made everyone laugh with my poor imitation. Besides, I
couldn't have acted as well as him. If I became dumb I
wouldn't be able to earn my living in the classroom and consequently I could only send my wife and children onto the streets.
However, Chun Won who is an honest man is most likely to
believe that Suh Rang has now really become dumb, if indeed
he ever doubted the genuineness of his dumbness. Well, the
two of them have different dimensions of thought and therefore he wouldn't worry about his being defeated by Suh Rang
again.'

'What do you think personally? Is Suh Rang pretending?'

'When you teach in a government school you can show two
kinds of reaction, both coming from your inferiority complex.
The first is that Suh Rang has really become dumb; the jealousy

of the one who cannot offer resistance when he should is the cause of this first reaction. The other is that to feel jealous makes life too sad, and although you cannot do it yourself you console yourself with the thought that you have the potential to do what others do. It is a kind of dancing to somebodys else's music. However, I am much inclined to find salvation in the latter.'

'Therefore you are suggesting that I too should believe it?'

'It is better to believe than disbelieve.'

'Still you can't console yourself by believing it. The question is how to act.'

'How to act? Well then, what do you want to do with Chun Won?'

'I can't get him out of my mind.'

'You'd better.' He was very firm and decisive. I couldn't find words to reply to him quickly enough before he continued. 'I advise you not to do anything, not because Chun Won is a friend of mine, nor because I want a quiet life as a teacher, nor again because you are young and lack experience. Acts of terrorism have no positive meaning, particularly when you think that we are all Koreans. They are the expressions of negative values. A young man must be ambitious. Why don't you try to develop your own ideas until they can be regarded as highly as Chun Won's or to open up new ground where you can be more influential than he? Why do you only think of attacking him?'

'Well, I am ...' I hesitated a little. 'I am entirely incapable of anything else.'

'The more reason to be studious. And you have to wait for a chance.'

'When do you think my chance would come?'

'You don't have to be so impatient. Instead of becoming an impulsive cane, you will have to aim at serving as a beam of the house.'

I couldn't go on any further. His advice that I should aim at becoming 'a beam of the house' gave me a typical teenage illusion that I had already become one. Now looking back on the conversation with the old experienced teacher, I was merely stripped of all my idealism by his persuasion. Nevertheless I am very grateful to him. Though he is now no longer in this world, I still remember him as an excellent teacher.

A year after the 1945 Liberation I came to the South from the North and got a job as a reporter covering social affairs. Many people emerged from underground movements and resumed active life. In the North I had seen enough of accusations, attacks and slanders against anyone who did not belong to the proletarian class, not only by the former collaborators with the Japanese but also by the leaders of nationalistic movements. In the South again the nationalist and communist camps joined forces in deriding and boycotting the former collaborators. Instead of sharing their burning hatred, I became weary of the human weakness of exempting oneself when judging the sins of human beings.

In this mood I came to be a little sympathetic towards Chun Won and his situation. Who could ever dare to stone him? My present habit of disregarding so-called 'public opinion' or 'majority opinion' is a hangover from this period. I no longer give unconditional support to the decisions of the majority. My colleagues on the newspaper attributed my sympathy for Chun Won to the fact that he and I had come from the same town. People, to my great distress, like to simplify life by seeing it in terms of the same town, the same school, the same class, etc.

My sympathy for Chun Won brought back to me the long forgotten thought of Suh Rang. It occurred to me that the fact that I had completely forgotten him was very strange. No sooner did I think of Suh Rang than I went to the arts editor, and I asked him about the man.

'Suh Rang? Who is he?' he asked. After I had explained he asked me again in a rather unconvinced tone, 'Ah, him, what do you want of him?'

'What does he do now?' I asked.

'What does he do? What can a dumb man do?' The editor didn't want to take my inquiry seriously.

'I heard that he had acted dumb.'

'There was such a rumour.' There was a cold, contemptuous smile on his lips. 'But it has proved to be wrong. Is the liberation of the country so great an event as to open the mute mouth of a dumb man?'

'I felt a strong blow of disillusionment, but in my heart of hearts something was defying my frustration. I toyed with an idea that Suh Rang might have had some personal reasons for remaining dumb and not appearing on the surface in a period as utterly chaotic as that was. And yet I failed to think of any reason for him to continue his dumb role at a time when even a stone, if it had a mouth, should open it. In vague expectation I went to see my old form master, who heartily congratulated me on my mild success in my journalistic career. We talked of the old days when we had gone hill-climbing. We also exchanged views about Chun Won. When I expressed my sympathy for Chun Won, he replied: 'That would lighten his guilty conscience. But perhaps he himself wants more severe criticism for what he has done.' Once again the wisdom of my teacher moved me deeply.

When our conversation drifted inevitably to the topic of Suh Rang, the teacher's face darkened. I hoped that he might have something different to say.

'Have you heard the true story behind the history of his dumbness?' I asked.

The teacher said nothing for a while. He rubbed his jaw and then said: 'It was our wishful thinking that we believed in his feigning of dumbness.'

'So he became a real mute then?'

'I am afraid so. I heard from someone that he went to see a doctor at the end of last year and started treatment for his illness.'

'Well, I am disillusioned.'

'It certainly is disillusioning. But to see the matter in close analysis, it was not only his personal problem, but ours as well. What is important here is that you and I believed that he was feigning, rather than accepting him as he actually was. So now you cannot say that an intelligent man is never swindled even when he is. Now before you decide whether he feigned or he really became dumb, you ought to be grateful for the opportunities of doubt he gave you.'

I tried hard to convince myself of the truth of what the teacher had said, but there remained a bitter taste in my mouth. In my journalistic career I had regarded it as my only source of joy to follow those patriotic leaders who had either emerged from underground or returned from abroad and to see their real faces and to hear their real voices. However, the more I met them the more disillusioned I became. And my disappointment in Suh Rang was as big a betrayal as a hole in my heart. Yet I did not give up hope in him and once wrote an essay about him in a magazine, but I received no response from the public.

When I was taking leave of my old master, he asked me: 'I presume that you wish to carry on in your present occupation?'

'I have developed an interest in politics.'

'Give it up!' His voice was as firm as it was on the day when he had told me not to take any physical action against Chun Won.

'There are people well suited to politics. You are not. My skin creeps when I think of what can happen to a strong individual in an organization. You could lose yourself by playing at politics; it could be the end of you.'

The old master, with whom I shared a secret bond over Suh Rang, perished against a dark stone wall next spring; while he was a professor he refused to sign a political statement, which led to a misunderstanding that he was opposed to the political group and a student from that group stabbed him to death. Twenty years later I had completely forgotten the poet, Suh Rang.

In my fifty years of life I have encountered from time to time an unexpected man, at an unexpected place and time, who has an unexpected story to tell me. Then I taste the joy of life to the fullest degree. A little while ago I had one of these experiences at an inn in a small town in Chung-chong Province, where I went to cover a certain story. It was the best experience I have ever had.

After supper I was reading the previous day's newspaper when I was suddenly seized with an acute pain of gastritis. The pain was so unbearable that I called a maid and asked her to buy me a lenitive. But when the medicine did not alleviate the pain, the young woman asked if she might call in a reputable doctor who happened to be in the same inn. I did not have time to think about the reasons why a famous doctor should stay at a small country inn. I scolded her for not having mentioned the doctor sooner.

When the woman brought the doctor to my room I was rather surprised. I had expected an old dignified person, but the man before me had a young, ruddy complexion with his forehead covered in hair down to his eyebrows, and a beard covering the lower part of his face. He also had youthful, lively eyes. He wore a loose, chestnut-coloured corduroy suit with a sweater of the same chestnut colour underneath. I said to him, trying to suppress my pain, that it seemed to be an attack of gastritis. Without examining me he took out a hypodermic from his bag, and asked: 'Do you drink a lot?'

When I replied that I indeed drank like a fish, he said, smilingly: 'Then perhaps one injection is not enough.'

He injected me with two doses of analgesic with great skill. He then proceeded to examine me, while I wondered to myself whether he was a quack, though I liked his unhesitating manner. The fact that he was staying in a small country inn, and so shabbily clothed seemed to prove that he was an impostor. He touched my stomach with his hand several times and said: 'I see you had an operation for appendicitis. Then it must be gastritis.'

Though his diagnosis was vague, I noticed that he had a beautiful voice. I also noticed that his eyebrows, eyes, nose and mouth were all beautiful, though they were half hidden behind the hair and beard. Of course there was no reason why a quack doctor should not be handsome, but somehow he looked different. There was something intelligent and refined about him. I felt attracted to him. In order to keep him longer I asked the young maid to bring a dish of apples. He did not refuse this offer, and his eyes twinkled.

In order to smooth over the awkward moments before the formality of exchanging names over the dish of apples, I asked him in a casual way: 'Did you drop in here on your way to somewhere?'

'No. I just wander about like this.'

'You wander about here and there?'

'While I go round to villages where there is no doctor, I occasionally come across a small town of this size.'

'Don't you want to settle down and open your own clinic?'

'No, it has become my habit to go round like this.'

'Isn't it tiring?'

'I have come to like it.'

'Where do you leave your family then?'

'I am alone.'

'Parents?'

'They have departed from this world.'

'Not married yet?'

'No,' he smiled.

When I realized that the conversation was drifting towards an inquisition I decided to face the formality of introduction. The woman brought a dish of apples and pears, and I asked him to help himself to the fruit. I apologized for my rudeness and introduced myself. The doctor in return pronounced his name.

'I am Suh Pah.'

I thought I didn't catch his name right, and repeated: 'Suh Pah?'

There was a twinkle of a smile in his eyes again, and he said: 'Suh is my surname, and Pah is the character for waves; I have only a one-character name.'

'Suh Pah!'

'My father gave me a different name, but as I began to go around the country, I used this name which I adopted. It somehow makes me feel closer to my father.'

'Suh Pah! It is a very impressive name.'

A short silence followed between the two of us, and I felt something at the back of my mind, although I couldn't say what it was exactly. *This name which I adopted. It somehow makes me feel closer to my father.* Something flashed in my mind, raising goose pimples all over my skin. I stared into his face, and with difficulty I got out: 'Then you are Mr Suh Rang's . . .' I couldn't finish the sentence.

The doctor lowered his eyes for a second and then said: 'Yes, I am his son.'

All I could say was, 'Ah! So you are!'

I couldn't say any more while waves of deep shock surged over me. It took me a few minutes before I was able to say in a trembling voice: 'That I should meet Mr Suh Rang's son here and now!'

He asked, 'Did you know my father?'

'I never met him, but I heard of him.'

'What did you hear of him?' he asked impatiently, pressing me for an answer. His clear bright eyes were burning with sincerity. I felt instinctively that I could solve the riddle which had hung round Suh Rang. 'Where should I start?' I hesitated, full of expectations. Another silence persisted for a short while before I finally spoke: 'What I know about Mr Suh Rang is nothing but rumours. Whether he acted dumb or whether some physical disability shut his mouth and ears is the thing I am most anxious to know.'

The doctor's eyes lost focus for a second and then they became bright again. He said: 'My father feigned it, then.'

'Ah, so did he?' I felt my clouded heart clearing and blue sky seemed to appear but only for a brief moment.

'Why then did he not open his mouth after the liberation in 1945?'

'It is because . . .' A shadow of pathetic agony crossed his face. 'Do you want to know why?' His eyes became vague again, as if he was looking at a distant place. 'It was when Seoul was recaptured by the UN Forces during the War. Father died in October that year. Just before his last moment he called me by my name.'

I strained every auditory nerve so as not to miss a word.

'When he uttered my name after he had stared at me for a long while, I was so shocked that I almost fainted. My father could speak! I tried with both hands to prevent my weak body from falling on the floor.'

After Suh Rang called his son by his name, he said, 'I am sorry.'

What the doctor told me that night is roughly as follows.

In the middle of his speech that day Suh Rang was suddenly seized with the illusion that he had heard the audience laugh at him; the waves of the illusion were so powerful that he had to stop. For a few seconds something was whirling in his head. When the spinning stopped and his head cleared, he had made a firm resolution that he would never speak again, that he would become dumb. No sooner had the resolution been made than he put one hand to his mouth and clutched his neck with the other. But when he returned from the Citizens' Hall and saw his wife, he regretted his wrong decision. What should he do with regard to his wife and his only son who was then fourteen? After tortuous inner struggles for a solution, he made up his mind that he would confide the secret at least to his own family.

However, a few days later, he changed his mind, not because he wanted to accomplish a perfect crime, but because strangely he felt a surge of strong love towards his wife when he saw the shadow of distress on her beautiful face and he also enjoyed a sense of trust in the sign of something deepening in his maturing son. There were times when the sense of compassion, which he felt as a Korean husband towards his Korean wife and son, who at the same time seemed more pleasant to look at and dearer than ever, overwhelmed him. Should he preserve this state? His aesthetic appreciation of the sadism in this *fin-de-siècle* situation made him take such a decision. His determination faded several times, but as the husband, the wife and the son learned to communicate with their hands, his original resolution hardened gradually. In the gestures of their hands desperate for perfect communication, and in the movements of their eyes in the effort to make up what the hands missed, he found a perfect form of human sincerity, more sincere than through the medium of spoken words. Suh Rang in the end had come to believe that words did not mean much; he had come to think that in communication between human beings at the highest level, words were obstacles.

When the Japanese detective Miwa came to him, he managed to push some pine-nuts which he happened to be chewing, deeply into his ears. Faced with the cunning detective, he decided to play the act in a more natural way. Miwa fired his pistol behind Suh Rang's back, but the pine-nuts in his ears made him show a much less sensitive response to the noise. His dog, which had for three years been like one of the family, fell to the ground covered in blood after jumping convulsively into the air twice. If he was completely motionless at the sight, it was because a heavy sense of guilt (that the dog had lost its life for him) momentarily so overcame him that he didn't know what to do. He became more deeply immersed in the sea of guilt, with his ears stopped with pine-nuts and the movements of his surroundings suspended. During the last phase of the Pacific War, Suh Rang remained like a deep-sea shell and managed to come through the cruellest phase of his life.

On the day of the Liberation he was in his room and clearly heard his wife, coming home from an outing, exclaim, 'Darling, they say that the war is over!' When she came into the room hurriedly she made hand gestures to tell him that the war had ended. He smiled at his wife; while she was waving her hands she looked attractive and lovely, but at the same time she looked so pathetic. The whole situation also seemed comic.

'Now I ought to make my sad wife happy,' he decided, and after a deep breath, he opened his mouth, 'Darling!' But the words did not come out. He tried again, 'Darling!' No sound. Feeling a bit confused he impatiently called, 'Darling!' Yet there was no sound. He utterly lost his head then. He raised his two hands into the air and shouted, 'Hurray!' No sound was audible, as before. His shocked eyes saw the embarrassed expression of his wife. He gathered all his strength and tried again and again. And he became more and more confused.

When his wife burst into tears in his arms, he was covered with sweat and his eyes were out of focus. For a long while he was unable to think and he felt utterly void. When he recovered his senses he said to himself, 'I am being punished for my deeds!' he held his bitterly crying wife in his arms for a long while. He held her tighter and tighter and that was all he could do. 'I am being punished mercilessly. I have lost the game completely. Justice has been done me!' He felt as if someone had been watching him deceive his own wife and son, and had hit him in the decisive moment. When he finally regained his composure, he felt like laughing, realizing that he had acted like a fool.

The next day his wife went out to see doctors with their son who was a student at a pre-medical school. Soon a rumour spread that Suh Rang had been receiving treatment. However, Suh Rang himself refused to see any doctor for treatment. Days and months went by.

One spring day, a year later, Suh Rang woke up from a nap and vaguely looked at the azaleas in full blossom outside the window. He suddenly called his wife, 'Darling!' Next moment he was very surprised; he heard himself calling his wife. 'Darling! Darling!' He heard his voice getting louder and louder. He called his son's name, and he felt his voice warm at his throat and lips. He stood and ran out into the hall calling for his wife and son. Waves of indescribable happiness flowed through him. Soon he realized that his son had gone to university and his wife had gone out shopping. He called his dog which had long been dead and there was no reply. With the recollection of his dead dog, his excitement abated.

A pedlar came to the bolted gate and shouted over the wall,

'Did you want seaweed?' Suh Rang crossed the garden and unbolted the gate. A stranger with bunches of seaweed on both his shoulders greeted him and said: 'This is the best quality. It is not loose or stiff.'

'I am sorry. I was calling my wife.'

'Oh, I see. I thought you had called me.'

'Well, let me see.' Suh Rang felt the seaweed with his hand and then bought a bundle. He felt happy that his voice had been heard by the pedlar.

Suh Rang, with the seaweed bundle, waited for his wife to return, feeling excited. But she was late because she had called in on her parents. Had she returned sooner, Suh Rang would have spoken in front of his wife and would have solved the problem of his dumbness. Her late return gave him time to think, and in the end he decided to remain as he had been. Suh Rang thought about the implications of resuming his speech. Long habit had made him happy to communicate with his wife by gestures, and he didn't find it inconvenient. He no longer needed words. His relations with people outside his home had long become meaningless. What did he want to say to people? Did he have to add more words to the world which had been already troubled by too many words? What would he gain by starting to speak again? Or what would he lose? Would it not be comic to be ecstatic over the recovery of the words which he had once voluntarily renounced or rather which he had been involuntarily robbed of? A comedy! It certainly was a comedy. Would it not be a revenge on the one who had taken words from him, to refuse them and remain silent? What were words?

When his wife came home Suh Rang had gone back to his previous dumb role. However, he felt a strong urge to talk again on one occasion – when his wife was on her death-bed. He wanted her to depart this world with the consolation of his words. He had loved her as if she was his own life and he had lived for her. But when he saw her, struggling to maintain the last thread of her life-force, focussing her dying eyes on him and trying to say something with her hands, summoning her last grains of strength, Suh Rang could not open his mouth. Instead he bade his last farewell to her with movements of his fingers.

'Then my father asked me whether I had felt a vocation for the medical profession. To my positive answer he expressed relief, saying that he suffered from a guilty conscience that I had chosen medicine on the score of his dumbness. At the same time it had made him feel extremely flattered.'

'That is the paternal love, I suppose.'

'He asked me whether I could love my patients. I answered that, to be honest, I did not know. He said then that man could not live alone and should not live alone. He said that man had to live inevitably in groups, and that to love another is never an easy task, let alone to love many.'

'That is quite true. It is easy to hate others, and it is an achievement if one can avoid hating others. Moreover, to love another person – to love others – is almost impossible.'

'You think so? It is impossible, isn't it?' The doctor asked with a strong voice as if in confirmation, with his sad, impatient eyes flickering.

I hesitated to answer him in a positive way that love was impossible. The doctor, without waiting for me to answer said as if he was talking to himself. 'Yes, it is impossible. How can one love another or many others? If someone says that it is possible, he is telling a lie.' In a subdued voice he continued, 'Since my father died what he said has bothered me a lot – his question whether I could love a patient or other human beings. To be frank with you, I cannot love others. I cannot love human beings *en masse*. Strangely, I cannot shut my eyes to the ugly sides of mankind. Spiritually as well as physically human beings have too many ugly sides, and I am not excluding myself here. To me ugliness itself is mankind.'

While I was listening to him I confirmed that the doctor was the real son of the aesthete Suh Rang; the father was sensitive to the beautiful and the son to the ugly. He continued in a quiet voice: 'Naturally I came to hate myself, but I did see once that the ugly human being could become as beautiful as a flame. During the war I was an army doctor and I met many army commanders who treated their soldiers like animals and who never hesitated to shoot them if they violated army rules. But once these commanders came into the hands of doctors they became good patients, as good as children. Yet as soon as they went out of hospital, they again returned to their former selves.'

The doctor and I laughed, but he soon resumed his story. 'I even had a murderer under my care. As a patient he seemed good and innocent, and I felt sorry for him.'

'I am sure you did.'

'Once I worked with a friend at his clinic. I saw, in the operating theatre, something beautiful in the trust of the suffering patient and in the devotion of the doctor who in utmost earnest was absorbed in his job. I wondered if human beings can carry on the same, beautiful relationship for ever. But I had to suffer from a bitter disillusionment a few days later when there was a wrangle over the medical fee. What looked so beautiful a human relationship became so ugly, which led me to the thought that human beings are good and beautiful only for a moment. This made me a wandering doctor. Whenever I go to a remote village where there is no resident doctor, I often find something beautiful in the patients. It often makes me wonder to see people in front of me so unbelievably good and beautiful. Of course I have had occasions when my heart sank when I found my medicines being stolen.'

I exclaimed in what was almost a groan: 'How greedy you are! You want to monopolize all the moments of human beauty and good!'

The doctor shook his head once and said, 'I think you are right. You can put it that way.'

The night was late. I ordered one more dish of apples. When the maid had brought the dish and left the room, he changed the position he was sitting in and became very serious.

'I would like to ask your pardon.'

'Why? I don't understand.'

'Though we have apparently met accidentally, it is not by chance at all.'

'No?'

'I saw your name in the register and I waited for this occasion.'

'But you couldn't have given me the gastritis which brought you to me.'

'No, I couldn't do that, but I meant to come and see you.'

'Then my gastritis brought me luck. Did I look beautiful as a patient?'

The doctor smiled and said, 'I read your old articles about my late father.'

'You did!'

'Your writing left a very strong impression on me. Several times I wanted to come and tell you the whole truth about my father, but the reason why I hesitated was because I was not sure whether the revelation of the truth was in accordance with his wish. Then I came to a new resolution that I had better keep the secret buried inside me. However, when I saw your name in the register I changed my mind.'

'On the contrary, if I had known that Mr Suh Rang had a son, I would have done my best to find him and make friends with him.'

'Perhaps I shouldn't have told you the story.'

'Not at all. By the way I heard that Mr Suh Rang enjoyed drinking.'

'Yes.'

'Do you want a drink?'

'No, thank you. Once alcohol gets inside me I may lose my head.'

'Without losing control there is no point in having drinks.'

The doctor refused to be persuaded.

'Do you intend to keep your bachelorhood into your old age?'

'It looks like it.'

'Do you find any human ugliness in woman?'

The doctor smiled again and said, 'No, but can you think of any woman who would accompany a wanderer like me?'

'Yes, I am sure.' I felt sorry for the fact that the doctor might not leave any descendants.

'May I ask you a blunt question? How do you deal with the problems you may face as a male?'

The doctor smiled contentedly. 'It seems that I have got into a habit. Lack of interest has given me a habit. Habit is terrible. Now I do not find it painful without it.'

'Perhaps it is a kind of sainthood.'

'Not at all.' The doctor paused a little while and then continued. 'I often commit mental adultery.'

'When, for instance?' I pressed him.

'Well,' he seemed to think carefully. 'For instance, on a hot summer country road I stop at a spring and ask a young woman for a gourdful of water. I feel a strong force of attraction towards the woman who offers me cool fresh water.'

'The force of gravity?'

'Is it funny?' The doctor flushed.

'Not at all. Please go on.'

'And there are occasions such as when a country girl adjusts her dress, turning crimson to her neck, in front of me with my stethoscope . . .'

'At that moment!' The doctor and I cried in unison and laughed heartily together.

This time I changed my position and said, 'Why do you move around with a single bag, instead of settling down in one place? Is it in the hope that you might experience some transitory beauty in a human being?'

'Well, I don't know,' said the doctor. 'No, I do not wander about to catch the transitory beauty of human beings. Put it this way; I feel a relationship with another human being has been established when I experience it.'

'In other words you can love another human being only in that moment, I presume?'

'No, I am not that arrogant, but perhaps it is simply that I cannot love another human being as many people can.'

I saw signs of vexed impatience on the doctor's face and I regretted and felt ashamed for having pressed for an answer just to convince myself, as if I was looking for the right clue in a commercial quiz.

Early next morning I saw him off as far as the bank of a river on the outskirts of the small town; he was on his way on foot to a small village about five miles away. We did not speak. There was no need for words between us. We felt contented just to walk together. At the river bank we parted with hackneyed farewells like, 'Take care of yourself and see you again soon.' But I knew for sure that we would not meet again, because neither he nor I wished to see each other again. He walked away along the bank, carrying a small brief-case, quickly, as if he were being pushed by the wind. While I watched him, I felt that he was carrying a heavy burden on his shoulders, along with a thick shadow of loneliness, which he himself had volunteered to bear or perhaps his poet father had handed down to him, or even ordinary people like us had forced upon him. It was, however, a burden somebody had to carry along.

In a brief moment of sadness I felt my heart becoming empty and yet strangely becoming full.

OBSCURITY

YI KWANG SU

Translated by Lyndal Weiler (in collaboration with Lee Eun-sook and Chung Chong-wha)

I had been imprisoned for three days when I was sent to the prison infirmary. The infirmary was not in a separate building but the rooms were located at the far end of the prison. The room which I entered was on the westernmost side, and was called Cell Number One. After the prison guard who took me there had left, a pale complexioned infirmary nurse with clear, bright eyes said to me, 'You are free to sit or lie down and it is all right if you speak quietly. But, if your voice is too loud the prison guards will make trouble for you.' The nurse then assigned me a place according to my number and left. I expressed my thanks to the nurse with an appreciative nod and then greeted the other two prisoners in the room with another nod of my head.

At that moment the prisoner who was nearest to me grabbed my hand in the old Korean way and, in a voice so loud that those in the adjoining cell could hear he said, 'Ah, you must be Mr Jin. I am Yun!' I recognized him also. He was in the detention room at C Police Station for about ten days while I was there, but he was transferred before me. Yun was just skin and bone but his voice was loud and every time he spoke he had used the word 'cock', so his cellmates referred to him as 'The Cock'. Whenever I recall this it is extremely difficult to suppress my laughter.

Sitting in the posture of the old Korean scholars, Yun expressed his concern about how I came to be imprisoned. Yun introduced me with praise to the old man sitting beside me. His name was Min and he was also skin and bone. Yun then opened his prison uniform to expose his stomach and legs, with his fingers he poked at his shin and ankle, and with his two hands he pinched his stomach, 'Look at this. It's all swollen. It's a little bit better now. When I was in Cell Number Eight in Block One it was much worse,' he said.

He then explained his ailments at tiresome length. It appeared that he knew the symptoms of his illness better than a doctor. And because the doctor didn't know what the illness was Yun lamented that he would probably only leave the prison as a corpse. According to Yun's own diagnosis the swelling was caused by eating nothing but rice gruel. His coughing, fever and diarrhoea were all caused from his anxiety over his wrongful imprisonment. He claimed that in order to be cured of his illness he needed to be released from prison to eat and drink as much food and wine as he possibly could. He then scowled and shouted that it was his accomplices and the doctor who were killing him.

Yun explained that a certain Mr Hyon and a certain Mr Im had conspired to mortgage the land of a man named Mr Kim (without his knowledge) as security for a loan of thirty thousand *won* from a money lender. Yun's only role was to carve the seals for the forged documents. He said, 'I don't know this bastard Hyon, but as for Im he was a very close friend. I am indeed the kind of person who would lay down his life for a friend. So I carved the seals. Mr Jin, did I ever take a single *won*? While Im and Hyon spent thousands of *won* between themselves, what crime did I commit?'

I knew that Yun's speech was not directed at me but at Min. There was a reason for this. Yun had said exactly the same things to me the first day we met at the police station detention room, but after he was taken to the detectives' room and interrogated for two hours he came out with his shoulders sagging and explained that Im and Hyon had promised him six thousand *won* if the conspiracy was a success. However, when the fraudulent plot was successful Hyon and Im found they were unable to use the seals which Yun had carved for them; instead they had to have new seals carved in Seoul. So, as a reward for his efforts, Yun was only given thirty *won*, food and wine, and an evening with a prostitute. I had to suppress my laughter once again when I thought about how Yun had lied to Min not knowing that I would be brought into their cell. I think Yun started speaking to me like this when I came into the cell because he had been telling Min that he was innocent and because I knew the truth and he had to try and cover up the lies he had told.

Skinny Min studied his bony fingers intently, pretending not to listen to what Yun fervently repeated day and night. He suddenly stood up and went to the privy, at which Yun shouted, 'Shitting again!' 'You're no better than me,' Min replied and continued to shit with great effort and concentration. The privy, which reminded me of an unpainted coffin, stood right next to where Min put his head at night. Min looked quite pitiful as his skeleton-like face showed the effort he was making while on it.

Yun, staring with narrow eyes at the back of Min's skinny neck, said, 'Mr Jin, that bastard there gets eighty sacks of rice grain from his land, has a grown-up son, and a wife who is only eighteen years of age. Even though he has a son and a wife, not even a dog comes to see him. Not even a single piece of clothing nor a bowl of rice is brought to him. In my case it would be understandable because my home is far away. But we'll wait and see. I have written a letter to my uncle who is a town mayor and he will send me at least thirty *won*. But Min comes from Shihung. Is it right that your wife and son don't show their faces here? Ha! He takes pride in the fact that his family name is Min. Are all Mins *yangban**? How on earth could someone who ignores their own husband or father be *yangban*?'

While Yun was verbally abusing Min like this Min just pretended that he couldn't hear. He had stopped groaning and he was sitting on the privy staring vacantly as if he had forgotten to get off it. Min's lack of response only made Yun more angry. He stood up abruptly, went to the privy, and with his fingers he poked Min in the ribs. Then, trying to scratch Min's pride he said, 'Well, what did I just say to you? If you stay like this you will die. If you haven't eaten you can't shit! If

---

*Yangban loosely refers to the people of the upper class.

you only have one mouthful of gruel how can you piss? Don't waste any more time, write a letter and ask for money to buy milk and eggs. What is the point of having money if you don't use it? Are you going to leave your money to a son who doesn't visit his dying father? Ha ha, now I know. Your eighteen-year-old wife will find a young boyfriend and have fun with your money.'

Min was unable to bear this any longer but without showing any sign of anger he calmly said, 'Well, why worry? I may live a little bit longer if I don't have to listen to your abuse and be subjected to your poisonous looks. There are certain things you can say but there are also things you shouldn't say. Why mention another man's wife? That is why I think countryfolk can't be helped.' Min maintained a calm composure but his sunken eyes held a poisonous look.

Yun repeated the same hurtful things to Min for days after that. When Min hated listening to these things he would close his eyes and pretend to be sleeping. Otherwise, he would stare through the window at the clouds in the summer sky. The calmer Min became, the more Yun would get heated and abuse him. As a last resort to make Min angry Yun would mention Min's eighteen year old wife at the end of every speech. The mention of his wife would at least bring a frown and a few unpleasant remarks from Min.

No matter how much Yun angered Min, Min pretended not to hear him and gave little or no response. When this happened Yun had the habit of attacking Min through speaking to me. He taunted Min by saying to me that Min ignores the doctor's advice, doesn't take his medicine, and is extremely stingy. Yun would go on endlessly about how the red on the tip of Min's nose must mean that the worms in his stomach are squirming around because his death was approaching, and how he would bet that Min's wife was already getting intimate with some young rogue.

Yun would only stop talking when he was sleeping or when his meal came. It seemed that Yun only lived for four things: eating, tormenting Min, shitting, and sleeping. And the only other thing he could do was complain about his illness and his accomplices. At any rate, Yun's mouth was seldom shut and even though his loud voice often brought about a command

from the prison guard Yun would hurl abuse at him as soon
as he left.

I never had a moment's peace because of Yun. Every word
he said had a strange way of getting on my nerves. His abuse
of Min, his constant whinging when we sat down to eat, his
slander of the prison guard, doctor, nurses, warden and his
accomplices, and his abuse without exception of any person he
spoke about, cut into me like a knife and pricked my fragile
nerves like a needle.

The thing I most wanted to do was to lie down in peace and
not have to think about anything, but Yun made it impossible.
I would sigh with relief when he had finished prattling on, but
my relief was shortlived, because Yun would then close his
eyes and start snoring. With the pillow placed under his neck,
his legs spread, belly exposed, eyes half closed and mouth wide
open, he snored loudly, sometimes making a kind of wheezing
sound as if he were suffocating. Otherwise, he would cough
and make a rasping sound as if he were plagued with whooping
cough.

It seemed to me that listening to his complaining was better
than putting up with his snoring and coughing. On one
occasion when Min quietly said, 'Not satisfied with tormenting
us while he is awake he must continue to make us miserable
even while he sleeps,' I could not help but laugh.

A patrolling guard shouted to Yun, 'Cover up your belly!
Prisoner No. 15, cover your belly, and your groin too. Why do
you always sleep during the day? You keep others awake at
night with your groaning on the privy.' Yun replied, 'Who's
sleeping?' and while rubbing his stomach and thighs he said,
'I have a fever so it is too hot to cover myself.' He then
covered himself with his uniform but as soon as the guard had
left he scowled and throwing open his uniform he said, 'Why
does he pick on me like that?' Min, pretending to be indignant,
said, 'Why don't you listen to the guard? It's no wonder you
shit day and night when you sprawl yourself out and expose
your belly. You even take someone's good words in a bad way.
Besides, what do you think you are doing, lying down exposing
your groin night and day?'

In comparison to the way Yun treated Min, he was extremely
kind to me. Knowing how difficult it was for me to move about
in my condition, he often did my work for me. Whenever I

would try to get up he would considerately say to me, 'If there is anything I can do for you please tell me. Why strain yourself?' When my private meals were delivered Yun would often insist that I exchange my millet and beans with his gruel. Purposely depriving me of my good quality food he would say, 'Well how can you possibly eat this millet and beans?' placing his gruel in front of me. I appreciated Yun's kind gesture but I did not agree with him. Firstly, because I did not want to break the regulations, and secondly, because the doctor had advised Yun to eat gruel.

After watching Yun and I argue about this for a while, Min, with a distasteful glance at his own bowl of gruel before him, would say, 'Hey you, why are you recommending that he eats stuff that smells like rat shit? Mr Jin, eat your food quickly! You know millet and beans are better than gruel.' When Min said something like this Yun would scowl and retort, 'You better stuff it down your throat or else you will die,' and then snatch my meal and begin eating it.

I had a guilty conscience about breaking the regulations, but at the same time I was sorry that I was rejecting his kind gesture. So I gulped down only one mouthful of gruel and returned to my bed with the excuse that I wasn't feeling well. Yun seemed to have eaten the rest of the gruel as well as all of my meal. Min only gulped down two mouthfuls of gruel before going to his bed to lie down. So Yun then ate his rice and soup while standing at the window to see whether or not the guard was coming.

Smacking his lips Min said, 'I would be fine if I could have just one glass of *paegal** and one bowl of beef tartar,' and then after a while he murmured again, 'If I could just have one sip of good *paegal* my stomach would be much better.' After eating the meal and the gruel and gulping down some water Yun said to Min, 'Ha! In your state you are talking about beef tartar again? Your guts can't even handle watery gruel and you want to eat beef tartar? You will drop dead immediately. The tip of your nose is all red. Worms are squirming inside you. In that state you will die.' If Yun's nose ran while he was cleaning the rice bowl he didn't wipe it with the back of his hand, but instead he would use three fingers to fling the mucus

---

*Paegal is a strong Chinese liquor.

anywhere and then continue cleaning the dish with the same hand.

Then when he starts to cough he doesn't turn his head away but leans closer to the dishes he is washing and coughs into them. He still insisted that he was the healthiest one among us. So he received the meals, washed the dishes and cleaned our eating place by himself. He seemed to think that he did these things exceptionally well. Also, when we heard the order after breakfast to get the privy ready, Yun would take it out and empty it. While doing so he grunted and complained that the privy was so heavy because Min shitted all night and all day. 'Well, listen here you,' said Min, 'I can't even eat one bowl of gruel a day, so how much shitting do you think I can do? It is you who eats two bowls of rice and two bowls of soup and gulps down two kettles of water. You are the one who shits on the privy all night and keeps us from sleeping.' What Min said seemed right to me.

On top of this, because Yun would finish off my rice and side dishes his indigestion was getting worse, and because over-ate he was always thirsty, therefore he went to the privy at least twenty times a day. 'The shit won't come out. If I poked it with a stick would it come out? If I want to shit, I have to eat,' he lamented several times during the day while looking at Min and me.

Yun's illness was getting worse and worse. I'm certain this was caused by his excessive eating. I was troubled because Yun's illness was getting worse for having eaten the food which was sent in to me, so I decided not to give the remainder to him. After eating what I could of my meal I placed what remained on the window sill before Yun's hand could reach for it. I earnestly said to Yun, 'If you eat this, something worse could happen to you. I counted the number of times you went to the privy with diarrhoea yesterday. Twenty-four times! Besides that, you also have a fever because you eat too much,' but he ignored me and snatched the bowl off the window sill and began eating.

I was forced to make a big decision. I decided that I would stop having some of my private meals sent in. So at dinner time I ate my special meals but at breakfast and lunch I ate the official meals. Because I was a patient in need of nutrition at any cost, this decision was painful for me. But to make my neighbour violate the regulations and make Yun's illness worse was something that I had to avoid.

Min knew why I had discontinued some of my special meals and on two occasions he chided Yun for his senselessness. Yun resented me because he thought I had discontinued the meals because I disliked him. Moreover, Yun's son sent three *won* in cash for Yun to buy milk, special meals and toilet paper. Since then Yun's attitude toward me became very cold. Before now, when I gave him advice, he listened to me quietly and would say, 'You are right, Mr Jin,' but now he would just glare angrily at me.

With the three *won* his son sent Yun bought a towel, soap and toilet paper. Once a week we were allowed to order things we needed. After we had ordered them it would take between one week and ten days for the things to arrive. Several times each day Yun would blame the prison authorities for the slowness of delivery. On the day the things arrived Yun would examine his towel, soap and toilet paper and complain, 'Damn Bastards! Is this supposed to be a towel? You couldn't even use this as a rag. And what about this soap? There is not even the slightest trace of fragrance in it at all.'

Min, unable to tolerate his whinging any longer, scolded, 'Well, did you ever use towels and soap like this in your house? You should have spent your three *won* on food. Why did you buy soap and a towel? What use do we have for soap in this place? Why do you buy towels when the prison already provides us with them? If you spend all of your money without thinking, you will spend the rest of your life being poor.' From that day Yun only used his soap to wash his face, but used mine whenever he washed his towel or his feet.

With his towel hanging on the towel line, his soap, tooth brush and tooth powder placed in the corner, toilet paper under his bedding, and rice and milk being sent in regularly, Yun had become very proud. He even bought himself a fan but complained several times a day that it was not a folding one like mine. Sitting cross-legged with his back straightened and his head held high he would beat the fan on the floor with a dignified air and continue talking about his favourite topics (the *yangban* and *sangnom**), complaining about his accomplices and the prison, or rebuking Min.

Yun seemed to think that his status was very high because he had two or three *won* worth of things sent in to him. Yun also thought that he no longer needed to be scared of the guards, he found great joy in telling the guard that he too was receiving special meals.

Once Yun started receiving private meals I once again ordered the special meals which I had previously discontinued. Because Yun and I were eating the best soft white rice, fish and stewed meat, I couldn't stand to watch Min eating the usual watery gruel. I could see him salivating as he looked from the bowl of gruel in front of him to the bowl of rice in front of me.

Soft, white rice ... only someone who has been imprisoned would know how precious a thing that rice was and how grateful I was for it. Its colour, its aroma, and the touch of it as you put it on your tongue with your chopsticks and taste it. You cannot help but feel that it is the most precious thing in heaven and on earth. Even the words 'white rice' sounded wonderful and divine. Whenever I felt grateful for having that marvellous rice I would put my hands together and look towards the heavens saying, 'May everybody have the pleasure of receiving such rice.'

On this occasion I forgot about the regulations and about Min's illness. I took one spoonful of rice and offering it to Min I said, 'Please chew it carefully.' Min took it and put it in his mouth. Did I imagine it or was Min's whole body actually shaking and his eyes really brimming with tears? Min ate every grain of rice without even leaving one speck and then he said, 'It was as delicious as sweet honey. How on earth could it be so delicious? I could die now and not have any regrets.' He seemed to want more, but instead of giving it to him I left some in the bowl. After eating all of his own portion Yun then stuffed down the remainder of my meal.

Yun's three *won* did not provide him with special meals for more than a week. The thirty *won* which Yun was confident about getting from his uncle, who was a mayor, did not arrive. Yun always said that if he died in prison his uncle would have

---

*Sangnom refers to lower class people.

435

to come and take care of his funeral which would cost him at least thirty *won*. Instead of spending thirty *won* after Yun's death, if he spent it when Yun was alive to let him eat what he wanted to, then he wouldn't die, and his uncle wouldn't have to come to the prison. Rather than spending thirty *won* for his funeral Yun thought it would be better if he used the money now. If he died and his uncle still didn't have money for the funeral then the prison authorities would take care of his cremation. For this reason, Yun said that it wasn't absurd to ask for thirty *won* and it would mean that he wouldn't have to cause any trouble for his relatives. Because Yun sent a letter to this effect he was quite sure he would receive the thirty *won*.

I sincerely hoped that Yun's mayor uncle would see Yun's logic and send the thirty *won*. I sincerely hoped for this because since Yun's private meals had stopped, Yun and Min would fight for my leftover food. Ever since I gave that spoonful of rice to Min, he asked for one spoonful of rice at every meal time. On hearing Min's request Yun would abuse Min and then tip over the rice bowl.

One day a big fight erupted between Min and Yun and they abused each other with words I couldn't possibly repeat. At that moment a prison guard was walking by. When he heard the commotion he chided Yun. When the prison guard had left Yun blamed Min for the scolding he had received and then abused him even more. As usual he said that Min would die in a few days, that his eighteen-year-old wife had already found a boyfriend, and that his son was worse than the dogs and the pigs.

I asked the prison guard to stop my private meals once again. But even by stopping my meals I was unable to improve the relationship between these two people. Since I stopped my private meals Min became as abusive as Yun. 'You petty thief. Did you forge the seals of the court in order to take someone's land in broad daylight? Did you not think that the dirty hand which had the seals carved would rot?' Min would attack. To which Yun would reply, 'Well what about the bastard who set fire to someone else's house? If you hate a man it would be better to just stab him with a knife. After burning the whole family to death, do you still expect to be pardoned of that crime? A person like you should kill your own children, so their evil genes cannot cause them to follow your example. If you let your children live they will burn down someone else's house.'

One day the prison guard opened our door and called, 'Number ninety-nine.' Because Yun was anxiously awaiting a letter from his uncle he seemed to mistake number ninety-nine for number fifteen. He stood up and said, 'Did a letter come for me?' 'Are you number ninety-nine?' the prison guard shouted. Min, the real number ninety-nine, was just staring through sunken eyes at the white clouds in the August sky as if no one would ever be calling him.

'Are you deaf, number ninety-nine?' the guard shouted. Yun then jabbed Min in the ribs and said, 'Are you dreaming with your eyes open? Can't you hear that God is calling you?' While still lying on the floor Min turned his head to look at the guard who was saying, 'Number ninety-nine, get all your things and come out.' As if seeing him for the first time, Min came to his senses and sat up. 'Are you releasing me?' His skeleton-like face shone with pleasure. 'If I say "come out", come out. If you come out you will know,' replied the guard. 'Has somebody from my house come to see me?' Min asked, his happy face somewhat disappearing. The tall nurse standing behind the guard said, 'You are changing rooms. Come out quickly with all your medicine bottles.' Min picked up his medicine bottles, towel and pillow and walked disappointedly towards the door.

At first Min did not understand the meaning behind the room change. But when the guard said, 'Leave your pillow. We are only going to the next room,' Min knew where he was being taken. He threw his pillow down dejectedly and his face which had momentarily shone with pleasure once again turned into that of a skeleton as he walked out the door. A moment later I could hear the door of the room next to this one being opened, closed, and then locked. I could imagine Min looking awkwardly at these people he was seeing for the first time as he groped around for a place to sleep.

As Yun placed Min's pillow under his own he started back-stabbing Min, 'Ah, what a relief to get rid of him! Shit, who can tolerate such a disgusting person? He didn't wash himself even once. Did you ever see him wash his face or brush his teeth in the morning? I don't know why he hated changing his clothes. Mr Jin, do you know why Min committed arson? Perhaps only because his family name is Min he served as a bailiff for a Lord Min in Seoul for several decades. As you have seen, Min is mean and stingy, so much so that the people under his control could not tolerate him. Who can have eighty sacks of rice without having exploited his subordinates? So, they went to Lord Min to complain about him. That is how he lost his position as bailiff last year, and a man called Kim became bailiff instead. Because Min thought that Kim had caused him to lose his position he met with Kim last Lunar New Year's Day and fought with him. Stupid Min was so upset that he went to Kim's house in the middle of the night and set it on fire. As it was the evening of the New Year's Day people who were still visiting with friends late into the night saw the fire and shouted, 'Fire!' They put out the fire, but had they not seen it Kim and his whole family would have died.'

While continuing with a speech about what an atrocious crime arson was, he saw the nurse come in and he stopped talking. After the nurse had left, Yun explained to me that the nurse himself had also been convicted of arson, 'Arsonists are wicked people. Setting fire to another person's house! These bastards and their offspring should be exterminated.' Then he let out a heavy sigh as if he were deeply grieved by the evil condition of mankind.

Whenever only Yun and I were in the cell there was no need to argue. At night, when the nurse who slept in our cell walked in, instead of calling Yun 'Mr Yun' the nurse would refer to him as 'Yun *sobang**'. Yun was annoyed at the nurse for doing this but knowing that there was no reason to hurt the nurse's feelings Yun avoided a direct confrontation with him. Only during the day when he and I were alone did he say, 'In Seoul language do you use the title *sobang* to refer to your senior? In our Cholla Province if you use the word *sobang* it means hired hand or servant.' He then watched me out of the corner of his eye. Because I knew it was a touchy issue for him I felt awkward about answering him, so I hesitated for a moment and then with a smile I said, 'Well maybe it would

---

*Sobang is a title usually used for a person of the lower class.

be more respectful if *nim** was added onto the end of *sobang*.'
'In our Cholla Province if you call someone *sobangnim* it
shows your respect. As you see, Mr Jin, that nurse always calls
me Yun *sobang*, so would that bastard also call his father and
uncle "so and so *sobang*"? If you compare our ages you'll see
that I'm old enough to be his father. He is so vicious.' Yun
said haughtily as if the person who ought to receive the reproof
was standing in front of him. That evening when the nurse
returned to our cell Yun was so angry that he didn't greet him
and gave him a dirty look instead.

Then one evening, when the nurse again called Yun 'Yun
sobang', a confrontation took place. 'What do you take me
for, calling me Yun *sobang*?' Yun protested. As if he were not
expecting this, the nurse stared at Yun with wide eyes and
laughed mockingly, 'What shall I have you called? Your profession is seal carving, so shall I call you "Mr Seal Carver"?
Your crime is fraud, so shall I call you "Mr Fraud"? You shit
all day and night, so maybe I'll call you "Mr Shitter". Or shall
I call you "sir"? Why do you behave so stupidly? You should
be thankful that I call you "Yun *sobang*". And how much
older than me are you?' And shaking his fist he continued, 'I
will call you "Yun the Bastard" if you continue to behave like
this.'

The bravery which Yun had at first had disappeared and he
became defeated. The prison nurse had proved to be quite an
adversary for Yun, and Yun realized that if he fought with the
nurse he might receive less medicine or none at all. So Yun
remained silent, but the prison nurse continued to abuse him
until he finally fell asleep.

The next morning, after our medical examinations were
finished, the tall nurse from our cell pointed Yun out with a
tilt of his chin to the short nurse from the next cell and said,
'That man got furious because I called him "Yun *sobang*." '
'Yun *sobang*, turn around. Then what shall we call you? Shall
I call you "Comrade Yun"? How about "*sondal†*"? Choose
which one you like the best,' the short nurse teased. Yun just
blinked his eyes and said nothing.

---

*Nim is a suffix which is added to a person's name as a way of showing
respect.
†*Sondal* is a social title endowed upon a person of lower middle class.

After this, Yun, who even before the Yun *sobang* incident had never been particularly liked by the nurses, came to be despised by them. If they were bored, the two of them would come into our cell so they could taunt Yun by calling him different names. After they had left Yun would turn to me and curse them, 'I hope those bastards rot to death in prison.' Everyday was miserable for Yun and yet another unpleasant incident awaited him. A man called Chong, who was also a defrauder and had shared Cell Number Eight in Block One with Yun, was transferred to our cell with a bad case of dysentery. I had heard Yun speak about Chong several times. Even though he had diarrhoea he still consumed too much milk and eggs, every time he spoke he told a lie and no matter how much advice he received he would always ignore it.

One day Yun and I went out to exercise. When we returned we saw a tall man with a pale face squatting over the privy in our cell and grinning at us. Yun was extremely displeased and after turning to me with his lips pursed he sat down in his place and started beating his fan. He said to the person sitting on the privy, 'So your diarrhoea hasn't stopped yet, eh? When we were in Cell Number Eight in Block One how many times did I tell you to be careful about what you eat? I left that cell three months ago and you still have diarrhoea.'

From what Yun was saying I took this man to be Mr Chong. Rising from the privy Chong did not seem to mind Yun's chiding. 'Mr Yun, we haven't seen each other in a long time,' he said with his whole face beaming as he seized Yun's hand, 'Are you still in the preliminary hearing stage?' Chong then turned and bowed deeply to me and said eloquently. 'My name is Chong Hong-dae. This must be a hard time for you.'

I judged from his accent that he was from Pyong-an Province but had learnt the standard Korean of Seoul. However, in the evening when the nurse who was from Inchon greeted him, he said his home town was Inchon. When he greeted another nurse who was from Cholwon in Kangwon Province he said his home town was Cholwon. Then, when he greeted a prisoner whose home town was Pyongyang he said he was from Pyongyang. At that time Yun turned to Chong, who was beside him and shaming him, and he said 'Why didn't you tell them your home town was Haeju as well? Anyway, how many home towns do you have?' It seemed that when Chong met people from a place that he had lived in for just one or two months he would say that that place was his home town.

Almost as soon as Chong had come into our cell he was saying, 'This cell is too dirty to live in,' he took off his coat and wiped the bowls with a rag and then looking under his bed he said, 'How can you live without cleaning this cell? It's too dirty to live in.' He then insisted on cleaning every inch of the cell. When Chong began to shake the mats, Yun grabbed his hand and said, 'Don't act as if you are the only person who cares about cleanliness. How can I stay sane with you behaving like this?' And that was the beginning of the continual bickering between Yun and Chong.

At supper time, Yun did not mind Chong getting up to receive the water pot, but when it was time to receive the rice and soup, Yun would not let Chong take it so he would get up quickly and push Chong aside to receive it from the window, causing Chong to take a step backward. 'Why do you push a man like that?' Chong asked, 'Wherever you go people dislike you. It doesn't matter to someone like me but you shouldn't behave like that with other people. They would slap you across the face.' He turned back to look at me and grinned, trying to show that he was a person who was not angered by such things, but he was unable to hide the anger in his eyes.

During supper the silence which reigned was merely the calm before the storm because after we had eaten and cleaned the dishes the bickering started up again. Chong criticized Yun for exposing his thighs, and for washing Chong's bowls in the water he had used for his bowls and mine, and for his coughing into the basin in which he had placed our bowls. Chong then washed our dishes again using new water from the pot and placed it carefully so that it wouldn't touch Yun's bowl. This made Yun mad, who screamed, 'You only think of yourself, why can't you think of others? If you use all the water in the pot what will we drink at night and what will we wash our faces with in the morning? A man should think of others, I tell you.' Chong ignored him and used almost all of the water in the pot to clean his rice bowl, soup bowl and chopsticks.

On one hand, Yun and Chong fought like this all of the time, but on the other, Chong was very polite to the nurse and I. It was almost like flattery. Also, there didn't seem to be anything he didn't know about agriculture, mining, Oriental

and Western medicine, and law. And because he spoke eloquently and told such good stories the nurses liked to be
around him.

Because Chong had the nurses' favour, instead of receiving
one bowl of gruel as he was supposed to, he received two
bowls of soup. In addition to this he received extra digestive
medicine or plasters and the like whenever he needed them.
When Chong asked a favour of them with that big grin on his
face, they could not refuse him.

Sometimes, when he had an extra portion of rice, he would
pick out all the good grains with his chopsticks and eat them,
and then after adding some salt to the remaining rice he would
wrap it up in a dish towel and begin kneading it to make rice
cake. After taking bites here and there from the parts which
looked delicious he wrapped up the remainder again to give
to the nurse when he returned to our cell at night. When he
gave the cake to the nurse he would always make a big show
of it.

Once, kneading some millet cake and munching it here and
there, Min looked at me and said, 'The nurses need to be fed
properly. They like it when I buy eggs and milk for them from
time to time. These young fellows are hungry day and night. I
have to bribe them like this so they will do me favours. If you
are on bad terms with the nurses they can bring you a lot of
harm. They report to the guards that the people I hate have
done bad things.'

'Hello, what is that? When Chong meets the nurse he
behaves as if he is meeting an uncle who he hasn't seen for
ten years, he flatters him as if he would chop off part of his
own flesh to feed him. As soon as the nurse leaves the cell
Chong again refers to him as "the bastard", it is not good to
be two-faced. I am not that kind of person. I only say things
which I could say to someone's face otherwise I say nothing
at all. It is not proper for a man to behave like you do. If you
are a real man you would not flatter a person to his face like
that. Also, if you want to make him a cake then make it with
fresh rice. You grind the grains with saliva-covered chopsticks
that have been in your mouth and when you are tired of eating
the cake you want to give it to someone else. It is not right to
do that. If you give it to someone else after doing that it is a
crime. Everything you do is just like that. If you really want

to give the nurse something you should buy him an egg with
your money. Ha! You stuff yourself with free rice and only
when you are tired of eating it you give it to someone else,
and then you boast about it. Why do you grin like that? If
you want to be a man then listen to the truth. When I see you
grinning like that it makes me feel so ill that I want to vomit.
Why do you smile like that? What is so good that you have
to smile about it?' Yun said harshly to Chong.

Chong was so taken aback that he was unable to speak
while Yun was making this speech. However, when Yun had
finished Chong managed to reply, 'You are saying exactly what
I want to say. Just cover your belly and sit down.'

That evening, after the nurse had finished his day's work,
he came rushing into the cell. 'Did you have a hard day? As
every day passes you are one day closer to your release. Console yourself with that thought. Three or four years will go
quickly. By the way, did I hear you arguing with Number 100
a while ago?' Chong said to him.

Number 100 is the number of the short nurse from the next
cell. I too had heard the sound of two people arguing earlier
on and calling each other bastards. The nurse changed into the
violet uniform worn by prisoners who were already serving
their sentence and sat down. Venting his anger he shouted as
if he wanted Number 100 in the next cell to hear, 'I wanted
to kill the bastard by tearing him to pieces but I stopped
myself. He makes me sick. What is he? He is only a prisoner
and a nurse like me. Ah, even though he only came here a
few days before me he still wants to give me orders. That
bastard is the son of a rat. Speaking of age, in age alone I
could be his older brother, in social status I am superior to
him. I was a clerk in a county hall, how can I have the same
status as a man who made his living with a yardstick? That
bastard! Today I stopped myself but if he does it again I'll
tear his mouth to pieces and break his legs. Even if a knife is
held to my throat I will say what I have to say and do what I
have to do.'

Chong, as if sympathizing with the nurse, clicked his tongue
and said, 'Calm down, Mr Shin, you must think of your respect-
ability. How could you fight with a baby? He is a bad person.
With eyes and a mouth like that he had such a venomous
appearance. His behaviour is so wicked. As soon as he is

released he will again set fire to someone's house and be sentenced all over again. How did he dare to do such a thing?'

At Chong's last words the nurse's eyes widened, and shaking his fist at Chong he said, 'Well, I too set fire to someone else's house. So what? Is cheating someone out of their money like you did all right? Are you saying that setting fire to someone else's house is worse? Your words are sickening. So I started a fire, what does it matter to you? Why do you grin like that? So what if Number 100 and I set fire to someone's house, what are you going to do about it?'

Chong's face reddened. While he was trying to flatter the nurse, he had made a mistake and as a result he was told off by the nurse. With a grin on his face once again, Chong tried to defend himself and said, 'No, did I say something wrong? You misunderstood.'

'Misunderstood? How could I have misunderstood,' the nurse, broke in. 'No, I didn't mean that. You lit the fire when you were drunk. You are not the kind of person who would do such a thing while you were sober. Mr Shin, because you are a tough person you may be able to kill someone if you were really angry, but because you are a manly man by nature you would not commit such a senseless crime as arson or fraud. I mean that your crime of arson is rather ambiguous. Number 100 committed arson while he was sober, that is the true crime of arson. That is what I mean ... now do you understand?' Seeing the nurse's anger subsiding he pulled out the rice cake which he had hidden in the rice bowl and gave it to the nurse saying, 'Please eat this.' 'I am so grateful to you for giving me this rice cake every day,' the nurse said as he took the cake.

After getting up for a minute to see whether the prison guard was coming or not, the nurse took a mouthful of the cake. At that moment Yun, who had been observing the interesting argument between Chong and the nurse with an occasional sideways glance, said, 'Alas, Mr Shin, don't eat that!' while waving his hand for emphasis. 'Why?' the nurse asked apprehensively as he went to his place and sat down with the rice cake still in his mouth. The prison nurse's place was next to mine, Chong's place was next to mine on the other side and Yun's was next to Chong's.

Yun sat cross-legged and beat his fan against his hand, 'If I tell you not to then don't. When have I lied to you? I am a man who tells the truth even if I am stabbed in the neck for it,' he said. Meanwhile, the nurse had swallowed the cake which he had in his mouth and while wrapping the remainder in toilet paper and placing it behind his back he said, 'Tell me, why shouldn't I eat it?' 'Why do you want to know the reason? I told you not to eat it because it would not be good for you,' Yun replied. 'I will not be satisfied until you tell me why. When I hear you insinuate like that it feels like fire burning inside me,' the nurse persisted.

At this moment Chong, with a most unpleasant look on his face, interrupted, 'Mr Shin, don't listen to these crazy words. Please eat it. By no means would I give Mr Shin something that he couldn't eat.' But the nurse was not convinced and demanded angrily, 'Yun *sobang*, please tell me quickly.' 'Why do you want to know? The only thing you need to know is that it is too unclean,' Yun replied. Chong was unable to tolerate this any longer and jerking himself to his feet he glared at Yun out of the corner of his eye and said indignantly. 'Why don't you just shut your trap?'

Yun ignored him and swaying his from side to side he said, 'I don't know but in your Pyong-an Province you may call a person's mouth a trap, however, in our Cholla Province a dignified person does not say such things. You were a man of religion for twenty or so years, how can you speak like that? After twenty years of religious life you give food which you have already licked to someone else, maybe if you had only ten years of religious life you would wipe your nose on it as well. Did I not tell you earlier that if you want to make someone something to eat you should do it with a spoon? But instead you stir it with chopsticks covered in spit, you eat all of the palatable yellow millet, you also pick out all of the beans and put them in your mouth and eat everything that is yellow, leaving only bluish, low quality millet and rotten beans. You wet the cloth with dirty water that you washed your chopsticks with, and then you make rice cake with the hand stained with your mucus. Even after that you take a bite here and there of the parts which look tasty, and then you offer the remainder to someone else. Having done that are you not afraid of heaven striking you with lightning? I'll tell you this much, if you give such things to other people it is inevitable that you will be punished. I am not the kind of person who likes to speak ill of others, Mr Shin, that is why I did not want to tell you this at first. I told you the truth. Although you come from Pyong-an province you ought to learn to say thank you, and if you can't do that then you should at least keep quiet. A person should not be as shameless as you.'

Chong's face became purplish and he made an expression as if he were incredulous and amused at the same time. 'I'm stunned! How can you make up these lies so shamelessly? I stir the rice with chopsticks so I can pick out the sand, rat shit, rotten beans and bad quality millet. Do I seem like a man who would tell Mr Shin to eat food which I had eaten or leftover? No, no, if you make up such lies your tongue will be cut out. Mr Shin, you must never listen to this crazy talk. Just eat it. If I am lying may I be struck down by lightning out of the clear blue sky,' said Chong and then he lay down as if had said all that he wanted to say.

My blood ran cold as I listened to Chong's untruthful oath. How could Chong swear so adamantly with two witnesses sitting right beside him? I felt deeply that the human heart and mind were unfathomably wicked. Could I ever interfere and bear witness? Chong assumed, and he was right, that because of my character he could feel safe in making up such a story. I did not have the courage to say, 'Mr Yun speaks the truth: Mr Chong is lying.' Chong clearly had the insight to know that I lacked such courage. As if Yun was also stunned by Chong's blatant lies, saying nothing, he sat down and looked the other way. As I lay motionlessly the prison nurse turned to look at me as if he expected that he would be able to find out the facts of the incident from me, but he seemed to find it difficult to ask me directly. Seeing that I was not going to say anything, the prison nurse picked up the cake and pushed it to the floor above Chong's head and smacking his lips he said to Chong, 'Here you are, you eat it! I don't want to make the two of you fight any more.' I admired the prison nurse's good judgement and in my mind I thought, 'Well done!'

However, this incident caused Chong to hold a deep grudge against Yun and little by little Chong would put him to shame. If Yun coughed Chong would tell him to turn his head away, cover his mouth and cough quietly. He would then say that Yun had such a nasty cough because he had such a wicked mind. Also, if Yun snored whilst taking a nap, Chong sometimes elbowed Yun in his side and said that because Yun had such a wicked mind he even bothered others while he was sleeping. And at other times he would tell Yun to stop tapping his fan and to wipe the dirty look off his face.

Whenever Chong said these things Yun would retort but he was never a match for Chong. Yun became so impatient with Chong's eloquent speeches that he lost almost every argument. Chong didn't lose to Yun in snoring either. Chong, with his protruding teeth and twisted lips, was an expert at snoring, but he declared that he didn't snore. It appeared that Yun, who by his nature slept a lot, didn't know that Chong snored. The prison nurse was the kind of person who would fall asleep the moment his head touched the wooden pillow. So, when Chong and Yun snored, I was the only one who suffered and was unable to sleep.

Yun was a soprano snorer, Chong was a baritone snorer, and I was the person who couldn't do anything but lie down with my eyes open, staring at the stars which shone into our cell. In addition to all of this, Chong hated Yun's bad breath so he always slept with his face turned towards me. Becaue I was ill I could only lie on my back to sleep, and I had to endure Chong's bad breath when he snored into my left ear. Food was rotting inside Chong's bloated stomach and I could not tolerate the disgusting smell of his breath ... hot, foul breath which he blew onto my left cheek all night long.

I wished to God that Chong would lie on his back but didn't dare to say it. I tried to imagine that it was a fragrant odour. If this was the breath of a young and beautiful woman would I consider it to be offensive? Isn't there shit and rotten food in a beautiful young woman's belly? Aren't we all equal? I started to make myself think like this so I could forget about the snoring and bad breath but I was unable to accomplish that in just one night. I also thought repeatedly about asking Chong to turn onto his back.

There were many nights when I would stay awake even until I heard the tapping of the wooden block from the Buddhist temple behind the prison. The block was tapped at half past three in the morning. Its 'tap, tap, tap' sound has a strong cleansing effect on a person's mind. Whenever I hear the tapping of the wooden block it reminds me of the Buddhist monk saying, 'May this sound spread throughout the world of Buddhists!' or 'May all mankind achieve enlightenment soon!'

If life is a 'sea of suffering' or a 'burning house', as the Buddhists say, then prison would have to be the most painful place of all. If you are ill in prison and spend endless amounts of time in the infirmary the suffering is three times worse. When I see suffering people in such agony I cannot help thinking that the concept of retribution for the deeds of a former life is so difficult to understand.

Just when I was about to go to sleep after hearing the early morning tapping of the block, Yun and Chong started taking turns at climbing onto the privy. Chong, who only thinks of his own welfare and never the feelings of others, was feeling happy about having slept well and so he started reading a book in a loud voice, washed his face with the water from the pot before the others could get up and use it, and then he massaged himself with a wet towel. He then started wiping the floors saying that it was good for exercise. I could not go back to sleep while he was making such a racket. Chong was spotted by the guard and told off for doing such things before it was time to get up but he still continued.

The day after the rice cake incident the short nurse came to our cell and started picking at the faults of the tall nurse without looking at any person in particular. He was talking about the fight he'd had yesterday. 'What did Long Legs say yesterday? Was he very angry? He's a crazy bastard. What will he gain if he picks a fight with me? If he wants to get more rice and coupons he won't get anything at all if he loses favour with me. While the prison guard and prison warden would believe my words, would they believe his? Without knowing this he picks a fight with me on any occasion. What a cheeky bastard! Even if he makes a scene I won't even blink. I just leave him alone. From time to time I try to irritate him and make him heated, and then I just watch him. Then, like a bull who has a stick poked up his arse-hole, he starts to roar. He roars until his voice becomes hoarse and then he calms down. Then I make him irritated again with words he does not want to hear. Again he goes crazy and shouts at the top of his voice. Then I leave him alone again. What can he do to me? Would he dare hit me? If he is caught by the prison warden he will be dealt with,' he then laughed as if this thought gave him

great pleasure. Perhaps the tall nurse had gone to the adminis-
tration block on an errand because he was not in the cell.

'That Number 9 is stupid. How could he pick a fight with
you? You are the head nurse, he should obey you,' said Chong.
'He's as stubborn as an ox. I tried to reason with him, but
does he understand? Day and night he just tells us that he was
a town clerk. You must get very annoyed with him, Number
100,' said Yun. The short nurse said, 'Does he know anything?
He knows nothing at all. Besides, he's slow, lazy and stupid.'
'You are right, I know that. You do all the work, what does
he ever do? Besides, he boasts too much,' Yun said. Chong
said, 'You should report him to the prison guard and have him
dismissed. I have had many people working under me but if
we could not get along, how could I have them working for
me? If I were you I would have him dismissed within three
days.' 'Even so, I would feel sorry for him and couldn't do it.
So I try to be as patient as I can. However, if he acts stupidly
I will not leave him alone,' said the short nurse.

At this moment the tall nurse came in with medicine bottles
and packets. The short nurse said, 'Today you will be changing
cells.' Because a typhoid patient was coming into our cell we
had to transfer into the next cell. The short nurse told us to
get ready quickly and then he rushed off as if he had, urgent
work to attend to.

The tall nurse called Yun 'Squire Yun', and Chong 'Scholar
Chong', in jest as he handed the bottles of liquid medicine and
packets of powdered medicine through the iron bars. Yun
received the medicine and, as usual, he said, 'No matter how
much of this medicine I take I won't get any better. If I could
have some good Oriental medicine my fever would go down,
my cough would stop, and the swelling would also go down,'
and sat down.

Chong got up after Yun, and pressing against the iron bars
he took the liquid and powdered medicine, as he was about
to go back to his place the tall nurse handed him one more
medicine packet. 'I brought it for you telling them that I would
eat it. Don't waste it. You think that if you take a lot you will
be okay, so you eat in one day what other people eat in three
days. Nobody can get you that amount of medicine,' said the
nurse. 'That is why I'm so very grateful. Will you give me
some alcohol-soaked absorbent cotton? Please give me more

449

this time. Can't you give me some alcohol? Please give me just one bottle of alcohol. I'll not forget my debt of gratitude to you when we get out into the world,' said Chong. 'Do you ask such things so that I will be severely punished?' asked the nurse.

Chong changed the subject and said, 'Even when I see Number 100 walking towards me he makes my skin creep. What kind of a person is he to give a hard time to a person who could almost be his older brother in age? If I were you I would do something about it.'

'Ah, if I used my fists that bastard son of a rat would be crushed,' the nurse said in rage. Yun, who saw that Chong was trying to flatter the prison nurse, said, 'Number 9, you are extremely patient. When I hear this abuse I grit my teeth in rage but you are extremely patient,' and then he sighed as if he were struck with admiration.

After a while the tall nurse brought in a handful of sanitary cotton saying, 'Divide it into three and then use it.' Chong rose to his feet quickly. Saying thank you in Japanese, he took the alcohol-soaked absorbent cotton from the nurse. Then he put it under his nose and after smelling it for a long time he set aside the two thirds of absorbent cotton which appeared to have been soaked in the most alcohol. I thought he was going to divide the remaining third into two and give it to Yun and I, but instead he divided it into three parts and gave one part to Yun. He added one part to a big lump of cotton he had saved and wrapped it up tightly in oiled paper and then he cleaned his face, head, hands and the soles of his feet with the remaining part, then threw it away. He had so much alcohol-soaked cotton wrapped up in oiled paper that he would wash his face, hands, and neck again many times in a day: he said it would make his skin nice and soft.

I thought that we would transfer after dinner but when it was almost evening, a short, plump prison guard came and opened wide the prison door and shouted, 'Transfer! Transfer!' The short nurse following him translated the order into Korean. Chong had intended to wrap up his pillow and aluminium rice bowl, but the prison guard shouted, 'No, you can't!' so Chong regrettably put them down. He barely managed to hide the alcohol-soaked cotton while the prison guard was not looking. We then walked out of the cell and into the next cell in single file wearing bamboo head baskets. The cell was locked once again.

Sitting on the most heated part of the floor, Min saw us come in and he smiled like a child. We had been separated for twenty days. In that period Min had become very thin and gaunt. It seemed that there were only sunken eyes on his face, they were eyes which did not seem to be able to move freely. His arms and hands hung limply under his pouch, his swollen veins stuck out, and his ankles were thicker than his calves. I wondered how he could be alive when he looked like a skeleton. In a loud voice I asked Min, 'What are you eating these days?' The reason I spoke loudly was because I thought Min would not be able to hear me if I spoke in a moderate tone.

While pointing to the milk bottle which was two thirds full. Min said, 'My brother-in-law in Seoul sent me five *won* so I can buy one bottle of milk every day but I cannot drink more than one mouthful. It tastes good but I can't swallow it. My brother-in-law is rich. With seven hundred sacks of rice grain he is well off. If I could get out of here I would go to my brother-in-law's house, he has a nice big guest room. Because his wife is my sister, he is good to me. If I could eat beef tartar and drink a glass of warm *paegal* it would lift my spirits.' It seemed that Min was just saying this so that he could boast about having a rich brother-in-law.

Yun, whose place was right beside Min's, tapped his fan and spoke garrulously, 'Your brother-in-law seems to be quite rich. Haven't you heard from your own home yet? Do as I told you, request an interview with the prison warden and make arrangements to sell the possessions in your house, so that you can use the money to buy whatever you want to eat: then hire a lawyer and apply for bail. When they see that you've become a living corpse they won't refuse bail. Now your upper cheeks have also turned red. It shows that you will not live longer than one month. How could you leave all of your money to an eighteen-year-old wife who pretends she doesn't know that her husband is dying? And what about your son? If I were you I would twist their necks and pull their heads off. Look at Min. His breath is shallow and hoarse. He's nearly dead. He's nearly dead!'

To which Min replied, 'It would be natural to ask me how I am if you hadn't seen me for a long time. Why is it that the

451

first thing you do is abuse me? I haven't had to listen to your abuse for a number of days and I was starting to feel a little more comfortable, why did you have to come back? Your hands and feet are swollen too, you won't live for even a few more days. Please stop this abuse,' and then he lay down with a sigh.

Besides Min, there was also a tall, stout young man in the cell named Kang, his belly was bandaged and he was sitting with his back against the wall. I heard recently that he worked for a local branch of a newspaper, he had been prosecuted for blackmailing a rich man who had indecent relations with his widowed daughter-in-law demanding sixteen hundred *won*. Kang was extremely hot-tempered and would not tolerate it when people offended him. He often gave Yun and Chong a hard time. If Yun picked on Min then Kang would scold Yun, and if Chong picked on Yun then he would also scold Chong. Yun and Chong resented Kang and gritted their teeth, while Kang held the two of them in contempt. Because the order we lay in was Yun, then Chong, then Kang, then me, there were many confrontations between Chong and Kang.

Kang, having graduated from technical school, was a knowledgeable person, and whenever Chong mercilessly attacked him with big words he pretended he knew the meaning of, Kang would say, 'You pick one word from here and one from there, and you pretend you know everything. You acquired the habit of cheating ignorant peasants in the countryside and you think you can do it here. Your lies are written all over your disgusting grinning face. You are now forty-five years old. Before you die, why don't you do something to prove you are a man? How dare you say you know about medicine and try to prescribe it for other people? You might try all other deceptions but don't ever try to practise medicine, which you know nothing about. You say you know about acupuncture, Chinese medicine, and Western medicine. Is there any person who can know that much about medicine? Your stomach must be in a mess because you have eaten so much food which you cheated from other people. Because you are so greedy, at one meal you eat two or three people's portions, and then you take medicine and water for digestion. You fart and belch and you are always vomiting, and the smell from all of this is killing everyone around you. If you eat like that, isn't it natural that your stomach will be bloated? Anything you say is nothing but lies. Why do you grin like that? Who said you are handsome? Do you think that if you keep rubbing your face with alcohol-soaked cotton that you will become handsome? The cotton is from a public institution. Did you ever use your money to buy a bottle of alcohol when you were at home? Already it seems impossible that you will ever behave like a real man before you die, so just shut your mouth!' Thus he rebuked Chong who was almost twenty years older than him.

One lunch time a bowl of dried anchovies was sent in. This bowl of anchovies was to be shared equally amongst everyone in the cell. They may have been called anchovies, but there were no whole pieces; the bowl was full of heads and tails, all broken to pieces, and, on top of that, straw, sticks and what not were mixed in. Still, in prison it was a delicacy which we only received once every two weeks. On the day the dish was sent in we were all as happy as if it were a holiday or somebody's birthday. Because Chong continued to be in charge of receiving the meals, he took the bowl of anchovies, and poking around at the anchovies he picked out the best ones and put them on his dish: he then put the rest onto our dishes. It seemed to me that if Chong didn't have half the bowl, he definitely had more than one third, but in Chong's eyes he had equally divided it into fifths.

Expecting lightning to come from Kang's mouth, I tried to neutralize the situation and said to Chong, 'Hey, it seems that the anchovies haven't been divided equally among us. Please try to dish them out again.' So Chong picked out the worst anchovies from his portion and then put them onto the other dishes; he then started eating his anchovies as if they were unbelievably tasty, picking out the best ones and eating them first.

Min, as if he were not interested in anything at all, scooped up one spoonful of gruel, ate it slowly, and then repeated the same action again, showing no interest at all in the anchovies. Kang did not touch the anchovies either, he ate his bowl of millet, and poured his portion of anchovies into Chong's dish. I too did not touch the anchovies.

Chong raised his head suddenly and, looking at Kang, said, 'Why don't you like anchovies?'

'I just don't like them. Keep them for your supper as well,'

Kang said and then without another word he had a mouthful
of water and went to his place to lie down. I do not know
what Kang was thinking but I was amused by this situation
and at the same time it aroused my curiosity. Chong also
seemed to be afraid of what Kang was thinking but he still ate
everybody's share of anchovies, almost half of which was salt,
and then he left some under the radiator for his dinner.

Chong seemed very satisfied with his meal, and smiling to
his heart's content he went to his place and lay down: a little
while later he was snoring. I think the overeating must have
made him sleepy. One dried, salty anchovy would give him
trouble even if he had a strong stomach. Kang also seemed to
know this and he was smiling. He unbandaged his stomach
and fanned the place where he'd had his operation. Then
getting up suddenly he walked over to the water kettle, shook
it and lifted up the lid to look inside. He offered a cup of
water to Yun and me, and then drank two cups of water
himself. With the remaining water he washed the towel which
he had used to wipe his stomach; then he dropped the empty
kettle to the floor and returned to his place.

Yun, watching what Kang was doing, said, 'Well done, Mr
Kang! When he wakes up he will find a fire burning in his
throat.' Saying this he opened the lid to check that not a single
drop of water was left and then returned to his place.

Chong snored as if he were suffocating; about an hour later,
he opened his eyes, sat up, and then ran to the kettle. Seeing
that there was no water in the kettle, he burst into anger,
threw the kettle to the floor and glared at Yun. Then, trying
to make trouble, he said, 'So, you drank all the water without
leaving a drop for me? I checked that there was water before
I went to sleep. You never think of other people, you always
just look after your own interests, that's why you shit day and
night.'

'Isn't that exactly what I should say to you? You are your
own worst enemy,' Yun said dignifiedly.

'I drank all of the water,' Kang declared. 'You ate all of the
anchovies so we had to fill our stomachs with water. Would
you only be satisfied if you could eat all of the anchovies and
drink all of the water by yourself?' Chong didn't say anything,
but it looked like he was about to die of thirst. He was restless,
he lay down and sat up again, he couldn't decide what to do.

He often got up and looked through the iron bars into the corridor so he could ask a prison nurse for some water but a nurse was nowhere to be seen. The prison guard and warden walked past twice, but Chong could not bring himself to ask either of them for water.

It seemed quite a long time before the short nurse finally came by. Chong rushed to the window with the kettle and said, his whole face smiling with adulation, 'Number 100, please give me some water. As I can't eat anything, I am dying of hunger, and I am so thirsty. We haven't got even one drop of water.'

'Where do you think you are? After having been in this prison for one year, don't you know the rules yet? It is not dinner time and that is the only time when you are allowed to get water,' said Number 100 smiling. Chong held the kettle high and shook it, 'That is why I asked you. Haven't you heard the proverb which says that he who gives a cup of water to a thirsty man is good and virtuous? Please give me just one cup. Is it impossible for you to quickly scoop some water from the tank?'

'Perhaps you deserve to be hungry and thirsty. If you were arrested for fraud, don't you think you deserve to suffer like this?' the nurse said. At that moment I think the nurse saw the prison guard approaching, for he left quickly. Chong dejectedly placed the kettle on the floor and sat down in his place.

The tall prison nurse, who was taking care of the typhoid patient in the next cell, was not allowed to walk past a certain point after curfew, so he stretched his neck to try and look into our cell. 'Mr Chong, shall I give you some water? Shall I give you some cold water with ice?' he asked and then showed Chong a handful of ice pieces which he was putting into a bag used to put on the head of a patient with a fever. Chong stood up quickly and went to stand under the iron grate, 'Number 9, give me a piece of that, ' he asked, holding out his hand.

'Why are you doing that? Aren't you afraid of getting typhoid? My hands are covered in typhoid germs,' said the nurse. 'Ahhh, disinfect your hands and then give me a piece of ice. I am very thirsty. Otherwise, put one scoop of water into this kettle. My chest is burning up,' Chong implored. The nurse replied, 'I heard just before that you ate all of the anchovies. You should just digest them. If you drink water you will just piss them out. You must digest them, it will make

455

your face smooth and glowing.' He then threw a piece of ice as small as his little finger. The ice hit the iron bar and dropped into the corridor, the nurse didn't seem to care and he returned to his cell with the ice bag.

Hanging his head, Chong returned to his place and sat down. 'Eat salt, you must eat salt if you have indigestion,' was Kang's prescription. For a brief moment Chong looked resentfully at Kang and tutted. 'Isn't there some water in the spittoon? You used it three times as much as we did when you brushed your teeth. There must be some water in the spittoon. You might just have to drink that,' Yun said

'You just ate too many salty things. It's not good for your insides for you to eat like that, you can't possibly stay in good health.' Saying this, Min gave Chong the bottle of milk which was on the floor above his head. 'Drink this,' he said.

'Thank you sir. May you get well and be acquitted as soon as possible,' said Chong; he then put his two hands together, bowed to Min, and drank the milk in one gulp. Chong made a speech, 'People should not behave like that. You should learn to look after other people. If you make people suffer, and then laugh, you will receive punishment from heaven. God sees everything.' After this, he seemed to give up the idea of trying to get water, and lay down on the floor.

'You are not human. You are thirsty because you ate too much. What will happen to you, now that you have drunk the milk as well? Ha! There will be a riot in your stomach. That's what happens to you when you are greedy. If you only eat as much as you are able to digest you won't have stomach trouble. You just eat and eat, if you go on like that your stomach will be completely ruined and you won't even be able to eat gruel. You know so damned much and yet you don't even know how to look after yourself. And you say to others that they will receive God's wrath. I will see you receive God's punishment at midnight tonight,' Kang said mockingly.

While this was going on it became dinner time again. Chong received private meals for dinner. Because of his stomach trouble he really should have fasted, but when his meal was brought in and he saw white rice, pancake, dried mackerel, and oxtail soup, he couldn't refuse it. 'You shouldn't eat too much for dinner,' I cautioned.

'What did I eat for lunch?' Chong replied crossly, 'Why are you all treating me like an irresponsible child?'

Chong finished all of his meal which had been sent in, as well as the left over anchovies, after which he gulped down three cups of water. 'Bed time!' came the order from outside, so all of us went to our places, lay down, and waited for sleep to come. Chong seemed to be having severe stomach trouble. He tried to get up twice to put some salt in his mouth and drink some water to relieve the indigestion. He also took three packets of digestion pills from my medicine envelope.

I was unable to sleep because I could hear the young typhoid patient groaning, and in his delirium he was babbling. He shouted that he wanted to go home; he cried loudly, saying, 'Sister, sister.' In a whisper the nurse next to me explained to me about the typhoid patient, 'That man is a college graduate. He is twenty-six years old. He opened a shop in Hwang-gum Street, but he was losing money. In order to get the fire insurance money he set fire to the shop. At the preliminary hearing the prosecutor recommended that he be sentenced to ten years' imprisonment. Upon hearing this recommendation he fainted in the dock. The doctor said he won't live much longer. He was orphaned, and he was brought up by his older brother's wife. That is why he calls for his sister. The man, is all right, but I don't understand why he would think of starting a fire as I had.' Meanwhile, the typhoid patient still called for his sister.

Chong vomited three times during the night. The cell was full of a sour fish smell from the anchovy vomit. Yun and Kang complained to Chong that they could not bear to live in such a filthy room. It seemed that Chong did not even have the energy to reply; as soon as he finished vomiting he returned to his place unsteadily, as if he were seasick, and slumped down. With this as a beginning, Chong vomited every two or three days. still, at each meal Chong ate twice as much as anyone else.

Whilst vomiting, Chong was seen by the prison guard. Chong explained to the guard that he hadn't eaten anything, and that he was vomiting because there was too much water gathered inside his stomach. Then turning towards us, he blabbered this excuse, 'Well, isn't it strange? I haven't eaten anything, and yet I have a belly full of water. If they would just release me for two weeks I could take medicine and cure this problem,' but nobody believed it.

It was obvious that Min was getting worse by the minute. Recently, he had not uttered a single word even when Yun picked on him. He fell twice when he was getting off the privy, his eyes could not move, and he lacked the energy even to close his mouth. We often raised our heads to look at him in the middle of the night in order to see if he was still breathing. Sometimes he would say that he wanted to eat white rice, but when he took one mouthful he would spit it out. 'I can't even taste this rice. I wish I could have one sip of *paegal*,' he said looking pathetic.

Min had a feeble existence. In a day he ate only one or two spoons of millet and drank two mouthfuls of water. One day the chief of the nurses came and examined him; he cleaned out the pus from Min's peritoneum and left. About two or three days later Min was released on bail. He was pleased to be going to his house, and while grinning from ear to ear he picked up his bundle of things and staggered out.

'Hmm! He will die as soon as he goes out,' Yun sneered. After a while the nurse helped Min to leave by holding his arm, and then returned. 'Min walks quite well. He was almost jumping up and down,' the nurse said smiling. 'If I was leaving on bail I would also get better,' said Chong wistfully, with a grin on his swollen face. 'What did I say? He can't survive very long with a red nose like that. And can he recover with such a bad temper? He didn't follow the doctor's advice. He didn't take the medicine prescribed to him. He is so obstinate,' said Yun. Chong rebuked Yun, 'Hmm, a dog smeared with shit is criticizing a dog covered in dirt. Who are you to criticize? You shit day and night, and eat all the time.'

'Ha ha ha ha, You talk too much with your precious mouth. You say exactly what other people should say to you, ha ha ha!' Kang said whilst laughing hysterically.

On the night Min left on bail I was sleeping, but I woke up when I heard some kind of sound. I realized that the typhoid patient in the next cell was dying. The choking and groaning sounds rang through the silent dawn air. It seemed that the prison nurse in the same cell was fast asleep because the only sound I could hear was the patient's breathing; there wasn't the slightest indication that anyone else was around. I woke up the nurse who was sleeping next to me and told him the situation. The nurse called the prison guard, who rang the alarm bell. The guard who was second in charge came, and, a little while later, the doctor arrived. No more than half an hour after the doctor gave him an injection, the typhoid patient drew his last breath.

The next morning we saw the young man's dead body being carried from the cell. It was a miserable sight. We could not see his face because it was bandaged; the only thing we could see was his long black hair which stuck out. He seemed to have cherished his hair; several months had passed since he came into the prison and he still hadn't cut his hair. If he were not in prison, the usual thing for a bachelor such as he to do would be to put fragrant oil in his hair, neatly part it, and have a cleanly shaven and powdered face. He had started a business in order to lead an enjoyable life, but he failed. When he failed, his love of money led him to think about setting fire to his house in order to take the insurance money. The natural result of the vice-like hold that greed had on him was that one day he decided to set fire to his house. After that, he was taken to the police detention cell and then to the prison, and there he ended his unbelievably terrible life.

I felt sorry about the death of this poor young soul. After watching his corpse being taken out the back door I put my hands together and bowed my head. I saw the sister-in-law who he had called in his delirium, with her husband, following the corpse in silence and wiping the tears from their eyes. The tall nurse who had taken care of the typhoid patient said that for two or three days before he died he would pray to Jesus Christ, and when he was sleeping he would call out, 'God! God!' and murmur, 'Jesus Christ who died on the cross for our sins, please forgive this criminal.'

The nurse said the young man was brought up in a Christian family and had graduated from middle school, technical school, and Bible college. I think that this young man did not entirely believe Jesus when he said that our main purpose in life should not be the acquiring of wealth, so he was tempted by the thought that money was the key to happiness and prosperity. He seemed to have come to his senses when he was nearly dead, and realized that Jesus Christ was right.

That day was very hot, the sun was shining brightly as we

took the rush mat, mattress, blanket and pillow, which had belonged to the man who had died, into the yard and hung them out. His pillow must have been damp because he was sweating so much just before he died. The tall nurse was wearing a gauze mask which covered his mouth, and was cleaning and disinfecting the dead man's cell. After finishing he scrubbed his hands with Cresol. 'It's terrible, my exertion and lack of sleep for the last fortnight achieved nothing. It's funny how I didn't see my mother when she died but I have seen an exorbitant amount of other people die,' he said with a laugh.

It had been a few days since the dead man was taken away, and Yun, Chong and I felt depressed. Yun's cough got worse, and in the afternoon his temperature went up to thirty-eight point seven degrees centigrade. Whenever he coughed he would spit his phlegm into the toilet paper and throw it away anywhere. When his fever went up he would become unconscious, and when he woke up from his slumber he gulped down some cold water. Even though Chong and I told him not to throw his phlegm wrappings wherever he pleased and use the spittoon instead, he never listened. He would take the toilet paper from under my mattress without asking; one day he took as many as forty or fifty pieces, spat into them, and threw them away.

Whenever Yun coughed, Chong, who was sitting beside him, shouted at him to turn his head the other way and cough. Yun, being such a malicious person, would then turn towards Chong and cough into his face. When the coughing subsided, Yun came back at Chong saying, 'Do you think I have tuberculosis? Why? My cough isn't a tuberculosis cough. My cough is clean. Stop twisting the truth.'

Eventually Chong saw the prison nurse and insisted to him that Yun's cough was serious and that he spat the phlegm everywhere. Chong urged the nurse to test his phlegm for germs. 'Test it, test it. Do you think I have tuberculosis? Although I look like this I have an iron constitution. It is just an ordinary cough, not a tuberculosis cough,' said Yun while looking at Chong out of the corner of his eye. Yun and Chong fought for the whole day because of this problem.

The next morning, during examination time, Chong went to the place where the doctor and prison nurse were, stood in front of them, and drew the doctor's attention to the fact that

Yun's cough was serious and he was coughing up a lot of phlegm which he spat everywhere. As soon as Yun came into the cell he said to Chong, 'Why do you have such a grudge against me? Every meal time you cheat me out of my rice, you use three pillows, and you vomit every night. If I told the prison guard these things you would pay dearly for it. You have such a stupid way of thinking; that makes you ill in spite of all the food you eat. Food is supposed to be digested and come out through your arse, but instead it rots inside you and comes out of your mouth. Look at your face. It is yellow and shows that you are about to die. Shall we bet on who will be carried out as a corpse first?' he challenged.

Three days later we found out the result of the test. The short nurse told us that '+ + +' was written on the paper. Yun looked blankly at the prison nurse and me, 'What do those tens mean?'* he asked anxiously. Chong interrupted, 'It means that tuberculosis germs are squirming inside you.'

'I didn't ask you,' Yun snubbed him and turned to the nurse again, 'There aren't any germs in my phlegm are there? What do those three tens mean?' The prison nurse smiled and said, 'It's all right. The doctor knows what is in your phlegm, I don't,' and left.

Chong moved his mattress five inches away from Yun's mattress and five inches closer to mine saying, 'Lay down closer to that wall. When you cough, cough towards the wall, and spit your phlegm into the spittoon. You don't listen to what others say. You must know there are tuberculosis germs in your phlegm, there are heaps of them. If there is only one + it means that you have a few tuberculosis germs, if there are two +'s, you have a lot, if there are three +'s, you have a huge amount of them. Now do you understand. So, try and think a bit about others and don't spit your phlegm just anywhere.' Listening to these words Yun's face turned pale, turning to me he asked in a trembling voice. 'Mr Jin, is that true?' All I said in reply was, 'Tomorrow the doctor will tell you.' I had nothing else to say.

When it was almost evening the short nurse came and said, 'Yun *sobang*, transfer! It will be good. You will have a big room all to yourself and you won't have to fight with Chong

*The Chinese character for 'ten' resembles the positive sign (+)

461

sobang. Pack your things quickly.' Hearing this, Yun sat up abruptly and stared at the nurse, 'Are you my worst enemy? You had my phlegm tested and now you want to move me to a cell where a man died? Are you saying that I should die? I won't go to that cell. What kind of bastard would come and take me to that cell? I will fight him to the death. You leave this dirty patient who shits through his mouth alone and instead you want to take a healthy man like me to a cell where a man died? Number 100, do you think you will go unpunished if you send me to a cell where a person died?' he shouted at the top of his voice.

'Why do you talk to me like that? How can I transfer you to another cell? If you have a contagious disease you should want to go to a place where nobody is, without having to be ordered to do so. Do you want others to be contaminated? You shouldn't think like that. If you are going to die soon you should behave well. Your behaviour is ill-mannered and annoying,' thus saying, the prison nurse left the cell huffing in contempt.

After the nurse left, Yun complained to Chong, saying that it was Chong who suggested that his phlegm be tested. Yun swore that he would see Chong carried out as a corpse first, but if by some misfortune he himself died first, he would haunt Chong after his death.

Chong said nothing for a while, but then a wide grin came to his face and he said, 'Ha! I wouldn't say that if I were you. Because you have such a bad and twisted mind you caught a bad disease. You bullied old Min so much and now his ghost has come back to get his revenge on you Ha! Why should I die? I will leave this prison alive and in good health. My case is coming to trial soon and when it does I will be found innocent. So don't you dare talk to me like that.' Having said this he lay down and started reading his Sutra book.

After meeting the prison chaplain, Chong got the Sutra from him and began reading it two weeks ago. He did not seem to have enough knowledge of Chinese to be able to read the Sutra written in the original Chinese characters, so he tried to figure out the meaning in his own way. Whenever he thought he'd worked out the correct meaning he would try to explain it to us. At other times he would recite the Sutra like a school boy, in a voice so loud that those in nearby cells could hear.

Regardless of whether it was after bed time or before wake-up time, and whether there were people sleeping or not, he would read the Sutra if he felt like it.

Once, when a nurse who was passing told him not to make such a big noise, Chong declared triumphantly. 'I'm reading the Sutra.' Listening to his occasional explanations it seemed to me that Chong had a rough idea about what the Sutra was saying, but he didn't show any indication that he was doing what the Sutra said to do. After two weeks of reading the Sutra he showed no signs of looking after the welfare of others.

On one occasion Yun said, 'Ha! Still you want to go to a better place when you die. Do you think you will get there just by reading the Sutra? You need to change your behaviour first.' While Yun was mocking Chong, Kang said, 'Leave him alone. For the first time in his life he is doing something good. Even if he just reads it, with the help of Buddha he may become a better person in his next life or the one after.'

'Yeah, leave me alone. It is said that if you abuse a person who reads the Sutra you will go straight to hell,' thus boasting Chong continued reading the Sutra in a loud voice. Worried that he would be sent to the cell where the young man had died, Yun became even more angry with Chong for reading the Sutra aloud, 'I hate listening to you. You have to think of other people. Please don't make so much noise.' Chong pretended not to hear him but after reading a few more lines he closed the book.

While lying on the floor, Yun turned his head towards me and asked my opinion, 'Mr Jin, if a person sleeps in a cell where someone has died, will that person die also?'

'Is there a room that someone hasn't died in or won't die in? In a hospital, as soon as a patient dies his bed is filled by a new patient. You will die when your time is up, regardless of where you sleep. Even if you want to die you won't be able to die, and even if you want to live longer you won't be able to live longer if it is not in your destiny. Don't get scared like that. Take it easy and recite the Sutra,' was my reply.

I thought that this would be the last opportunity I would have to speak to Yun, so to show my sincerity I deliberately sat up and spoke to him. Before I knew what kind of reaction Yun had to what I said, the cell door opened and the prison guard ordered, 'Number 15, transfer!' The short nurse next to the prison guard was grinning as he shouted, 'Come out. Bring all your things with you.'

Yun sat up in his place abruptly, 'Sir, I am not suffering from tuberculosis. My cough is a clean cough,' was his plea. The prison guard ignored him and ordered him to go out quickly. Yun, so angry that he was trembling, transferred back to Cell Number One, abusing the prison guard and nurse as he went.

Chong muttered, 'Oh, it's good that he is gone. What kind of a person behaves like that? He is a venomous snake. He doesn't think about other people. He coughs anywhere and spits his phlegm anywhere. We should disinfect our cell. Can we live in it if we don't disinfect it?' He saw that the blanket Yun had left behind was a brighter colour than his own, and he quickly swapped his for Yun's and covered himself with it. He also put the aluminium bowl that Yun had used inside his own bowl. It looked like he was doing it because he was afraid someone else would beat him to it.

Kang sat and watched this with a blank look on his face, and then he scolded, 'You say we should disinfect our cell and yet you use the blanket and bowl of a sick man. What do you think you are doing? You are so quick to point out other people's faults. What you say about Yun applies to you.' Chong looked a little ashamed and said, 'Well all I have to do is hang the blanket in the sun tomorrow and wash the crockery with alcohol-soaked cotton,' He then continued reading the Sutra whilst rocking back and forth.

Looking back, it seems to me that Chong was reading the Sutra not so that he could go to a better place after he died, but so he would be acquitted at his forthcoming trial. Because, after he was sentenced to one and a half years' imprisonment, he read the Sutra much less diligently than before the appeal, when he never seemed to stop reading it.

I don't know how many times Chong told us that he was innocent, and that his prosecutor and his accomplices would be sympathetic towards him. Chong said that he was found guilty because the judge was a Nagamura and not a Yamashida, and that in the appeal court trial his innocence would most certainly be proven. He tried to justify himself to the guard who told him that the appeal would be very much against him. He said that he was wrongly accused and that he was not afraid of his one and a half year sentence but he was determined to fight for the court to clear his name. He seemed to be moved by his own speech.

Not long after, Kang was sentenced to two years' imprisonment. Chong, half-flatteringly, recommended Kang to appeal the decision, Kang said, 'I won't appeal. A man deserves two years imprisonment if he has received a higher education and then taken another's money through blackmail.' That night, when the prison guard asked him whether or not he was going to make an appeal, Kang said in Japanese, 'I will accept it,' giving up his right to appeal. And the following morning, before Kang was transferred to the main prison, he revealed to me his concern about his parents who were over seventy years old, and swore that he was going to become a new person during his time in prison.

'He is so silly,' Chong criticized after Kang had left; he seemed to be recalling that Kang had scolded him many times for what he said. In comparison to Kang, who had given up his right to appeal and accepted his sentence willingly, Chong, who had committed blackmail, still insisted that he was innocent. This behaviour made Chong appear even uglier, and as a result, the prison guards and nurses despised Chong.

When Chong had gone to the writing room to fill out an application for bail, the short prison nurse came and stood outside our cell, 'Bastards who cheat other people mustn't have any sense of shame. Chong had no land to sell but he lied to others that he did, he took five thousand *won* for a deposit, out of which he put one thousand *won* into his own pocket, and now he says that his one and a half year sentence is unfair. Ha! On top of that he is now asking for bail. The prosecutor and prison authorities hate that kind of man and he won't be released until he dies,' he said.

The days when Chong received favours from the nurses for his flattery were gone. His health deteriorated and as time went on he looked more pitiful and lonely.

One day I went into the prison yard with Chong to exercise; it was about twenty days after Yun had been transferred. The season when the dahlias bloom had already passed and the chrysanthemums were starting to bloom. Chong, wearing nothing but his underwear, was running, but I was unable to move my body so I just stood in the one place, looking down at the fading rose moss flowers and letting the sun warm my skin.

The mornings and evenings had been cool, the cosmos flowers were drooping because of the frost which had come down in the morning, but the afternoon was warm and sunny. While looking down I heard someone call out, 'Mr Jin.' When I raised my head I saw Yun's head poking out of the window of Cell Number One. His face was yellow and swollen and his narrow eyes had become even narrower. Instead of greeting him I just gave him a small nod, even that was against the rules. If the prison guard had seen this I would have been reprimanded.

'Mr Jin! I am definitely going to die soon. That's why my face is so swollen like this. Last night I dreamt that I was wearing mourning clothes made of coarse, yellow, hemp cloth, I had my hat on and I was walking in Chongno. Do you think that was a dream about my approaching death?' Yun's voice was so gentle it made me tearful.

The next day, when Chong and I went out to exercise again, Yun looked out through the window at us as he had done the day before, 'Money came from my uncle. Should I eat eggs or should I drink milk? Whatever I eat I can't digest,' he said.

A few days later, Yun spoke to me again, 'Today the doctor asked me if any of my family members died from being bloated. My father was bloated just like me before he died.' After saying this he seemed to be in utter despair and let out a heavy sigh. As if not wanting Chong to hear, he waited until Chong was out of hearing range before he asked me. 'If you want to pray to Buddha do you just say "Namu Ami Tabul"?' I sat up quickly, put my hands together, and bowing slightly I said, 'Namu Ami Tabul.'

Yun tried to put his hands together as I had done, but as soon as he saw Chong coming toward him he put his hands down abruptly. When Chong went away once again, Yun said, 'Mr Jin, if I recite "Namu Ami Tabul" are you sure that I will go to Paradise and not to hell after my death?' he tried to open his narrow eyes as wide as possible and look straight at my face. I had never been asked such a grave and responsible question in my life. As a matter of fact, I didn't know how to answer this question myself, but on this occasion I couldn't say no, even if it meant that I was lying and would go straight to hell. So, shaking my head vehemently three or four times, I answered decisively, 'Pray with all your heart. How could Buddha's words be lies?' Before disappearing from the window, Yun shook his head many times and bowed deeply.

After this incident I heard Yun order milk and eggs, and a few days later I heard him complain again that he was unable to digest the milk. We noticed that his health was deteriorating gradually, and when we went out to exercise there was no sign of Yun at the window. From what the nurse said, his illness was getting worse and worse. In the last few days his body temperature had shot up to as high as thirty-nine degrees centigrade. The doctor had given up and was going to release him soon.

One night after bed time I was looking out the window when I heard people dashing and stomping through the corridor. The fat prison warden and the dark-complexioned guard were standing outside the door of Cell Number One. A stranger wearing a long grey coat was also there, obviously he was Yun's uncle, the mayor. Soon afterwards I saw Yun walking out of his cell wearing his white padded jacket and leaning on the tall nurse.

The short nurse who had been leaning against the window returned to his place and lay down. He said, 'Finally he has been released on bail. Even if he goes home they say he won't survive another month.'

'I wish I could be released on bail too!' said Chong with a deep sigh.

Three months after I had been released from prison I met the short nurse who had been released on parole. He told me that Min and Yun had died, and Kang was still in prison doing carpentry work. Chong's indigestion had got worse and he got nephritis and pleuritis so he was moved to the hospital in the main prison. There was no chance that his appeal would he heard before he died.